Outrage

Outrage

The Rise of Religious Offence in Contemporary South Asia

Edited by Paul Rollier, Kathinka Frøystad and Arild Engelsen Ruud

First published in 2019 by
UCL Press
University College London
Gower Street
London WC1E 6BT

Available to download free: www.uclpress.co.uk

Text © Contributors, 2019
Images © Contributors, 2019

The authors have asserted their rights under the Copyright, Designs and Patents Act 1988 to be identified as the authors of this work.

A CIP catalogue record for this book is available from The British Library.

A CIP catalogue record for this book is available from The British Library. This book is published under a Creative Commons 4.0 International license (CC BY 4.0). This license allows you to share, copy, distribute and transmit the work; to adapt the work and to make commercial use of the work providing attribution is made to the authors (but not in any way that suggests that they endorse you or your use of the work). Attribution should include the following information:

Rollier, P., Frøystad, K., and Ruud. A.E. (eds,). 2019. *Outrage: The Rise of Religious Offence in Contemporary South Asia*. London: UCL Press. DOI: https://doi.org/10.14324/111.9781787355279

Further details about Creative Commons licenses are available at
http://creativecommons.org/licenses/

Any third-party material in this book is published under the book's Creative Commons license unless indicated otherwise in the credit line to the material. If you would like to re-use any third-party material not covered by the book's Creative Commons license, you will need to obtain permission directly from the copyright holder.

ISBN: 978–1–78735–529–3 (Hbk.)
ISBN: 978–1–78735–528–6 (Pbk.)
ISBN: 978–1–78735–527–9 (PDF)
ISBN: 978–1–78735–530–9 (epub)
ISBN: 978–1–78735–531–6 (mobi)
DOI: https://doi.org/10.14324/111.9781787355279

Contents

List of figures	vii
List of abbreviations	viii
List of contributors	ix
Note on diacritics	xi
Acknowledgements	xii

1. Introduction: Researching the rise of religious offence in South Asia 1
   Paul Rollier, Kathinka Frøystad and Arild Engelsen Ruud

2. 'We're all blasphemers': The life of religious offence in Pakistan 48
   Paul Rollier

3. The rise of religious offence in transitional Myanmar 77
   Iselin Frydenlund

4. Religious outrage as spectacle: The successful protests against a 'blasphemous' minister 103
   Arild Engelsen Ruud

5. Affective digital images: Shiva in the Kaaba and the smartphone revolution 123
   Kathinka Frøystad

6. 'Durga did not kill Mahishasur': Hindus, Adivasis and Hindutva 149
   Moumita Sen

7. The languages of truth: Saints, judges and the fraudulent in a Pakistani court 178
   Asad Ali Ahmed

8. Blasphemy and the appropriation of vigilante justice
    in 'hagiohistoric' writing in Pakistan 208
    Jürgen Schaflechner

9. Afterword: On the efficacy of 'blasphemy' 236
    Ute Hüsken

Index 249

List of figures

Figure 6.1	Bhabatosh Sutar's work in Chetla Agrani Club, Kolkata, 2012. Source: author	158
Figure 6.2	Representations of Asur village, FE Block, Kolkata, 2016. Source: author	160
Figure 6.3	Families taking selfies against the backdrop of the Asur village, FE Block, Kolkata, 2016. Source: author	160
Figure 6.4	Durga *murti* in the *pandal*, FE Block, Kolkata, 2016. Source: author	162
Figure 7.1a-c	Representations of the photographs of Yousaf Ali, as they appeared in the *Khabrain* newspaper. Stock image	200

List of abbreviations

BJP	Bharatiya Janata Party (India)
BNP	Bangladesh Nationalist Party
ECHR	European Court of Human Rights
FIR	First Information Report
ICT	Information and Communication Technology
IPC	Indian Penal Code
JNU	Jawaharlal Nehru University
MaBaTha	*Ah-myo Batha Thathana Saun Shaung Ye a-Pwe*, or the Organisation for the Protection of Race and Religion (Myanmar)
MaHaNa	State Sangha Mahanayaka Committee (Myanmar)
NLD	National League for Democracy (Myanmar)
OIC	Organisation of Islamic Cooperation
PPC	Pakistan Penal Code
SLORC	The State Law and Order Restoration Council (Myanmar)
SPDC	State Peace and Development Council (Myanmar)
ST	Sunni Tehreek (Pakistan)
TLP	Tehreek-i Labbaik Pakistan (Pakistan)
UNHCR	United Nations Human Rights Council
USDP	Union Solidarity and Development Party (Myanmar)
ICJ	International Commission of Jurists
HRCP	Human Rights Commission of Pakistan
NCJP	National Commission for Justice and Peace
OHCHR	Office of the United Nations High Commissioner for Human Rights
UNHRC	United Nations Human Rights Council

List of contributors

Asad Ali Ahmed is a sociocultural anthropologist who has taught at the Pratt Institute and at Rutgers and Harvard universities. His principal work examines the relationship of the political and the religious, as mediated by language and law, in colonial and postcolonial Pakistan. He is also the co-editor of *Love, War and Other Longings: Essays on Cinema in Pakistan* (OUP, 2019).

Kathinka Frøystad is a social anthropologist and Professor of Modern South Asian Studies at the University of Oslo working on religious offence, ritual crossings and other aspects of religious complexity. Her works include *Blended Boundaries: Caste, Class and Shifting Faces of 'Hinduness' in a North Indian City* (OUP, 2005), as well as a number of articles and book chapters.

Iselin Frydenlund is Associate Professor of Religious Studies at MF Norwegian School of Theology, Religion and Society, and Director of the MF Centre for the Advanced Study of Religion. Her research area is Theravada Buddhism in Sri Lanka and Myanmar, and she specialises in questions concerning the relationship between Buddhism, nationalism, politics and violence.

Ute Hüsken is Professor and Head of the Department of Cultural and Religious History of South Asia at Heidelberg University. Her main fields are Buddhist and Hindu studies, ritual, festival studies and gender studies. Her major books include *When Rituals Go Wrong* (Brill, 2007) and *Viṣṇu's Children* (Harrassowitz, 2009).

Paul Rollier is a social anthropologist and Assistant Professor of South Asia Studies at the University of St Gallen. His research interests lie in the anthropology of religion, politics and the everyday in South Asia. He recently co-authored *Mafia Raj: The Rule of Bosses in South Asia* (Stanford University Press, 2018).

Arild Engelsen Ruud is Professor of South Asia Studies at the University of Oslo. He writes on issues of democracy and politics in South Asia, specifically West Bengal and Bangladesh. He is author of *Poetics of Village Politics: The Making of West Bengal's Rural Politics* (OUP, 2003), co-editor of *Power and Influence in India* (Routledge, 2010) and *South Asian Sovereignty: The Conundrum of Worldly Power* (Routledge, forthcoming) and co-author of *Mafia Raj: The Rule of Bosses in South Asia* (Stanford University Press, 2018).

Jürgen Schaflechner is Assistant Professor at Heidelberg University and holds a PhD in South Asian Literary Studies and Anthropology (2014). His research and teaching focuses on cultural and postcolonial theory, the politics of religious and ethnic minorities in the Islamic Republic of Pakistan and the role of documentary film in anthropological research.

Moumita Sen is a visual studies scholar and currently a Postdoctoral Fellow at the Department of Culture Studies and Oriental Languages at the University of Oslo. Sen is the co-editor of *Nine Nights of the Goddess: The Navaratri Festival in South Asia* (SUNY Press, 2018) and is working on a book from her award-winning doctoral dissertation on aesthetics, religiosity and political patronage among clay-modellers of West Bengal.

Note on diacritics

The contributors to this volume draw on a variety of South Asian languages. Foreign words have been romanised without diacritics, with the exception of chapter 8, which is primarily based on the translation of Urdu texts.

Acknowledgements

Early versions of many of the essays in this volume were presented at a workshop entitled 'Reassessing the rise of offence politics in South Asia', held in Oslo in December 2016 and funded by the Department of Culture Studies and Oriental Languages (IKOS), University of Oslo. We would like to thank the workshop participants, the South Asia Symposium and the IKOS Religion and Politics network, as well as the anonymous reviewer recruited by UCL Press for useful comments to earlier drafts.

1
Introduction: Researching the rise of religious offence in South Asia

Paul Rollier, Kathinka Frøystad and Arild Engelsen Ruud

In 2011 a dinner party conversation in New Delhi ended with the following joke. An Indian dog and a Pakistani dog happened to meet at the Indo-Pak border. Fatigued but determined, the Indian dog trudged across to Pakistan. Surprised, the Pakistani dog asked: 'Why did you do that? Didn't they treat you well in India?' The Indian dog explained: 'All I ever got to eat was rice and lentils, lentils and rice, never any meat. I cannot take this any more, so now I am moving to Pakistan.' To its surprise, however, the Pakistani dog then crossed the border in the opposite direction. When asked why he had decided to move to a meatless diet, the Pakistani dog explained: 'Back home I am not even allowed to bark!'

With this joke, the host of the dinner get-together put a sardonic end to a conversation that had revolved around a growing sensitivity to expressions that offend religious sentiments across South Asia. In Pakistan the governor of Punjab, Salman Taseer, had recently been assassinated for criticising the draconic blasphemy legislation that made it possible to issue death sentences even for unwitting disrespect of the Prophet. In Bangladesh, over a hundred Jamaat-e-Islami activists had been arrested for defending their leader's comparison of his struggles with the suffering of the Prophet. Some years earlier, both countries had seen large-scale protests and violence in connection with the so-called Danish cartoon controversy. Meanwhile in India, hardly a week now went by without a news report about an artist, scholar or politician criticised, charged or assaulted for hurting religious sentiments, particularly Hindu ones. What was going on?

At the dinner party, possible parallels were suggested and discussed. The joke was the host's gentle way of shifting attention from parallels to differences of kind. Whereas the growth of religious offence controversies in India was giving rise to a public critique of the legislation that enabled them, such a critique had become too dangerous to be voiced in Pakistan – as it would also do in Bangladesh a few years later. Needless to say, this was not a joke that elicited laughter.

Eight years on, the relevance of this joke and the conversation that prompted it has only intensified. Why did allegations of hurt religious sentiments become so pronounced across South Asia and religious traditions after the turn of the millennium? Our primary aim is to throw light on the circumstances that came together to pave the way for this development. Drawing on detailed case studies of recent religious offence controversies in India, Pakistan, Bangladesh and Myanmar, we look for commonalities in the structural conditions that mark the entire region, and that cut across national and religious differences. One of these is the legacy of colonial law, which a number of scholars before us have examined. Clearly this legacy, and the legal amendments that have been made since the break up of British India, are crucial for understanding the particular shapes religious offence controversies take in the individual countries.

With their strikingly different political history and distinct postcolonial attention to issues of religious denomination, identity and sentiment, all four countries have come to experience heightened sensitivity to religious offence in the last few years. This is what makes Myanmar particularly interesting in this context and has prompted us to include it here. In spite of decades of a nationalist and autocratic military regime, once a semblance of democracy and open public sphere is re-established Myanmar proceeds to experience expressions of religious hurt in the same terms as India, Pakistan and Bangladesh, with their relatively longer histories of open public space. Although outside the purview of the present volume, the same could be said of postwar Sri Lanka, where pro-Sinhalese Buddhist groups have become increasingly active in denouncing perceived insults to their religion.

The contributions collected in this volume are particularly attentive to four conditions that have nurtured religious offence controversies in South Asia. First, to the implications of the rapid introduction of social media and smartphones; second, to how the arrival, deepening or decline of democracy has influenced the articulation of political and religious rivalry; thirdly, to how an increasingly 'split public' (Rajagopal 2001, 2009; Sunstein 2017; Udupa and McDowell 2017) reinforces the mutual suspicion between religious and secular reasoning; and finally, to the growing demands for recognition – not only among marginalised communities within South Asia, but also among adherents of hegemonic South Asian religious traditions. Though our list of changing structural conditions could undoubtedly have been expanded further, these four give a fair indication of the contextual canvas spanned out for the case studies detailed in the following chapters.

To document the beginning of the recent rise of religious offence controversies in South Asia in numerical terms is difficult. Quantitative exercises such as charting verdicts, lawsuits or First Information Reports (FIRs – reports that initiate legal proceedings) of alleged religious offence in comparable ways in the four countries would virtually be methodologically impossible. Furthermore, to our knowledge there is no reliable, provision-specific, publicly available data pertaining to the registration of blasphemy offences in any of the countries examined. The few quantitative overviews that we do have concern Pakistan, which has the strictest blasphemy legislation in the region. However, these are generally confined to cases that have been reported in the press and/or that came to the attention of human rights groups (Ahmed 2018; HRCP 2017, 96; Julius 2016, 100; see Siddique and Hayat 2008, 323–5). For what it is worth, this set of data indicates that there have been over a thousand cases of 'religious offence' in the country since the mid-1980s, with an increase from the 2000s onwards. This observation also seems credible for India, while the escalation appears to have begun somewhat later in Bangladesh and Myanmar. One of the main difficulties in quantifying this upsurge lies in the fact that recorded statistics of these cases, even if available, would not include the multitude of religious offence controversies handled outside the legal system – nor probably those cases not reported by the media, which necessitates a reflection on mediatisation.

Media play a dual role in offence controversies. Firstly, they constitute a medium through which allegedly offensive material can be manufactured and easily circulated to a growing proportion of the population. With the expansion of print media (books, newspapers, pamphlets, etc.) and the shift from state-controlled broadcasting to commercial TV channels in the early 1990s, the internet and mobile phones from the mid-1990s and social media and smartphones from the mid-2000s, the ongoing digital revolution represents a formidable source of unpredictability that generates a contradictory movement of enhanced visibility and growing containment (Udupa and McDowell 2017). Secondly, and importantly for the understanding of escalation, the media constitute a public sphere in which offence controversies are reported and heatedly debated. Even minor religious offence controversies in terms of legal repercussions can attract considerable public attention. This is particularly so in instances involving art and celebrities, art demanding a particularly extensive freedom of expression and celebrities being well-known already – not to mention the combination of the two. Instances in which films, novels or paintings are met with lawsuits, threats or violence frequently receive wide coverage.

In combination, conventional and new media thus work as a giant megaphone. Offence controversies constitute highly marketable news and the complex media ecology is a significant reason for their prominent place in South Asia's public life. Our point of departure reflects this dual analytical gaze. Though partly relying on a positivist notion of a quantifiable (at least in principle) increase, we equally rely on the exponentially growing attention to these controversies across the South Asian mediascape.

Scholarship on the rise of religious offence in South Asia has so far been preoccupied with case studies, country-specific developments and reflections about their cause and impact. While these are necessary starting points, this volume hopes to encourage reflections that transcend individual cases and countries and so push the transition to a field of scholarship in which contributors engage with, debate and critique one another's arguments, methodologies and theoretical presuppositions. One element of this is to deepen the awareness of the relations between South Asian and European battles over religious offence beyond the topic of colonial law, and to problematise the concepts from which we depart, including 'religious offence' and its roots in the inscrutable notion of 'blasphemy'.

Conceptual reflections and global historisation

Dependent as it is on the truths that a community cherishes (Lawton 1993, 4), the concept of blasphemy is notoriously imprecise. In Hebrew the term relates to the Abrahamic taboo of taking the name of God in vain (Lawton 1993, 14). In Greek this notion translates as *blasphemein*, to harm (*blaptein*) by the act of speech (*pheme*); it stands in profound contrast to *euphemein*, meaning to utter apt words or keep silent during the performance of rituals (Dacey 2012, 17; Lawton 1993, 14). In the Abrahamic context, therefore, blasphemy is generally understood as the opposite of a declaration of faith, and by extension as the betrayal of God's covenant (Bretherton 2016; Nash 2007, 2; Levy 1981). But this offence need not necessarily be oral in nature, as evidenced by a recently unearthed 2800-year-old latrine in Israel, purposely built on a site of pagan worship so as to desecrate 'false' gods (Ganor and Kreimerman 2017).

Together with physical desecration and iconoclastic profanity, blasphemy should be conceived as part of a continuum of religious offences instantiated in a variety of ways through words, gestures, images and so on. Thus, while recognising the distinction between 'blasphemy' and 'sacrilege' in English, for practical purposes we use these terms interchangeably.[1] We also recognise that these terms and their vernacular equivalents carry a judgement made on someone's communication. We should not therefore assume that any transgressive act has occurred: our ethnography suggests that sometimes the offensive act, utterance or artefact exists only in the accuser's imagination. Further, in certain contexts the incriminating evidence – a blasphemous remark, for instance – cannot be repeated directly for fear of committing yet another act of blasphemy.[2] Hence we find it useful to follow Favret-Saada's invitation to treat allegations of blasphemy as a system of places, meaning that the locutor making the advent of a blasphemy case possible is not the 'blasphemer', a mere addressee, but rather the 'denunciator' (Favret-Saada 1992, 258).

In Europe, the meaning of blasphemy has evolved considerably, depending on the accepted boundaries between legitimate and forbidden forms of dissent (Nash 2007). Encompassed by the notion of heresy during much of the medieval period (Bretherton 2016), fifteenth- to seventeenth-century Christian Europe saw a proliferation of legislations to eradicate outrageous speech and iconoclastic gestures (Christin 1992; Delumeau 1978). However, efforts to suppress blasphemy were powered more by theological concerns over heresy and the state's attempts to secure its own claim to power over ecclesiastical courts than by an increase in actual acts of blasphemy (Cabantous 2002, 58–9; Loetz 2009; Martignoni 2005). In this context historians have variously interpreted the suppression of blasphemy as signalling the emergence of the modern state, an excessive instrumentalisation of religion by monarchical power and, by the nineteenth century, class conflicts (Boudet 1996, 49; Delumeau 1978; Marsh 1998).

The dangerous efficacy of blasphemy was over time relegated to the realm of unreason. From a liberal secular perspective, the belief in blasphemy is often dismissed as a relic of the past or as an anachronistic aberration (Al-Azmeh 2013; McGarry 2014; Viswanathan 1998, 240) embraced by those, often Muslims, who fail to grasp the importance of freedom and the true nature of signs (Keane 2009; Mahmood 2009).[3] Yet the global resurgence of blasphemy-related controversies over the last decades (Cumper 2017, 138), including in liberal democracies, calls into question its alleged demise.

While these controversies remain often formulated in religious terms, we may also discern the re-emergence of blasphemy in a secular garb – a crime increasingly understood and debated as a form of disrespect for humans and their religious sensibilities, rather than as an offence to the sacred (Favret-Saada 2017). What was once punished as blasphemy now tends to be viewed as religious hatred and discrimination, as a violation of rights against a particular group or individual on the basis of its religion or belief (see Dacey 2012; Bretherton 2016). Conversely, accusations of blasphemy (in the religious sense) are increasingly framed as an assault on liberal societies' attachment to freedom of expression (e.g. Eriksen and Stjernfelt 2012; Gubo 2015; cf. Cumper 2017, 164). The main case for such freedom holds that even harmful speech should be protected, because doing so has a desirable impact on democratic development (Danbury 2017). While censorship only heightens curiosity and invites transgression, the argument goes, freedom of speech ensures a 'marketplace of ideas' where truth can emerge and thus ultimately protect individuals against the abuse of state power (cf. Baker 1989).[4]

Yet the challenges posed by new technologies of media and communication to the regulatory capacity of states complicate this assessment. In a so-called 'post-truth' era of algorithmic governance and 'social media echo chambers', the liberty to voice one's opinion online, for instance, cannot be dissociated from concerns over the internet serving as a potential incubator of violence and as an instrument in the pursuit of power (Price and Stremlau 2017, 318). Similarly, in secular yet religiously/ethnically diverse Western societies, such as those of Europe, defendants of an unbridled right to free expression must contend with those for whom this right conflicts with their freedom of religion, and who may therefore seek redress for perceived religious slights.

The legal articulation between these two rights has become highly contested. In Europe there is no consensus on whether the beliefs of religious communities should be given legal protection.[5] While some argue that protecting religions against defamation could act as a safeguard against the discrimination of minorities, others contend that doing so would compromise the right to free expression and foster religious intolerance.[6] In recent years the compromise position consists in replacing blasphemy laws with incitement-to-religious-hatred legislations, thereby protecting *members* of religious communities from vilification, rather than their beliefs.[7] The liberal understanding of free speech holds that persons only can be protected from defamation, not what they think or worship (Dierkens and Schreiber 2012, 171; de Saint Victor 2016).

But distinguishing between inciting hatred towards beliefs and towards believers can prove difficult in practice (Cumper 2017, 156). In addition, this distinction rests on a historically specific understanding of what a person's proper relationship to belief and rituals should be, rather than a universal one (Mahmood 2009; Mahmood and Danchin 2014). Religion is here conceived as a set of beliefs to which the individual gives ascent, so that religious symbols appear as external and inconsequential to the supposedly true locus of religiosity, one's interiority. Blasphemy is therefore not perceived as a real offence. As such, it is often met with allegations of majoritarian prejudice on behalf of religious minorities.

As Saba Mahmood has remarked, 'minorities often contest the discriminatory practices of secular law through the same legal instruments that enshrine majoritarian privilege' (2015, 176).[8] It should therefore not be surprising that international structures of governance, such as the United Nations Human Rights Council (UNHRC) and the European Court of Human Rights, have become key sites for the re-articulation of blasphemy in recent decades. Pakistan, in particular, has played an important role in this process. Since the late 1990s it has sought to recast 'blasphemy' into the discourse of human rights, so as to counter negative stereotypes towards Muslims (Rehman and Berry 2012; Bettiza and Dionigi 2015, 634–7; Zuber 2015).[9] Acting on behalf of the Organisation of Islamic Cooperation (OIC) at the UNHRC, the Pakistani delegation successfully tabled resolutions aimed at criminalising the 'defamation of religions'.[10] While Western democracies saw these attempts as eroding the universal right of freedom of expression and as potentially reinforcing discrimination towards minorities and doctrinal dissidents, the OIC pointed to the existence of a number of religious insult provisions in EU countries.[11] In 2011, after years of tussle, the OIC finally accepted the general shift away from the notion of 'defamation of religion' towards that of 'discrimination', anti-'hate speech' and 'incitement' to religious hatred and violence (OHCHR 2011). This shift is grounded in the distinction between verbal attacks on religious individuals or groups and attacks on religious symbols and religions as such (Temperman and Koltay 2017, 7; Parmar 2015, 382).

Of particular interest is the fact that Pakistan and the OIC, while still striving to impose a global ban on the 'defamation of religions', also emphasised the need to promote cross-cultural 'tolerance' and 'interfaith harmony' (cf. Parmar 2015, 380). This strategic recourse to a discourse of tolerance may seem surprising in light of the discriminatory effects of blasphemy laws. But as Wendy Brown suggests, the idiom of tolerance is generally an expression of domination (Brown 2006, 204). Talk of tolerance often functions through the essentialisation of cultural and religious differences, so as simultaneously to incorporate and sustain the otherness of the tolerated element (Brown 2006, 28). In its long-standing attempt to translate domestic blasphemy laws into an international legal norm, the OIC's strategic embrace of such liberal language allows it to universalise its call to shield religious sensitivities from insult.

Moreover, Pakistan's stance on defamation at the UNHRC and its recourse to notions of 'interfaith harmony' and 'tolerance' is in keeping with South Asia's legal traditions on free speech and its limits. As discussed below, colonial regulations on speech and expression were devised in the name of public order, and purportedly aimed at fostering 'communal harmony' among easily excitable subjects. Central to these were the proscription of incitement to religious hatred and offences to religious sentiments. In the postcolonial period, 'reasonable restrictions' of the constitutional right of free speech have also included state security, public order, friendly relations with foreign states, public decency and morality and caste discrimination (cf. Pohjonen and Udupa 2017, 17).[12]

The history of religious offence and its regulation in South Asia is deeply intertwined with Western developments and debates on blasphemy; in several respects it prefigures these developments. Thus the recasting of blasphemy into an idiom of hurt religious sensibilities, which emerges in the late twentieth century in Europe (Favret-Saada 2017), is already discernible in India in the 1920s and 1930s (of which more below). This is no coincidence. Asad Ahmed's work shows that the concerns that presided over the drafting of anti-blasphemy provisions during the colonial era were directly inspired by nineteenth-century liberal and utilitarian projects of legal reform (Ahmed 2009, 2016). Rather than simply being triggered by irreducible cultural differences heightened by new technologies of communication and migration flows, the recent globalisation of blasphemy controversies is predicated upon the rise of the modern state and its grammar of governance. This effected a reorganisation of religious life and a reconceptualisation of 'religious offence', notably through the enactment of colonial laws, to which we now turn.

Law and turning points

Scholars of blasphemy working in the Euro-American world commonly point to the Rushdie affair of the late 1980s as a turning point.[13] The sheer novelty of a transnational blasphemy controversy helped to portray this affair as an upheaval generating an indisputable 'before' and an 'after'

(Grenda, Beneke and Nash 2014, 7). The affair also serves as a reference point for studies of later confrontations between free speech and artistic freedom (e.g. Klausen 2009; Grillo 2007a, 2007b; Ball 2017), as if it were the mother of religious offence controversies. In this way, organised expressions of outrage towards artistic representations deemed injurious to religion appear as the preserve of Muslims – a view which overlooks the fact that the moralist stance of anti-Rushdie protesters directly draws on a rhetoric forged by Christian fundamentalists in Europe since the 1960s (cf. Favret-Saada 2017).

Seen from a South Asian perspective, however, the Rushdie affair is of lesser magnitude as a turning point. To be sure, it was the first large-scale transnational offence controversy involving South Asians at home and abroad. The affair was moreover seminal in that it united South Asian Muslims with Muslims in other parts of the world in a common debate (though not necessarily a common stand) long before the galvanising effect of the so-called 'war on terror'. And in India, where the book was banned from importation, it triggered criticism of the Congress government for 'appeasing' the Muslim minority. As such, the Rushdie affair is a major reference point in South Asian discourses on censorship as well. Yet in this region the Rushdie affair was neither the first of its kind, nor necessarily the most consequential. For South Asianists, the Rushdie affair is rather part of a series of events that originated in British India and forked out in the independent states after decolonisation. Henceforth events in each South Asian country began to acquire greater density, especially from the 1980s or 1990s onwards, though not simultaneously, to the same degree or in full sync. To give a better understanding of these uneven parallels, we need to go back to the mid-nineteenth century.

In the scholarship on religious offence controversies in South Asia, a significant turning point was the establishment of a common Indian Penal Code (IPC) for the entire population of British India in the 1860s; this now forms the basis of the criminal codes in India, Pakistan, Bangladesh, Myanmar and Sri Lanka, as well in other former British colonies (see Yeo and Wright 2016 [2011], 3). Whereas the Mughals (1526–1857) primarily settled disputes by arbitration, their British successors held it important to develop a uniform legislation. Initially they had relied on whatever legal traditions were in place, spanning from bodies of customary law, Islamic jurisprudence traditions, the Anglo-Hindu laws, various parliamentary charters and acts, East India Company regulations and English common law (Skuy 1998; Patra 1961). The next step was to draft a legislation that would be applicable and acceptable to all sections of society and thus help to maintain 'social order'.

Although drafted by Macaulay in the 1830s, this legislation was not enacted until 1862, having acquired more urgency after the great Indian uprising of 1857. For Macaulay and his colonial successors, the challenge was to allow for extensive religious freedom and critique while preventing religious intimidations. The relevant four sections made it an offence to destruct and defile places of worship and sacred objects (section 295), to disturb rituals (section 296), to trespass burial grounds or places of worship (section 297) and to utter words or to make sounds and gestures with a view to 'wound' someone's 'religious feelings' (section 298).[14] In addition, in another chapter, section 153 aimed to prevent deliberate provocations of the kind that might instigate interreligious rioting.[15]

With this new law, all human punitive rights were transferred to the courts. By the same stroke all the religious traditions found in this heterogeneous subcontinent were given equal protection. In this respect the IPC was ahead of English blasphemy legislation, which only protected the Church of England until it was abolished in 2008. In the decades that followed, section 153 was nevertheless found wanting; it was supplemented in 1898 with 153-A, which criminalised attempts to promote 'feelings of enmity' between religious communities.[16] Decades later, however, the intense communal polarisation that followed in the wake of the Independence movement, aided by an increasingly affordable printing technology, gave rise to a mode of transgression that turned out to be unpunishable by existing law. This mode of transgression – satirical writing about the Prophet or Hindu deities – was epitomised by the *Rangila Rasul* pamphlet. This affair, and two other similar controversies,[17] became a second turning point in the modern history of offence controversies in the region, and decisively shaped the way in which 'blasphemy' and 'religious sentiments' came to be conceived, adjudicated and experienced over the next hundred years.

Published in Lahore in 1924, the Urdu pamphlet *Rangila Rasul* ('The colourful Prophet') claimed to describe intimate events of the life of the Prophet. Written and published by members of the Arya Samaj (Thursby 1975, 40), this caricature contained satirical poems about the Prophet and his multiple marriages. Its overall message was that his teaching, which constitutes the essence of Islam, 'was derived from his sexual "experiences"' (Raj 2015, 150). Highly popular and soon translated into several languages, within months the publication spurred the mobilisation of Muslims for whom the pamphlet amounted to a defamation of their Prophet and religion. Mahatma Gandhi, by criticising it, contributed to making *Rangila Rasul* better known (Nair 2013). The uproar soon became so tumultuous that the government of Punjab attempted to stop it (Thursby 1975, 41).

The Hindu publisher was arrested and prosecuted for attempting to promote enmity between different classes of colonial subjects (section 153-A of the IPC). The judicial process concluded in 1927 with an acquittal. The Lahore High Court ruled that sections 298 and 153-A did not criminalise the *verbal* defamation of religions and did not apply to *deceased* religious leaders (Ahmed 2009, 182; Thursby 1975, 45).[18] The court added that if such expressions were to be criminalised, a further section would have to be added.

This decision caused further protests. The ability to display wounded feelings during these protests and mosque gatherings was part of a 'politics of self-expression' grounded in notions of cultural authenticity and virtuous emotions (Daechsel 2006; Pernau 2015); it was voiced in a language that drew heavily on Urdu poetry and its images of burning hearts and unrequited love (Gilmartin 1991, 1998). Two years after the acquittal Ilmuddin, a young Muslim carpenter from Lahore, murdered the Hindu publisher. His subsequent trial and execution for murder attracted the intervention of eminent leaders and intellectuals, such as Muhammad Ali Jinnah and Allama Iqbal. With time Ilmuddin acquired the status of an Islamic hero and saint, and close to a century later served as an exemplar for Salman Taseer's murderer (Schaflechner, chapter 8).

With *Rangila Rasul* a new form of urban politics was born. It centred on the mobilisation of communities through the performance of affective attachment to both material and abstract religious symbols: mosques, cows, printed scriptures and religious figures among others (Gilmartin 1991, 1998; Freitag 1989; Scott 2015). The well-publicised legal processes around publications such as *Rangila Rasul* often brought increased sales to the pamphlet, tract or newspaper in question (Thursby 1975, 48; Scott 2015, 294).

Disappointed over the lack of a legal weapon that could stop hurtful publications in the future, Muslim leaders appealed to the Governor of Punjab. For the government, the judgements handed in cases of provocative writings failed to clarify whether a deliberate insult to a religion or to a deceased religious figure amounted to the intentional promotion of enmity between communities (Thursby 1975, 6). Eager to pacify protesting Muslims and prevent further cases, in 1927 the government proposed a 'Religious Insults Bill' which aimed to criminalise not only spoken offence but also any representation intended to 'outrage' religious feelings (Barrier 1974, 101; Thursby 1975, 61; Stephens 2014). In its original form, section 295-A reads as follows:

> Whoever, with deliberate and malicious intention of outraging the religious feelings of any class of His Majesty's subjects, by words, either spoken or written, or by visible representations, insults or attempts to insult the religion or the religious beliefs of that class, shall be punished with imprisonment of either description for a term which may extend to two years, or with fine, or with both.[19]

Once this section was passed into law, the Indian subcontinent was equipped with one of the strictest regulations of religious offence that the world had ever seen. After 1947, these regulations (sections 295, 295-A, 296, 297 and 298) were incorporated in the respective penal codes of the now independent states of India, Pakistan, Myanmar and, from 1971, Bangladesh.[20]

Commenting in the aftermath of the *Rangila Rasul* affair on Muslim susceptibilities and the risk of social upheaval, the Punjab Governor wrote that an attack on the Prophet 'stung them to the quick' and that they 'could not bear' to see this repeated (quoted in Thursby 1975, 41). Scholars have suggested that such statements, and the wording of section 295-A, are premised on the colonial assumption that Indian society was essentially religious and that its confessional pluralism demanded a neutral and rational arbiter. Colonial subjects were thought to be susceptible to volatile religious passions and vulnerable to religious insults, which in turn would lead to social disorder (Ahmed 2009, 179; Ramdev et al. 2016). Born out of an active engagement with the local conditions, this piece of legislation, and subsequent legal restrictions on expressions that cause real or perceived harm, could become a means to instil restraint and to discipline 'native' religious sensitivities (Adcock 2016, 343). Ironically local religious publics using these laws nowadays often fail to recognise the colonial origin of these notions of blasphemous and seditious libel.

Summing up our argument thus far, the Rushdie affair is less significant in the history of blasphemy controversies if seen from South Asia. For South Asianists, more significant turning points are the colonial implementation of blasphemy legislation in the 1860s and its subsequent strengthening, particularly the addition of section 295-A in 1927. The next turning points occurred after Independence and were thus country-specific. Before we can return to this volume's ambition of identifying some of the conditions that nurtured the rise of blasphemy controversies *across* the South Asian region, a summary of country-specific developments is in order. As is well known, the four countries considered in this volume – India, Pakistan, Bangladesh and Myanmar – pursued different political paths after decolonisation, which had a direct impact on the kind of public expressions that were permitted.

India

Under the aegis of Jawaharlal Nehru, India became a socialist republic dedicated to industrialisation, modernity and secularism. Though its Muslim population shrank greatly following the establishment of Pakistan, India remained a composite society and its proportion of Muslims was still around 10 per cent (Joshi, Srinivas and Bajaj 2003). A main priority for independent India was to reconstruct a polity that could prevent new fragmentation along religious lines and also inculcate respect for religious others.

At the same time other developments suggested that these steps were inadequate. In the south, Periyar E. V. Ramasamy's reinterpretations of the *Ramayana* emphasised the negative traits of Lord Rama. In 1956 he burned images of Rama in public (Richman 1991) to mobilise Dravidians against Brahmanism. In the same year Aubrey Menen published a novelistic *Ramayana* interpretation– *Rama Retold: A Secular Retelling of the Ramayana* (1956) – which was every bit as provocative as that of Periyar (cf. Chandran 2017, 60–5). And in the 1960s interreligious riots were suddenly on the rise again – spearheaded by mobs that, according to Hasan, were 'headed not very infrequently by RSS volunteers' (1988, 827). One of the outcomes of this was a further tightening of the religious offence regulations. In 1961 section 295-A was expanded with an 'or otherwise' phrase, and in 1969 section 153-A was considerably extended. The result was that there hardly remained a thinkable religious transgression left to criminalise.

The 1970s were marked by far more dramatic events than religious offence controversies, including the brief but dramatic war with Pakistan that culminated with independence for Bangladesh, an emergent Sikh insurgency in Punjab and the increasingly authoritarian rule of Indira Gandhi. During the 21-month Emergency period, the state maintained strict control over all publications and public utterances, as it would continue to do for another 15 years with radio and TV broadcasting. This may explain why Rushdie's novel *The Satanic Verses* shocked the few Indians who read it before restrictions were imposed. One of these was the well-known author and journalist Khushwant Singh; he advised Penguin India not to publish the work in India since it was so hurtful and tasteless that it could inspire massive riots (Waldrop 1999; Frøystad 2013, 199).

In the decades that followed, the number of blasphemy controversies picked up, first slowly and then with increasing speed and mediatised intensity. By now there is a vast scholarship detailing specific cases (e.g. Date 2007; Laine 2014; Pennington 2016; Sarma 2014; Sethi and Sengupta 2014; Taylor 2011; Ramaswamy 2011; Laine 2011; Copeman 2012; Dharwadker 2012), so we will instead emphasise interrelated trends. Firstly, the weight has shifted from pre-publication to post-publication regulation, and thus from clearances to complaints. This development began with the termination of the state monopoly on television and radio broadcasting in the early 1990s; it continued with an expanding television universe followed by internet connectivity on large and small screens. Feature films and documentaries still need clearance by a censor board prior to public screening, but the liberalisation of the rest of the mediascape is more than sufficient to make the scope for potential transgressions virtually infinite.

Secondly, legal redress is increasingly sought for alleged offences against Hinduism. As Hindu nationalism has metamorphosed into one of India's most persuasive political ideologies, blasphemy controversies increasingly reflect alleged offences against Hindu sentiments (Bailey 2014; Taylor 2014; Thapar 2014; Tripathi 2009). True, such cases are hardly new (as illustrated by the *Ramayana* reinterpretations of Periyar and Menen) and offences against minority religions are still suppressed (as illustrated by the ban on the book *Islam, a Concept of Political World Invasion by Muslims* from 2003). Yet the re-emergence of a self-assertive Hinduism has clearly multiplied the number of incidents in which Hindus claim their deities and religious feelings have been disrespected.

Thirdly, religio-political organisations and pressure groups play a growing role in initiating political campaigns and legal proceedings against alleged transgressors. As Chandran poignantly remarks, censorship has become 'democratised' (Chandran 2017, 2010). The prosecutor's role is no longer monopolised by the state but dispersed across the political and societal spectrum – with the effect that alleged transgressions, which could formerly be handled with discretion, frequently turn into massive spectacles of demonstrations, protests, campaigns and vigilante attacks.

Fourthly, religious offence controversies have spread from the domains of politics and art to academia, beginning with the violent and legal campaigns against D. N. Jha's documentation of the deep roots of beef consumption in India and continuing with attempts to block the works of James Laine, Wendy Doniger and Jeffrey J. Kripal. Though the higher courts support academic freedom, a long-drawn-out legal battle is nevertheless a 'punishment' in its own right (cf. Dhavan 2008). An interrelated development is the protests against allegedly offensive university course readings. Though institutions generally seek to uphold the principle of academic freedom, such attacks nevertheless create considerable cross-pressure at a time when the government shares the protesters' ideological position.

Lastly, a fifth trend is worth noting. Due to the above developments, many Indian intellectuals have expressed growing worries about retaining a regulation of religious offence so extensive that even the most careful politician, activist, artist or academic working on questions of religion risks hurting someone's religious sentiments. So a new critical debate has begun: one that discusses whether regulating religious offence produces more blasphemy controversies than it prevents, and if it would be better to do away with this kind of regulation. Yet since India's legal regulation still appears to have considerable popular support (cf. Singh 2018a, 2018b), and certain politicians advocate harsher punishment rather than deregulation, the debate is likely to be long drawn out. As indicated in our opening joke, however, it is noteworthy that India is not among the South Asian countries where questioning the wisdom of regulating religious offence has become a dangerous thing to do.

Pakistan

Like the other countries considered in this volume, Pakistan inherited the religious offences provisions contained in the IPC. But in contrast to them, in Pakistan these laws were substantially enhanced to include offences directed towards specific holy names, objects and feelings. Aside from colonial legal provisions, Pakistan also inherited the memory of past controversies and an emotional repertoire of protest against blasphemy (Blom 2008). The *Rangila Rasul* affair, which took place in Lahore, shaped a local imaginary of heroic sacrifice that would suffuse controversies for the century to come. This imaginary revolves around the celebration of iconic slayers of blasphemers (Ilmuddin d. 1929, Cheema d. 2006, Qadri d. 2016; cf. Schaflechner, chapter 8) and is primarily conveyed through shrines, movies, television series, street banners and popular literature. Yet the first decades following Pakistan's independence only saw eight formal cases of blasphemy accusations (Julius 2016, 101).

With the rise of religious parties in the late 1970s, and calls for the establishment of the *Nizam-e-Mustafa* (Rule of the Prophet), Muslimness increasingly came to be defined by the state. While the Prime Minister

Zufliqar Ali Bhutto (1971–7) had already made concessions to Islamic parties, it was under Zia-ul-Haq's regime (1977–88) that blasphemy was cast as a capital offence (Talbot 1998, 241–4). Under his state-led process of Islamisation, five additional clauses were added to the Pakistan Penal Code, all of them pertaining to offences against Islam. These include the physical desecration of the Quran (section 295-B, life imprisonment), insulting the relatives or companions of the Prophet (section 298-A, three years) and insulting in any way the Prophet himself (section 295-C, mandatory death sentence since 1991).[21]

These legal additions led to an increase in the number of individuals charged with blasphemy, from a handful of cases before the mid-1980s to over a thousand charged under religious offence sections since (HRCP 2017, 96; Julius 2016, 100; Siddique and Hayat 2008, 323ff). Although no one accused has so far been executed, over 53 suspected blasphemers have been killed since 1986 at the hands of zealots or vigilante mobs (ICJ 2015, 11).

The occurrence of blasphemy accusations is predominantly localised in Punjab, where the majority of Pakistan's Christians and Ahmadis live, and in lower middle-class areas, where false accusations have become a lethal instrument in socioeconomic conflicts. Human rights groups and scholars have repeatedly denounced the discriminatory nature of these laws, pointing out that individuals with mental health problems are probably disproportionately targeted (Husain 2014), and that the majority of those killed following an allegation are non-Muslims.[22]

Most sentences for religious offence are overturned at the High Court level, and the accused acquitted on the ground that the charges were concocted and spurred on by family feuds, business quarrels, land disputes or religious rivalry (ICJ 2015, 7). Legal scholars suggest that the deliberate wording of these provisions fails clearly to define the types of behaviours that could amount to defilement (Siddique and Hayat 2008; Forte 1994). Consider the broad reach of section 295-C:

> Whoever by words, either spoken or written, or by visible representation or by any imputation, innuendo, or insinuation, directly or indirectly, defiles the sacred name of the Holy Prophet Muhammad (peace be upon him) shall be punished with death, or imprisonment for life, and shall also be liable to fine.

The lack of a reference to the offender's psychological state or intention to offend in this section partly accounts for the fact that the legal proceedings for 295-C are often constrained by the near-impossibility of repeating or displaying the inculpating words or representation, lest that would amount to a reiteration of blasphemy (see Rollier, chapter 2).

Large swathes of the population, including the country's *ulema* and religious organisations, regard this section as a divine decree and the cornerstone towards the instauration of a more Islamic society. The religious right, with the support of Islamist militants, forcefully oppose any attempt to hold a debate on these laws. The very act of criticising these sections of the Penal Code is often held to constitute in itself an act of blasphemy. In 2011 the Governor of Punjab was killed by his bodyguard, Mumtaz Qadri, for criticising the misuse of Pakistan's anti-blasphemy provisions (see Schaflechner, chapter 8). This assassination marks a new turn in Pakistan's tryst with blasphemy. The murder trial of the bodyguard and his execution in 2016 were accompanied by massive street protests in support of him – a man lionised by protestors for his readiness to break state laws to uphold that of God. In this context of religious fervour and outrage, holding blasphemy trials becomes increasingly perilous. Judges, the accused and their counsels are subjected to intimidation and occasionally to attacks by members of extremist Islamist groups (ICJ 2015, 7; UNHRC 2013, 13–14).[23] The resultant atmosphere, and the judiciary's concern for public sentiments in these cases, serve to impede the proper delivery of justice.

This surge in blasphemy accusations over the last two to three decades should be understood within the global economy of religious offence, in which sections of Pakistan's state and society expect their country to spearhead a worldwide Muslim campaign against blasphemers, as it did at the UNHRC for over a decade. Hence each international blasphemy crisis – around the Danish cartoons in 2005, the 'Innocence of Muslims' video in 2012 and the Charlie Hebdo cartoons in 2015 – translates locally into lively expressions of outrage and protests in which emerging religious publics stage their attachment to the defence of Islam.

Blasphemy accusations as they have occurred over the last few years should be seen in connection with two new trends. First, Pakistan has witnessed the spectacular emergence of a powerful political movement, the Tehreek-i Labbaik Pakistan (TLP). Established with the likely assent of the military (Sethi 2017) in the aftermath of Qadri's execution, the TLP is dedicated to the rigorous punishment of blasphemers. While the movement had already proven its capacity for disruptions through massive street protests in 2017, the 2018 general elections provided it with the opportunity to demonstrate the appeal of its anti-blasphemy narrative among voters of traditional religio-political parties (Khalid 2018).

No longer merely an instrument in interpersonal rivalry, allegations of religious transgression are increasingly woven into political discourse and wielded in conjunction with concerns over 'national security'. This brings the regulation of blasphemy closer to the traditional pattern of censorship that has affected media circles and dissident voices in the country, especially (though not only) during periods of military rule (Boquérat 2016). In short, accusations of blasphemy form part of a series of established devices to restrict the freedom of expression. This evolution is taking place in the context of a second trend whereby the military, to pursue its counter-terrorism strategy, has seen its punitive capacity enhanced, notably through the creation of military courts to try civilian suspects and the practice of enforced disappearances (OHCHR 2017, 4; ICJ 2018).

Bangladesh

When Bangladesh became independent from Pakistan after the 1971 war, the new constitution listed secularism as one of its four founding principles. This was a reflection of the ideological orientation that had underpinned at least a significant part of the liberation war and that came to influence subsequent events in this situation of double postcoloniality. Those who held Islam to be the defining ideological foundation of a Muslim majority country were forced into retreat. The main Islamic party, the Jamaat-e-Islami, was banned, while organisations and individuals thought to have been on the wrong side of the war lost positions and influence.

Though the independent government made some concessions to pan-Islamic sentiments, partly in response to the severity with which the oil crisis hit this devastated nation, nowadays these early years are often seen as a time when the constitution's liberal and secular ideals were held high. Nonetheless, as early as 1973 the poet Daud Haidar was accused of having insulted the Prophet in a poem. He was imprisoned, his ancestral home burnt and one of his relatives killed; later Haidar was forced into exile.

The outrage against Daud Haidar had ignited protests and it saw the first Islamist demonstration after Bangladesh's war of independence. Though a singular incident, it is nonetheless suggestive of a religiosity that ran counter to the more public secularism (Riaz 2004). After the bloody coups of 1975, religion as central to the nation's identity was re-emphasised and upheld by the military governments that ruled the country for the next 15 years. In a series of amendments, the epithet 'Islamic Republic' was attached to the country's name, the Bismillah added as a preamble to the Constitution and other religious references were introduced. In spite of religiously conservative leanings of the ruling clique, however, Bangladesh did not see the same turn to conservative Islam as did Pakistan, remaining instead largely open and liberal.

Accusations of religious offence resurfaced, however, with the reintroduction of democracy in 1990. The election winner, the Bangladesh Nationalist Party, established an alliance with Jamaat-e-Islami. Soon after a case was filed against professor and known atheist Ahmed Sharif. He belonged to the educated elite establishment and was a former freedom fighter, both of which made it unthinkable for a recently established government to take him on. A year later, however, Taslima Nasreen was accused of insulting Muslims in her novel *Shame*. By this time the government was more comfortably in power (Riaz 2008), and Nasreen was also junior compared to Sharif. A bounty was offered for her head, tens of thousands protested in street demonstrations and she was summoned by the court. Eventually Nasreen fled the country. After this more incidents took place, including the banning in 1995 of what is considered the first scholarly feminist work in Bangladesh (*Naree* by Humayun Ahmed).

In the same period Ahmadis were increasingly targeted: cases of physical assault took place and their publications were banned by the government. This period also witnessed increased Islamist assertion in the countryside, including a series of fatwas against working women and an expanding number of mosques and madrasas.

Overall these relatively smaller incidents did not seem to challenge the secularism of the state. Laws protecting Islam had not been introduced; the Ahmadis, although often subject to random cases of violence and oppression, were not legally defined as non-Muslim; and food was still available behind screens during Ramadan, the month of fasting. But after 2009 the dynamics seemed to change and two opposing identities of national ideology asserted themselves.

Acting on election pledges and responding to a long-standing demand, the government instituted the so-called International War Crimes Tribunal to try war criminals from the war of independence. Four years on, the sentencing of a well-known Islamist leader to life imprisonment for his war crimes set off massive protests within days. In February 2013 hundreds of thousands of protesters assembled at the Shahbag crossing in central Dhaka, demanding that he be hanged instead (De 2015); they feared that the prison sentence would simply be overturned with a change of government. The scale of the demonstrations spurred the government to ensure a retrial in which he received the death penalty. The government, on the verge of being accused of relaxing on its pledge to try the war criminals, had clearly shifted gear following the Shahbag demonstrations. He was later executed. In all, 30 individuals have received the death penalty and six have been executed.

The scale and success of the Shahbag protests set in motion a counterreaction (Roy 2018; Zaman 2018). From January 2013 onwards a dozen individuals were accused of blasphemy, atheism or apostasy; seven of them were killed. In addition, a number of other people were killed for deviating religious beliefs. The perpetrators belonged to fringe Islamist organisations, but, as with the Shahbag protests, these incidents spurred a dynamic of action and reaction between an Islamic interpretation and a secular progressive interpretation of the nation's identity. Surveys picked up a broad antipathy against atheists and bloggers that the government had also noticed (Fair, Hamza and Heller 2017); four bloggers were duly arrested for hurting religious sentiments and making derogatory remarks against religion. Soon an Islamist organisation called Hefazat Islam came to the fore with its demand for legislation against blasphemy. Rather than refuting the demand, the Prime Minister retorted that legislation protecting religion already existed in the Bangladesh Penal Code (Sáez 2018). Not satisfied, Hefazat organised a giant demonstration in Dhaka in May 2013, to which possibly 100,000 participants were bussed in from all over the country to support its demands, including prosecution of the 'atheist bloggers'. The potential fall-out was nipped in the bud when the demonstrators were chased out of town in a surprise move at night by the police.

However, in its second consecutive term in power, Awami League has made concessions to Islamists, and in particular to Hefazat. These include a revision of school textbooks, the removal of an allegedly idolatrous statue of the lady of justice outside the Supreme Court and the decision to declare a graduation degree from the Hefazat's madrasas as equivalent to government school degrees.

Although Bangladesh does not possess a blasphemy law such as that existing in Pakistan and envisioned by the Hefazat, Islamist organisations have been increasingly successful in setting the terms of what constitutes intolerable religious offence in the public sphere. In recent years this has led to a series of incidents following accusations of blasphemy, including the 2014 case involving the cabinet minister Latif Siddique (discussed by Ruud in chapter 4).

Myanmar

Myanmar (known as Burma before 1989) is often not included under the epithet South Asia, but it is still the inheritor of the same legal system, known originally as the Indian Penal Code. British Burma was separated from British India in 1937 and followed a different trajectory thereafter. It had a new constitution, a different independence movement and a very different experience during the Second World War; it also, after a brief period of electoral democracy, suffered a lengthier period as a brutal military dictatorship. In spite of this the Myanmar Penal Code remained intact, and sections 295-A and 298 have come to be used in courts to regulate issues of religious sensibility. As discussed earlier, section 295-A was originally a 1927 amendment intended to protect religious minorities. However, in Myanmar (as well as in Sri Lanka), it has come to be used as a device by which to protect majority Buddhist sentiments against minorities.

There has been a relevant debate over the place of 'blasphemy' in Buddhist thought. One line of argument suggests that there is no place for blasphemy within Buddhism. Scriptures, and in particular the *Brahmajala-sutta*, hold that material culture or objects have no real sacred value; as objects of attachment they can only create obstacles for the individual's quest for merit and distort the mind. In effect, the argument goes, it is not possible to offend a true Buddhist. Against this, in many ways, urban interpretation (Fuller 2016) is the more popular religiosity that attributes protective power to the Buddha, the *dhamma* (Buddhist teachings) and the *sangha* (the community of monks). Paul Fuller points out that Buddhist objects are part of what has been termed 'apotropaic Buddhism', which constitutes 'a constant feature' in Buddhist history and in which objects, texts and teachings are regarded as having protective or magical qualities. 'An image of the Buddha [which in a way is not simply an image, but *is* the Buddha, a surrogate Buddha, as it were], has the power to protect and avert danger' (Fuller 2014; italics original).

Although Buddhism played a central role in both pre-colonial and colonial Burmese identity, a fact evidenced by Myanmar's early twentieth-century revivalist movement (Winfield 2010; Cox 2010), there were nonetheless few legal cases of religious offence in either Lower or Upper Burma, at least in the colonial era documents. These few cases were often related to interpretational issues among Buddhist monks rather than to offence caused by members of other religions.

A significant development, however, was the so-called shoe controversy, which helped to tie the fledgling independence movement to the country's more traditional Buddhist symbols and identity (Charney 2009). The controversy involved the exemption for European visitors to pagoda precincts to remove their shoes. This exemption was seen by many Burmese Buddhists, nationalists and traditionalists alike, as a sign of disrespect. Having simmered for many years, the shoe controversy finally became a nationwide issue in 1916. Protests, publications and public pressure eventually forced the colonial authorities to allow trustees of pagodas to bar visitors who did not remove their shoes. The controversy was one element, albeit of great significance, which inspired many Burmese to connect colonialism to a sense of moral decline among Buddhists. Its significance lay particularly in that it politicised and mobilised both lay people and Buddhist monks in protests that lasted into the 1920s and 1930s.

However, Buddhism-based political unrest was soon eclipsed by the emergence of a new class of secular-oriented intellectuals. Educated in British-inspired institutions, this intelligentsia soon took the lead of the independence movement (both against the British and later against the Japanese), and later formed the core of independent Myanmar's political elite. After Independence, Buddhism played a minor role in politics, even if ideas of making Buddhism a national religion were contemplated (Charney 2009, 101ff); this was even more the case during the first decades of the military regime, with its muscular and notionally socialist nationalism. From the late 1980s, in particular after the botched 1990 election, the regime sought increasingly to appropriate Buddhism and Buddhist symbols as a means of legitimising its rule. Pagodas and temples underwent reconstruction as the regime sought to reinforce a connection between the nation-state and Buddhism. In the same period there was also a significant mobilisation of monks against the regime (Gravers 2012), and what amounted to a struggle over moral power took place.

This struggle over moral power did not spill into political mobilisation on issues of religious offence, however. A recent study (Ashin and Crosby 2017) shows that between 1980 and 2017 there were only 17 rulings concerning heresy (*adhamma*) and malpractice (*avinaya*) in state-regulated Buddhist courts. Most of the accused were monks. There is no mention in the constitution of state preference for Buddhism, and the State Sangha Act (1990) enables state control over the *sangha*, in particular 'unruly' anti-regime monks.

After the 2007 'Saffron Revolution', which saw the first major mobilisation of monks alongside lay protesters, and in particular after the dissolution of the military regime and the junta in 2010–11, religion has come to occupy a more prominent role in political mobilisation. It is also in this period that accusations of religious offence have been raised – notably in the two cases involving bar owners who used inappropriate depictions of the Buddha and that of the writer and opposition politician who claimed that the Buddha was not Burmese. Both cases are investigated by Frydenlund (chapter 3).

Analytical perspectives: Beyond methodological nationalism

The countries considered in this volume have followed radically different political paths following the dissolution of the British Empire. Moreover, the religious traditions that dominate in the four countries are radically different from one another. Nevertheless the respective nationalist ideologies in all four countries have all become increasingly flavoured by religion during the past decades, and all four countries have experienced a perceptible rise in religious offence controversies.

What are we to make of these similarities? Are they coincidental? The question is yet to be addressed within the scholarship of blasphemy and religious offence, which has tended to focus on individual countries – a perspective that unwittingly promotes methodological nationalism by naturalising national borders (cf. Glick Schilller 2006, 613). We believe that much can be gained for scholars of blasphemy accusations in India to look across the border to Pakistan and Myanmar, or for scholars of religious offence in Pakistan to look to India and Bangladesh, and so on. In this way we can attempt to track the commonality of these countries with respect to religious offence controversies beyond the IPC and their colonial pasts.

This volume is an attempt – possibly the first one – to think beyond methodological nationalism and to consider the denominators and similarities that cut across national, political and religious differences. However, the development of a politics of blasphemy in fairly similar directions across these lines requires a more explicitly formulated analytical point of departure to come properly into view. To indicate the analytical directions we consider fruitful for reflecting on growth beyond national, political and religious contexts, we begin with those that have deepest academic trajectories before moving on to explore those we believe deserve more attention in future research.

Persisting importance of law

Recent scholarship has drawn attention to a range of important legal effects. Ramdev, Nambiar and Bhattacharya have argued that section 295-A has facilitated an 'outrage prone economy of "feeling"' which right-wing nationalists in India now regard as part of their national character (Ramdev, Nambiar and Bhattacharya 2016, xxi). Through it, they contend, religion was made legally immune from criticism and outrage was turned into a constitutive affect through which to lay political claims. Importantly, the process of 'immunising' religion from criticism in the name of vulnerable religious sentiments may be (retroactively) constitutive of these very feelings. Similarly, Mazzarella and Kaur argue that, far from merely containing religious sentiments, censorship and laws limiting certain forms of expression can be 'a generative technology of truth' (Mazzarella and Kaur 2009, 5) that produces normative modes of attachment to the divine. According to Pinney, law here functions in an 'iatrogenic' manner – that is, as generating the very problem it attempts to prevent (Pinney 2009; see also Abbas 2013; Adcock 2016; Siddique and Hayat 2008). Rather than simply preventing the targeted offence, these scholars claim, laws incite the display of wounded sentiments and warrant its strategic mobilisation in response to perceived offences. These laws, Ahmed writes, 'demanded both the demonstration of emotionality and its containment and regulation through judicial process' (Ahmed 2009, 173).

Elaborated further by Scott, this led to the development in colonial India of a thriving 'extralegal legal culture' – evidenced, for instance, by the legal language deployed by offended groups to narrate their emotional experience and make it politically legible (Scott 2015, 301). Extended to contemporary India, this perspective illuminates how Hindu nationalists who petition the courts to limit what can legally be written or taught about Hinduism describe their emotional reaction to the 'offence' in a language that directly reflects the wording of the law (Adcock 2016, 330; Pennington 2016). The analytical perspective deployed in this volume draws on this perspective to accentuate how seemingly visceral and spontaneous displays of outrage are often fundamentally shaped by colonial law and the administrative apparatus of South Asia's postcolonial states.

While this perspective captures well the paradoxical outcome of regulating public expressions, it is too mechanistic to shed light on the banal fact that there are also numerous transgressions that have *not* been construed as offensive. An alternative, which many of our contributors endorse, is to think of law as having a 'crystallising' effect. Like a catalyst, it enables people to make their discontent, ambitions, rivalry or even greed manifest by offering a 'site' for articulating 'widely different interests and grievances, often only remotely connected with the event itself', to borrow Grillo's formulation (Grillo 2007b, 21). Within this perspective, law is primarily *trans*formative rather than formative. It enables action, but never from a clean slate.

Whichever perspective one sides with, scholars of offence controversies in South Asia agree that the law and its wordings are of tremendous importance. This is why so many scholars refer to the addition of 295-A as a seminal turning point – much as the Rushdie affair or the Chevalier de la Barre affair (Cabantous 2002, 127–32) are treated in the scholarship of religious offence in the Euro-American world. That said, a quick recapitulation of the *Rangila Rasul* case and the anti-Rushdie agitations in Britain also brings up an approach to the role of law that has received less attention. Here law is seen as a desired state of protection that a minority group can envision and is willing to fight for. Whereas Indian Muslims in the 1920s agitated for a law that protected the Prophet and won, British Muslims in the 1980s agitated for universalisation of the English blasphemy legislation, but lost.

Blasphemy accusations as politics

Alongside legal history and the implications of law, the analytical perspective that has deepest pedigree in the study of South Asian censorship controversies is undoubtedly political instrumentalism. Anchored in rationalist perspectives emphasising human agency (whether individual or institutional) and goal-driven behaviour, the underlying question is approximately as follows: who would have something to gain from instigating a censorship controversy – and what would that 'something' be? This line of inquiry has a clear continuity with studies of interreligious riots in India, where instrumentalist perspectives came to enjoy a prominent position in the 1990s.

In his poignant investigations of riots in north India, Brass (1997; 2003) departs vehemently from former studies which suggested that collective violence somehow erupts spontaneously. Instead he insists that riots are 'a grisly form of dramatic production' (Brass 2003, 15) involving preparation, rehearsals and particular individuals whose skill lies in their ability to orchestrate riots. Drawing on these insights, Elcheroth and Reicher argue that mass street mobilisations and communal violence in India have become a standard practice in the Indian political repertoire (Elcheroth and Reicher 2017, 157). Applied to the study of blasphemy controversies, this approach can be used to illuminate at least four questions: who are the actors that gain from these controversies; what is the role of the state therein; how is offence dramatised as political theatre; and, lastly, whether these controversies can facilitate the emergence of new kinds of publics?

Answering the first of these questions is not as straightforward as it may seem. Certainly many scholars draw attention to how majority communities appear more eager to initiate blasphemy cases than others. But the language of religious sentiment and the laws regulating blasphemy and 'hate speech' have also been harnessed by marginalised groups to secure justice, not least in India (Ramdev et al. 2016, xxxvi; see also Frøystad 2016). Although the 'winners' of blasphemy controversies cannot therefore be deduced *a priori*, evidence suggests that the legal provisions tend to be availed of by those who can simultaneously display a credible threat of disruption to substantiate the veracity of the outrage. As such these individuals and groups – usually numerical majorities or economic and social elites – are far more likely to see their petition for censorship and castigation answered by the state (Adcock 2016; Viswanath 2016, 355). With the participation of skilled organisers and provocateurs – for example, Dinanath Batra in India or the TLP and the Sunni Tehreek in Pakistan – 'any disrespect can be portrayed as blasphemy and lay itself to popular mobilizations – which may translate into votes' (Jaffrelot 2008, 2). The regulation of religious offence therefore appears as a preferential system in which only the powerful may draw direct dividends from staging their affective sensitivity.

In Pakistan, Bangladesh and Myanmar, religious minorities very rarely seek legal redress for offensive acts against their religion. By contrast, religious minorities in India have been able to deploy hurt religious feelings to gain concessions from the state, but atheist and agnostic groups have not (Padmanabhan 2016, 355). Thus, depending on whose sentiments were outraged, blasphemy regulations do not operate uniformly. Further, while these laws can theoretically be availed of by any citizen of India, Bangladesh and Myanmar, Pakistan possesses provisions to protect one religion in particular, Islam, and to discriminate specifically against another, the Ahmadi sect. To sum up, the regulation of religious offence tends to privilege the dominant classes in a given society and also to reinforce the state's coercive powers to curb dissent – or at least to give it moral or religious legitimacy.

Another perspective on blasphemy controversies as politics concerns the ambiguous role of the state. Calls for redress are almost always directed at the state and its legal institutions. Called upon to arbitrate, the state may respond by recognising the sacred nature of that which was allegedly offended and by 'protecting' the injured party. The role of the state has often been conceived as a benevolent arbiter that does its best to maintain peaceful coexistence between religious communities (cf. Frøystad 2013). However, as Adcock (2016) points out, the arbiter's 'tolerance' can also entail cultural and political regulation. Its legal apparatus produces normative judgements on what counts as religiously offensive, and what should remain unspeakable (Butler 1997, 96ff).

Moreover the state can draw on local concerns over blasphemy and 'hate speech' to widen its regulatory reach – as when the Pakistani state banned YouTube (from 2012 to 2015) and blocked individual online content purportedly to protect local Muslim sentiments.[24] Similarly, Mazzarella and Kaur also draw attention to the historically constituted conflation in India between moral and political regulation of blasphemy, sedition and obscenity (Mazzarella and Kaur 2009). Of course, similar perspectives are also applicable beyond South Asia, as Saeed demonstrates in her analysis of how the Egyptian and Turkish states used the Charlie Hebdo controversy as an opportunity to tighten control over media and bestow legitimacy to its disciplinary actions (Saeed 2015, 39).

A third perspective on blasphemy controversies as politics elucidates how protests are staged as political theatre. Inspired by dramaturgical and performative perspectives developed by Goffman (1969), Schechner (1988), Tilly (2006) and others, this optic is useful for bringing out how participants in anti-blasphemy protests often draw on local repertoires forged during the colonial period and in the course of successive protests (e.g. Blom 2008). It also brings out how protesters must stage and embody their hurt to make it visible in order to obtain legal redress – without which, as noted by Cefaï, there can be no collective action (Cefaï 2007, 163, quoted in Blom and Jaoul 2008, 2; Ramdev et al. 2016, xxvii).

For Pakistan, it also helps to tease out the long tradition for heroising assassins of blasphemers. Recalling the protests in the UK following the publication of his book *The Satanic Verses*, Rushdie describes how protesters' 'faces were performing anger for the cameras ... rejoicing in their anger, believing their identity was born of their rage' (Rushdie 2012, 128). Whether the protesting community is a minority (e.g. British Muslims in the UK or Hindu nationalists in the US) or a powerful segment of society (e.g. Hindu nationalist organisations in India), it must foreground its vulnerability, its sense of hurt and need for state protection as a strategy for political assertion.

A fourth perspective on blasphemy controversies as politics pertains to how they nurture the emergence of new kinds of publics and political communities, and new modes of envisioning political sovereignty. The prominence of blasphemy can fruitfully be interpreted as symptomatic of a 'politics of identity', whereby marginalised communities deploy a language of hurt to demand safeguards or the acknowledgement of a historical injustice or cultural singularity. While some scholars analyse such processes in terms of assertiveness of formerly disenfranchised communities (as does Sen, chapter 6), others warn against the resulting fragmentation of citizenship and established political communities into privatised 'constituencies of blood' (Al-Azmeh 2013).

Scaled up, some also point out how blasphemy accusations bring about a new assertiveness and unify global communities across territorial divides. This process could be seen during the Rushdie affair, but the emergence of new media has now made such processes even easier. As Saeed has argued (2015), alleged transgressions such as the Danish cartoons (2005–6) and the Charlie Hebdo caricatures (2015) bring dispersed Muslim communities into a global conversation that helps to reinforce a transnational and trans-sectarian Muslim identity, if not 'new forms of ethical and political practice for a global arena' (Devji 2006). The same is true of diasporic Hindu formations; as Zavos (2008) and Anderson (2015) have argued, their 'performative expressions of outrage' against M. F. Husain's paintings, or against an offensive stamp, helped to make Hinduism visible in the UK and gave coherence to an idiosyncratic inflection of Hindu nationalism in Europe.

Analysing blasphemy controversies as politics can yield a plethora of insights – but they can also easily fall short in isolation. The cultivation of an emotionality of hurt and the emergence of new technologies of communication play vital roles in this regard. Let us now move on to perspectives that analyse these developments in their own right.

Affect and blasphemy

Elucidating how emotions are influenced by law and dramatised to increase the likelihood of a ban does not exhaust the role of sentiments in religious offence controversies. To understand what moves people to tear down transgressive posters, march through the streets in scorching heat, thrash 'blasphemers' or merely appeal to their community leaders to take action, it is equally necessary to lend an ear to the protesters. When engaging with them, theories of affect appear particularly useful. The strand that has gained most currency for such purposes is the Spinozian brand taken up by Deleuze and Guattari, given further momentum by Massumi (1995) and thereafter refined by a number of scholars (see Seigworth and Gregg 2010).

One of the advantages of the notion of affect is that it captures the indirect and non-reflective thinking (cf. Thrift 2004, 60) that moves people to act. In contrast to 'emotions', a term generally used in reference to inner sentiments (but see Blom and Tawa Lama-Rewal, in press 2019), affect explicitly refers to sentiments that prompt immediate action. Yet due to their non-reflective status, the resultant actions are not always predictable and thus not easily pinned down by instrumentalist perspectives. However, such unpredictability does not result in affect-related behaviour being entirely random. It is almost always cultural, sometimes in ways that can be thoroughly naturalised, as in the case discussed by Schaflechner (chapter 8). It is also worth noting that affect can be 'tamed' and choreographed to suit a standard protest repertoire, as suggested in Ruud's analysis (chapter 4) of how collective outrage can be staged for television cameras.

Applied to the study of religious offence controversies, the theory of affect can help us to understand why reactions to a given transgression can become so intense – even if a rumoured transgression is all it takes, as in the cases described by Blom (2008), Kublitz (2015) and Ruud (chapter 4). Blom's work is particularly enlightening since it illuminates how some of the young men in Lahore who protested against the 2006 *Jyllands-Posten* cartoons were taken by surprise by the strength of their own reactions. Schaflechner's chapter extends this analysis by discussing how such reactions, including the killing of 'blasphemers', are moulded by a history of past emotions connected to blasphemy, and by a specific literary genre that magnifies such affective response.

Theories of affect can also illuminate the *rise* of religious offence controversies. As Mazzarella has argued (Mazzarella 2012), modernity's attempts to promote rational deliberation and suppress affect are perhaps now giving way. Affect is returning to the political domain with full force, partly because of the ways in which mediatisation transforms the economy of attention. Consequently, politics is increasingly becoming a matter of affect engineering (Thrift 2004, 64). A meme combining wickedness with humour can create larger ripples than even the most eloquent political oratory. A key question is thus how and why people come to develop such devoted and uncompromising attitudes (cf. Atran 2016), often within remarkably short spans of time. As Frøystad suggests (chapter 5), part of the answer is the growing reliance on visual communication enabled by increased smartphone connectivity. To make sense of such processes, we underline the importance of mediatisation, which the next section approaches through the optic of materiality.

Materiality and mediatisation

Though several scholars have noted the significance of materiality and mediatisation for bringing about religious offence controversies in South Asia, few have moved beyond mentioning it in passing. In our view, the medium and replicability of the alleged transgression deserve far closer attention. Consider, for instance, that M. F. Husain's paintings of Hindu goddesses from the 1970s did not spark any controversy until they were reproduced in a critical article in a magazine in 1996. This fact exemplifies not only how religio-political organisations may actively look for transgressions to rally around, but also how mediatisation multiplies a message in ways that dramatically increase the likelihood of a successful 'transgression hunt'.

Similarly, scholars have remarked how in the last decades of the colonial era, controversies around publications such as *Rangila Rasul* and *Satyarth Prakash* were made possible by the formidable growth of affordable print technology at the time (e.g. Scott 2015; Nair 2013). The same applies to Periyar's controversial *Ramayana* interpretations, which he disseminated on inexpensive paper through his own journals, magazines and printing press, allowing for the extensive coverage of his grievances and campaigns (Richman 1991, 180). The transition from finite modalities of replication and circulation, such as the print medium, to the unbound possibilities afforded by digital networks, invites us to look beyond the question of replicability and to take materiality equally seriously as symbolic content, legal affordances and political processes.

Materiality approaches – as developed in social anthropology – examine how humans and their material surroundings are mutually constitutive (Miller 2005). By attuning our senses to how human sociality is conditioned by its material surroundings, artefacts and images, they seek to elevate materiality from its subordinate role. In this way we can 'think through things' (cf. Henare, Holbraad and Wastell 2007) and follow their effects, which necessitates that we pay close attention to their meanings – whether common sense or surprising.[25] By introducing this orientation more explicitly into the scholarship of religious offence controversies, we can better appreciate how these controversies may be shaped by the properties of the medium through, or on which, the alleged offence is committed, documented and reproduced. For instance, what difference does it make whether an alleged offence is spoken, written, drawn or gestured – and thereafter possibly multiplied by being telecast, printed or digitalised?

Addressing such questions goes far beyond rehearsing the contrast between disallowing visual representations of the divine (as in Islam and

Judaism) or encouraging them, as in most Hindu traditions. In chapter 7, for example, Asad Ali Ahmed examines how legal courts in Pakistan can transform alleged religious offences from verbal remarks into typed witness statements and judgements that repeat, preserve and multiply them, with profound implications for the defendant. Shifting to the smartphone revolution in India, Frøystad examines in chapter 5 how the emergence of digital devotion in the shape of sharing and commenting on religious images may create a marked 'split affect' in the case of innovative or daring images – particularly if their circulation crosses religious boundaries.

In short, the magnitude of a blasphemy accusation partly rests on the material form, reproducibility and potential circulation of the alleged transgression. Though an insulting utterance, a burnt Quran, a sacrilegious theatre play or an eaten cow cannot be readily reproduced, a video, an image or a novel in digital format can easily be disseminated globally through digital channels, thus altering the economy of outrage in South Asia and beyond.

A quick glance at recent scholarship on media and mediatisation helps us appreciate just how much the public sphere has burgeoned and democratised from the days of print newspapers. Consider India, where until 1991 the state monopolised broadcast media with a view to 'educate, inform and … help maintain national unity', leaving only the privately owned printed press to exercise critical journalism (Thussu 1999, 126). Since the end of the state monopoly, private broadcast has grown exponentially and now totals over 800 television channels (Government of India 2018). In Pakistan, where television broadcasting was liberalised in 2000, there are over 130 channels, whereas Bangladesh has at least 26 (Udupa and McDowell 2017, 2). In Myanmar most television channels remain state-owned and, though the government has created an opening for private channels and satellite television, these are still under tighter regulation than in the other countries considered here.

To this we must add the internet revolution followed by the advent of social media. Today active social media users account for one-third to one-fifth of South Asia's population.[26] Across the region, internet connectivity has developed through mobile phones rather than computer screens (Udupa and McDowell 2017, 2–3). A steadily growing proportion of South Asia's diverse population thus participates in this burgeoning media swirl at the same time as new connections are forged across countries and with their diasporas. These developments, as eloquently pointed out by Udupa and McDowell, have reconfigured political participation in profound ways, not least by forging a new kind of pluralism that 'places antagonism, passions and collective forms of identification at the center of democratic politics' (Udupa and McDowell 2017, 4).

This has a number of implications for how religious offence controversies begin and unfold. Firstly, social media enables the proliferation of potential transgressions and allows a degree of anonymity to its users, which reduces the threshold for sharing transgressive content. Secondly, the expansion of the mediascape has led to the emergence of 'cultures of counterfeit' and piracy, where copies circulate without necessary reference to an original (Comaroff 2007, 137; Sundaram 2010). This means that it is increasingly difficult for the state to stop the circulation of a pirate and online copy of a banned text, film or expression. Conversely, it renders it impossible for a given community to impose its taboos on a global scale. Thirdly, the growing possibilities for sharing visual images and videos enhance affectivity. And lastly, the expansion of new media technologies makes religious offence controversies simultaneously local and global. Though usually anchored in a specific local context, they can more easily be delocalised and transposed, particularly if the accuser is part of a wider transnational network or community (e.g. Taylor 2011).

In this regard, it should be noted that these new media facilitate the spatial circulation of *both* 'offensive' material *and* outrage, as we saw as early as in the affair of *The Satanic Verses*.[27] Herein we also find a counter-intuitive point: outraged publics not only communicate their indignation, but may also circulate the incriminated material to persuade co-religionists to protest. Just as an official ban often turns out to be the best way to publicise a book or a film (Scott 2015, 298; Kaur and Mazzarella 2009, 9), the outraged party often gives visibility and fame to that against which they protest. These observations notwithstanding, Favret-Saada's observation that there is a marked discrepancy between the potential controversies that escalate and those that fall into oblivion (Favret-Saada 1992, 257) is equally apt today. Accusations that find popular traction are typically the culmination of complex sets of actions over time that often go undetected (cf. Ghosh 2016; Favret-Saada 2004), which resonates with our earlier point about law as a 'crystalliser' of discontent.

We leave it to our contributors to continue these reflections. For now, let us conclude that there are numerous reasons why scholars of religious offence controversies need to be more attentive to mediatisation and other aspects of materiality, and should examine texture, replicability and circulation as closely as contested meanings and political contexts. One of them is the ongoing 'media revolution', which strikes us as crucial for the escalation of blasphemy controversies. That being said, it is now time to introduce the chapters that follow.

***

Chapter outline

Although the four countries covered in this volume – Pakistan, India, Bangladesh and Myanmar – are very different in terms of religious traditions and political culture, they are also united by certain elements of colonial history. For the sake of simplicity, we use the epithet 'South Asia' to indicate our regional focus, even though we are acutely aware of the ambiguous regional status of Myanmar.[28] Yet our aim is not to monitor the history of blasphemy controversies in a given political region, but rather to bring up case studies that help us reflect on their rise across stark differences of political regimes and religious orientations. Each contributor focuses on an individual case or type of accusation of a religious offence, on the ground that the complexity of the rise needs to be understood by means of in-depth investigation. Each contributor has also been asked to emphasise dimensions of their case that help to illuminate the rise of religious offence controversies beyond it – and, if possible, beyond the national context in which it is enveloped. It is this labour of identifying the 'drivers' of contemporary offence controversies that led us to single out the analytical frameworks spelled out in the previous sections.

The first of these, the framing role of the law, is investigated in particular in Paul Rollier's paper on the growing anti-blasphemy agitation in Pakistan. He addresses the relationship between the law and people's concrete engagement with the risk of desecration. He draws attention to the way in which people's relationship with desecration rests on a distinct mode of apprehending holy words and objects. Encoded in law, this relationship ultimately demands vigilance towards the potential blasphemer in each and every person. In a Pakistani court, this leads to a situation in which the adjudication of blasphemy allegations is caught in a circular logic that paradoxically magnifies the offence.

More generally, Rollier notes how the rhetoric of, and sensitivity towards, religious offence translates into everyday practices and attitudes – and now extends to all religious communities, which confers on it a quasi-ecumenical quality. This in turn helps us to understand how the idiom of outrage has become so widespread in South Asia. The framing role of the colonial-era law plays a significant role, and we shall see the law making its appearance in several of the chapters. Moreover, the very personal sense of grievance when symbols and objects are said to be 'attacked' helps to explain why irreverence, mocking or deliberate insult cannot be let pass by many. A further observation in Rollier's chapter is that the misuse of anti-blasphemy laws and the performance of outrage have become a weapon in interpersonal disputes, and are increasingly wielded by competing religious entrepreneurs and politicians to gain visibility and relevance.

This aspect of religious outrage is further explored in detail from the other end of South Asia, Buddhist-majority Myanmar. In chapter 3, Iselin Frydenlund details two cases of blasphemy accusations and judicial proceedings there. Her analysis focuses on how, in this fledgling electoral democracy, accusations of blasphemy are being negotiated and pushed through media, the judiciary and in political mobilisations by representatives of majoritarian religious organisations. Frydenlund points to a wider political context, in which a certain form of cultural change is seen as a postcolonial invasion, resistance to which becomes defence of traditional values. There is also a historical context formed by the so-called 'shoe controversies' in the colonial era which, as mentioned earlier, helped to set Buddhism and respect for its symbols at the centre of the nation's independence struggle. These combine to fuel blasphemy controversies in a situation where the newfound democracy faces political power tussles as well as the commercialisation of religious symbols.

Similarly chapter 4, in which Arild Englesen Ruud investigates accusations launched against a government minister in Bangladesh, sees the suddenness of the charges and their success in light of electoral democracy and the ideological conflict at the heart of the postcolonial republic. Here the ruling party has sought at times to portray itself as the custodian of a secular polity, willing to accommodate the needs of minorities and non-believers, and at other times as the representative of a generally religious populace. The story of the conflict over the nature of the state is old, but increasingly characteristic of much of South Asia's late twentieth- and early twenty-first-century history. Modi's rise to power in India is perhaps the globally most appreciated expression of this change, but its antecedents derive from the cow protection movement of the nineteenth century and the various reform movements within all major religious denominations in the region. For Bangladesh, the conflict lies at the core of its modern identity. Ruud locates the sudden success of the protests in the highly visible mobilisation by the secularists in the years before the minister made his statements. This prehistory, in which the government's position had been ambiguous and indecisive, enabled Islamist groupings to seize their opportunity. Helped by activist social media, the message of outrage was spread within days.

Social media is another core theme in this collection. The role played by social media in spreading accusations of blasphemy or potentially offensive content is suggested in several of the contributions, but it is most thoroughly investigated by Kathinka Frøystad in chapter 5. Her case study focuses on visual images disseminated via mobile phones and on the viscerality of digital images. Here, as in several of the other chapters, the outrage is caused by visual rather than textual or oral content: it is about depictions rather than statements. In Ruud's Bangladeshi case, Latif Siddique's controversial statement in New York was filmed and circulated on YouTube and on television. Rather than the statement itself, what was found offensive was the circulation of its video recording and the fact that it entered people's homes and daily lives. In Frydenlund's Burmese case, it was the depiction of the Buddha with earphones that instilled a sense of outrage. Frøystad's case is about memes or photoshopped images circulated via mobile phones.

Frøystad takes the two parallel revolutions – the rapid expansion of smartphones and the rise of blasphemy controversies – as her starting point. She merges these fields of enquiry by examining how smartphones contribute to the rise of blasphemy accusations, and illustrates how circulating religious images on smartphones, such as memes in which deities are portrayed in novel or daring ways, may be deemed offensive if they 'spill out' to the wrong audience. Frøystad pays particular attention to the capacity of social media for large-scale circulation and inexpensive image transmission in societies characterised by 'split publics', thus producing radically contradictory 'affects' in societies marked by political tension and anxiety. The case in question follows the historical trajectory of a narrative about the Kaaba in Mecca as a former (or in some versions, present) Shiva temple. Despite the narrative's existence in textual and verbal forms at least since the 1940s, it did not result in blasphemy controversies before being transmuted to digital visual images.

In most of our chapters it is representatives of the majority community who most vocally express their outrage and grievances against blasphemers. In Pakistan and Bangladesh these are usually Muslims claiming to represent the *ummah*; in Myanmar these are members of the Buddhist majority and their community of monks, the *sangha*, who object most fiercely to the perceived offence. As for India, the denouncers are often Hindus, especially proponents of Hindutva, though they can also be representatives of minority religions, as in Frøystad's chapter.

Several chapters also bring out how secularists and non-believers can be disproportionately targeted: a writer who denounces the *sangha*'s nationalist understanding of Buddhism (chapter 3), a boastful minister (chapter 4), and Governor Taseer in Pakistan, killed by his bodyguard for denouncing the country's harsh blasphemy laws (chapter 8). Their relaxed interpretation of religion was understood as secular and representative of Western-inspired values and lifestyle. All were seen as part of a wider ideological or cultural divide, and as representing a non-national or even anti-national ethos.

This topic is most thoroughly investigated in chapter 6. Here Moumita Sen explores the nascent worship of Mahishasur, hitherto considered by most to be the demon slain by the goddess Durga and who is now celebrated with gusto in a religious festival particularly popular in Kolkata. Increasingly, however, and quite rapidly, the cult of Mahishasur has gained popularity among Adivasis throughout West Bengal, as well as among leftist groups in places such as Jawaharlal Nehru University and elsewhere. The cult itself, and the support it has gained, have roused the anger of groups professing more traditional interpretations. These include some among the Hindu nationalists, most notably Smriti Irani, a BJP minister, who has claimed that worshippers of Mahishasur are anti-national. As in other chapters, the offended parties often use set stylistic devices to stress their sense of outrage.

In chapter 6, the minister's insistence on raising the issue in parliament is set against the canvas of the politics of ethnicisation in India. Sen's study underlines the importance of emergent Adivasi assertion and newfound identity in confronting an increasingly hard-line Hinduisation propagated by the Hindutva forces; acknowledging the role of both is crucial to understanding this rise of the politics of offence.

Sometimes both parties to the controversy are part of the same religious community, as in the case investigated by Asad Ali Ahmed. In this complex and puzzling case, Ahmed explores the layers of interpretation and mutually conflicting ontologies at stake in the controversy. Specifically, he deals with the trial of a Sufi teacher ridiculed in the English language press, dismissed in a meandering judicial system and maligned by religious scholars, who accuse him of blasphemy. But the story is also about translation across a real and imagined cultural divide. The study locates a driver in the different registers, or even ontologies, involved in blasphemy accusations: the English language world of the Pakistani elite, the Urdu-speaking world with its own religious interpretations upheld in the state instruments of law and court, and the religious and spiritual world of the Sufi and of the Sufi's antagonists. The one is anathema to the sensibilities of the other – a situation which is not unlike that found in other countries (think of the India v. Bharat debate) and which underlines the vast distances in cultural anchorage found in South Asian societies.

While in Ahmed's chapter the offended party is Deobandi, Jürgen Schaflechner points out in chapter 8 that blasphemy accusations in

Pakistan are often pushed by Barelwis, who have a mass following and are often misrepresented as open-minded Sufis. To Barelwis, Schaflechner writes, disrespect of the Prophet is intolerable and their veneration of Muhammad unsurpassed. He points out that within the devotional Barelwi tradition and cosmology, the Prophet is elevated to a position of unconditional devotion. For Barelwis, the Prophet is considered to be 'the perfect man' (*al-insan al-kamil*). As Schaflechner investigates the most well-known cases of blasphemy allegations in the country, those involving Asia Bibi, a Christian woman, and Governor Salman Taseer, he is intrigued by the post mortem veneration of the Governor's murderer, his bodyguard Mumtaz Qadri. The author reminds us of the existence of a vast corpus of hagiographic literature eulogising lay Muslims who daringly lost their lives in an attempt to punish blasphemers. Schaflecher also brings out the contagious nature of blasphemy accusations: once Asia Bibi has been accused of blasphemy, any form of support extended to her becomes problematic. Governor Salman Taseer was not murdered because he had committed blasphemy, but because he was critical of a law that protected the Prophet.

Finally, Ute Hüsken's thoughtful Afterword to this volume points out some alternative and potentially fruitful disciplinary and conceptual avenues to investigate the rise of religious offence politics. One of these, she writes, consists in approaching blasphemy controversies through the lens of ritual studies, so as to appreciate better *how* they work on us as humans and as society through their performative efficacy. She also points out, rather optimistically, that the 'accelerated connectivity' characteristic of our era indeed facilitates the expansion of blasphemy controversies, but may also be harnessed to further mutual understanding.

As the cases studies in this volume make clear, the politics of religious offence has become a significant phenomenon in contemporary Pakistan, India, Bangladesh and Myanmar. To explain its prevalence and its emergence, we have indicated a series of important, and to an extent unrelated, developments that in combination have caused this 'perfect storm': the rapid introduction of social media and smartphones, the deepening of democracy and its effect on political and religious rivalry, the mutual suspicion between religious and secular reasoning and, finally, the growing demands for recognition among both marginalised and hegemonic communities. These are developments that have a profound impact on society. Whatever the next turn will be in the history of religious offence controversies in South Asia, it will be deeply anchored in these developments.

Notes

1. This is further motivated by the terms commonly used by our interlocutors in South Asia to denote religious offence, such as *tauheen*, *behurmati*, *ninda* and *pakhandi*, which are broadly synonymous with 'insult' and 'disgrace', be it performed through oral, visual or physical means.
2. Think of the stoning scene in Monty Python's *Life of Brian*: a crowd is about to stone Matthias to death because he has uttered the name of God, 'Jehovah'. But the accused turns to the priest and starts to question his sentence: 'Look, I don't think it ought to be blasphemy, just saying "Jehovah"'. 'He said it again!' shouts the angry crowd. As Matthias repeatedly utters the name of God, the priest exhorts him: 'I'm warning you. If you say "Jehovah" once more…'. He claps his hand over his mouth, but it is too late: a stone hits him. Despite his attempt to control the unruly offended crowd, the priest is eventually stoned to death.
3. On the notion of blasphemy in Islam and its overlap with apostasy, see Stewart (n.d.), Forte (1994) and Izutsu (2002, 99–101).
4. On the different argumentative traditions in support of 'free speech', see Danbury (2017).
5. Article 9 of the European Court of Human Rights for instance, which guarantees the right to freedom of thought, conscience and religion, may conflict with others' right to freedom of expression (Article 10). On the different European approaches to the limitation of freedom of expression, see Leigh (2011) and Trispiotis (2013).
6. The former UN Special Rapporteur on freedom of religion or belief, Asma Jahangir, expressed these concerns very clearly (Limon, Ghanea and Power 2017, 652–3).
7. Consider, for instance, the 2008 abolition of the British law against blasphemy and the simultaneous enactment of the Racial and Religious Hatred Act (Barendt 2011; Sandberg and Doe 2008). On the shift from blasphemy laws to anti-hate speech legislations, see Temperman and Koltay (2017).
8. This line of thinking proposes to take the recent return of blasphemy controversies as a vantage point to question the 'patterns of liberal restriction' that underlie the 'situation of hegemonic secularism' prevalent in the West (Asad, Brown and Mahmood 2009, 30, 105). Less a means to restrict free speech, 'blasphemy' is seen as reflective of the shape that free speech arguments take in a given context (35).
9. On the notion of religious offence at the European Court of Human Rights, see Lewis (2017).
10. See, for instance, UNHRC (2008).
11. As of 2016, seven out of 45 European countries still possessed anti-blasphemy provisions of some sort (Theodorou 2016). In 2012, 32 states in the world possessed such laws (PEW 2012).
12. The right to freedom of expression is enshrined in article 19 of the Indian, Pakistani and Burmese constitutions and in article 39 of Bangladesh's, as well as in Article 19 of the Universal Declaration of Human Rights.
13. Salman Rushdie, a celebrated British author of Indian descent, had come under fire for his unfavourable parody of Prophet Muhammad in his 1988 novel *The Satanic Verses*. Immediately after its publication, it was banned from importation in India. The controversy acquired global resonance following the effort of diaspora circles in England to communicate their outrage to the rest of the Muslim world, including Iran, whose ayatollah issued a fatwa against Rushdie in the shape of a death threat. Not only was Rushdie now in danger wherever he went, but so were those associated with his work: his Japanese translator was killed and his Norwegian publisher injured.
14. '295. Whoever destroys, damages, or defiles any place of worship, or any object held sacred by any class of persons with the intention of thereby insulting the religion of any class of persons, or with the knowledge that any class of persons is likely to consider such destruction, damage, or defilement as an insult to their religion, shall be punished with imprisonment of either description, for a term which may extend to two years, or with fine, or with both.'

    '296. Whoever voluntarily causes disturbance to any assembly lawfully engaged in the performance of religious worship or religious ceremonies, shall be punished with imprisonment of either description, for a term which may extend to one year, or with fine, or with both.'

    '297. Whoever, with the intention of wounding feelings of any person, or of insulting the religion of any person, or with the knowledge that the feelings of any person are likely to be wounded, or that the religion of any person is likely to be insulted thereby, commits any trespass in any place of worship or on any place of sepulture or any place set apart for the performance of funeral rites or as a depository for the remains of the dead, or offers any indignity to any human corpse, or causes disturbance to any persons assembled for the performance of funeral ceremonies, shall be punished with imprisonment of either description, for a term which may extend to one year, or with fine, or with both.'

'293 [a typo for 298]. Whoever, with the deliberate intention of wounding the religious feelings of any person, utters any word or makes any sound in the hearing of that person, or places any object in the sight of that person, or makes any gesture in the sight of that person, shall be punished with imprisonment of either description, for a term which may extend to one year, or with fine, or with both.' (Morgan and Macphearson 1863, 217–21).

15. '153. Whoever malignantly and wantonly, by doing any thing [sic] which is illegal, gives provocation to any person, intending or knowing it to be likely that such provocation will cause the offence of rioting to be committed in consequence of such provocation, be punished with imprisonment of either description, for a term which may extend to one year, or with fine, or with both; and if the offence of rioting be not committed, with imprisonment of either description, for a term which may extend to six months, or with fine, or with both.' (Morgan and Macphearson 1863, 127–8).

16. '153-A. Whoever by words, either spoken or written, or by signs, or by visible representations, or otherwise, promotes or attempts to promote feelings of enmity or hatred between different classes of Her Majesty's subjects shall be punished with imprisonment which may extend to two years, or with fine, or with both.' (LawyerServices. In, n.d.).

17. One around Pandit Kalicharan Sharma's *Vichitra Jivan* (published in Agra in 1923) and the other around Devi Sharan Sharma's *Sair-i-Dozakh* (published in Amritsar in 1927). See Thursby (1975).

18. Additionally there was the problem of *intention*: the publisher stated that his aim had never been to hurt anyone, but merely to make Muslims aware of the dubious morality of the person they venerated.

19. In its present form, the penalty is of two years' imprisonment in Myanmar and Bangladesh, three years in India and ten years in Pakistan.

20. The wording of these sections is the same across penal codes (including Sri Lanka) with one notable exception: the offence of insulting religion or religious beliefs carries a maximum two year sentence in Bangladesh and Myanmar, three years in India and ten years in Pakistan. Another small difference consists in the additional words 'or otherwise' in the Indian section 295-A.

21. Two of these five sections, namely 298-B and 298-C, are designed to criminalise the ritual markers of the Ahmadi community, whose members had been officially declared 'non-Muslims' in 1974. The legal reforms undertaken in the 1980s, which also included the creation of sharia courts and the *hudood* ordinance, was part a broader policy of Islamisation (or Deobandization) of society. See Nasr (2001, 130–57). For a detailed overview of the parliamentary debates that led to these reforms, see Ahmed (2018); on the possibility of further reforming these laws, see Hoffman (2014) and Rumi (2018).

22. To be more precise, blasphemy accusations rarely target Sunni Muslims. Over the last three decades Shias and Ahmadis, who represent about 20 per cent and 0.3 per cent of the population, were the accused in 70 per cent of all cases under sections 295-B, 295-C and 298, while Christians and Sunnis were the accused in 15 per cent of these cases respectively (figures derived from HRCP 2017, 96 and Julius 2016, 98). On blasphemy controversies in relation to religious minorities in Pakistan, see also Abbas (2013), Gregory (2012), Shakir (2015) and Siddique and Hayat (2008).

23. Judges are sometimes coerced to sentence the accused without evidence and lawyers attacked or pressured deliberately to misrepresent their clients (see UNHRC 2013, 13–14).

24. In the case of media restrictions, the blasphemous is treated on a par with content that the state deems un-Islamic or anti-national. In 2017 it issued over 1,000 requests to Facebook to restrict access to specific content, resulting in the shutdown of 177 pages for violating local anti-blasphemy laws or condemning Pakistan's independence (Facebook 2017b). India issued over 10,000 complaints, and had over 1,000 pages shut down for violating local laws relating to defamation of religion and hate speech (Facebook 2017a).

25. Though made popular by the work of Gell (1998) and Latour (e.g. 1999, 2005), scholars disagree on the depth of this perspective's intellectual roots. For Miller (2005), they seemingly only extend back to Bourdieu's celebrated analysis (1977) of how the architecture of the Kabyle reproduced their thinking. For Høstaker (2015), they date back to the paleontology of Leroi-Gourhan (1911–86), which discussed how early humans externalised tasks to things, which in turn influenced their lives in profound ways.

26. In 2018 India had 250 million active social media users, Pakistan 35 million, Bangladesh 30 million and Myanmar 18 million (Kemp 2018a, 2018b).
27. Favret-Saada writes that shortly after the publication of *The Satanic Verses* in the UK, local Muslim organisations disseminated relevant sections of the book among ambassadors of Muslim countries in London (1992, 251). Henceforth the campaign expanded to the Middle East, Africa and back to South Asia.
28. We are also aware of the omission of Sri Lanka, Nepal and Bhutan. In addition, both the Maldives and Afghanistan are at times listed as part of South Asia.

References

Abbas, Shemeem Burney. 2013. *Pakistan's Blasphemy Laws: From Islamic Empires to the Taliban*. Austin: University of Texas Press.

Adcock, C. S. 2016. 'Violence, passion, and the law: A brief history of Section 295A and its antecedents.' *Journal of the American Academy of Religion* 84 (2): 1–15.

Ahmed, Ali Asad. 2009. 'Spectres of Macaulay: Blasphemy, the Indian Penal Code, and Pakistan's postcolonial predicament', in *Censorship in South Asia: Cultural Regulation from Sedition to Seduction*, Raminder Kaur and William Mazzarella, eds, 172–97. Bloomington: Indiana University Press.

Ahmed, Ali Asad. 2016. 'Of panopticons, pannomions and the corpo-real: Bentham, blasphemy and the Indian Penal Code'. Paper presented at the South Asian Seminar Series, Cornell University, 25 April 2016.

Ahmed, Asad. 2018. 'Law and order: A brief history of the anti-blasphemy laws'. *The Herald*, February (updated 10 May) 2018. https://herald.dawn.com/news/1154036, accessed 13 June 2018.

Al-Azmeh, Aziz. 2013. 'Post-modern obscurantism and the lure of blasphemy', in *Blasphemy as Political Game*. Geneva Graduate Institute. Keynote lecture on author's academia.edu webpage.

Anderson, Edward. 2015. "Neo-Hindutva": the Asia House M. F. Husain campaign and the mainstreaming of Hindu nationalist rhetoric in Britain.' *Contemporary South Asia* 23 (1): 45–66.

Appignanesi, Lisa and Sara Maitland. 1989. *The Rushdie File*. London: Fourth Estate.

Asad, Talal, Wendy Brown and Saba Mahmood. 2009. *Is Critique Secular? Blasphemy, Injury, and Free Speech*. Berkeley: University of California Press.

Ashin, Janaka and Kate Crosby. 2017. 'Heresy and monastic malpractice in the Buddhist court cases (Vinicchaya) of modern Burma (Myanmar).' *Contemporary Buddhism* 18 (1): 199–261.

Atran, Scott. 2016. 'The devoted actor: Unconditional commitment and intractable conflict across cultures.' *Current Anthropology* 57 (Supplement 13): S192–S2013.

Bailey, Greg. 2014. 'Indology after Hindutva.' *South Asia: Journal of South Asian Studies* 37 (4): 700–7.

Baker, C. Edwin. 1989. *Human Liberty and Freedom of Speech*. New York; Oxford: Oxford University Press.

Ball, John Clement. 2017. 'Capital offences: Public discourse on satire after Charlie Hebdo.' *Genre* 50 (3): 297–317.

Barendt, Eric. 2011. 'Religoius hatred laws: Protecting groups or belief?' *Res Publica* 17 (1): 41–53.

Barrier, N. Gerald. 1974. *Banned: Controversial Literature and Political Control in British India, 1907–1947*. Columbia: University of Missouri Press.

Bettiza, Gregorio and Filippo Dionigi. 2015. 'How do religious norms diffuse? Institutional translation and international change in a post-secular world society.' *European Journal of International Relations* 21 (3): 621–46.

Blom, Amélie. 2008. 'The 2006 Anti-"Danish cartoons" riot in Lahore: Outrage and the emotional landscape of Pakistani politics.' *South Asia Multidisciplinary Journal* 2008 (2).

Blom, Amélie and Nicholas Jaoul. 2008. 'Introduction: The moral and affectual dimension of collective action in South Asia.' *South Asia Multidisciplinary Academic Journal* 2008 (2).

Blom, Amélie and Stéphanie Tawa Lama-Rewal, eds, In press, 2019. *Emotions, Mobilisations, and South Asian Politics*. New Delhi: Routledge India.

Boquérat, Gilles. 2016. 'Pakistan's power game and the new media landscape', in *Pakistan's Political Labyrinths: Military, Society and Terror*, Ravi Kalia, ed, 40–58. New York; London: Routledge.

Boudet, Jean-Patrice. 1996. 'La genèse médiévale de la chasse aux sorcières, jalons en vue d'une relecture', in *Le Mal et le Diable: Leurs Figures à la Fin du Moyen Age*, Nathalie Nabert, ed, 35–52. Paris: Beauchesne.
Bourdieu, Pierre. 1977. *Outline of a Theory of Practice*. Cambridge: Cambridge University Press.
Brass, Paul. 1997. *Theft of an Idol: Text and Context in the Representation of Collective Violence*. Princeton, NJ : Princeton University Press.
Brass, Paul. 2003. *The Production of Hindu–Muslim Violence in Contemporary India*. Seattle: University of Washington Press.
Bretherton, Luke. 2016. 'Blasphemy', in *New Dictionary of Theology: Historical and Systematic, 2nd ed*, Martin Davie, Tim Grass, Stephen R. Holmes, John McDowell and Thomas A. Noble, eds, London; Downers Grove: Inter-Varsity Press.
Brown, Wendy. 2006. *Regulating Aversion: Tolerance in the Age of Identity and Empire*. Princeton, NJ; Oxford: Princeton University Press.
Butler, Judith. 1997. *Excitable Speech: A Politics of the Performative*. New York; London: Routledge.
Cabantous, Alain. 2002. *Blasphemy: Impious Speech in the West from the Seventeenth to the Nineteenth Century*. New York: Columbia University Press.
Cefaï, Daniel. 2007. *Pourquoi se mobilise-t-on? Les théories de l'action collective*. Paris: La Découverte.
Chandran, Mini. 2010. 'The democratisation of citizenship: books and the Indian public', *Economic and Political Weekly* 45(40): 27–31.
Chandran, Mini. 2017. *The Writer, the Reader and the State: Literary Censorship in India*. New Delhi: Sage Publications.
Charney, Michael W. 2009. *A History of Modern Burma*. Cambridge: Cambridge University Press.
Christin, Olivier. 1992. 'Le statut ambigu du blasphème au XVIe siècle.' *Ethnologie française* 22 (3): 337–43.
Comaroff, John L. 2007. 'Law and disorder in the postcolony.' *Social Anthropology* 15 (2): 133–52.
Copeman, Jacob. 'The mimetic guru: Tracing the real in Sikh – Dera Saccha Sauda relations', in *The Guru in South Asia: New Interdisciplinary Perspectives*, Jacob Copeman and Aya Ikegame, eds, Abingdon: Routledge.
Cox, Laurence. 2010. 'The politics of Buddhist revival: U Dhammaloka as social movement organiser.' *Contemporary Buddhism* 11 (2): 173–227.
Cumper, Peter. 2017. 'Blasphemy, freedom of expression and the protection of religious sensibilities in twenty-first-century Europe', in *Blasphemy and Freedom of Expression: Comparative, Theoretical and Historical Reflections after the Charlie Hebdo Massacre*, Jeroen Temperman and András Koltay, eds, 137–52. Cambridge: Cambridge University Press.
Dacey, Austin. 2012. *The Future of Blasphemy: Speaking of the Sacred in an Age of Human Rights*. New York: Continuum.
Daechsel, Markus. 2006. *The Politics of Self-Expression: The Urdu Middle-Class Milieu in Mid-Twentieth Century India and Pakistan*. London: Routledge.
Danbury, Richard. 2017. 'Where should speech be free? Placing liberal theories of free speech in a wider context', in *Speech and Society in Turbulent Times: Freedom of Expression in Comparative Perspective*, Monroe Price and Nicole Stremlau, eds, 171–91. Cambridge: Cambridge University Press.
Date, Vidyadhar. 2007. 'Politics of Shivaji: The James Laine affair.' *Economic and Political Weekly* 42 (20): 1812–14.
de Saint Victor, Jacques. 2016. *Blasphème: brève histoire d'un 'crime imaginaire'*. Paris: Gallimard.
De, Sanchari. 2015. 'Context, image and the case of the Shahbag movement.' *Contemporary Social Science* 10 (4): 364–74.
Delumeau, Jean. 1978. *La Peur en Occident (XIVe–XVIIe siècles): Un Cité Assiégée*. Paris: Fayard.
Devji, Faisal. 2006. *Back to the Future: Cartoons, Liberalism, and Global Islam*, Open Democracy, 12 April 2006. https://www.opendemocracy.net/en/liberalism_3451jsp/.
Dharwadker, Vinay. 2012. 'Censoring the "Ramayana"'. *PMLA* 127 (3): 433–50.
Dhavan, Rajeev. 2008. *Publish and be Damned: Censorship and Intolerance in India*. New Delhi: Tulika Books.
Dierkens, Alain and Jean-Philippe Schreiber. 2012. *Le Blasphème: Du Péché au Crime?* Bruxelles: Éditions de l'Université de Bruxelles.
Elcheroth, Guy and Stephen Reicher. 2017. *Identity, Violence and Power: Mobilising Hatred, Demobilising Dissent*. Basingstoke: Palgrave Macmillan.

Eriksen, Jens-Martin and Frederik Stjernfelt. 2012. *The Democratic Contradictions of Multiculturalism*. New York: Telos Press.

Facebook. 2017a. 'India.' https://transparency.facebook.com/government-data-requests/country/IN, accessed 23 August 2017.

Facebook. 2017b. 'Pakistan.' https://transparency.facebook.com/government-data-requests/country/PK, accessed 23 August 2018.

Fair, Christine, Ali Hamza and Rebecca Heller. 2017. 'Who supports suicide terrorism in Bangladesh? What the data say.' *Politics and Religion* 10(3): 622–61.

Favret-Saada, Jeanne. 1992. 'Rushdie et compagnie: Préalables à une anthropologie du blasphème.' *Ethnologie française* 22 (3): 251–60.

Favret-Saada, Jeanne. 2004. *Le Christianisme et ses Juifs 1800–2000*. Paris: Éditions du Seuil.

Favret-Saada, Jeanne. 2017. *Les sensibilités religieuses blessées. Christianismes, blasphèmes et cinéma 1965–1988*. Paris: Fayard.

Forte, David F. 1994. 'Apostasy and blasphemy in Pakistan.' *Connecticut Journal of International Law* 10 (1): 27–68.

Freitag, Sandria B. 1989. *Collective Action and Community: Public Arenas and the Emergence of Communalism in North India*. Berkeley: University of California Press.

Frøystad, Kathinka. 2009. 'Communal riots in India as a transitory form of political violence: Three approaches.' *Ethnic and Racial Studies* 32 (3): 442–59.

Frøystad, Kathinka. 2013. 'Cosmopolitanism or iatrogenesis? Refections on religious plurality, censorship and disciplinary orientations', in *Navigating Social Exclusion and Inclusion in Contemporary India and Beyond: Structures, Agents, Practices*, Uwe Skoda, Kenneth Bo Nielsen and Marianne Qvortrup Fibiger, eds, 19–40. London: Anthem Press.

Frøystad, Kathinka. 2016. 'A fine balance: Censoring for respect and social harmony', in *India's Democracies*, Arild Engelsen Ruud and Geir Heierstad, eds, 183–222. Oslo: Universitetsforlaget.

Fuller, Paul. 2014. 'Blasphemy and offence in Burmese Buddhism.' *DVB online*, 14 December 2014, http://www.dvb.no/analysis/blasphemy-and-offence-in-burmese-buddhism-myanmar/46504.

Fuller, Paul. 2016. 'The idea of "blasphemy" in the Pali canon and modern Myanmar.' *Journal of Religion and Violence* 4 (2): 159–81.

Ganor, Sa'ar and Igor Kreimerman. 2017. 'Going to the bathroom at Lachish.' *Biblical Archaeology Review* 43 (6): 56–60.

Gell, Alfred. 1998. *Art and Agency: An Anthropological Theory*. Oxford: Clarendon Press.

Ghosh, Shohini. 2016. 'The alchemy of hate and hurt', in *Sentiment, Politics, Censorship: The State of Hurt*, Rina Ramdev, Sandhya Devesan Nambiar and Debatitya Bhattacharya, eds, 55–68. New Delhi: Sage.

Gilmartin, David. 1991. 'Democracy, nationalism and the public: A speculation on colonial Muslim politics.' *South Asia: Journal of South Asian Studies* 14 (1): 123–40.

Gilmartin, David. 1998. 'Partition, Pakistan, and South Asian history: In search of a narrative.' *Journal of Asian Studies* 57 (4): 1068–95.

Glick Schilller, Nina. 2006. 'Beyond the ethnic lens: Locality, globality, and born-again incorporation.' *American Ethnologist* 33 (4): 612–33.

Goffman, Erving. 1969. *The Presentation of Self in Everyday Life*. London: Penguin.

Government of India. 2018. 'Permitted private satellite TV channels', https://www.broadcastseva.gov.in/ChannelListDemo, accessed 25 September 2018.

Gravers, Mikael. 2012. 'Monks, morality and military: The struggle for moral power in Burma – and Buddhism's uneasy relation with lay power.' *Contemporary Buddhism* 13(1): 1–33.

Gregory, Shaun. 2012. 'Under the shadow of Islam: The plight of the Christian minority in Pakistan.' *Contemporary South Asia* 20 (2): 195–212.

Grenda, Christopher S., Chris Beneke and David Nash. 2014. *Profane: Sacrilegious Expression in a Multicultural Age*. Berkeley: University of California Press.

Grillo, Ralph. 2007a. 'Artistic licence, free speech and religious sensibilities in a mulitcultural society', in *Law and Ethnic Plurality: Socio-Legal Perspectives*, Prakash Shah, ed, 107–25. Koninklijke: Brill.

Grillo, Ralph. 2007b. 'Licence to offend? The Behzti affair.' *Ethnicities* 7 (1): 5–29.

Gubo, Darara. 2015. *Blasphemy and Defamation of Religions in a Polarized World: How Polarized Fundamentalism is Challenging Fundamental Human Rights*. Maryland: Lexington Books.

Hasan, Mushirul. 1988. 'Indian Muslims since independence: In search of integration and identity.' *Third World Quarterly* 10 (2): 818–42.

Henare, Amira, Martin Holbraad and Sara Wastell. 2007. *Thinking Through Things: Theorising Artefacts Ethnographically*. London: Routledge.

Hervik, Peter. 2011. *The Annoying Difference: The Emergence of Danish Neonationalism, Neoracism, and Populism in the Post-1989 World*. Oxford: Berghahn.

Hoffman, Matt. 2014. 'Modern blasphemy laws in Pakistan and the Rimsha Masih case: What effect – if any – the case will have on their future reform.' *Washington University Global Studies Law Review* 12 (2): 371–92.

Høstaker, Roar. 2015. 'We have always been posthuman', in *The 40th Annual Meeting of the Social Studies of Science Society (4S)*. Denver, Colorado.

Human Rights Commission of Pakistan. 2017. 'State of Human Rights in 2016', http://hrcp-web.org/hrcpweb/wp-content/uploads/2017/05/State-of-Human-Rights-in-2016.pdf, accessed 8 June 2017.

Husain, Muzaffar. 2014. 'Blasphemy laws and mental illness in Pakistan.' *The Psychiatric Bulletin* 38 (1): 40–4.

International Commission of Jurists. 2015. *On Trial: The Implementation of Pakistan's Blasphemy Laws*. International Commission of Jurists. http://www.refworld.org/docid/565da4824.html, accessed 9 August 2017.

International Commission of Jurists. 2018. *Pakistan: Widespread Practice of Enforced Disappearance must be Addressed*. https://www.icj.org/pakistan-widespread-practice-of-enforced-disappearance-must-be-addressed/, accessed 9 January 2018.

Izutsu, Toshihiko. 2002. *Ethico-religious Concepts in the Qur'ān*. Montreal; Ithaca, NY: McGill-Queen's University Press.

Jaffrelot, Christophe. 2008. 'Hindu nationalism and the (not so easy) art of being outraged: The Ram Setu controversy.' *South Asia Multidisciplinary Academic Journal* 2008 (2): 1–17.

Joshi, A. P., M. D. Srinivas and Jitendra Bajaj. 2003. *Religious Demography of India*. Chennai: Centre for Policy Studies.

Julius, Qaiser. 2016. 'The experience of minorities under Pakistan's blasphemy laws.' *Islam and Christian-Muslim Relations* 27 (1): 95–115.

Kaur, Raminder and William Mazzarella. 2009. *Censorship in South Asia: Cultural Regulation from Sedition to Seduction*. Bloomington: Indiana University Press.

Keane, Webb. 2009. 'Freedom and blasphemy: On Indonesian press bans and Danish cartoons.' *Public Culture* 21(1): 47–76.

Kemp, Simon. 2018a. 'Digital in 2018 in Southeast Asia, Part I – North-West.' https://www.slideshare.net/wearesocial/digital-in-2018-in-southeast-asia-part-1-northwest-86866386, accessed 23 August 2018.

Kemp, Simon. 2018b. 'Digital in 2018 in Southern Asia.' https://www.slideshare.net/wearesocial/digital-in-2018-in-southern-asia-86866282, accessed 23 August 2018.

Khalid, Imran. 2018. 'Changing trends of religious vote in Pakistan.' *New Age*, 19 September 2018. http://www.newagebd.net/article/50912/changing-trends-of-religious-vote-in-pakistan.

Klausen, Jytte. 2009. *The Cartoons that Shook the World*. New Haven: Yale University Press.

Kublitz, Anja. 2015. 'The cartoon controversy: Creating Muslims in a Danish setting', in *In the Event: Towards the Analysis of Generic Moments*, Lotte Meinert and Bruce Kapferer, eds, 107–125. London: Berghahn.

Laine, James W. 2011. 'Resisting my attackers, resisting my defenders: Representing the Shivaji narratives', in *Engaging South Asian Religions: Boundaries, Appropriations, Resistances*, Matthew Schmalz and Peter Gottschalk, eds, 153–72. New York: SUNY Press.

Laine, James W. 2014. 'Censorship in brown and white.' *South Asia: Journal of South Asian Studies* 37 (4): 708–16.

Latour, Bruno. 1999. *Pandora's Hope: Essays on the Reality of Science Studies*. Cambridge, MA: Harvard University Press.

Latour, Bruno. 2005. *Reassembling the Social: An Introduction to Actor-Network Theory*. Oxford: Oxford University Press.

Lawton, David. 1993. *Blasphemy*. Philadelphia: University of Pennsylvania Press.

LawyerServices.In., n.d. 'Addition of new section after section 153, Act XLV, 1860', http://www.lawyerservices.in/INDIAN-PENAL-CODE-AMENDMENT-ACT-1898-SECTION-5-Addition-of-new-section-after-section-153-Act-XLV-1860.

Leigh, Ian. 2011. 'Damned if they do, damned if they don't: The European Court of Human Rights and the protection of religion from attack.' *Res Publica* 17 (1): 55–73.

Levy, Leonard Williams. 1981. *Treason Against God: A History of the Offense of Blasphemy*. New York: Schocken Books.
Lewis, Tom. 2017. 'At the deep end of the pool: religious offence, debate speech and the margin of appreciation before the European Court of Human Rights', in *Blasphemy and Freedom of Expression: Comparative, Theoretical and Historical Reflections after the Charlie Hebdo Massacre*, Jeroen Temperman and András Koltay, eds, 259–93. Cambridge: Cambridge University Press.
Limon, Marc, Nazila Ghanea and Hilary Power. 2017. 'Freedom of Expression and religions, the United Nations and the "16/18 Process"', in *Blasphemy and Freedom of Expression: Comparative, Theoretical and Historical Reflections after the Charlie Hebdo Massacre*, Jeroen Temperman and András Koltay, eds, 645–80. Cambridge: Cambridge University Press.
Loetz, Francisca. 2009. *Dealings with God: From Blasphemers in Early Modern Zurich to a Cultural History of Religiousness*. Farnham: Ashgate.
Mahmood, Saba. 2009. 'Religious reason and secular affect: An incommensurable divide?' *Critical Inquiry* 35 (4): 836–62.
Mahmood, Saba. 2015. *Religious Difference in a Secular Age*. Princeton, NJ: Princeton University Press.
Mahmood, Saba and Peter Danchin. 2014. 'Immunity or regulation? Antinomies of religious freedom.' *South Atlantic Quarterly* 113 (1): 129–59.
Marsh, Joss. 1998. *Word Crimes: Blasphemy, Culture, and Literature in Nineteenth-Century England*. Chicago: University of Chicago Press.
Martignoni, Andrea. 2005. 'Langue blasphèmatoire et geste iconoclaste. Blasphèmes et pouvoirs dans la Terre Ferme vénitienne à la fin du Moyen Age.' *Studi Veneziani* XLIX: 79–112.
Massumi, Brian. 1995. 'The autonomy of affect.' *Cultural Critique* 31 (2): 83–109.
Mazzarella, William. 2012. 'Affect: What is it good for?', in *Enchantments of Modernity: Empire, Nation, Globalization*, Surabh Dube, ed, 291–309. London: Routledge.
Mazzarella, William and Raminder Kaur. 2009. 'Between sedition and seduction: Thinking censorship in South Asia', in *Censorship in South Asia: Cultural Regulation from Sedition to Seduction*, Raminder Kaur and William Mazzarella, eds, 291–309. Bloomington: Indiana University Press.
McGarry, Molly. 2014. 'Base, vile and depraved: Blasphemy and other moral genealogies.' *Qui Parle: Critical Humanities and Social Sciences* 22 (2): 31–56.
Miller, Daniel. 2005. 'Materiality: An introduction', in *Materiality*, Daniel Miller, ed, 1–50. Durham: Duke University Press.
Mishra, Pankaj. 2016. 'Welcome to the age of anger'. *The Guardian*, 8 December 2016. https://www.theguardian.com/politics/2016/dec/08/welcome-age-anger-brexit-trump, accessed 31 January 2018.
Mishra, Pankaj. 2017. *Age of Anger: A History of the Present*. New York: Farrar, Strauss and Giroux.
Morgan, Walter and Arthur George Macphearson. 1863. *The Indian Penal Code (Act XLV of 1860) with notes*. Calcutta: C. G. Hay & Co.
Nair, Neeti. 2013. 'Beyond the "communal" 1920s: The problem of intention, legislative pragmatism, and the making of Section 295A of the Indian Penal Code.' *Indian Economic and Social History Review* 50 (3): 317–40.
Nash, David. 2007. *Blasphemy in the Christian World: A History*. Oxford: Oxford University Press.
Nasr, Seyyed Vali Reza. 2001. *Islamic Leviathan: Islam and the Making of State Power*. New York: Oxford University Press.
National Commission for Justice and Peace. 2013. *Human Rights Monitor 2012–13: A Report on the Religious Minorities in Pakistan*. Lahore: National Commission for Justice and Peace.
Office of the United Nations High Commissioner for Human Rights. 2011. 'Combating intolerance, negative stereotyping and stigmatization of, and discrimination, incitement to violence, and violence against persons based on religion or belief. UN draft resolution of Pakistan (on behalf of the Organization of the Islamic Conference)', https://digitallibrary.un.org/record/701464, accessed 14 September 2018.
Office of the United Nations High Commissioner for Human Rights. 2017. 'Concluding observations on the initial report of Pakistan'. 23 August 2017. http://tbinternet.ohchr.org/_layouts/treatybodyexternal/Download.aspx?symbolno=CCPR/C/PAK/CO/1&Lang=En
Padmanabhan, Mukund. 2016. 'How far can you go?', in *Sentiment, Politics, Censorship: The State of Hurt*, Rina Ramdev, Sandhya Devesan Nambiar and Debatitya Bhattacharya, eds, 3–14. New Delhi: Sage.

Parmar, Sejal. 2015. 'Uprooting "defamation of religions" and planting a new approach to freedom of expression at the United Nations', in *The United Nations and Freedom of Expression and Information: Critical Perspectives*, Tarlach McGonagle and Yvonne Donders, eds, 373–427. Cambridge: Cambridge University Press.

Patra, Atul Chandra. 1961. 'A historical introduction to the Indian Penal Code.' *Journal of the Indian Law Institute* 3 (3): 351–66.

Pennington, Brian K. 2016. 'The unseen hand of an underappreciated law: The Doniger affair and its aftermath.' *Journal of the American Academy of Religion* 84 (2): 323–36.

Pernau, Margrit. 2015. 'The virtuous individual and social reform: Debates among North Indian Urdu speakers', in *Civilizing Emotions: Concepts in Nineteenth-Century Asia and Europe*, Margrit Pernau, Helge Jordheim and Orit Bashkin, eds, 169–86. Oxford: Oxford University Press.

PEW. 2012. 'Laws penalizing blasphemy, apostasy and defamation of religion are widespread', PEW Research Center, http://www.pewforum.org/2012/11/21/laws-penalizing-blasphemy-apostasy-and-defamation-of-religion-are-widespread/, accessed 14 September 2018.

Pinney, Christopher. 2005. 'Things happen, or: From which moment does that object come?', in *Materiality*, Daniel Miller, ed, 256–72. Durham: Duke University Press.

Pinney, Christopher. 2009. 'Iatrogenic religion and politics', in *Censorship in South Asia: Cultural Regulation from Sedition to Seduction*, Raminder Kaur and William Mazzarella, eds, 29–62. Bloomington: Indiana University Press.

Pohjonen, Matti and Sahana Udupa. 2017. 'Extreme speech online: An anthropological critique of hate speech debates.' *International Journal of Communication* 11: 1173–91.

Price, Monroe and Nicole Stremlau. 2017. 'Conclusion: Philosophies and principles in turbulent times', in *Speech and Society in Turbulent Times: Freedom of Expression in Comparative Perspective*, Monroe Price and Nicole Stremlau, eds, 317–24. Cambridge: Cambridge University Press.

Raj, Richa. 2015. 'A pamphlet and its (dis)contents: A case study of Rangila Rasul and the controversy surrounding it in colonial Punjab, 1923–29.' *History and Sociology of South Asia* 9 (2): 146–62.

Rajagopal, Arvind. 2001. *Politics after Television: Hindu Nationalism and the Reshaping of the Public in India*. Cambridge: Cambridge University Press.

Rajagopal, Arvind. 2009. 'A "split public" in the making and unmaking of the Ram Janmabhumi campaign', in *The Indian Public Sphere: Readings in Media History*, Arvind Rajagopal, ed, 207–27. New Delhi: Oxford University Press.

Ramaswamy, Sumathi, ed, 2011. *Barefoot Across the Nation: Maqbool Fida Husain and the Idea of India*. New York: Routledge.

Ramdev, Rina, Sandhya Devesan Nambiar and Debatiya Bhattacharya. 2016a. 'Sentimental sovereignties: Hurt and the political unconscious', in *Sentiment, Politics, Censorship: The State of Hurt*, Rina Ramdev, Sandhya Devesan Nambiar and Debatiya Bhattacharya, eds, xv–1. New Delhi: Sage Publications.

Rehman, Javaid and Stephanie E. Berry. 2012. 'Is "Defamation of Religions" passé? The United Nations, organisation of Islamic cooperation, and Islamic State practices: Lessons from Pakistan.' *George Washington International Law Review* 44 (3): 431–72.

Riaz, Ali. 2004. *God Willing: The Politics of Islamism in Bangladesh*. Lanham, MD: Rowman & Littlefield.

Riaz, Ali. 2008. 'Constructing outraged communities and state responses: The Taslima Nasreen saga in 1994 and 2007.' *South Asia Multidisciplinary Academic Journal* [online], 2.

Riches, David. 1986. 'The phenomenon of violence', in *The Anthropology of Violence*, David Riches, ed, 1–17. Oxford: Basil Blackwell.

Richman, Paula. 1991. 'E. V. Ramasami's reading of the Ramayana', in *Many Ramayanas: The Diversity of a Narrative Tradition in South Asia*, Paula Richman, ed, 175–201. Berkeley: University of Califormia Press.

Roy, Anupam Debashis. 2018. 'Shahbag stolen? Third force dynamics and electoral politics in Bangladesh.' *South Asia Research* 38 (3s): 1–24.

Rumi, Raza. 2018. 'Unpacking the blasphemy laws of Pakistan.' *Asian Affairs* 49 (2): 319–39.

Rushdie, Salman. 2012. *Joseph Anton: A Memoir*. London: Random House.

Saeed, Sadia. 2015. 'The Charlie Hebdo affair and the spectre of majoritarianism.' *Economic and Political Weekly* 50 (23): 37–41.

Sáez, Lawrence. 2018. 'Bangladesh in 2017: Bloggers, floods, and refugees.' *Asian Survey* 58 (1): 127–33.

Sandberg, Russell and Norman Doe. 2008. 'The strange death of blasphemy.' *Modern Law Review* 71 (6): 971–86.
Sarma, Deepak. 2014. 'The Doniger difficulty: Colonial Cotton and Swadeshi sensibilities.' *India Review* 13 (3): 287–9.
Schechner, Richard. 1988. *Performance Theory*. London: Routledge.
Scott, J. Barton. 2015. 'Aryas unbound: Print Hinduism and the cultural regulation of religious offense.' *Comparative Studies of South Asia, Africa and the Middle East* 35 (2): 294–309.
Seigworth, Gregory J. and Melissa Gregg. 2010. 'An inventory of shimmers', in *The Affect Theory Reader*, Melissa Gregg and Gregory J. Seigworth, eds, 1–25. Durham: Duke University Press.
Sethi, Aarti and Shuddhabrata Sengupta. 2014. 'Toward a reader's uprising: Reflections in the wake of assaults on books and authors in today's India.' *India Review* 13 (3): 290–9.
Sethi, Najam. 2017. 'Capitulation or orchestration', *The Friday Times*, 1 December 2017, http://www.thefridaytimes.com/tft/capitulation-or-orchestration/, accessed 17 September 2018.
Shakir, N. 2015. 'Islamic shariah and blasphemy laws in Pakistan.' *The Round Table: The Commonwealth Journal of International Affairs* 104 (3): 307–17.
Siddique, Osama and Zahra Hayat. 2008. 'Unholy speech and holy laws: Blasphemy laws in Pakistan – controversial origins, design defects and free speech implications.' *Minnesota Journal of International Law* 17 (2): 303–85.
Singh, Amit. 2018a. 'Conflict between freedom of expression and religion in India – A case study.' *Social Sciences* 7 (article no.108): 1–17.
Singh, Amit. 2018b. *The Conflicts of Freedom of Expression and Religion*. Mumbai: People's Book Shop.
Skuy, David. 1998. 'Macaulay and the Indian Penal Code of 1862: The myth of the inherent superiority and modernity of the English legal system compared to India's legal system in the nineteenth century.' *Modern Asian Studies* 41 (3): 615–31.
Stephens, Julia. 2014. 'The politics of Muslim rage: Secular law and religious sentiment in late colonial India.' *History Workshop Journal* 77 (1): 45–64.
Stewart, Devin J., n.d. 'Blasphemy', in *Encylopedia of the Qur'ān*, Jane Dammen McAuliffe ed, Leiden: Brill.
Sundaram, Ravi. 2010. *Pirate Modernity: Delhi's Media Urbanism*. Oxford; New York: Routledge.
Sunstein, Cass. 2017. *#Republic: Divided Democracy in the Age of Social Media*. Princeton NJ: Princeton University Press.
Talbot, Ian. 1998. *Pakistan, a Modern History*. London: C. Hurst.
Taylor, McComas. 2011. 'Mythology wars: The Indian diaspora, "Wendy's children" and the struggle for the Hindu past.' *Asian Studies Review* 35 (2): 149–68.
Taylor, McComas. 2014. 'Hindu activism and academic censorship in India.' *South Asia: Journal of South Asian Studies* 37 (4): 717–25.
Temperman, Jeroen and András Koltay. 2017. 'Introduction', in *Blasphemy and Freedom of Expression: Comparative, Theoretical and Historical Reflections after the Charlie Hebdo Massacre*, Jeroen Temperman and András Koltay, eds, 1–21. Cambridge: Cambridge University Press.
Thapar, Romila. 2014. 'Banning books.' *India Review* 13 (3): 283–6.
Theodorou, Angelina E. 2016. 'Which countries still outlaw apostasy and blasphemy?' PEW Research Center, http://www.pewresearch.org/fact-tank/2016/07/29/which-countries-still-outlaw-apostasy-and-blasphemy/, accessed 14 September 2018.
Thrift, Nigel. 2004. 'Intensities of feeling: Towards a spatial politics of affect.' *Geografiska Annaler* 86 (B): 57–78.
Thursby, Gene. 1975. *Hindu-Muslim Relations in British India*. Leiden: E. J. Brill.
Thussu, Daya Kishan. 1999. 'Privatizing the airwaves: The impact of globalization on broadcasting in India.' *Media, Culture & Society* 21 (1): 125–31.
Tilly, Charles. 2006. *Regimes and Repertoires*. Chicago: University of Chicago Press.
Tripathi, Salil. 2009. *Offence: The Hindu Case*. Calcutta: Seagull.
Trispiotis, Ilias. 2013. 'The duty to respect religious feelings: Insights from European Human Rights law.' *Columbia Journal of European Law* 19 (3): 499–552.
Udupa, Sahana and Stephen D. McDowell. 2017. 'Introduction: Beyond the "public sphere"', in *Media as Politics in South Asia*, Sahana Udupa and Stephen D. McDowell, eds, 1–17. London: Routledge.
United Nations Human Rights Council. 2008. 'Combating defamation of religions.' https://digitallibrary.un.org/record/624080?ln=en, accessed 14 September 2018.

United Nations Human Rights Council. 2013. 'Report of the Special Rapporteur on the independence of judges and lawyers, Addendum: Mission to Pakistan (A/HRC/23/43/Add.2), 4 April, 2013.' http://www.refworld.org/docid/51b9a0794.html, accessed 16 September 2018.

Venkatesan, Soumhya. 2014. 'From stone to god and back again', in *Objects and Materials: A Routledge Companion*, Penny Harvey, Eleanor Conclin Casella, Gillian Evans, Hannah Knox, Christine McLean, Elizabeth B. Silva, Nicolas Thoburn and Kath Woodward, eds, 72–81. New York: Routledge.

Viswanath, Rupa. 2016. 'Economies of offense: Hatred, speech, and violence in India.' *Journal of the American Academy of Religion* 84(2): 352–63.

Viswanathan, Gauri. 1998. *Outside the Fold: Conversion, Modernity, and Belief*. Princeton, NJ: Princeton University Press.

Waldrop, Anne. 1999. 'Gud, og jeg vet ikke hva.' *Samtiden* 1999 (5–6): 112–22.

Winfield, Jordan Carlyle. 2010. 'Buddhism and Insurrection in Burma, 1886–1890.' *Journal of the Royal Asiatic Society* 20 (3): 345–67.

Yeo, Stanley and Barry Wright. 2016 [2011]. 'Revitalising Macaulay's Indian Penal Code', in *Codification, Macaulay and the Indian Penal Code: The Legacies and Modern Challenges of Criminal Law Reform*, Barry Wright and Wing-Cheong Chan, eds, 3–18. Oxon: Routledge.

Zaman, Fahmida. 2018. 'Agencies of social movements: Experiences of Bangladesh's Shahbag movement and Hefazat-e-Islam.' *Journal of Asian and African Studies* 53 (3): 339–49.

Zavos, John. 2008. 'Stamp it out: Disciplining the image of Hinduism in a multicultural milieu.' *Contemporary South Asia* 16 (3): 323–37.

Zuber, Valentine. 2015. 'La liberté religieuse est-elle la clé de l'universalisation des droits de l'homme? Quelques éléments de réflexion pour une recherche globalise', in *Polarisations Politiques et Confessionnelles: La Place de l'islam dans les "Transitions" Arabes*, Anna Bozzo and Pierre-Jean Luisard, eds, 211–20. Rome: RomaTrE-Press.

2
'We're all blasphemers': The life of religious offence in Pakistan

Paul Rollier

Introduction

In 2016, at a village mosque in northeastern Punjab, a local imam rhetorically asked his audience whether anyone among them did not believe in the teaching of the Prophet. Mishearing, a teenager raised his hand. At once, the cleric accused him of blasphemy. The boy went home, cut off his blasphemous limb and walked back to the mosque with his severed hand on a tray (BBC 2016). A year later, in an unrelated development, hundreds of protesters were injured when the police attempted to disperse an anti-blasphemy sit-in that had put Islamabad on near lockdown (Masood 2017). Throughout the country activists had been demanding that the government sack its Law Minister, whom they accused of undermining the country's stringent blasphemy laws, and hence of challenging the status of the holy Prophet Mohammad.

Whether culminating in acts of self-mutilation or countrywide protests, the issue of blasphemy seems to have become an inexorable trait of Pakistan's socio-religious landscape. It was not always so. Under the colonial-era laws regulating 'offences against religion', there were only a handful blasphemy charges filed. But since the extension of these laws and the introduction of harsher penalties in the 1980s, there have been over 1,000 formal cases of blasphemy accusation, and over 60 suspected blasphemers have been killed extra-judicially, most of them members of religious minorities. It is as if the law indeed spawned, rather than curbed, its targeted offence.

These developments take place at a time when new media, mass education and a state-led process of Islamisation in the country have prompted a deepening 'objectification' of religion (Eickelman 1992, 643), evidenced by the salience of popular debates over what constitutes proper belief and religious practice. In this context, the recent proliferation of blasphemy controversies encompasses ever more behaviours, expressions and sections of society in its ambit. Anti-blasphemy laws have become a deadly weapon in interpersonal disputes, with the mere allegation of blasphemy often arousing mob violence. What is more, organised religious lobbies, political organisations and established politicians increasingly wield such imputations, or the threat thereof, to undermine their opponents' credibility or to stifle dissent.

In this chapter, I reflect on the social processes and cultural assumptions that underlie the growing anti-blasphemy mobilisation in Pakistan. Among scholars and informed observers, the dominant analysis of this phenomenon foregrounds the ways in which the law is instrumentalised by a range of actors for petty reasons. Yet this interpretation, I would argue, does not exhaust the range of practices and beliefs that facilitate the recent rise of blasphemy allegations. International coverage of this mobilisation tends to focus on the iconic victims of these accusations, such as Asia Bibi (see chapter 8), and on the spectacular acts of violence that occasionally surround these cases. This angle comforts liberal indignation and gives rise to the perception that Pakistan's issue with blasphemy ultimately reflects irreducible antagonisms between Islamists and liberal seculars, or between the Muslim majority and marginalised minorities. Instead, I argue that concerns over desecration transcend this partitioning; they do not only stem from theological or discursive positions regarding the true and correct understanding of religious beliefs and practices, or from the proper limits of the right to freedom of expression. In particular I emphasise how, in a context of pronounced inequalities, competition over scarce resources – from land and money to asylum status abroad – and the quest for political relevance and for control over public space facilitate the salience of blasphemy controversies. Further, I draw attention to the way in which people's relationship with desecration rests on a distinct mode of apprehending holy words, objects and images. This relationship, encoded in law, ultimately demands vigilance towards the potential blasphemer in each and every individual.

***

Existing research on the issue has revealed how the passionate invocation of 'love' towards the Prophet Muhammad, which lies at the heart of anti-blasphemy rhetoric and violence, must be understood in relation to colonial laws, designed to protect the 'religious sentiments' of erstwhile Indian subjects, and to the elaboration of stringent anti-blasphemy laws in the postcolonial period (Nair 2013; Saeed 2015; Scott 2015; Stephens 2014; see also chapter 1). Another strand of scholarship has documented the arbitrary nature of blasphemy accusations, the widespread violations of fair trial in these cases (e.g. International Commission of Jurists 2015) and the poor design of the existing legislation (Ahmed 2018; Forte 1994; Siddique and Hayat 2008). All of them observe that those who do not belong to the dominant religious strand, such as Shias, Ahmadis and Christians, are disproportionately affected by these laws. Sunni Muslims, who represent about 70 per cent of Pakistan's population, account for only 15 per cent of those accused of blasphemy.[1] But to appreciate the vitality of the anti-blasphemy movement, we must elucidate the emic understanding of blasphemy's relationship to law, the anxiety that surrounds its commission, its relation to people's ideas about language and the divine and the impact that these provisions may have on everyday social relations and behaviours.

To explore these issues, I draw on my ethnographic experience in some working-class neighbourhoods of Lahore, where I have been carrying out intermittent fieldwork on religion and politics since 2008. My interlocutors for this research include a range of actors implicated to varying degrees in blasphemy disputes, from lay Muslims occasionally protesting against 'blasphemous' movies or caricatures to relatives and lawyers of incarcerated defendants in cases of religious offence.

The variegated nature of these accusations is bewildering. They may, for instance, concern an allegedly burnt Quran, an inappropriate comment between friends, an offending 'like' or a poem on a Facebook post or a direct insult to a revered religious. We should not assume, however, that blasphemy accusations necessarily follow a transgressive deed or utterance. Inverting this sequence, and treating blasphemy as an empty or floating signifier, allows us not to lose sight of the well-documented fact that allegations of blasphemy often turn out to be spurious or based on fabricated evidence – a point even acknowledged by the Supreme Court of Pakistan.[2] Analytically, too, it would be misleading to suppose that something is designated as 'blasphemous' on account of its distinctive content. As Favret-Saada suggests, 'blasphemy' comes to exist through an act of judgement (Favret-Saada 1992, 257), and blasphemy controversies usually unfold within a distinct field of interlocution marked by four positions: an accuser {X}, a 'blasphemer' {Y} and an authority {Z} likely to take sanctions on the basis of an institutional apparatus {MI}, which encompasses existing repertoires of theological, cultural and legal interpretations and sanctions. Turning the 'blasphemer' into the addressee, rather than as the starting point of blasphemy controversies, the paradigm becomes:

{X} to {Z}, by virtue of {MI}: « {Y} has said: '*God is n*'» (Favret-Saada 1992, 258)

In the Pakistani context the legal authority {Z} entrusted to take sanctions, the state apparatus, does not hold a complete monopoly over justice. Clerics too may act as an informal {Z} when issuing their opinion or verdict (*fatwa*) on a particular accusation. And often the accusers {X}, be they activists, politicians, clerics or private complainants, consider that the authority {Z} entrusted to take sanctions fails to do so promptly or effectively. So much so that {X} and {Z} may collapse into each other, for instance in the case of blasphemy-related mob violence or the extra-judicial killing of the accused. The story of the severed hand with which I opened this chapter suggests a unique folding of these positions: following the accusation of the cleric {X}, the accused teenager {Y} becomes the sanctioning authority {Z} and dissociates himself from {Y}, probably to avoid being ostracised, if not killed. Further, the position of social actors may change from one controversy to another: an accuser may approach clerics or the courts as one of the authorities qualified to take sanctions, but at times religious leaders and members of the judiciary are themselves the initiators of the accusation.

This chapter begins with those who claim to be the authorised representatives of the person – the Prophet Muhammad – or the thing – printed verses of the Quran – that was purportedly desecrated, namely religious entrepreneurs. I show that although close to 85 per cent of the accused are non-Sunni Muslims,[3] the salience of blasphemy controversies partly stems from heightened intra-Muslim competition between Sunni sub-sects vying for relevance and visibility. This has contributed to making the rhetoric of religious offence pervasive *across* religious communities, leading to a growing number of common people susceptible of construing certain utterances or actions as blasphemous, which in turn further reinforces the position of religious entrepreneurs. However, this dynamic process and the institutional apparatus ({MI}) mobilised to set it in motion are premised upon certain assumptions about language and about the ability of objects to materialise the divine.

These assumptions are cultural, for they are shared across religious denominations, and become most apparent when attending to the way allegedly blasphemous content – '*God is n*' in the above scheme – is actually manipulated or eluded both during blasphemy controversies, as well as in everyday contexts. Hence in the second and last sections of this chapter I focus on these manipulations – first in the context of court documents to show how the adjudication of blasphemy paradoxically magnifies the offence, then in more mundane environments. The latter enables me to explore the linguistic and corporeal hexis that organises my interlocutors' everyday engagement with the risk of desecration. This allows me to argue for an interpretative model of the rise in blasphemy accusations that would connect the politics of religious offence and its legal inflection to the nondiscursive, embodied practices and attitudes that inform people's apprehension of blasphemy.

Anti-blasphemy competition

One could easily misinterpret the proliferation of blasphemy disputes as a consequence of new modes of suppressing political dissent. It is true that in a context of growing social media and private news outlets, an increasing proportion of blasphemy allegations are made in relation to online content. Though members of religious minorities remain disproportionately targeted by these charges, since 2015 Muslim student activists, human rights campaigners and even renowned journalists have fallen victim to such allegations (Ahmed and Abbas 2017). With the active support of conservative TV anchors and militant religious organisations the state itself, through its telecom and media regulators, now endeavours to monitor and censor online activity for sacrilegious content.[4] Surprisingly, however, it is only over the last few years, with the rising number of internet users, that blasphemy laws have been explicitly used as a tool of political censorship to muzzle progressive voices.

The issue of blasphemy started gaining importance in the late 1980s, and therefore predates the advent of mass media. More significantly, this growth is concomitant with a heightened rivalry between Sunni sub-sects (*maslak*) in the country. Since the era of Zia-ul-Haq, military patronage and Saudi largeness have strengthened Deobandis and other puritanical strands over the numerically dominant Barelvi or Sufi *maslak* commonly associated with a spiritual and quietist interpretation of Islam.[5] A number of analysts conjecture that Barelvi groups are now seeking to reverse this trend by becoming more vocal and politically active, notably around the issue of blasphemy (Khan 2011; Khan and Shams 2017; Ur Rehman 2016). While in Deobandi milieus the concern over blasphemy was historically confined to anti-Shia groups, for Barelvis this has been more pronounced and directly stems from their doctrinal orientation. In contrast to Deobandi and Ahl-e-Hadith followers, whom they traditionally blame for lacking respect towards the Prophet, Barelvis attribute extraordinary qualities to Muhammad; they often claim to be the genuine 'lovers of the Prophet' (*ashiq-e-rasul*), always ready to lay down their lives to protect his honour and sanctity (*namoos*).

In urban Punjab, where I carried out my research, this sensitivity towards religious irreverence is ubiquitous. Amid the profusion of commercial advertisements and political placards on city walls and rickshaws, one regularly finds posters of the Sunni Tehreek, a Barelvi organisation, that include the following slogan: 'There is only one punishment for blasphemers of the Prophet: beheading (*tauheen rasalat ki ek saza, sar tan se juda*)'. Sure enough, these calls for brutal intransigence towards blasphemers upset common assumptions about these Sufi-leaning Muslims, often portrayed as Pakistan's antidote to Islamism. But Barelvis claim that such intransigence is testimony to their exceptional love ('*ishq*) for the Prophet, as evidenced by the romantic symbols deployed during their anti-blasphemy protests, from heart-shaped posters to flowers and Valentine's Day cards.

The recent mobilisation around the trial of Mumtaz Qadri (2011–16), himself a Barelvi, has offered the movement unprecedented visibility across public space (see chapter 8). Qadri sympathisers within the lawyers' community in Punjab were in fact instrumental in airing anti-blasphemy outrage, and many of them remain committed to the wide application of the blasphemy laws (Reuters 2016). Some of the plaintiffs in the cases that I studied in Lahore were represented pro-bono by such activist lawyers.

This is not to suggest that Barelvi groups, and the Sunni Tehreek in particular, have a monopoly over blasphemy accusations. Among the cases that I studied, some of the accusers were clerics or followers of the Ahl-e-Hadith and Deobandi schools. Charges of blasphemy can indeed originate from, and be directed towards, Muslims of all persuasions. Conversely the loud display of religious outrage has proved to be a rallying point that cuts across sectarian and political affiliations, especially when 'blasphemy' is attributed to a non-Muslim person or to a foreign country. This is manifest when considering the colossal protests in 2006 against the caricatures of the Prophet, the 2012 riots against the movie *Innocence of Muslims* and the 2015 anti-Charlie Hebdo rallies (Blom 2008; Walsh 2012). These countrywide protests brought together Muslim religious groups and scholars of almost all persuasions and sects, including Shias, Ahl-e-Hadith, Deobandi and Barelvi groups (e.g. Popalzai et al. 2012), not to mention secular politicians (Dawn 2015).

Notwithstanding intense theological and political disputes among themselves, all religious schools in the country are unanimous in their support of the blasphemy laws and capital punishment for offenders. Blasphemy controversies are therefore both a site of competition between religious organisations and clerics vying for visibility and political relevance and also one of the few points of consensus, allowing them to displace and externalise their differences. Such unanimity can be traced to the older anti-Ahmadi movement, to which Pakistan's blasphemy laws are intimately connected (Ahmed 2010). This movement similarly drew together Sufi-leaning and more reformist Sunni and Shia Muslims for the sake of defending the ultimate nature of Muhammad's prophecy.

Allegations of blasphemy silence the accused, and often empower both denunciators and those defending the alleged transgressor. Chief among the former are clerics who, on the basis of their theological competence, are frequently involved in the registration of blasphemy-related First Information Reports (FIR)[6] – either by persuading the complainant to register it (e.g. *State v. Sawan Masih*) or by forcing the police into doing so (Amnesty International 2016, 29). In one case that I studied in detail, clerics from a militant Ahl-e-Hadith organisation laid siege to a police station to have a suspected blasphemer arrested under three distinct charges. Reluctant at first, the police officer eventually agreed to register the FIR after clerics threatened to burn down his station.

For lawyers too, these controversies can be opportunities for career advancement. Consider the most mediatised case in recent decades: that of Asia Bibi, a Punjabi Christian woman sentenced to death in 2010 and finally acquitted in 2018. Her legal team has changed a number of times over the last seven years. Among Lahori lawyers, rumour has it that the case has been sold for profit a number of times among Bibi's legal teams. Her one-time lawyer, whom I interviewed, also served as a prosecutor in a high-profile case involving the assassination of a suspected blasphemer. He sees himself as resolutely Sunni and advocates a more diligent application of the blasphemy laws, rather than their amendment. He was initially reluctant to take up Asia Bibi's defence and to prosecute the assassin. 'Working on these cases feels like wearing a suicide vest', he said, pointing to the armed policeman dozing under a tent outside his house. 'But then I was told about the money, so I accepted.' Being a Muslim lawyer with rather conservative views (he mentions in passing his admiration for Hitler) certainly serves the interests of his Christian client.[7] These various actors may not necessarily act cynically for venal ends. But it is important to recognise that situations of blasphemy accusation do generate concrete opportunities. They cannot be analysed solely through the lens of an ideological antagonism between progressive and conservative worldviews, nor through that of an irreducible divide between Pakistan's Muslim population and its religious minorities.

Even less sensational cases similarly entail competitive dynamics, as if blasphemy controversies were a form of market. This is particularly evident among Punjabi Christians. Perceived for the most part as 'untouchables' on account of their ancestral association with 'impure' occupations (O'Brien 2006), Punjabi Christians are significantly overrepresented among victims of blasphemy accusations (Julius 2016, 97–9). A Christian accused of blasphemy usually receives the support of local Christian charities and human rights associations, in the form of legal aid and allowances. In turn, these organisations draw on international support – whether through ecclesiastical networks, international human right associations or European governments. These local actors' success in gaining international assistance depends on their ability to advertise their work.

Upon receiving news of an allegation involving a Christian, such agencies seek to act as benevolent protectors, frequently presiding over the surrender of the accused to the police. They then typically exhibit online photographs of themselves next to the accused and declare their commitment to provide free legal assistance to the Christian victim. Many relatives of convicted blasphemers that I met had received the visit and occasional help of such charities. But they often resented these 'social workers' of a higher social standing, saying that, like the accusers, they must be deriving considerable benefit from the misfortune of the accused, notably in the form of privileged access to foreign networks of patronage. At the same time, within their own immediate community, the accused were themselves viewed as profiting from the situation, for instance by trying to secure asylum abroad. Among this poor and marginalised community, each allegation of blasphemy against one of their own ignites an outbreak of backbiting and positioning, enhances competition for scarce resources and weakens relations of trust within the community.

In sum, the scale of Pakistan's anti-blasphemy movement is predicated upon an intersectarian consensus over the inadmissibility of blasphemy. Competing *maslaki* strands seize the issue of blasphemy to gain visibility and political relevance. Blasphemy accusations create situations in which, aside from acts of violence, opportunities arise for a series of actors who do not operate solely on the basis of theological and ideological commitment, but also on the basis of their religious, caste and class identity – as well as their position within the judicial process, to which I now turn.

Handling blasphemy in court

When Pakistan gained independence in 1947, the country inherited the 1860 colonial Indian Penal Code and its amendments, which included provisions designed to protect all religions and everyone's 'religious feelings' from insult and outrage.[8] Several sections were subsequently added during the military dictatorship of Zia-ul-Haq (1977–88). First, in 1980, section 298-A proscribed the use of 'derogatory remarks' against the Prophet Muhammad's wives, his immediate relatives and his close companions. A few years later section 295-B was introduced to prevent the desecration of the printed Quran and other quranic inscriptions, followed by section 298-B and 298-C prohibiting Ahmadis from using Islamic terminologies, calling themselves Muslims or propagating their faith. Lastly, section 295-C was added to protect the honour and the 'sacred name' of the Prophet. It states that:

> Whoever by words, either spoken or written, or by visible representation or by any imputation, innuendo, or insinuation, directly or indirectly, defiles the sacred name of the Holy Prophet Muhammad (peace be upon him) shall be punished with death, or imprisonment for life, and shall also be liable to fine. (Pakistan Penal Code, 1860)

Taken together, these sections of the penal code are known as the 'blasphemy laws'. Legal scholars have noted important shortcomings in the drafting and design of these provisions (Ahmed 2018; Siddique and Hayat 2008; Forte 1994). Section 295-C, for instance, lacks an explicit intent requirement and, with phrases such as 'imputation, innuendo, or insinuation', fails to define clearly the types of behaviours that could amount to defilement. The broad reach of this section makes it susceptible to misuse on the part of complainants motivated by property dispute, personal feud or religious rivalry. Surviving an allegation of blasphemy depends to a large extent on the religious identity and social capital of both accuser and accused. While leading Muslim journalists or religious scholars may succeed in containing such allegations (e.g. Gannon 2017), this is rarely the case for working-class defendants. Though no one sentenced on charges of blasphemy has so far been executed, over 55 suspected blasphemers have been killed by zealots while under trial or shortly after their acquittal (International Commission of Jurists 2015, 11). In many cases high court judges enter acquittals on the basis of weak witness testimonies and technical irregularities. But presumed blasphemers are almost never exculpated on the ground that what they said, wrote, gestured or insinuated was deemed below the threshold of blasphemy, or because they did not intend to blaspheme.[9] The contours of the law are so vague that, as the novelist Mohammed Hanif puts it, 'no Pakistani has a clear idea what constitutes blasphemy' (2011).

The extent of popular attachment to the figure of the Prophet and to the legislation 'protecting' it, together with the risk of angering protest-prone Sunni formations, impel public opinion to remain in favour of the legal status quo. For these formations and their activists, to amend what they call the 'Sanctity of the Prophet Act' (Namoos-i-Risalat Act) prefigures nothing less than the undoing of Pakistan and social chaos. Its enforcement by state authorities, they claim, ideally serves a dual purpose. Firstly, it prevents responsible Muslims from having to kill blasphemers themselves (Forte 1994, 50; Qureshi 2008). Secondly, the ambiguous legal definition of blasphemy allows for its use as a surrogate for the Islamic prohibition against apostasy, for which there is no law in Pakistan: converts from Islam to Christianity can therefore be arrested for their apostasy and incarcerated on charges of blasphemy (Forte 1994, 58). As a result, a government attempting to initiate a debate on the law, or to limit its misuse, would have to confront the threat of nationwide street protests by religious parties and activists, who never fail to denounce such initiatives as a plot to undermine the Islamic fabric of the nation.[10]

To appreciate what is at stake one should retrieve the emic valency of the offence. First, and this is a key distinction with European Christian contexts, in Pakistan to blaspheme is not so much to utter insults against God, but rather to harm the sanctity of God's revelation, the Quran, or the honour of its last Prophet – and by extension that of the Prophet's companions and relatives.[11] Therefore blasphemy here encompasses not only written and spoken words, but also physical contact with the Quran, or with objects marked with quranic verses. So while scholars generally treat 'blasphemy' as stemming from an act of communication, be this linguistic, oral or written, visual or musical, we must here think of it as also including non-verbal and non-communicative actions pertaining to tangible matter. Indeed, the complainant need not see or hear the offence for it to be recognised as such, since section 295-C states that even 'imputation, innuendo, or insinuation' that 'indirectly' desecrate the name of the Prophet can be constitutive of the offence (Siddique and Hayat 2008, 351).

This porosity between verbal blasphemy and physical desecration enlarges the field of potential offence to a host of everyday situations that can be used as pretexts to press charges. For instance, dropping a Quran from one's shopping bag or disposing of a visiting card bearing the name 'Muhammad' have in the past formed the basis for blasphemy cases. So has a child making a spelling mistake and inadvertently writing 'execrating' the Prophet, instead of 'praising' him (*laanat* and *naat*). Other instances include photocopying a textbook with torn pages, thereby juxtaposing the name of the Prophet with the word 'cheat', and shouting slogans against a police officer named Umar Daraz, thereby defiling Umar, the second Sunni caliph of Islam. Cases such as these, which have resulted in legal proceedings or even mob violence against the accused, exemplify the extent to which intentionality may be irrelevant to the commission of the offence. Imputed metaphors, fortuitous appositions, inferred homologies and mere absentmindedness are increasingly construed by the general public as valid ground to lay charges of blasphemy.

From a legal standpoint, the proof of intent to blaspheme is not a prerequisite to convict someone under section 295-C.[12] Such absence of a criminal intent requirement makes this provision particularly susceptible to abuse. Similarly, outside the courts vigilante groups show a total disregard for their victims' intention to offend or absence thereof. As a result imputations of blasphemy, like those of witchcraft and sorcery in other contexts, are almost impossible to deny, since the veracity of an accusation tends to be gauged by the effect allegedly caused by the offence, rather than with reference to the accused's intention to offend. Narratively, guilt therefore tends to be a consequence rather than the cause of a condemnation.

Consider the following case. A group of Christian boys applies liquid medicine to a wounded donkey. Its trickle forms a shape on the donkey's skin, possibly resembling the Arabic letters for 'Muhammad'. The boys and the donkey are subsequently arrested on the basis of desecrating a holy name by writing it on an animal (Marshall and Shea 2011, 87). The agency of the blasphemer somehow recedes behind fortuity and impersonal forces: he or she becomes accountable for homophonies, a slip of the tongue, mental illness or even the force of gravity pulling a scrap of paper towards the floor and forming shapes on non-humans.

The dangerous materiality of the blasphemous necessarily affects its treatment in court. For instance, prosecution witnesses have sometimes refused to produce or to repeat the incriminating evidence, on the basis that doing so would amount to desecration (e.g. *State v. Salamat Masih* 1995, 815). Similarly, a number of lawyers that I have met recounted how probing into purportedly offensive words could expose them to the very same allegation of blasphemy. Hence some of them forgo the possibility of cross-examining the accuser, since that would entail repeating the offensive words. Reflecting on this behaviour, a judge once commented that 'in the process of administration of justice, we need to be secular' (Aqeel 2014). Though adjudicated in secular criminal courts, in blasphemy cases the courtrooms are usually thronged with the complainant's supporters, including pro-bono lawyers as well as hardline clerics and their followers. The loud presence of clerics and militants is intimidating for the accused as well as for lawyers and judges, who are legitimately concerned about their own safety if they dare to acquit the accused.

A defence lawyer recounted to me that one day in the Lahore High Court, while reproducing the incriminating evidence in his notebook, clerics in the audience started fuming and openly called on the judge to stop the commission of blasphemy. This circular logic is kept at bay so long as lawyers, judges, court clerks and the spectators appreciate in good faith the distinction between the words allegedly used by the accused and the act of merely reporting these words for forensic purposes. The impossibility of having a public debate over what exactly amounts to blasphemy, as well as the expanding scope of blasphemy controversies, both hinge on the tenuousness of the quotation marks that signal this distinction. Under these circumstances, how is blasphemous language contained and secured to avoid its proliferation?

To answer this question, I examine the linguistic mechanisms used to neutralise the incriminating evidence within judgement sheets. These legal documents are not verbatim records of the discussions taking place during trial. As they are designed for a wider audience than those present in court, it becomes all the more necessary to neutralise or secularise the reference made to the blasphemous kernel – what Favret-Saada terms '*n*' – lest it should be construed as a reiteration of the offence. In the extracts below, I have sought to isolate this '*n*' within written verdicts typed out for the historical record, which were shown to me by lawyers working on these cases. It must be noted that the court judgements considered are often multilingual and bear the mark of an unacknowledged work of translation (see chapter 7).[13]

> Blasphemic and sarcastic words written by the accused were so pathetic, painful and heart burning that this court was not inclined to mention or to reproduce but nevertheless as this is "Corner Stone" of the whole structure of the instant case, so this court seems quite imperative to mention here these words. However, these words are being written with the heavy heart and by seeking advance pardon from Almighty Allah and the Holy Prophet Hazrat Muhammad SAW. Even otherwise this court is guided by the saying of an Islamic

> jurist which is as, *"naql kufr, kufr na bash"'* [in Urdu script], "reporting of kufar is not kufar". These blaspehmic, sarcastic and derogatory words and writings are as,
> [a] *suar ki azan band karo* [in Urdu script]
> [b] *Pakistani suar ki ummah* [in Urdu script]
> [c] *Madni di ma di...* [in Urdu script]
> [d] *Muhammad di ma di...* [in Urdu script]
>
> [a] "stop pig's azan" (call for prayer)
> [b] Pakistanis are the Umma of pigs
> [c] Abused to the mother of Madni
> [d] Abused to the mother of Hazrat Muhammad (SAW)
>
> (*State v. Zulfiqar Ali* 2014, 12–13)

Before reluctantly reporting the incriminating words in the above extract, the judge, or his scribe, seeks Allah's forgiveness and signals that the 'reporting of unbelief is not unbelief' – two strategies drawn from the practice of early Mughal historians working on Hindu Sanskrit text.[14] The blasphemous kernel is inconsistently isolated from the rest of the text by way of quotation marks (in the English translation of the first expression) and ellipsis (in the third and fourth expressions in Urdu). While both Urdu and Punjabi language favour indirect quotes, here quotation marks and line breaks are inserted in the text effectively to insulate, authenticate and unambiguously attribute the utterance to someone else. This is not always the case, however. Consider the absence of quotation marks in the following indirect quote:

> The appellant uttered derogatory remarks against the Holy Prophet Hazrat Muhammad (Peace Be Upon Him) by stating that (Maaz Allah) [God forbid] the Prophet of the Muslims fell ill one month prior to his death and the insects nourished in His mouth and ear. She further stated that your Prophet (PBUH) married Hazrat Khadija (R.A.)[15] just for her wealth (...) She further stated that Holy Quran is not the book of God but a man-made book.
> (*State v. Asia Bibi* 2014, 2)

A quotation implies a series of signs, protocols and typographical cues that signal the fictive nature of the person saying 'I' and mark the distinction between the use of a word or an utterance and its mere mention. Since the absence of quotation marks can radically transform the citation of blasphemy into its performance, other cues are inserted to mark this distinction. In the above example the expression *maaz allah* (God forbid) fulfils this function. Now consider the following judgement extracts:

> The intention of the accused can also be assessed from the words used by him that:
>
> *"Mera yasu masih sacha hai, voh aega. Voh allah ka beta hai (na'uzu bi'llah) musulmanon ka nabi jhuta hai aur mera yasu*
> *masih sacha hai vohi bachaega"* [in Urdu script]
>
> [My Jesus the Messiah is truthful, He will come. He is the son of Allah (we seek refuge in Allah). The prophet of Muslims is a liar, and my Jesus the Messiah is truthful and will save us] (my translation, P.R.)
> (*State v. Sawan Masih* 2014, 2)
>
> [He] uttered filthy remarks against the Holy Prophet (P.B.U.H.) (Nauz-Billa) as under:
>
> *"me panjtan ka singer huon aur musulmanon muhje maaro"*
>
> [I am a singer of the Prophet's family, you Muslim people, beat me up] (my translation, P.R.)
> (*State v. Younas Masih* 2013, 8)
>
> Masih started talking in a loud voice and said that:
>
> *"Hamara yasu masih sacha hai voh aega aur voh musulmanon aur isayon ko bachaega aur (na'uzu bi'llah) ye bhi kaha ki musulmanon ka nabi jhuta hai"* [in Urdu script]
>
> [Our Jesus the Messiah is truthful, He will come, and He will save Muslims and Christians and (we seek refuge in Allah) he also said that the prophet of Muslims is a liar] (my translation, P.R.)
> (*State v. Sawan Masih* 2014, 2,4)

Here quotation marks are used in conjunction with the expression *na'uzu bi'llah* or *nauz-billa* (we seek refuge in Allah). This pleonastic device aims at insulating the dangerousness of sacrilegious words and at distancing the author from the reported utterance. Outside the domain of the court as well, I noticed that my interlocutors would pronounce these formula whenever discussing in Urdu or Punjabi the issue of blasphemy, whether with me or among themselves, presumably to ward off its offensive force.

These precautions appear all the more salient in a Punjabi-language environment, known as it is by its speakers for its rich repertoire of insults and swear words (Zaidi 2010, 35). The significance of these formulae is further attested by their common use across religious communities. Uttered in everyday situations as a safeguard against the omission of certain words, or against misspeaking of religion, *na'uzu bi'llah* and *maaz allah* are part of a set of everyday Arabic formulae used by both Muslims and non-Muslims in Pakistan.[16] This set also includes *sallallaahu alaihi wa sallam* (or SAW), which in the above extracts figures in English as 'Peace be Upon Him' (or PBUH), as well as *radhiallahu 'anha* (RA), 'may Allah be pleased with her'. Invariably written or pronounced right after taking the name of the Prophet, the invocation SAW/PBUH pervades everyday conversation. In certain contexts and milieus, its omission in fact almost verges on the blasphemous.[17] More than merely replicating quotation marks, the insertion of these expressions in court documents could be read as oral amulets designed to subdue the inauspiciousness of the blasphemous utterance. Within and beyond court documents, *na'uzu bi'llah* and PBUH are akin to *euphemia* – that is, 'words of good omen' that function as antidotes to blasphemy more effectively than mere ellipses and euphemisms (see Austin 2011, 45–6; Benveniste 1974).

Used in blasphemy trials in early modern Europe, this linguistic strategy is not peculiar to South Asia. It usually denotes an attempt on behalf of court scribes to defuse the quasi-magical charge of blasphemy and the attendant danger of divine retribution.[18] Secular courts may have taken on God's task of punishing blasphemers, but they must still proclaim their own vulnerability to God's retribution for the same crime. More importantly, these formulae are a precautionary measure indicating the mere reporting of the offence, lest others in the courtroom and beyond construe the omission of such antidotes as an endorsement of the blasphemy. Its use allows court scribes, lawyers and judges to position themselves as external to the commission of the offence while striking a compromise between the judicial need for optimal evidence and the necessity of observing the taboo.

In contrast to an understanding that treats verbal and visual signs as mere vehicles for the transmission of information, the semiotic ideology under consideration rests on the assumption that language and signs have potent transformative effects and cannot be abstracted from the social relations in which they arise. What this examination of court document reveals is that the virulent anti-blasphemy mobilisation in the country, and the popular consensus over the necessity to uphold blasphemy laws, imply a presumption of linguistic efficacy, if not the recognition of blasphemy's power to bring about prodigious disruptions.[19] This points to a first oddity: the act of adjudicating over blasphemy not only requires its manifestation in the courts, but also entails the affirmation, or at least the recognition of, its power.[20]

Blasphemy, then, is a peculiar kind of offence likened to a contagious substance. If suspected blasphemers are not killed before reaching the courts, adjudicating over their offence entails conjuring it into existence. Blasphemous evidence is transported, stored and analysed by forensic experts. In the courtroom, material traces of sacrilege must be produced and witnesses must utter blasphemous words, all of which can be denounced as blasphemous by the complainants' supporters if they play in favour of the accused. Sometimes pieces of blasphemous evidence are even fabricated to inculpate the accused (see, for instance, *State v. Usman Rasheed* 2017). The regulation of blasphemy, then, paradoxically entails its material proliferation.[21] Following Favret-Saada, for whom blasphemy controversies originate in the act of denunciation rather than in any blasphemous utterance (Fahret-Saada 1990, 127; 1992, 258), we may say that in the present context forensic content is produced retroactively, so to speak.

Extending the realm of blasphemy

In October 2017 the National Assembly passed an amendment to the Election Act 2017 which affected the wording of a declaration form for election candidates. The words 'I solemnly swear' in the finality of prophethood (*khatm-i-nabuwat*) were replaced with 'I believe' and references to the status of Ahmadis were omitted. Already galvanised by the popular mobilisation in support of Mumtaz Qadri a year earlier, Barelvi clerics and activists protested against the amendment, seeing it as a conspiracy to 'appease' Ahmadis, and calling for the sacking of the Law Minister. Despite the government claiming that the issue of wording was a 'clerical error' and restoring the declaration to its original form, protestors staged a three-week-long sit-in (*dharna*) just outside the capital. Over 8,000 police and paramilitary troops were mobilised to disperse protestors, killing at least six of them and wounding hundreds.

Ultimately aimed at the legal and political transformation of Pakistan into an Islamic state, their newly created Barelvi movement succeeded in securing the support of certain sections of the state, who thereby hoped to settle scores with rival state institutions (Kakar 2017; Masood 2017). Here I want to draw attention to the movement's name – the Tehreek-e-labbaik ya rasool Allah – and how this name conditioned the way one could talk about the movement. Roughly translated as the 'Movement of the Prophet's followers', *labaik* in fact refers to a type of prayer uttered by pilgrims during the *haj*. The first word of this prayer, *labaik*, condenses the affirmation of divine unity: 'Here I am, O Lord! What is Thy command?' (Martin 2005, 7158). In television interviews and public interventions, commentators and politicians critical of the protests found it awkward to name and condemn the movement without appearing to be irreverent to its literal meaning. Soon they resorted to paraphrases and acronyms to castigate the ongoing protests safely.[22]

The above vignette illustrates how the reverence owed towards sacred words was strategically harnessed to make a political intervention immune from criticism. This was predicated not only by an enforced presumption of linguistic efficacy, as seen earlier in relation to the precautious wording of court judgements in blasphemy trials, but also by a certain relationship of subjection to holy words, and to the doctrine encapsulated herein. This was made clear to me on multiple occasions in the course of my fieldwork, especially in my interactions with members of communities overrepresented in blasphemy trials.

I regularly met Aftab, a middle-aged Lahori police constable of Christian faith. His brother-in-law was incarcerated for allegedly writing anti-Islamic comments on a book. While conversing with Aftab and his relatives – all of them Christian Punjabis – I noticed their avoidance of the Prophet's name, Muhammad, whenever they broached the topic of Islam. So instead of saying that someone 'spoke about the Prophet Muhammad *Sallallaahu alaihi wa sallam*', they would say that he 'spoke about Bashir'. Once, during a visit to his home, I asked Aftab about this substitution. He pointed to the thin wall separating us from his Muslim neighbour and replied, smiling: 'In this society, we're all blasphemers (*gustakh*)'. I observed the same artifice among another group of Christian friends, albeit using a different name than 'Bashir'. They reasoned that it was a much safer means of talking freely, lest eavesdropping Muslims should hear them pronounce the sacred name without the appending formula, or misconstrue their utterance as an insult to the Prophet.[23]

The strategy of verbal avoidance displayed in specific situations by Punjabi Christians and Muslim political commentators illustrates how holy words gain authority over their speaking subjects and assertively demand that one be vigilant to its tangible utterance. By pronouncing 'Muhammad' or 'Labaik', one is decisively projected into a discursive space bound by strict rules and stipulated roles for all speaking subjects. Unlike scientific discourse, which carries with it rules only relative to the form and content of statements, doctrinal allegiance directly implicates its speaking subject and effects two types of subjection. It 'binds individuals to certain types of enunciation and consequently forbids them all others; but it uses, in return, certain types of enunciation to bind individuals amongst themselves, and differentiate them by that very fact from all others' (Foucault 1981, 63–4). Muslim commentators of the protests could not easily pronounce the name of the movement since to do so would bind them to their own pledge of allegiance towards Islam and the *ummah*, and would therefore prevent a frontal critique of the movement. Punjabi Christians, on the other hand, were shown to deny themselves access to a holy name of Islam because it would subject them to the exclusionary rules of enunciation that come with it, and over which they have no say.

This latter example of verbal avoidance points to the subtle ways in which these constraints permeate the most mundane domains of life. These effects are not solely verbal, however, and confining these dynamics to a linguistic framework would fail to account for the material and sensuous lineaments of this enforced sensitivity. When the Muslim call for prayer (*azan*) resounds, for instance, one lowers one's voice or falls silent, out of 'respect' for the amplified sacred utterance. Similarly, possessing anything that bears quranic verses demands a certain type of attitude and comportment, what Hirschkind in a different context called a 'quranically tuned body' (2006, 76). This gives rise to an ecology of the sacred written into bodily attitudes: the holy scripture may dispense spiritual blessings (*baraka*) and talismanic protection on its beholder, but it demands adoring attention to both its message and its material form. For instance I observed that some of my interlocutors would hand me their quranic amulet before going to the bathroom. And on two occasions friends reprimanded me for keeping a volume of the Quran on a shelf next to other books, rather than being wrapped and kept separately. In fact the last few years have seen over a dozen Pakistanis being killed by mobs for allegedly treating copies of the Quran as ordinary objects, an offence punishable with life imprisonment (section 295-B of the Penal Code).

A series of regulations and ordinary acts of piety surround the day-to-day handling of the sacred text. Individual copies of the Quran (*musahaf*) must be held in a state of ritual cleanliness (*wuzu*) or stowed separately from other objects, and must never be allowed to touch the ground, be sat upon or used as a pillow. Evidently an old or damaged *musahaf* cannot be disposed of like other waste. Such 'martyred' (*shaheed*) copies, as they are called, must be disposed of with reverence;

so too must any object inscribed with quranic verses. In Pakistan these should either be wrapped in cloth and buried in the ground, or drowned in water for the ink to be washed away.

As for the printing and publication of Qurans, it is subjected to cautious supervision and inspection, not only for errors in the text, but also to ensure the material quality of the object itself. In Punjab, the Auqaf and Religious Affairs Department issues scientific guidelines concerning the production of Qurans, reserving the right to test the exact grammage, thickness, opacity and tensile strength of the paper used – and in the case of digital Qurans, the quality of electronic devices (Government of Punjab 2011). For their part, concerned citizens turn to social media, where videos of Quranic pages floating in gutters or lying amidst garbage abound.

The presence of Islam in public and private spaces circulates and proliferates in sensorial and tangible ways. A plethora of quranic expressions are painted or engraved on houses, on rickshaws and trucks, on tombstones and shopfronts. They are worn as amulets and pieces of jewellery, amplified through the call to prayer and electronic Quran reciters, aired on Islamic TV and radio programmes and shared on WhatsApp groups and Facebook posts. With this exponential growth, the attendant anxiety over desecration centres on an ever greater realm of materialised words and objects.

As they are magnified or turned into artefacts, sacred words acquire new properties that facilitate not only their dissemination, but also their desecration. The more quranic inscriptions proliferate on diverse mediums, the more likely they are to be misused, displaced, lost or dirtied. Because quranic revelation takes place through and within matter, its reproduction, commodification and proliferation makes the sacred increasingly contingent upon the plasticity of signs. A verse of the Quran printed on paper, for instance, makes the sacred contingently 'bundled' with other qualities, such as flammability (c.f. Keane 2003, 414); this in turn allows for its physical desecration, for instance setting the sacred on fire.

Since verses of the Quran can be reproduced on almost any support and medium, one learns to handle seemingly ordinary objects with care.[24] A banner, a visiting card, a newspaper or a children's book may well contain holy verses or a mention of the Prophet's name. I frequently observed people of all creeds picking up a stray newspaper or a piece of paper lying on the pavement and placing it on an elevated spot, out of precautionary reverence – or perhaps to forestall a possible accusation of desecration. Handling religious posters, burning paper and disposing of its ashes, discarding a newspaper or a children's book, or even going to the toilet when one is wearing an amulet, are trivial situations truly pregnant with desecrating potential.

The material forms taken by Quranic revelation may be thought of as possessing agency to the extent that they are enmeshed in causal relations that are read as reflecting human intentions. Think, for instance, of the imputations of blasphemy that originated in a visiting card falling on the floor, a newspaper lying on the ground or a dripping substance forming shapes on the body of an animal. It is insofar as we impute human intention to such situations that these material forms gain agency over us. This insight offers a counterpoint to the prevailing instrumentalist analyses of Pakistan's blasphemy affairs in terms of the self-interested misuse of the law.

What lends so much potency and danger to these affairs is the interplay between a legal apparatus and the concrete, tangible manifestations given to the sacred through spoken words and material objects. As observed earlier in this chapter, the adjudication of blasphemy accusations must necessarily contend with the material, sensuous and linguistic forms through which the sacred is mediated and allegedly defiled. What is crucial here is that the causal relations which are imagined to exist between humans, sacred objects and holy words, and which are solidified through legal ties, are taken to be extensible.

Consider the self-referentiality ascribed to Pakistan's anti-blasphemy provisions by Mumtaz Qadri – the Barelvi bodyguard who killed the governor of Punjab on the basis of the latter's rude criticism of section 295-C of the penal code (see Haq 2010). While the said section protects the Prophet's 'sacred name', during his trial Qadri argued that to challenge this 'sacred provision of law' was in itself 'tantamount to directly defiling the sacred name' of the Prophet (*State v. Mumtaz Qadri* 2015a). In a different case altogether, a judge observed that rather than protecting Pakistani citizens' 'religious feelings', section 295-A was designed to protect Muslims' 'sacred feeling' (*State v. Muhammad Azam* 2011). As if through the effect of contamination, the realm of inviolable sacredness delineated by law is extrapolated to encompass the law itself, and the religious sentiments of one segment of the citizenry.

This process is discernible across the religious landscape, with diverse formations in the country lobbying for a legal extension that comforts their distinct theological position. Each school of thought, or rather its most vocal representatives, specialises in defending the honour of a specific Islamic figure, or set of figures. As observed earlier, Barelvi clerics and activists portray themselves as the true lovers of the Prophet. Shias, on the other hand, seek to protect the sanctity of Ali and of the Prophet's immediate relatives (*ahl-e-bait*). As for anti-Shia Deobandi organisations, they have been campaigning for capital punishment in the case of insults to the Prophet's companions (*sahaba*). Their proposed bill focuses specifically on the 'honour' (*namoos*) of the *sahaba* because of Shias' ritual propensity to curse these figures.[25]

Although far less common and audible, but no less significant, this demand is also found among non-Muslim communities. Given their vulnerability to the blasphemy laws, I was initially surprised to hear some of my Christian interlocutors insisting that the legal protections granted to Muhammad and the Quran also be extended to Jesus and the Bible.[26] Even bishops have made this argument (Forte 1994, 58), probably in the hope that rights granted to Christian beliefs might secure civil rights to community members.

Since the late 1980s religious entrepreneurs of all creeds see the extension of the legally sacred along particularistic lines as a source of influence and exclusive rights for their respective denomination. Though locked in theological and social antagonisms, these groups have more in common than meets the eye. This forces us to de-provincialise the putative affinity between Islam (or one of its sects) and religious susceptibility. It also encourages us to recognise the issue of blasphemy as a cultural and political idiom premised on a *shared* semiotic ideology and constructed through a particular historical configuration of power and its articulation in law. Rhetorically, this idiom manifests itself through a limited vocabulary used across the denominational spectrum: an outraged community demonstrates its unrivalled affective attachment towards a specific figure and vows to defend its 'honour'. Forged during the colonial period in the context of communal mobilisations (Gilmartin 1991), the dramatised display of emotional commitment to religious symbols has gradually been accepted by all as the ultimate locus of community identity.

While I was documenting a Catholic pilgrimage in Punjab a few years ago, an incident brought home to me the quasi-ecumenical nature of this idiom. A Muslim passer-by was suspected of having surreptitiously trashed flex-board effigies of the Virgin Mary. Reflecting on the incident, a furious Catholic pilgrim exclaimed: '[this effigy] is a sacred thing, we're ready to lay our lives for it!'[27] In this context, the use of the expression to 'lay one's life' (*jaan dena*) directly mirrors the ubiquitous Muslim slogan graffitied and chanted in the wake of blasphemy accusations: 'We're ready to sacrifice our lives for the dignity of the Prophet Muhammad'.[28]

Asked what he meant, he and his companions described how 'intolerable' (*naqabil-e-bardasht*) such insults felt to them.

This turn of phrase also happens to be a part of the established lexicon used by anti-blasphemy Muslim activists. 'We can endure anything', some of them chanted in a recent protest, 'but we won't tolerate (*bardasht*) the slightest thing said against the Prophet' (Ali 2017). Members of a community overrepresented among victims of blasphemy allegations were thus deploying the very same idiom of outrage, passion and intransigence over sacrilege that is so often directed against them. It is as if the critique of this hegemonic idiom of offence could only exist within its given terms, rather than from an autonomous, external or secular domain of dissent. Similarly, the Supreme Court recently vilified demonstrators who had laid siege to the capital to protest the rephrasing of the electoral law – a change of words that they deemed abusive to Islam. In its formal statement, the bench noted that in propagating violence and using 'filthy-abusive language' against the government and in the name of Islam, protestors had themselves been 'denigrating the glory of Islam' (Iqbal 2017). As for the Law Minister, under pressure from protesters to resign, he sought to reaffirm his Muslim credentials by stating that he and his family were 'ready to lay down [their] lives for the honour of the Prophet' (Khattak 2017).

This sacrificial trope is grounded in the notion that such emotional attachment transcends rationality and self-control (Gilmartin 1991), so that the confrontation with an act of sacrilege is sometimes said to short-circuit one's ability to reason (*logic fail ho jata hai*).[29] If a sign of true Muslimness lies in the inability to think rationally in these situations, or to 'digest' blasphemy, as a judge once put it (*State v. Muhammad Azam* 2011, §17 and 20), failing to be overwhelmed by righteous anger can easily be taken as reflective of a defective religious sensibility.

Cultivating this sensibility calls for retributive forms of violence, since the willingness to die often entails the readiness to kill, and vice versa (e.g. Ilm uddin, Mumtaz Qadri). How else can we make sense of the theatrical brutality occasionally meted out to suspected blasphemers, such as dismembering and immolation? In extreme cases the accusers become the avenger of the injured symbol, inflicting upon their victim the very injury befallen to the symbol: bodies are dismembered like torn pages, or sometimes burned alive when the alleged offence involved burning a Quran. The victims' bodies are isomorphically desecrated in the retributive attack, sometimes to the point of self-injury, as in the case of the severed hand with which I opened this chapter.

Conclusion

Tracking the material life of blasphemous matter shifts the focus away from the dominant legalistic, instrumentalist and linguistic paradigms, and allows us to recognise that the repression of 'blasphemy' has tangible effects beyond the mere suppression of offensive words. It makes its presence felt in the way one thinks, feels and relates to religious artefacts. I have shown that the process of repressing 'blasphemy', by way of legal adjudication for instance, is in fact what brings its forensic content – '*God is n*' – into being in the first place, almost retroactively. Or, to put it in Favret-Saada's terms, blasphemy is not the starting point, but rather the narrative end of the sequence.

This productive tension between regulation and the proliferating offence is seized by the self-appointed representatives of that which has allegedly been offended. These controversies are thus turned into a site of competitive rivalry for religious organisations, clerics or politicians vying for political relevance or eager to discredit an opponent's claim to moral and religious probity. Premised on the reinforcement of the blasphemy laws in the 1980s and 1990s, and situated in a context where the issue of religious offence has been mythologised and charged with considerable emotive weight since the early twentieth century, this process has arguably generated an ever-growing sensitivity towards blasphemy among lay people of all shades.

Intensified by the fact that always more holy persons, places, words and objects could theoretically be added to the protective purview of the law, a growing number of actors aspire to expand its scope along particularistic lines as a potential source of exclusive rights. These dynamics, I argue, are grounded in certain assumptions about the power of words and objects to instantiate the divine, which in turn calls for a distinct mode of engaging with them, even in 'secular' courts. Far from being abstract principles, these assumptions give shape to a verbal and gestural hexis that permeates even the most mundane facets of life and which demands utmost vigilance towards the potential blasphemer in us. What makes blasphemy such a potent idiom for political mobilisation, then, is this entanglement of anti-blasphemy laws with the proliferating sensible forms through which the sacred is made manifest and occasionally defiled. In short, blasphemy accusations constitute a productive arena where discourse is turned into matter and written onto bodies and tongues. Herein dissenters can be legitimately killed, and each community can cultivate its exclusivist vision of religious citizenship.

Notes

1. Though representing less than two per cent of the population, Ahmadis and Christians taken together were the accused in half of all blasphemy cases during the period 1986–2012 (NCJP 2013, 204). Within the remaining half, two-thirds were Shia Muslims (Julius 2016, 98), who otherwise represent from 10 to 25 per cent of Pakistan's total Muslim population.
2. Quoting the Legal Aid Society (Karachi), the bench noted that: 'the majority of blasphemy cases are based on false accusations stemming from property issues or other personal or family vendettas rather than genuine instances of blasphemy and they inevitably lead to mob violence against the entire community' (*State v. Mumtaz Qadri* 2015b, 26).
3. See note 5.
4. Following a three-year ban on YouTube, purportedly to protect citizens from watching an anti-Islam film, *Innocence of Muslims*, the Pakistan Telecommunication Authority (PTA) is now in a position to force YouTube and Facebook to block content 'violating local laws prohibiting blasphemy, desecration of the national flag, and condemnation of the country's independence' (Facebook 2016; Rasmussen and Wong 2017). PTA also encourages consumers to police cyberspace and to report 'blasphemous URLs'. With over 30 million active Facebook users in the country, a growing number of blasphemy controversies now originate in cyberspace (see chapter 5). While people have been sentenced for blasphemous text messages and smartphone videos in the past, in 2017 death sentences were awarded for acts of blasphemy on Facebook and WhatsApp for the first time. For a legal assessment of digital regulations in relation to blasphemy in Pakistan, see Mir (2015).
5. Pakistan's population is overwhelmingly Muslim, with Christians, Hindus, Ahmadis and Scheduled Castes accounting for less than four per cent of the population, according to the 1998 census – although these figures probably reflect an under-reporting of religious minorities (Khan 2018). Barelvis or Sufis are estimated to account for 50 to 60 per cent of the Muslim population, Deobandis and Shias for 15 to 20 per cent respectively and Ahl-e-Hadith (also known as Salafis or Wahhabis) for about 5 per cent of the population (Syed et al. 2016, 28, 188, 231). Barelvis, Deobandis and Ahl-e-Hadith are Sunni sub-sects that emerged in the late nineteenth century. Very schematically, the Barelvis (also known as Ahl-e-Sunnat wa Jamaat) are associated with a shrine-based form of devotionalism close to Sufism. Deobandis, by contrast, tend to adopt a more literalist interpretation of the Quran and Sunnat. Even more literalist, the Ahl-e-Hadith sub-sect favours a narrow and direct use of the Quran and the *hadis* and rejects Sufi institutions and practices (Metcalf 1982).
6. The First Information Report (FIR) includes the complainant's description of an offence that comes under police jurisdiction.
7. A leading 'liberal' Muslim journalist recently accused of blasphemy similarly hired the services of a lawyer who had previously defended Islamist militants, so that the judge could feel safe exonerating the accused journalist (Gannon 2017).
8. These are sections 295 and 295-A of the 1860 Indian Penal Code. For details, see chapter 1.
9. For an exception to this, see Forte (1994, 349).
10. There have been a number of propositions to amend the law, for instance by introducing procedural changes to the way in which allegations of blasphemy could be registered (Gregory 2012, 203). Lately the judiciary has taken steps in this direction, notably by seeking to penalise false accusations of blasphemy, which currently entails a mere Rs 1,000 fine.
11. This is what Christian theologians referred to as 'mediate' instances of blasphemy, rather than 'immediate' ones that target God directly (Delumeau 1989, 17). In common parlance in Urdu the act of blasphemy is referred to as *tauheen-e-risalat* (defaming the apostleship), *behurmati* (disgrace, lit. the absence of honour) and *gustakh-e-rasool* (rudeness towards the messenger). What is injured here is explicitly the honour and dignity (*izzat, hurmat, namoos, shaan*) of the Prophet or of the Quran.
12. On this point, see Siddique and Hayat (2008, 342, 348). While other sections of the Pakistan Penal Code dealing with blasphemy and desecration (295-A, 295-B, 298-A) include a reference to criminal intent (*mens rea*), 295-C does not. However, lawyers that I have interviewed explained that in the context of bail applications, judges do occasionally consider whether or not the accused intended to commit the offence. On the question of criminal intent in blasphemy cases, see International Commission of Jurists (2015, 31).

13. Although English is the official language of the laws and legal judgements in the country, in practice both English and Urdu are used in court documents and proceedings – especially at the district level (trial courts), where proceedings may also take place in regional languages. The judge may express him or herself in English, use Arabic for quranic passages and employ Urdu in both Nastaliq and roman scripts for poetic effect and to quote witness statements. Although in the cases under consideration the accused were Punjabi-speakers, and presumably if they did blaspheme would not have done so in any other language, their mother-tongue is rarely, if ever, reported in the judgement sheet. The work of translation may be designed to attenuate the supposed crudeness of Punjabi, thereby 'disinfecting' the document, or simply to make it available to a wider readership. Conversely, there are instances where the incriminating words are quoted in Urdu, but are not translated in English.
14. See Truschke (2016, 203–28). See chapter 6, where Sen alludes to a member of the Indian parliament using a similar formula: 'may my God forgive me for reading this'.
15. R.A. stands for *radhiallahu 'anha:* 'may Allah be pleased with her'.
16. On *na'uzu bi'llah*, see Schimmel (1994, 91). Other very commonly used Arabic formulae include *ma sha' allah* (may God preserve him/her/it from the evil eye), *astagfiru'llah* ('God forbid') and *subhana'llah* ('I extol the perfection of God').
17. *Sallallaahu alaihi wa sallam* is known as a *tasliya*, that is, a 'plea that Muhammad's intercession be accepted by God on behalf of his followers' (Rippin n.d.).
18. Court scribes would insert formulae such as *'absit verbo blasphemia'* (may these words be exempt of blasphemy) or ask for God's forgiveness, lest repeating a blasphemous utterance should cause harm and bring about God's vengeance (e.g. Loetz 2009, 154–5).
19. On the articulation between 'semiotic ideology' (Keane 2003) and Muslims' claims to injury in reaction to blasphemy, see Mahmood (2009). This notion that blasphemy could bring about Pakistan's destruction is well expressed by one of the architects of the blasphemy laws: such provisions, he writes, can prevent 'chaos in the society, splitting the unity of mankind against the Divine scheme of things' (Qureshi 2008, 83). As a general feature of religious language, this assumption of linguistic efficacy is not unique to Pakistan. However there is a distinctive South Asian trajectory to this assumption, owing to its crystallisation in colonial law, wherein Indians were conceived as having 'a predisposition toward mental agitation and hurt sentiments in response to loaded words, offensive gestures, and transgressions of hierarchical order' (Ahmed 2009, 180).
20. Judges and ecclesiastical authorities in high medieval and early modern Europe faced a similar dilemma. Documents dealing with and condemning blasphemy were almost always silent on the exact wording of the blasphemous utterance, presumably to avoid reiterating the injury (Christin 1992, 339; Casagrande 1987, 234–5).
21. The same process was discernible in 1988 at the beginning of *The Satanic Verses* controversy, with British Muslim organisations disseminating passages of the book to their members and to ambassadors of Muslim countries in London (Favret-Saada 1992, 251).
22. I am grateful to Amélie Blom for drawing my attention to this.
23. As per sections 298-B and C of the Penal Code, Ahmadis are legally banned from 'posing' as Muslims and from using Islamic terminology. The same does not apply to Christians. In fact, the recourse to everyday Islamic expressions (e.g. *mashallah, allah hafiz, inshallah* etc.) is relatively common among Punjabi Christians in their interactions with both co-religionists and Muslims.
24. On the *quran* as material object, see George (2009), Starrett (1995) and Suit (2013).
25. Their proposed bill seeks to extend section 298-A of the Penal Code. Since the early twentieth century, Shias' ritual insults to the first four caliphs (*tabarra*) and Sunnis' retaliatory *madh-e-sahaba* (verses recited in praise of the Sunni caliphs and *sahaba*) have been at the centre of sectarian polemics and violence in the region (Jones 2012, 186–221). To this day, Deobandis's investment in anti-blasphemy mobilisation in Pakistan appears to be guided by this concern over disrespect towards the *sahaba*, what they term *gustakh-e-sahaba*.
26. A handful of Sikhs and Hindus have filled complaints under sections 295 and 295-A of the Penal Code over the last five years. Asad Ahmed (2018) has recently demonstrated how the introduction in 1980 of section 298-A in particular has set in motion this logic of extension. Contrary to existing colonial legislations on religious offence, which only set out general principles applicable to all religions, this new section specifies and names those religious personages that were henceforth protected by law, thus leaving all others unprotected.
27. *Ye muqaddas cheez hai, ham iske lie jaan de denge.*

28. *Namoos/hurmat-e-risalat par jaan bhi qurban hai.* This slogan is generally put up and chanted by Barelvi activists.
29. Here is the response reportedly given by outraged students to their liberal teacher: 'Teacher! We Muslims can't reason anymore when it comes to the question of the honour of the Prophet' (my translation of the author quoting her students in Urdu: *'teacher, namoos-e-rasool per aa ker her Musalman ka logic fail ho jata hae'*). See Abu Bakr (2011).

References

Abu Bakr, Aaishah. 2011. 'Hypersensitivities – the Salman Taseer issue.' Last modified 22 January 2011. http://thevoiceofyouth.com/2011/01/22/hypersensitivities-the-salman-taseer-issue/.
Ahmed, Asad Ali. 2009. 'Specters of Macaulay: Blasphemy, the Indian Penal Code, and Pakistan's postcolonial predicament', in *Censorship in South Asia: Cultural Regulation from Sedition to Seduction*, Raminder Kaur and William Mazzarella, eds, 172–205. Bloomington: Indiana University Press.
Ahmed, Asad Ali. 2010. 'The paradoxes of Ahmadiyya identity: Legal appropriation of Muslimness and the construction of Ahmadiyya difference', in *Beyond Crisis: Re-evaluating Pakistan*, Naveeda Khan, ed, 273–314. New Delhi: Routledge.
Ahmed, Asad Ali. 2018. 'A brief history of the anti-blasphemy laws.' *The Herald*, February 2018; uploaded 31 October 2018. https://herald.dawn.com/news/1154036.
Ahmed, Issam and Gohar Abbas. 2017. 'Pakistani right cries "blasphemy" to muzzle progressives.' *Agence France Press*, 17 January 2017. https://finance.yahoo.com/news/pakistani-cries-blasphemy-muzzle-progressives-044842744.html.
Ali, Kalbe. 2017. 'Who is Khadim Hussain Rizvi?' *Dawn*, 3 December 2017. https://www.dawn.com/news/1374182.
Amnesty International. 2016. 'As good as dead: The impact of the blasphemy laws in Pakistan.' Accessed 8 January 2017. https://www.amnesty.org/download/Documents/ASA3351362016ENGLISH.PDF.
Aqeel, Asif. 2014. 'Pakistan court upholds death penalty for Asia Bibi despite serious legal loophole in trial.' *World Watch Monitor*, 17 October 2014. https://www.worldwatchmonitor.org/2014/10/3430018/.
Austin, Norman. 2011. *Sophocles' Philoctetes and the Great Soul Robbery*. Madison: University of Wisconsin Press.
BBC. 2016. 'The boy accused of blasphemy who cut off his hand.' *BBC*, 19 January 2016. http://www.bbc.com/news/world-asia-35341256.
Benveniste, Emile. 1974. 'La blasphémie et l'euphémie', in *Problèmes de linguistique générale* (2), 254–7. Paris: Gallimard.
Blom, Amélie. 2008. 'The 2006 anti-"Danish cartoons" riot in Lahore: Outrage and the emotional landscape of Pakistani politics.' *South Asia Multidisciplinary Academic Journal* 2. http://samaj.revues.org/1652.
Casagrande, Carla. 1987. *I peccati della lingua: Disciplina ed etica della parola nella cultura medievale*. Rome: Instituto della Enciclopedia Italiana.
Christin, Olivier. 1992. 'Le statut ambigu du blasphème au XVIe siècle.' *Ethnologie française* 22 (3): 337–43.
Dawn. 2015. 'Bilour's publicity stunt: A reward for the heirs of Charlie Hebdo attackers.' *Dawn*, 3 February 2015. https://www.dawn.com/news/1161252.
Delumeau, Jean. 1989. *Injures et blasphemes*. Paris: Imago.
Eickelman, Dale F. 1992. 'Mass higher education and the religious imagination in contemporary Arab societies.' *American Ethnologist* 19 (4): 643–55.
Facebook. 2016. 'Government request report.' Accessed 6 December 2016. https://govtrequests.facebook.com/country/Pakistan/2016-H1/.
Favret-Saada, Jeanne. 1990. 'Ethnologie religieuse de l'Europe.' *Annuaire de l'École pratique des hautes études, section des sciences religieuses* 99: 125–30.
Favret-Saada, Jeanne. 1992. 'Rushdie et compagnie: Préalables à une anthropologie du blasphème.' *Ethnologie française* 22 (3): 251–60.

Forte, David F. 1994. 'Apostasy and blasphemy in Pakistan.' *Connecticut Journal of International Law* 10 (1): 27–68.

Foucault, Michel. 1981 [1970]. 'The order of discourse', in *Untying the Text: A Post-Structuralist Reader*, Robert Young, ed, 48–78. Boston: Routledge and Kegan Paul.

Gannon, Kathy. 2017. 'Blasphemy charges create climate of fear for Pakistani media.' *Associated Press*, 18 March 2017. https://apnews.com/767fe3b15a9b413b88bb459d24e42b45/blasphemy-charges-create-climate-fear-pakistani-media.

George, Kenneth M. 2009. 'Ethics, iconoclasm, and Quranic art in Indonesia.' *Cultural Anthropology* 24 (4): 589–621.

Gilmartin, David. 1991. 'Democracy, nationalism and the public: A speculation on colonial Muslim politics.' *South Asia: Journal of South Asian Studies* 14 (1): 123–40.

Government of Punjab (Auqaf and Religious Affairs). 2011. *The Punjab Holy Quran (Printing and Recoding) Rules*. Accessed 5 February 2016. http://www.punjabcode.punjab.gov.pk/public/dr/THE%20PUNJAB%20HOLY%20QURAN%20(PRINTING%20AND%20RECORDING)%20RULES,%202011.doc.pdf.

Gregory, Shaun. 2012. 'Under the shadow of Islam: The plight of the Christian minority in Pakistan.' *Contemporary South Asia* 20 (2): 195–212.

Hanif, Mohammed. 2011. 'Pakistan: Silence has become the mother of all blasphemies.' *The Guardian*, 3 March 2011. https://www.theguardian.com/world/2011/mar/03/pakistan-silence-blasphemy-mohammed-hanif.

Haq, Ayesha Tammy. 2010. Interview: Salmaan Taseer, Governor of Punjab. *News Line Magazine*, December 2010. http://newslinemagazine.com/magazine/interview-salmaan-taseer-governor-of-punjab/.

Hirschkind, Charles. 2006. *The Ethical Soundscape: Cassette Sermons and Islamic Counterpublics*. New York: Columbia University Press.

International Commission of Jurists. 2015. *On Trial: The Implementation of Pakistan's Blasphemy Laws*. International Commission of Jurists. Accessed 9 August 2017. http://www.refworld.org/docid/565da4824.html.

Iqbal, Nasir. 2017. 'SC rejects use of foul language for Islamic cause.' *Dawn*, 3 December 2017. https://www.dawn.com/news/1374247.

Jones, Justin. 2012. *Shi'a Islam in Colonial India: Religion, Community and Sectarianism*. New York: Cambridge University Press.

Julius, Qaiser. 2016. 'The experience of minorities under Pakistan's blasphemy laws.' *Islam and Christian–Muslim Relations* 27 (1): 95–115.

Kakar, Farman. 2017. 'Barelvi activism.' *The News*, 26 November 2017. http://tns.thenews.com.pk/drives-barelvi-activism/.

Keane, Webb. 2003. 'Semiotics and the social analysis of material things.' *Language & Communication* 23 (3–4): 409–25.

Khan, Muhammad Ismail. 2011. *The Assertion of Barelvi Extremism*. Hudson Institute. Accessed 10 November 2015. https://www.hudson.org/research/9848-the-assertion-of-barelvi-extremism#footNote25.

Khan, Saman Ghani. 2018. 'Mosaic nation: What made the census flawed and controversial.' *The Herald*, 20 February 2018. https://herald.dawn.com/news/1153901.

Khan, Sattar and Shamil Shams. 2017. 'Pakistan's Barelvis – Transformation from peaceful to violent?' *Deutsche Welle*, 11 December 2017. http://www.dw.com/en/pakistans-barelvis-transformation-from-peaceful-to-violent/a-41744277.

Khattak, Inamullah. 2017. 'NA passes Elections (Amendment) Bill 2017 to "strengthen" Khatm-i-Nabuwwat clauses.' *Dawn*, 16 November 2017. https://www.dawn.com/news/1370903.

Loetz, Francisca. 2009. *Dealings with God: From Blasphemers in Early Modern Zurich to a Cultural History of Religiousness*. Aldershot: Ashgate.

Mahmood, Saba. 2009. 'Religious reason and secular affect: An incommensurable divide?', in *Is Critique Secular? Blasphemy, Injury, and Free Speech*, Talal Asad, Wendy Brown, Judith Butler and Saba Mahmood, eds, 64–100. Berkeley: Townsend Center for the Humanities, University of California.

Marshall, Paul and Nina Shea. 2011. *Silenced: How Apostasy and Blasphemy Codes are Choking Freedom Worldwide*. Oxford: Oxford University Press.

Martin, Richard C. 2005. 'Pilgrimage: Muslim pilgrimage', in *Encyclopedia of Religion (2nd edition)*, Mircea Eliade and Lindsay Jones, eds, London: Macmillan.

Masood, Salman. 2017. 'Pakistan calls in army to help restore order after violent clashes in Islamabad.' *The New York Times*, 25 November 2017. https://www.nytimes.com/2017/11/25/world/asia/pakistan-protests-khadim-hussain-rizvi.html.

Metcalf, Barbara D. 1982. *Islamic Revival in British India: Deoband 1860–1900*. New Delhi: Oxford University Press.

Mir, Waqqas. 2015. *Blasphemy in the digital age: a research study by Digital Rights Foundation*. Digital Rights Foundation. Accessed 30 January 2016. http://digitalrightsfoundation.pk/blasphemydigitalage/.

Nair, Neeti. 2013. 'Beyond the "communal" 1920s: The problem of intention, legislative pragmatism, and the making of section 295A of the Indian Penal Code.' *Indian Economic and Social History Review* 50 (3): 317–40.

NCJP (National Commission for Justice and Peace). 2013. *Human Rights Monitor 2012–13: A Report on the Religious Minorities in Pakistan*. Lahore: National Commission for Justice and Peace.

O'Brien, John. 2006. *The Construction of Pakistani Christian Identity*. Lahore: Research Society of Pakistan.

Pakistan Penal Code (Act n° XLV of 1860). Accessed 5 January 2015. https://www.oecd.org/site/adboecdanti-corruptioninitiative/46816797.pdf.

Popalzai, Shaheryar, Sidrah Moiz Khan and Ema Anis. 2012. 'Ishq-e-Rasool Day: 20 killed, over 200 wounded in protests across Pakistan.' *The Express Tribune*, 21 September 2012. https://tribune.com.pk/story/440300/ishq-e-rasool-day-observed-across-pakistan-live-updates/.

Qureshi, Muhammad Ismail. 2008. *Muhammad: The Messenger of God and the Law of Blasphemy in Islam and West*. Urdu Bazar Lahore: Nuqoosh.

Rasmussen, Sune Engel and Julia Carrie Wong. 2017. 'Facebook was where Pakistan could debate religion. Now it's a tool to punish "blasphemers".' *The Guardian*, 22 July 2017. https://www.theguardian.com/technology/2017/jul/19/facebook-pakistan-blasphemy-laws-censorship.

Reuters. 2016. 'Pakistani lawyers' group behind spike in blasphemy cases.' *Reuters*, 7 March 2016. http://www.reuters.com/article/pakistan-blasphemy-lawyers-idUSKCN0W905G.

Rippin, Andrew. n.d. 'Taṣliya', in *Encyclopaedia of Islam: Second Edition*, edited by Peri Bearman, Thierry Bianquis, C. Edmund Bosworth, E. van Donzel and Wolfhart Heinrichs. Leiden: Brill Online Books and Journals. Accessed 9 January 2016.

Saeed, Sadia. 2015. 'Secular power, law and the politics of religious sentiments.' *Critical Research on Religion* 3 (1): 57–71.

Schimmel, Annemarie. 1994. *Deciphering the Signs of God: A Phenomenological Approach to Islam*. Albany: State University of New York Press.

Scott, J. Barton. 2015. 'Aryas unbound: Print Hinduism and the cultural regulation of religious offense.' *Comparative Studies of South Asia, Africa and the Middle East* 35 (2): 294–309.

Siddique, Osama and Zahra Hayat. 2008. 'Unholy speech and holy laws: Blasphemy laws in Pakistan: Controversial origins, design defects, and free speech implications.' *Minnesota Journal of International Law* 17 (2): 303–85.

Starrett, Gregory. 1995. 'The political economy of religious commodities in Cairo.' *American Anthropologist* 97(1): 51–68.

State v. Asia Bibi. 2014. *Criminal Appeal 2509/2010*. Lahore High Court, 5 November 2014.

State v. Muhammad Azam. 2011. *Cr. P.L.A No. 04/2011*. Supreme Appellate Court of Gilgit-Baltistan, 25 May 2011.

State v. Mumtaz Qadri. 2015a. *Criminal Appeal n°90 of 2011*. Islamabad High Court, 9 March 2015.

State v. Mumtaz Qadri. 2015b. *Criminal Appeals n° 210 and 211*. Supreme Court of Pakistan, 27 October 2015.

State v. Salamat Masih. 1995. *28 p.Cr 811*. Lahore High Court, 23 February 1995.

State v. Sawan Masih. 2014. *Case FIR n°112/13*. Lahore Sessions Court, 27 March 2014.

State v. Usman Rasheed. 2017. *Criminal Appeal No.76-J of 2013*. Lahore High Court, 10 January 2017.

State v. Younas Masih. 2013. *CRL Appeal n°711/2007*. Lahore High Court Lahore, 27 February 2013.

State v. Zulfiqar Ali. 2014. *FIR n°314/2008*. Lahore Sessions Court, 14 July 2014.

Stephens, Julia. 2014. 'The politics of Muslim rage: Secular law and religious sentiment in late colonial India.' *History Workshop Journal* 77 (1): 45–64.

Suit, Natalia K. 2013. 'Mushaf and the material boundaries of the Qur'an', in *Iconic Books and Texts*, James W. Watts, ed, 189–206. Sheffield: Equinox Publishing.

Syed, Jawad, Edwina Pio, Tahir Kamran and Abbas Zaidi. 2016. *Faith-based Violence and Deobandi Militancy in Pakistan*. London: Palgrave Macmillan.

Truschke, Audrey. 2016. *Culture of Encounters: Sanskrit at the Mughal Court*. New York: Columbia University Press.

Ur Rehman, Zia. 2016. 'In Qadri's fate, Barelvis see their redemption.' *The News*, 3 March 2016. https://www.thenews.com.pk/print/102383-In-Qadris-fate-Barelvis-see-their-redemption.

Walsh, Declan. 2012. '19 reported dead as Pakistanis protest Muhammad video.' *The New York Times*, 21 September 2012. http://www.nytimes.com/2012/09/22/world/asia/protests-in-pakistan-over-anti-islam-film.html.

Zaidi, Abbas. 2010. 'A postcolonial sociolinguistics of Punjabi in Pakistan.' *Journal of Postcolonial Cultures and Societies* 1 (3): 22–55.

3
The rise of religious offence in transitional Myanmar

Iselin Frydenlund

Religious offence in transitional Myanmar

In recent years two cases of 'religious offence' have come into prominence in Burmese public debate.[1] In both cases the accused were found guilty of offending Buddhism and sentenced to prison and hard labour. Both cases were passed after strong mobilisation by a recent Buddhist monastic organisation called the MaBaTha (an acronym for *Ah-myo Batha Thathana Saun Shaunq Ye a-Pwe*, or the Organisation for the Protection of Race and Religion). Of crucial concern to the MaBaTha and their supporters was the notion that Buddhism is in peril. The aim of the MaBaTha – and the separate but interlinked 969 network – is to protect Buddhism (or more specifically, the *sasana*)[2] from perceived internal as well as external threats. The means by which Buddhist protectionist movements seek to secure and protect the *sasana* range from educational programmes for children to preaching, public marches, signatory campaigns – and even, as we shall see, to legal activism and Buddhist interest litigation.

Being geared towards the production of normative religious beings, trials serve as an important 'religion-making' technology (Mandair and Dressler 2011), drawing distinct boundaries and often distinguishing between 'good religion' and 'bad religion'. Buddhism has a strong monastic legal tradition for regulating 'proper' from 'improper' monastic practice, ritual purity, succession lines and property issues through legal judgement. Furthermore, in South and Southeast Asia, the 'responsible Buddhist king is expected to inject state authority into monastic affairs when appropriate' (Carbine 2016, 105).

In pre-colonial Buddhist states, then, both the monastic order of monks and nuns (the Sangha) and the state acted as 'religion-makers'. Yet 'blasphemy' seems at that time not to have been of great concern. While notions of disrespect towards the Buddha or 'wrong views' (*adhamma*) can certainly be identified in Buddhist canonical scriptures (including the monastic law, the *vinaya*), disrespect or wrong views have not generally been the subject of legal sanctions, nor of state regulation in pre-colonial Buddhist states. With the advent of the colonial state, new forms of legal codification of religion were adopted, as well as introduction of the very concepts of 'religion' and 'religious offence'.

This chapter traces the historical trajectories of state regulation of religious offence and blasphemy – or what is constructed as 'good religion' and 'bad religion' – in Burma/Myanmar, reaching from British colonialism to present-day practices. It shows how the legal regulation of religious offence, blasphemy and heresy has served various political as well as religious interests. The religious aspect is not to be forgotten, as the military regime's institution of Buddhist courts in 1980 functioned not only as an instrument for state control of the Sangha, but also served a particularly conservative and scripturalist strand of elite monasticism, rejecting dissenting voices as heretical. Therefore the British Penal Code's regulations of 'offence of religion', as well as the strong Burmese Buddhist legal tradition (of which the Buddhist courts are one variation), have together contributed to a legal-religious environment by which 'religious offence' or 'false views' (*adhamma*) could be sanctioned by the state.

The question raised in this chapter is why exactly the two cases were selected to be the object of accusations, and not, for example, inflammatory speech against Muslims, which dominated public debate during the same period. MaBaTha monks have compared Muslims to snakes and cuttle fish; for example U Wirathu has claimed that they engage in 'sexual jihad' and that mosques are 'enemy bases' (Frydenlund 2019). In 2014 and 2015 such statements were not charged with 'Deliberate and malicious acts intended to outrage religious feelings of any class by insulting its religion or religious beliefs'. We therefore need to understand when, how and why certain cases are conceptualised as 'religious offence' or 'wrong views' (*adhamma*), and what interests such classifications might serve.

At one level, it can be argued that the two 'religious offence' cases against Buddhism from 2015 express deep-felt insecurities about the future of Buddhism in times of rapid change. The political transition from 2011 onwards brought about rapid social, economic and political changes in Myanmar, and cases brought to the court regarding 'religious offence' against Buddhism could be seen as action taken to protect traditional culture. From this perspective, the rise of new forms of Buddhist nationalism and their concern for protecting Buddhism can be explained as a local response to the forces of globalisation. This insight is important, but yet insufficient for our understanding of how and why 'religious offence' cases came into central view just after the country opened up after 50 years of military rule. Rather, it is suggested in this chapter that the two prominent 2015 'religious offence' cases indicate that religious offence legislation is now used for Buddhist interest litigation in new and unprecedented ways in Burmese history.

Case 1: The Buddha with headphones

The first case involved a dual British/New Zealand citizen, Phil Blackwood, and two Burmese citizens, Tun Thurein and Htut Ko Ko Lwin. All were found guilty on 17 March 2015 of 'insulting religion' for a psychedelic bar advertisement depicting the Buddha wearing headphones and accompanied by the text 'Bottomless Frozen Mararita [sic] K 15000'. On the eve of 9 December 2014, Blackwood posted the ad on Facebook to promote cheap drinks at the V Gastro Bar, located in the up-market Bahan Township. The ad went viral and, after having received several complaints Blackwood removed the image and posted an apology. Following complaints made by the MaBaTha to the Bahan police station, the police took action. Only hours later Blackwood (the general manager), Thurein (the bar owner) and Lwin (the bar manager) were arrested and sent to Insein prison, just outside Myanmar's former capital, Yangon. The actual involvement of Blackwood's colleagues in the posting remains unclear.

Blackwood, Thurein and Lwin were charged under Myanmar's Penal Code, Chapter XV, 'Of Offences relating to religion', under sections 295 and 295-A. According to the judge, Blackwood's apologies in court did not remove his guilt of having 'intentionally plotted to insult religious belief'; he deemed moreover that Blackwood should have known (after spending three years in the country) that this would hurt Buddhist feelings. On 17 March 2015 the three men were sentenced to two and a half years in prison with hard labour by the Bahan Township Court, under sections 295-A and 188 of the Penal Code (charged with disobedience to public servant [sic]).[3] The first charge under section 295 was later dropped. The exact reason for this remains unclear. One possible explanation could be that the court did not consider the digital image of the Buddha with headphones to represent the destruction of a real 'object considered sacred', as defined in section 295.

Case 2: 'The Buddha was not Burmese'

On 23 October 2014, a few weeks before the arrest of Blackwood, Thurein and Lwin, the writer and National League for Democracy (NLD) activist Htin Lin Oo gave a speech at a literary festival in Chaung-U Township in Sagaing Division. In this speech he criticised the use of Buddhism to promote discrimination. Shortly afterwards a ten-minute edited video appeared on social media, causing outrage among 969 and MaBaTha monks. On 4 December the activist was charged by the Chaung-U Township Court, after a complaint was filed against him by township officials, under section 295-A on 'Deliberate and malicious acts intended to outrage religious feelings of any class by insulting its religion or religious beliefs' and section 298 on 'Uttering words, etc; with deliberate intent to wound religious feelings'. In his speech Htin Lin Oo points out that the Buddha was not Burmese, not Shan, not Karen, nor belonging to any of Myanmar's 'national races' for that matter.[4] So, he concludes, 'if you want to be an extreme nationalist and if you love to maintain your race that much, don't believe in Buddhism'. The speech concludes by stating that 'Our Buddhism is being destroyed by these people wearing robes'.

Htin Lin Oo was detained at his first court hearing on 17 December after being denied bail. More than 11 hearings were subsequently held in the beginning of 2015, during which he was repeatedly denied bail. His supporters had hoped he would avoid trial because he had publicly apologised to monks of the Chaung-U Township at his fifth hearing on 15 January, among other things performing a full prostration in honour of the local head of the Sangha.[5] However, this was not sufficient for the Immigration Department chief U Tun Tun Khine, who first filed the case against him. After what was later talked of as an ongoing saga of hearings, the verdict was reached on 2 June 2015. Htin Lin Oo was acquitted of the charge of 'wounding religious feelings', but found guilty of the charge of 'insulting religion'. He was sentenced to two years in prison.

Both the Blackwood, Lwin and Thurein case and the Htin Lin Oo case soon turned into a human rights issue for human rights and pro-democracy groups such the UN, the International Commission of Jurists, Amnesty International and Burma Campaign UK, who saw the accused as political prisoners whose right to freedom of expression had been violated (see e.g. Sherwell 2015). After pressure from the government of New Zealand, Blackwood was released in January 2016, as one of 102 political prisoners who were granted presidential amnesty by President

Thein Sein. The other three Burmese prisoners were released by the new NLD government during 2016.

Both cases attracted huge national and international media attention. In Myanmar the cases were considered so politically sensitive that the accused had difficulty in finding defence lawyers. Furthermore, the legal court documents are not official, and it has so far been impossible to access them. This discussion is based upon the media reports and interviews with relevant actors during the controversy.

Buddhist blasphemy?

The 969 and MaBaTha monks conceptualised the picture of the Buddha with headphones, as well as Htin Lin Oo's speech, as being offensive to Buddhism. This raises the question about notions of disrespect in Buddhism, and to what extent such notions of disrespect can help us explain the two 2015 'religious offence' cases.

Drawing on Steven Collins's concept of the 'Pali imaginaire' (an ideology of order found in the Pali texts), Paul Fuller (2016) has suggested that the Pali imaginaire can explain (at least in part) why the monks were offended by the bar advert and by Htin Lin Oo's speech. If by blasphemy we mean slander or harm to sacred persons or objects, we will find that Pali canonical texts contain narratives describing, as well as condemning, such acts. For example, slandering of the *dhamma* had a direct relationship to sins considered forms of harm to the Buddha, such as confiscation of property or desecration of sacred objects. Such acts would result in the most horrific karmic consequences, leading directly to hell, but they did not result in *human* distribution of punishments (Jenkins 2016). This is important to remember, as Fuller rightly reminds us, because modernist Buddhism – as well as orientalist constructions of Buddhism – have resulted in popular conceptions of Buddhism as being overwhelmingly concerned with non-attachment, and which therefore should be not concerned with insult, defamation and hurt feelings.

Importantly, however, legal sanctions of disrespect are not frequent in Pali canonical texts. False claims of superhuman qualities result in expulsion from the order, but 'wrong views' (*adhamma*) or insults expressed towards Buddhism are significantly not subject to legal sanctions.[6] Certainly there is mention of disrespect with regard to the practice of 'turning-the-bowl'. This act, known in Pali as *pattanikkujjana-kamma*, can be performed against lay people considered morally unworthy of making donations to the Sangha in eight specific cases: these include disrespect of the Buddha, the Sangha or the Dhamma.[7] 'Offence' against Buddhism then has *moral* consequences, either through karmic retribution or through a form of 'religious boycott'. Importantly, such sanctions are only applicable to a defined Buddhist community; they would not be the source of legal consequences for non-Buddhists. It should also be mentioned that little is known about the practice of *pattanikkujjanakamma* in Buddhist history, suggesting that it has not been of major concern to the Buddhist literati.[8]

In spite of textual evidence of notions of disrespect, or practices across the Buddhist world of reverence of the Buddha image, drawing a direct line from canonical and traditional notions of disrespect to contemporary *legal* 'religious offence' cases is problematic. Firstly, the MaBaTha monks did not make explicit reference to canonical texts, so it remains an open question to what extent it was the 'Pali imaginaire' or other legal traditions that informed their views. Secondly, there is the question of representation. The two cases mostly attracted attention from radical monastic organisations such as the MaBaTha, while other monks such as Aria Bhivamsa – who in fact testified in defence of Htin Lin Oo during his trial – questioned MaBaTha's legal understanding and strategy (*Frontier Myanmar* 2014). If notions of slander and religious offence are important in the 'Pali imaginaire' and traditional Buddhist cultures, why did only the 969 and the MaBaTha engage in this issue? I suggest that rather than seeking for answers in Buddhist traditions of respect and disrespect we have to look for explanations in modern constructions of law and religion in Myanmar. Furthermore, we need to unpack the specific political context of the cases which, as we shall see, eventually turned alleged disrespect into matters of state law.

Constructing religious offence and blasphemy by law

As previously noted, in South and Southeast Asia there seems to be little evidence to suggest that Buddhist law was particularly concerned with slander and 'blasphemy'.[9] Rather, in Burma (as in British India and British Ceylon), legal measures against 'religious offence' were introduced under British colonial rule. In the following account I will explore particular developments of law under British colonial rule, and later under postcolonial authoritarian rule, to show how colonial law designed to protect communal harmony eventually became an instrument for securing the interests of the military state.

The British politics of religious 'non-interference'

Burma was a province of British India, and Indian rules and regulations applied to Burma too. The Indian Penal Code (1860) was adopted by Burma in 1861 and is still current law in Myanmar.[10] The Penal Code does not regulate religion in specific ways, but contains five sections pertaining to 'religious offence':

- 295. Injuring or defiling place of worship, with intent to insult the religion of any class.
- 295-A. Deliberate and malicious acts intended to outrage religious feelings of any class by insulting its religion or religious beliefs.
- 296. Disturbing religious assembly.
- 297. Trespassing on burial places etc.
- 298. Uttering words etc with deliberate intent to wound religious feelings.

Section 295-A was added by colonial authorities in 1927 to curb communal tension in India, and was soon applied to British Burma. As elsewhere in British India, colonial legislation in Burma regarding 'religious offence' was aimed at ensuring interreligious harmony between its *subjects* (and not between the subjects and the state); it sought to protect the religious feelings of *all* citizens (see chapter 1). In Burma, this was in line with the British policy of 'non-interference' in the religious domain. This implied a form of state secularism, with no legal preference for one religion over another; it also sought to ensure that 'religion could not be used in the service of the projects of the colonial state' (Turner 2014, 13).

Neutrality was far from the reality on the ground, however. The colonial era was marked not only by Christian missionary activities and politics of colonial difference (such as the chief commissioner of Burma's insistence on the Burmese being barefoot in court), but also by negotiations and contestations over the meaning of 'religion' and the 'secular', as exemplified by the so-called 'shoe controversy'. This controversy concerned the wearing of shoes in Buddhist sacred space, particularly at pagoda platforms. Burmese Buddhists took offence at the British ruling to exempt Europeans and Americans – and later also local Muslims – from the rule requiring removal of shoes at such platforms; they viewed this as an offence and a threat to the *sasana*. Furthermore the British colonial model of 'religion' conceived the *sasana* as fitting into the universalised category of 'religion'. The *sasana* was deprived of its privileged status, which eventually resulted in calls for protection of Buddhist sacred sites and symbols against sacrilege.

However, British legal records[11] indicate that 'religious offence' cases were not frequent. This in turn suggests that section 295 to 298 were not an important legal instrument for either the British or the Burmese Buddhists in the larger schemes of contestation and negotiation over the status of religion in the colony. In addition, the media material from the turn of the century examined by Alicia Turner (2014) contains few references to court cases. The question of how to respect 'religion' or *sasana* was strongly contested, but the British viewed the so-called 'shoe controversy' or the *shiko*[12] debate as threats to colonial order (Turner 2014, 129–30), thus making charges of sedition more applicable. For example, U Dhammaloka – an Irish convert to Buddhism and an anti-colonial activist in Burma at the beginning of the twentieth century – was threatened with charges of sedition for asking an off-duty Indian officer to remove his shoes at the Shwedagon Pagoda (Turner 2014, 124). But the Buddhists did not charge the British with 'religious offence' for wearing shoes at pagoda platforms – not perhaps surprising given power asymmetry and colonial difference.

The following cases from British legal libraries in Burma give a glimpse into how the British judges ruled with regard to 'religious offence'. The Judicial Commissioner of Lower Burma (1872–92)[13] mentions only one single case where section 295 of the Penal Code had been applied in a lower court. The case *Queen Empress v. Nga Po San* concerned a case in which bells had been stolen from a Buddhist pagoda – a theft which, according to the local court, 'must have been done with the knowledge that Buddhists would regard this damage to the pagoda as an insult to their religion'. The Judicial Commissioner notes, however, that the accused had not removed the bells himself, but rather had tried to sell on stolen goods: this, according to the Commissioner, would not make him culpable of insulting Buddhism. The case was not re-opened, but the judgement that section 295 was not applicable in the case of theft of religious artefacts was passed on to the lower courts.

In another case from Upper Burma in the same period, the question of intent is at stake. In the case *Queen Empress v. Nga Po San and Mi Kin* the accused were charged of having sexual intercourse within temple premises. The couple were found guilty of charges of 'religious offence' under section 295. However, according to the Commissioner – and with reference to the *Rutna Mudali* case from British India in 1887 – section 295 did not apply as the accused most probably wanted to keep this a secret; it was not an act 'with intent to insult'. Therefore, according to the Commissioner, the couple instead should be convicted of trespassing under section 297. He argued that it 'was a trespass to enter it for the purpose for which the accused entered it, and the accused must have known that the religion of the Buddhists who worshipped at the pagoda was likely to be insulted thereby'.[14]

As discussed above, the British had exempted themselves from the practice of removing shoes at pagodas – a situation that had deeply offended the Buddhists. The two cases discussed here thus reveal an apparent contradiction in British policies on 'religious offence': what qualified as 'religious offence' under colonial rule depended upon British sensibilities with regard to theft and sex in temple premises, but not to footwear. In 1919 the Buddhists eventually won the 'shoe controversy', an event often said to have marked the beginning of the end of British colonialism in Burma. As Alicia Turner has shown, protection of the *sasana* was more important to anti-colonial aspirations at the turn of the century than national independence.

Burma was separated from India in 1937, but self-government did not imply independence from Britain. The 1930s were marked by political instability, labour strikes and – in 1938 – severe anti-Indian/anti-Muslim riots. The forerunner to the riots was the publication of the book *Moulvi-Yogi Awada Sadan*. It contained three parts, written by two Muslims and one Buddhist, all engaging in religious polemics against the religious 'Other'. The book, published in 1931 but only discovered by Burmese media in 1938, was presented as largely anti-Buddhist and eventually banned after the inception of riots. The Buddhist author had died in 1931, so only the two Muslims were charged with violation of 295-A and 298, after intense pressure from Buddhist associations.

At a mass rally held at the Shwedagon Pagoda on 26 July 1938, a resolution was passed calling for vigorous action to be taken against Maung Shwe Hpi, the publisher of the work. If not, 'this meeting warns Government that steps will be taken to treat the Muslims as enemy No. 1 who insult the Buddhist community and their religion and to bring about the extermination of the Muslims and the extinction of their religion and language'.[15] Importantly, however, the charges were dropped and the British judge ruled that the 1938 riots were not caused by the book but were rather due 'to the agitation of the Burmese Press'.[16] Also, *The Final Report of the Riot Inquiry Committee* from 1939 concluded that the blasphemy controversy was a piece of 'unscrupulous political opportunism' with the aim to 'embarrass a particular Ministry'.[17] Furthermore, the religious legitimacy of the rioters was called into question, and the *Report* even claimed that monks participating in the riots represented 'an insult to Buddhism'.[18]

Except for this case, colonial 'religious offence' legislation was not to be used by Buddhist activists until nearly a century later, when political liberalisation allowed space for Buddhist interest litigation. In the intervening years, 'religious offence' legislation came to be one out of many tools used against public enemies under military rule.

Post-independence: Law as a policy tool for the military state

Military rule in Burma resulted in changes in the judiciary remarkably different from developments in India or Sri Lanka. The 1947 Constitution had established a liberal democratic state, specified the fundamental rights of citizens and guaranteed judicial independence, but during the socialist and one-party regime of General Ne Win (1962–88) the judiciary lost its independence. The regime did not abandon the colonial laws, but superimposed a new doctrine that the role of the court was to reveal the 'truth', and to do so by 'trumping all old doctrines from Anglo-Indian law' (Cheesman 2011, 813). Within this socialist legality 'socialist rights' were given primacy over 'individual rights' (the latter being seen as bourgeois); the law was viewed as an instrument to safeguard the interests of the socialist state. Furthermore, by the mid-1970s the regime had succeeded in eradicating all professional judges in Burma.

In spite of its socialist ideological framing, however, more than anything the Ne Win regime represented military authoritarianism, which penetrated socio-legal structures to an even greater extent than Ayub Khan's Pakistan (Cheesman 2011). Its pragmatism meant that it got rid of the judges trained in the Anglo-Indian legal tradition, but kept colonial laws for its own pragmatic and strategic use. The judiciary did not respect *habeas corpus*, the public had little access to courts and secrecy became the hallmark of the judiciary. By the 1980s trials had disappeared from public media (Cheesman 2015, 119).

How did the military regime rule with regard to 'religious offence'? Firstly, it should be noted that the Ne Win regime hardly referred to Buddhism, while the 1974 Constitution mentions no state preference for Buddhism. It is strictly secularist, stating that 'Religion and religious organisations shall not be used for political purposes' (Article 156-C). The Constitution grants equality before the law and religious freedom, but limits those rights with reference to 'national solidarity and the socialist social order' (Article 153-B). Simultaneously, Buddhism – particularly the Sangha – was the subject of increased legal regulation, to control so-called 'unruly' monks and subsequently to curb monastic resistance to the regime.

Ne Win also institutionalised a specific Buddhist monastic court system. As we shall see, this is concerned with the 'heresy' of monastic fraternities charged for holding 'deviant' doctrines, but it rarely engages with the secular Penal Code and its 'religious offence' legislation. While more research is needed to establish a clear pattern of how 'religious offence' legislation was applied during Ne Win rule, preliminary research indicates that cases were few. 'Public enemies' were rather charged with the Unlawful Associations Act, the Emergency Provisions Act and Penal Code sections on sedition and treason (Cheesman 2015). The section 295 to 298 do not seem to have been in frequent use. Given ethnic minority armed resistance to the Burmese state, these provisions were certainly not considered an appropriate instrument for minority protection against the military regime's 'Burmanisation' policies against the country's numerous ethnic and religious minorities. On the contrary: religious minorities were under strict surveillance. For example, the Ministry of Religious Affairs has for decades imposed close censorship of translations of the Bible and the Quran into the Burmese language, with the particular aim of excluding Pali Buddhist loan words.

The new junta (1988–2011), led by the State Law and Order Restoration Council (SLORC) and the State Peace and Development Council (SPDC),[19] was to abandon socialist ideology altogether. The SLORC/SPDC made 'law and order' its new slogan; this did not imply the rule of law, but rather subsuming law *to* order (Cheesman 2015). In this period a new hierarchy of judges (comprised of bureaucrats and administrators) resurrected a system marked by non-independence and 'unrule' of law. As Cheesman points out, in contrast to the Ne Win years soldiers were no longer necessary in the courtroom as the civilian judiciary was fully subordinated to military interests (Cheesman 2011, 825).

The post-1988 period also witnessed a shift from Ne Win's secularism to an increasingly pronounced religious nationalism (Schober 2011). This shift came after the violent crackdown in 1988 on the student movement and pro-democracy monks, when the SLORC needed to repair its relations to the Sangha, eventually resulting in a state-sponsored Buddhist nationalist ideology (Schober 2011, 88–90). This re-orientation is expressed in the 2008 Constitution Article 361, which grants Buddhism a special position as the majority religion.

The 2008 Constitution strikes a balance between Buddhist constitutionalism on the one hand and recognition of Christianity, Islam, Hinduism and Animism and secularist orientations on the other.[20] Although it does not actually grant Buddhism the status of state religion, post – 1988 re-orientations towards Buddhist symbols and institutions indicate that Burma had become a *de facto* Buddhist state. In the post-1988 period, massive human rights violations took place in Myanmar; cases against public enemies were made under any law, 'often based on completely wild claims' (Cheesman 2015, 115). The extent to which it is possible to discern a particular legal reasoning with regard to 'religious offence' cases in this period is thus uncertain. According to the Assistance Association for Political Prisoners (AAPP), prior to 2000 the state made little use of section 295 to 297 of the Penal Code, preferring to use Unlawful Association or the Emergency Acts against political opponents. However, from the beginning of the 2000s the state did increasingly apply section 295 to 297 in 'softer cases' against monks, as this drew less international attention and thus allegedly improved Burma's poor human rights reputation by decreasing the number of *defined* political prisoners.[21]

During the first years of the 2000s two particular 'religious offence' cases are worth discussing as they provide insight into how the regime made use of such legislation against 'unruly' Buddhist monks. The first instance, in 2003, relates to the conviction of U Wirathu, who at the time had already begun his clandestine nationalist and anti-Muslim activities within the Sangha[22] and who later became the international face of radical Buddhist ideology and so-called 'Buddhist extremism'.[23] He was charged under section 295 for instigating anti-Muslim violence during the 2003 riots in Kyaukse (central Myanmar), but was released in 2012 as part of President Thein Sein's political reform process.

Severe anti-Muslim violence occurred in Mandalay in 1997 and again in Kyaukse in 2003, and the military regime could neither risk new instances of communal conflicts beyond their control nor the growth of nationalist networks of young and militant monks. As previously mentioned, the SLORC had initiated pro-Buddhist policies. However, one of the unintended consequences of this new propagation of Buddhism was increased tension between Buddhist and Muslim communities not affected by the civil war – conflicts that were eventually to backfire on the government (Human Rights Watch 2009).

The second important instance concerns 'religious offence' charges against monks and nuns who participated in the 2007 so-called 'Saffron Revolution'. Thousands of Buddhist monks and nuns took to the streets to peacefully protest against deteriorating living standards, but their actions were met with massive violence from the regime. Thousands were detained and hundreds disappeared, while others died in custody. In most cases monks and nuns were charged with disturbing public order (Human Rights Watch 2007 and Human Rights Council 2007). U Gambira, perhaps the most famous monk of the Saffron Revolution, was charged (among other things) for violations of sections 505-A and 505-B of the State Offence Act (threatening the stability of the government); Immigration Act 13/1 (reportedly a reference to his visit to Thailand in 2005); Illegal Organization Act 17/1; Electronic Act 303-A; and Organization Act 6. He was not, however, charged with 'religious offence'. In fact, only a few monks and nuns were charged under sections 295 and 295-A for 'religious offence'.

In those cases, monastics had in fact not taken to the streets during the massive demonstrations. Rather, the security forces had raided their monasteries at night in search for monks in hiding (Human Rights Watch 2009). Perhaps the regime decided to charge them with 'religious offence' because it was difficult to accuse monastics arrested in a monastery (defined sacred space) of 'Unlawful Association' in public space; certainly the reasoning behind this charge remains obscure. In another case a monk waiting outside the court that was hearing a case against Aung San Suu Kyi in 2009 found himself charged under section 295-A for planning self-immolation (despite the lack of any evidence to support this claim, or any explanation as to why self-immolation would classify as a 'religious offence').

In short, during SLORC/SPDC rule political prisoners faced charges under a wide range of sections from the Penal Code, including 'religious offence'.[24] This was more the exception than the rule, but the fact that it was used at all shows that 'religious offence' legislation was one of the numerous tools that the military regime applied to curb monastic unrest, opposition or violence. As we shall see, as Myanmar moved towards political liberalisation from 2011 onwards, the nature of such cases would eventually take on a new significance.

Protecting 'orthodoxy' from 'heresy': The Buddhist court system

Before moving to the transitional period (2011–) another aspect of Myanmar's legal system has to be discussed, as it in very specific ways contributes to a legalistic approach to the classification of religious difference. This is the Buddhist state court system (called *vinicchaya*),[25] which is unique to Myanmar. This court has absolute authority in doctrinal matters and constitutes a particular Buddhist legal culture that shapes and formats Buddhist thought and practice in decisive ways.

Soon after Independence attempts were made to institute a centralised Buddhist court system (referred to as the Vinicchaya Act from 1949). Again, such attempts failed during the early years of Ne Win's rule as part of its secularist orientations (Maung Maung 1988); *vinaya* transgressions were only to be dealt with within each monastic lineage, or *gaing*. Without a state-backed supra-*gaing* structure in place, no rulings regarding heresy (*adhamma*) could be made. It was not until 1980 (still under Ne Win's rule) that a specific legal system to deal with *vinaya* cases came into place at the national level. In these Buddhist courts Buddhists (mostly monks) are charged with heresy (*adhamma*), and malpractice (*avinaya*), under the jurisdiction of the State Sangha Mahanayaka Committee (referred to as the MaHaNa). This body, established under Ne Win in 1980, oversees the regulation and conduct of the Sangha. This Buddhist court system has been a significant feature of both the maintenance of the *sasana* by the Sangha and the control of the Sangha by successive military governments (Ashin and Crosby 2017).

Between 1980 and 2017, 17 rulings were made in cases concerning alleged heresy and malpractice at the national level of the *vinicchaya* system (Ashin and Crosby 2017). In most cases the accused are monks (in two cases former monks) who have been found guilty of *adhamma*, charged with wrong understanding of meditation, Buddhist cosmology or of the concept of *karma*. In only one case is the accused a lay person, and in that very exceptional case it was the followers of a meditation master who wanted to 'verify' the master's teachings after his death. In one case the accused was found guilty after his death. Shin Ukkattha (1897–1978) had been one of Burma's leading modernist intellectuals, but in 1981 his teachings were deemed to be 'un-Buddhist' by the court.

In all 17 cases the accused have been found to be guilty and, with few exceptions, they have accepted the court's decisions. In only two cases have the accused refused to accept the verdict. In such cases, several laws are at the courts' disposal,[26] which state that anyone disobeying the *vinicchaya* court can be sentenced to up to six months' imprisonment. This happened to the nun (*thilashin*) Saccavadi. She accepted the court's refusal of full ordination for women as *bhikkhunis*, but refused to *apologise* to the court for having been fully ordained as a *bhikkhuni* in Sri Lanka.

Another legal instrument at hand to ensure compliance is the Penal Code, especially section 295 to 298. So far this has only been applied in the most recent case, namely the Mopyar case from 2011. Its leader, the monk Shin Nana (later referred to as U Mopyar, a reference to his sky-blue outfit) had been found guilty back in 1983 of making false superhuman claims (which, according to the *vinaya*, requires expulsion from the order). Being denied the status of a monk, Shin Nana wanted to establish a new *gaing* (sect), based on his particular 'doctrine of present action'. Based upon a ruling from 2011, the Mopyar *gaing* was officially outlawed by the state on the grounds that U Mopyar taught *adhamma*, or 'wrong teachings' (Ashin and Crosby 2017). His negation of karmic causality of reward and retribution seems to have been of particular concern to the monastic guardians of Theravadin orthodoxy. This case is particularly interesting as the court still treated the accused as a Buddhist (although he had himself denounced Theravada Buddhism) and as a monk (in terms of honorific titles used), even though he had been formally defrocked for more than 30 years and had even served a three-year sentence for being a 'false monk'.

U Mopyar continues his activities, but his followers now operate clandestinely due to the high risk of severe sanctions. For our purpose here, it is noteworthy that when U Mopyar did not comply with the rulings of the *vinicchaya* court he was then charged under sections 295 and 295-A of the Penal Code for acts 'intended to offend religious feelings', as well as for insulting Buddhism. In fact, his activities were deemed to be an attempt to destroy Theravada Buddhism. Furthermore, U Mopyar was also charged under section 5J of the Emergency Provisions Act for behaviour deemed to be a threat to national security (Kawanami 2017).[27] Interestingly in this case secular state law functions as a 'back-up' resource when the *vinaya*, or other specific *vinacchaya* court regulations,[28] fail to regulate 'deviant' behaviour.[29]

The Buddhist court system in Myanmar is thus mostly a legal mechanism for the Sangha hierarchy to uphold specific notions of purity and orthodoxy, within a defined sphere of religious specialists. Cases involving lay people – Buddhist or non-Buddhist – with regard to 'religious offence' fall under the Penal Code. They are usually dealt with in secular courts although, as the Mopyar case illustrates, a case can move from being considered an internal doctrinal matter to being defined as an 'insult' or 'offence' and thus as an external threat to Buddhism. The driver of this system, as pointed out by Ashin and Crosby (2017), is the wish to protect the *sasana* from impurity and corruption, based on a specific form of Buddhist scriptural fundamentalism unique to Myanmar. In addition, state mechanisms for legal regulation of religion, both religious and secular, are potential tools for the exercise of political power – both by the military regime and, as we shall see, by monastic formations such as the MaBaTha.

Myanmar's political liberalisation and the politics of 'religious offence'

After more than half a century under military rule, Myanmar has since 2011 experienced a rapid political transition and an opening up to the outside world. The reformist agenda of President Thein Sein's semi-civilian government implied the release of Aung San Suu Kyi from house arrest and increased freedom of expression and association, as well as the freedom to form political parties. It also saw the release of hundreds of political prisoners, including Buddhist monks. Myanmar's first free (but not fair) elections in 25 years were held in 2015.[30] Aung San Sui Kyui and the NLD made a historic landslide victory, and the election result was accepted by both the ruling Union Solidarity and Development Party (USDP) and the military. During 50 years of military dictatorship, 'Rule of Law' became one of the most important appeals by the pro-democracy movement. The need for legal reform was undisputed and, from 2011 onwards, the semi-civilian government initiated broad legislative reforms, with steps being taken to review and amend laws.[31]

Yet, in this wave of political liberalisation and legal reform, the first transition years of democratic reform also witnessed new media regulations and continued restrictions on the press.[32] Furthermore – and contrary to liberal expectations – in 2015 the Parliament and the President passed legislation that implied increased regulation with religion, most notably the so-called 'race and religion laws'. The laws were passed due to mobilisation of the MaBaTha and were specifically designed – according to the laws' main designer and campaigner U Wirathu – to protect Myanmar from 'Islamisation'.[33] These laws, which partly override previous Buddhist and Muslim family laws, seek to regulate marriages between Buddhist women and non-Buddhist men, to prevent forceful conversion through state control of conversion from one religion to another, to abolish polygamy and extra-marital affairs and to promote birth control and family planning in certain regions of the country.

'Protect your religion!' — The rise of Buddhist protectionism

Since 2012 anti-Muslim sentiment, hate rhetoric and the politics of fear have dominated public discourse in Myanmar. While it is clear that anti-Muslim sentiments can be traced back to the colonial era, recent anti-Muslim attitudes are more systematic (Schissler et al. 2017). Such sentiments have been explained as the outcome of government and/or military initiatives, but they must also be considered as a reaction to the ontological insecurity experienced as a result of rapid economic and social changes since Myanmar's reform process began (Walton et al. 2015). Tropes of decline and deracination are central to Buddhist eschatology, and calls for the protection of the *sasana* against imminent external or internal threats are a recurrent theme in Buddhist history. Obviously the nature of such perceived threats has changed over time;

the current 'myths of deracination' are tied to larger concerns about open borders, illegal immigrants (as the Rohingyas are claimed to be), the 'Islamisation' of Myanmar and the possible eradication of traditional culture.

In response to these fears, a cluster of interrelated Buddhist protectionist movements was formed in 2012 and 2013, the most important being the MaBaTha. As previously noted, monastic mobilisation had not been allowed back in 2007, but the transition process created new space for monastic mobilisation in the public domain. Buddhist protectionist groups in particular benefited from this new space, as the semi-civilian regime of Thein Sein saw such Buddhist protectionist groups as beneficial to its interests (Frydenlund 2017).

As we have seen, public law was weak under military rule and the possibilities for Buddhist interest litigation curbed. Certainly the *vinicchaya* court was important for *vinaya* regulation and doctrinal issues from the 1980s onwards, but it was not until the years following the 2011 political reforms that Buddhist activists could engage in public law to secure the *sasana*. A close analysis of early MaBaTha activities shows that the MaBaTha monks from the very beginning considered law an important tool for the *protection* of the *sasana*, and from 2013 onwards the promulgation of the 'race and religion' laws was top priority. Given the legacy of state codification and legal regulation of religion and ethnicity in Myanmar,[34] in addition to the strong Buddhist legal culture, the legalistic approach taken by the MaBaTha is unsurprising.

The 'race and religion' laws came to play an important role in the 2015 elections, as the USDP presented itself as the protector of the laws in contrast to the NLD. Moreover, the elections influenced the timing of the legal process, with monks pushing for the laws to be signed by the President before the elections, fearing that the laws would not be passed in the case of an NLD victory. Therefore one might argue that the success of Buddhist legal activism was contingent upon the transitional regime's struggle for electoral victory. In addition, the 'race and religion' laws influenced the ways in which religion informed the electoral campaign. Back in 2014 the MaBaTha had declared its neutrality vis-à-vis party politics. In 2015, however, they urged people not to vote NLD on the grounds that it was too Muslim-friendly as the NLD had voted against the laws in Parliament. Moreover, USDP campaign posters explicitly mentioned the laws and the MaBaTha issued flyers urging the people to vote for parties that supported the laws (Frydenlund 2017).

It was within this context of transition, political competition, uncertainty, violence against Muslim minorities, rise of Buddhist protectionist groups and Buddhist legal activism that writer and NLD activist Htin Lin Oo challenged the MaBaTha, and Blackwood, Thurein and Lwin posted the bar advert depicting the Buddha with headphones on Facebook. It is my contention that, similarly to the 2015 race and religion laws, the recent blasphemy cases serve as a useful device for the promotion of certain legal-political Buddhist interests. The MaBaTha, with increasing confidence due to regime support and protection, responded swiftly to both cases, and propagated that legal action was necessary against alleged offence against Buddhism.

In both cases MaBaTha monks pushed for legal prosecution of the offenders. As previously mentioned, it was MaBaTha monks who complained to the police in the V Gastro Bar case. In the Htin Lin Oo case, charges were pressed by the local Immigration Department of U Chaung Township (central Myanmar), but in close collaboration with local MaBaTha activists. Furthermore, the MaBaTha asked the NLD for disciplinary action against Htin Lin Oo, which resulted in his dismissal as NLD information officer (Mann 2014).

In both cases 969 and MaBaTha monks attended the public spectacles outside the respective courtrooms – something that would have been unthinkable just a few years before. During military rule the judiciary ruled on the principle of secrecy, which meant closed trials and the disappearance of trials from public media, particularly from the 1980s onwards. During the political liberalisation restrictions decreased, and journalists were given more access to the courts than before. Also, although press freedom was still under heavy pressure, court cases were again reported in the media.

Increased press freedom in Myanmar after 2011 made it possible for journalists to report from the courts, which resulted in high public visibility of the two cases. Furthermore, with MaBaTha monks becoming active users of social media, their position on the two cases attracted major attention on social media like Facebook and YouTube.

Although newly acquired press freedom made it possible to report on the cases, heavy pressure was put on the media and the courts. Journalists complained that the monks behaved in a threatening and intimidating manner, with the aim to scare them off covering the cases (Mann 2014). There were also rumours that leading MaBaTha monks pressurised both judges and lawyers involved in the two cases. Only weeks after the Htin Lin Oo verdict in June 2015, the MaBaTha at its annual conference in Insein published a 12-point statement in which they demanded blasphemous (*pyit mhar saw kar thaw*) attacks against monks to be stopped.[35] This statement was released only four months before the elections, and at a time when the MaBaTha monks had dropped their self-declared political neutrality and asked people not to vote for the NLD.

The Htin Lin Oo case: Challenging the MaBaTha

Being a prominent columnist and NLD activist, the political context of his case was not lost upon Htin Lin Oo. After receiving his sentence in June, he commented to the press that 'What I said was for love and peace between different communities with different faiths'. He added that 'I received two years' imprisonment for that, but I won, because I can reveal the people behind all of these haters. From my case, the whole country now knows who is the black hand behind the scenes' (Mann 2015). Htin Lin Oo was obviously referring to the military, and his belief that his imprisonment was the result of the military curbing the opposition in the run-up to the November 2015 elections.

Shortly after the verdict President Thein Sein decided to give presidential amnesty for 6,966 prisoners, but Htin Lin Oo's name was not on the list. The presidential amnesty was arranged the day before a sacred Buddhist full moon day, and just months before the parliamentary elections in November. Furthermore, the verdict – as well as the amnesty – took place as the President was in the final stages of signing the 'race and religion' laws proposed by the MaBaTha. As previously discussed, President Thein Sein and the USDP actively supported the MaBaTha and the 969. By promoting this and other legal claims made by the MaBaTha during the election campaign, the USDP could stand a chance against the NLD. From the government's point of view, support of the MaBaTha would enhance their chances of electoral success.

From the MaBaTha point of view, 'race and religion' legislation and blasphemy cases were tools in protecting the *sasana* and securing Buddhist rights. During the run-up to the 2015 elections, the MaBaTha monks used their religious authority to bolster support for the USDP. Conversely it branded NLD and Aung San Suu Kyi as Muslim-friendly. Their attack on Htin Lin Oo must therefore be understood as a strategy of delegitimising NLD politicians who appeared 'Muslim-friendly' and who criticised the MaBaTha agenda from a Buddhist point of view – for example, by arguing that Buddhism should not be used for identity politics.

Htin Lin Oo may have been particularly vocal and strident in his comments, but he was by no means alone in his criticism. Numerous Buddhist monks and nuns offered an alternative to MaBaTha's protectionist agenda, arguing that Buddhist philosophy and psychology (as expressed in the *abidhamma* literature) explicitly hold that ethnicity, culture and even religion are simply categories of the human mind.[36] However, explicit criticism in public was considered dangerous. Monks who publicly challenged the MaBaTha, such as the well-known Moe Thu (a pen name) in Burmese dailies or on social media came under heavy pressure from MaBaTha sympathisers – in some instances they were met with closed temple doors and death threats.[37]

The V Gastro Bar case: global economies, local sensibilities

The depiction of the Buddha with modern technological gear such as headphones disturbed Buddhist practices of regarding the Buddha image as sacred, requiring the utmost respect and care. Adding to the perceived offence was the explicit link made between the Buddha and alcohol consumption, perceived as offensive due to the Buddhist precept of refraining from the consumption of intoxicants. Given Myanmar's traditional religious culture, the strong reactions against the bar's advertisement were no surprise. There was a widespread opinion among Burmese Buddhists that the ad had deeply offended their religious sensibilities.

According to Lt.-Col. Thien Win, the head of Bahan police station, Blackwood explained during interrogation that 'he did it because using the Buddha in ads is in fashion internationally and he thought it would attract more attention' (Kyaw Phyo Tha 2014). As such, the Blackwood, Thurein and Lwin case reflects an issue concerning Buddhist activist groups not only in Myanmar, Thailand and Sri Lanka, but across the globe – namely the commercial use of images of the Buddha.

The V Gastro Bar case thus fits into a wider arena of Buddhist legal-cum-political activism that takes issue with the commercialisation of Buddhist symbols, such as Buddha tattoos and Victoria's Secret Buddha bikinis in Sri Lanka, Buddha bars in Paris and Monaco, and Buddha heads (lacking the full body) kept in bathrooms or doormats depicting the Buddha.[38] Across the Buddhist world, such commercialisation of Buddhism is perceived as disrespectful, but is, it should be noted, mostly a concern for radical Buddhist protectionist groups – such as the MaBaTha in Myanmar, the Bodu Bala Sena (BBS) in Sri Lanka or the softer lay movement Knowing Buddha Organisation (KBO) in Thailand. The last of these groups works for the education of non-Buddhists in dealing with Buddha images and artefacts, opposing the commercialisation of Buddhist symbols and explaining why Buddha tattoos, for instance, are seen as disrespectful.

The groups are local Buddhist activist groups, but increased mobility and digital communication contribute to a growing sense of interconnectedness and sharing of 'protectionist concerns' across the Buddhist world.[39] Myanmar's neighbouring countries had been exposed to the global tourist industry and global circulation of artefacts for decades. However, due to 50 years of isolation and socialist economy, the Burmese were not exposed to this until 2011–12, after the opening up of the economy and a newly booming tourist industry.

Looking at the V Gastro Bar case from a historical perspective, one could even argue that economic liberalisation resulted in a form of neo-colonialism, brought in by foreign companies and foreign tourism, that sparked just another offence to traditional Buddhist culture. In this light, it appears not too different from the shoe controversy at the beginning of the twentieth century. As in that incident Buddhist symbols became a focus of resistance, provoking defence of traditional values.

The rise of Buddhist interest litigation in transitional Myanmar

However, the reason why Blackwood and his colleagues ended up in court, were denied bail, sentenced to two and a half years with hard labour and denied presidential amnesty in July 2015 has less to do with Buddhist sensibilities in the general population, I suggest, than with new forms of Buddhist legal activism, monastic politics, electoral competition and the lack of an independent judiciary. If we compare Myanmar to Sri Lanka, for example, Buddhist groups there have failed in their attempts to get tourists with Buddha tattoos on their bodies convicted for religious offence. In fact, in a ruling from 2017, the Supreme Court ruled that Buddha tattoos were not illegal in Sri Lanka.[40] The concern over commodification of Buddhist symbols is shared, but the case of Myanmar illustrates the importance of existing regimes of legal codification of religion (for example, through the *vinicchaya* courts) for how actors think of 'religious offence' as an option for resolving disputes – or even how certain speech acts are classified as 'religious offence' in the first place. Furthermore, the case of Myanmar highlights the importance of shifting political contexts for the ways in which 'religious offence' legislation is conceptualised and applied in courts.

The Htin Lin Oo case illustrates the latter point even further. His criticism of the MaBaTha was articulated from a Buddhist normative point of view with no articulated intention of misusing Buddhist symbols, nor of insulting Buddhism, except for loudly challenging contemporary ethno-religious politics. In this case the Penal Code was used to silence lay critique of nationalist monks and to marginalise the very few voices at the time who publicly dared to confront the 969 and the MaBaTha. The MaBaTha legal campaigns (including the 'race and religion' laws and the two 'religious offence' cases) were aggressive and noisy; human rights activists and lawyers who challenged MaBaTha sympathisers (both lay and monastic) claimed they were met with abusive language and threats.

In his study of Buddhist constitutionalism in Sri Lanka, Schontal raises the question as to why 'an equally active climate of Buddhist-interest litigation' cannot be identified in Myanmar or Thailand (Schontal 2016). In Sri Lanka, he points out, a strong culture of public law and Buddhist constitutionalism encourage a climate for Buddhist-interest litigation. As we have seen, the state in Myanmar is a *de facto* Buddhist state, but due to military rule and lack of rule of law, public law has been weak, and Buddhist-interest litigation hardly present until 2015.

The conjuncture of economic and political liberalisation, as well as a new media reality in post-2011 Myanmar, created new spaces for monastic engagements in public life, including legal activism. Some groups benefited more from these new freedoms than others, however, and the Thein Sein government's protection of the 969 and the MaBaTha meant that the judiciary – which in the Myanmar case is not independent from the executive power – was more in tune with Buddhist groups under government protection than monastic groups associated with the opposition.

This point is further illustrated by the fact that the MaBaTha lost much of its government support after the NLD victory in 2016, and that the MaHaNa subsequently reduced its support to the MaBaTha, ruling that the name was not in compliance with the 1990 Law on Sangha regulation.[41] Furthermore, on 10 March 2017 – following allegations of anti-Muslim hate speech – the MaHaNa banned U Wirathu from public speaking and preaching for one year. The decision was made a few days after U Wirathu had publicly expressed support for the assassins of Myanmar's leading constitutional lawyer, U Ko Ni, who was of Muslim background. In the weeks before the verdict monks from the 2007 'Saffron Revolution' had argued in public that U Wirathu's support for the assassins was an 'offense to Buddhism' (Htun Khaing 2018). The MaHaNa ruled that U Wirathu had 'repeatedly delivered hate speech against religions to cause communal strife and hinder efforts to uphold the rule of law'.[42] The very next day U Wirathu delivered a 'silent sermon' against MaHaNa's ban. During the sermon his mouth was symbolically covered with two pieces of coloured tape, images of which went viral on social media.

As we have seen, Burma/Myanmar has a strong legacy of legal regulation of religion, both in secular and Buddhist law. In addition, as Kari Telle notes with reference to Indonesia (Telle 2017), discourses on offence and deviancy are thriving in the new and highly mediatised reality, facilitated by the liberalisation of the public sphere. The social media circulation of 'offence against Buddhism' – be they Facebook bar adverts, anti-nationalist speeches or militant anti-Muslim sermons on YouTube – fosters the impression of an increasing offence which needs to be contained through rulings and lawsuits. But as Myanmar stumbles between political liberalisation and continued military rule, 'religious offence' constitutes an open legal category contingent upon rapidly shifting political realities.

Notes

1. I will discuss various sections that regulate insult of religion in the Burmese context. When speaking about charges made under section 295 to 298 of the Penal Code, I refer to these collectively as 'religious offence' cases. Heresy and 'wrong views', according to the Buddhist courts, are referred to as *adhamma*.
2. The Pali word *sasana* (in Burmese: *thathana*) refers to the teachings, practices and institutions established by a particular *buddha*. It is understood to exist for a particular period of time before it disappears altogether.
3. Two years for offence of religion and six months for disobeying a civil servant.
4. YouTube clip, https://www.youtube.com/watch?v=0piWM3c_5sg.
5. See more at: http://www.mizzima.com/news-domestic/u-htin-lin-oo-face-trial-insulting-religion#sthash.y6ouZrx8.dpuf and https://democracyforburma.wordpress.com/2015/01/16/burma-myanmar-htin-lin-oo-paid-respect-to-monks-and-asked-for-their-forgiveness/.
6. I thank Jens Borgland for sharing his *vinaya* expertise with me.
7. *Pattanikkujjana Sutta* in the *Anguttara Nikaya*.
8. In modern times Buddhist monks in Myanmar have engaged in turning-the-bowl on three specific occasions: against the Communist Party in 1950, against the SLORC regime in 1990 and during the 'Saffron Revolution' in 2007.
9. By 'Buddhist law' I refer to the *vinaya* and the genre of written law known as *dhammasattha* ('treatise on law'), a corpus genealogically related to broader South and Southeast Asian written legal traditions. In Christian Lammerts' impressive work on *dhammasattha* texts in Burma in the period 1250–1850 there are few, if any, traces of blasphemy cases (Lammerts 2018). However, this does not rule out the possibility of legal sanctions of disrespect towards the Buddha, the Dhamma and the Sangha; we just do not yet have evidence of these.
10. The so-called Burma Code is a vast body of laws from 1818 to 1954. See https://myanmar-law-library.org/law-library/laws-and-regulations/burma-codes/.
11. Catalogues searched that yielded no findings on section 295 to 298 are the Rangoon Law Reports 1937, 1938. When religion does appear as a subject for legal reasoning, the cases concern property rights or questions regarding religious identities. The latter was of importance due to Burma's legal plural system with regard to family law. For examples, there are cases that discuss to what extent Chinese Buddhists would fall under Burmese Buddhist family law (based on the traditional *dhammasatha* tradition).
12. *Shiko* is a traditional form of respect. Burmese Buddhists defined this as 'religion' in order to avoid having to comply with British demands that Burmese had to *shiko* British teachers in the colonial education system.
13. 'Selected Judgments and Rulings', from Myanmar Law Library, at https://myanmar-law-library.org/law-library/case-law/selected-judgements-of-lower-burma-1872-1892/.
14. Criminal Revision No. 1235 (1894) in *Upper Burma Rulings 1892–1896*, Vol I., from Myanmar Law Library.

15. 'Translation of the Resolution Passed at the Meeting on the Shwedagon Pagoda on the 26th July 1938', Appendix II (X), in *The Final Report of the Riot Inquiry Committee* (1939).
16. Quote from the *Sun* newspaper, which followed the trials closely, and quoted in Phyo Win Latt (2018). I thank Phyo Win Latt for sharing his paper on the 'blasphemous book' with me.
17. *The Final Report...*, p. 292.
18. *The Final Report...*, p. 278.
19. In 1997 SLORC changed to the State Peace and Development Council (SPDC).
20. The 2008 Constitution bans 'religion' (however defined) from politics; it also prohibits the use of religion for electoral purposes (Art. 121). Moreover, members of religious orders are not entitled to vote or to form political parties (Art. 392 (a)). Furthermore, the Political Parties Registration Law No. 2/2012, 6(d) prohibits political parties from 'writing, speaking, and campaigning causing the conflicts and violence among the individual, groups, religions and ethnics'.
21. Information provided by the Assistance Association for Political Prisoners, January 2019.
22. Interviews with U Wirathu in the documentary film *Venerable W* (2017). In the film he also explains that he realised the dangers of Islam after reading the book *In Fear of Our Race Disappearing* (1997), which during certain periods was banned by the military censorship. He started public preaching about the dangers of mixed marriages in 2001 (personal interview with U Wirathu, 2014).
23. He came to international fame after being on the cover of *Time Magazine*, June 2013, with the title 'The Buddhist Face of Terror'. *Time Magazine* (Europe, Middle East and Africa edition, 1 July 2013) 182(1) cover.
24. See, for example, the numerous reports published by the Assistance Association for Political Prisoners (Burma).
25. *Vinicchaya* in Pali means to make a judgement. In the Burmese context it refers to judgements regarding *dhamma* and *vinaya* practice. Within the monastic legal system a distinction is made between ordinary *vinaya* issues and allegations of *adhamma* and *avinaya* (usually referred to as *vivadadhikarana* in Pali).
26. The court used the Vinaya Dharmakan Disputes Settlement Law No 3/1980 and the Protection of Decisions in Vinaya Dharmakan Disputes Law No 9/1983. In addition, the court has several state laws at its disposal, most importantly the Law relating to the Sangha Organisation 20/1990.
27. There is another case from 2014 in which section 295-A was used as a 'back-up' in a monastic property dispute between the MaHaNa and two famous monks ('the London Sayadaw case'). The court later dismissed charges of 'religious offence', but upheld charges of disobeying the MaHaNa under the Law Relating to the Sangha Organisation.
28. The Act to Protect Vinicchaya Judgements (1983) and the Sangha Organisation Act (1990).
29. In most cases, the accused accept the rulings of the court (Ashin and Crosby 2017).
30. This qualification rests on the fact that the Constitution reserves 25 per cent of the seats for the military, the Rohingya population are disenfranchised and that the security situation in several ethnic minority areas prevented people from casting their votes.
31. For example, the Wireless Telegraphy Act (1934), the Printer and Published Registration Act (1962) and the Law Relating to the Forming of Organisations (1988).
32. For example, the section 66-D of the Telecommunications Law, which was adopted in 2013 with the aim of improving the climate for foreign investors, has also been used to crack down on individuals who express opinions on social media that meet with official disapproval. Section 66-D reads: 'Using a telecommunication network to extort, threaten, obstruct, defame, disturb, inappropriately influence or intimidate'. The law has been used to restrict freedom of expression online and has been heavily criticised by journalists and human rights organisations.
33. For more detail on the legal-political process of the laws and how the notion of 'religious freedom' was used to protect Buddhism, see Frydenlund (2017, 2018).
34. The state recognises 135 'national races'. The 135 list does not have an official legal status: it is a document produced by the regime in the early 1980s, and is interpreted in conjunction with the highly controversial 1982 Citizenship Law. The Rohingya population is denied citizenship based on lack of recognition as a 'national race'.
35. *Myanmar Times*, 23 June 2015.
36. Interviews with Buddhist monks engaged in inter-faith activities and NLD monks in Yangon and Mandalay, June 2014 and February 2015.
37. Several of my interlocutors had received serious threats during 2014 and 2015 for their criticism of the 969 and the MaBaTha. Fieldnotes, Yangon, Bago and Mandalay, 2014–15.

38. For example, 'Buddha doormats' have been of great concern to Buddhist activists in Norway.
39. See Walton and Schonthal (2016) and Frydenlund (2019) for debates about the local-regional dimensions of the new forms of Buddhist nationalism.
40. Two British citizens have been deported from Sri Lanka due to their Buddha tattoos. However, in the Naomi Coleman case the Supreme Court ruled in November 2017 that Buddha tattoos were not illegal in Sri Lanka, and she was given £4000 in compensation.
41. However, the MaHaNa did not condemn the organisation and its activities themselves (Walton and Tun 2016).
42. The MaHaNa ruled that if he did not respect the ban, legal measures would be taken. U Wirathu was not convicted of having breached the ban (he skilfully manoeuvered this by re-posting old speeches and giving 'silent sermons'), and to what extent the MaHaNa in the case of violation would have resorted to 'religious offence' legislation in the Penal Code remains unclear.

References

Legal libraries

'Criminal Revision No.1235 (1894)', in *Upper Burma Rulings 1892–1896*, Vol.I., Myanmar Law Library.
Rangoon Law Reports 1937, 1938, Myanmar Law Library.
'Selected Judgments and Rulings ', Myanmar Law Library.
The Final Report of the Riot Inquiry Committee (1939). Rangoon, Supt, Govt Printing and Stationary, Burma.

Secondary sources

Ashin, Janaka and Kate Crosby. 2017. 'Heresy and monastic malpractice in the Buddhist court cases (vinicchaya) of modern Burma (Myanmar).' *Contemporary Buddhism* 18 (1): 199–261.
Carbine, Jason A. 2016. 'How King Ramadhipati handled his boundary case: Sima, sasana, and Buddhist law.' *Buddhism Law & Society* (1): 105–64.
Cheesman, Nick. 2011. 'How an authoritarian regime in Burma used special courts to defeat judicial independence.' *Law & Society Review* (45): 801.
Cheesman, Nick. 2015. *Opposing the Rule of Law: How Myanmar's Courts Make Law and Order*. Cambridge: Cambridge University Press.
Frontier Myanmar. Anonymous. 12 November 2015. 'Mandalay monks criticise Ma Ba Tha.' http://frontiermyanmar.net/en/news/mandalay-monks-criticise-ma-ba-tha.
Frydenlund, Iselin 2014, personal interview with U Wirathu, Mandalay, Myanmar. Translated from the Burmese to English.
Frydenlund, Iselin. 2017. 'Religious liberty for whom? The Buddhist politics of religious freedom during Myanmar's transition to democracy.' *Nordic Journal of Human Rights* 35 (1): 55–73.
Frydenlund, Iselin. 2018. 'The birth of Buddhist politics of religious freedom in Myanmar.' *Journal of Religious and Political Practice* 4: 107–21.
Frydenlund, Iselin. 2019. 'Buddhist Islamophobia. Tropes. Themes. Actors', in *Handbook of Conspiracy Theory and Contemporary Religion*, Asbjørn Dyrendal, David Robertson and Egil Asprem, eds, Leiden: E. J. Brill.
Fuller, Paul. 2016. 'The idea of "Blasphemy" in the Pāli canon and modern Myanmar.' *Journal of Religion and Violence* 4 (2): 159–81.
Global Freedom of Expression. Colombia University. 2018. 'The case of V Gastro Bar (Philip Blackwood, Htut Ko Ko Lwin, and Tun Thurein)'.
Htun Khaing. 2018. 'As preaching ban on U Wirathu ends, split in the Sangha widens.' *Frontier Myanmar*, 14 March 2018. https://frontiermyanmar.net/en/as-preaching-ban-on-u-wirathu-ends-split-in-the-sangha-widens.

Human Rights Council. 2007. 'Report of the Special Rapporteur on the situation of human rights in Human Rights Watch.' *Crackdown. Repression of the 2007 Popular Protests in Burma*, vol.19, no.18(C).

Human Rights Watch. 2007. *Crackdown. Repression of the 2007 Popular Protests in Burma*. vol 19, no. 18 (C).

Human Rights Watch. 2009. *The Resistance of the Monks. Buddhism and Activism in Burma*. September 2009: New York, US.

Human Rights Watch. 2009. 'The resistance of the monks: Buddhism and activism in Burma.' *Human Rights Watch*.

Jenkins, Stephen. 2016. 'Debate, magic, and massacre: the high stakes and ethical dynamics of battling slanderers of the Dharma in Indian narrative and ethical theory.' *Journal of Religion and Violence* 4 (2): 129–57.

Kawanami, Hiroko. 2017. 'Mòpyar Gaing: A case study of a heterodox sect in modern Myanmar.' Paper presented at the International Association for Buddhist Studies XVIII Congress, 20–25 August 2017, Toronto, Canada.

Kyaw Phyo Tha. 2014. 'Police arrest New Zealander, 2 Burmese for promotion insulting Buddhism', 11 December 2014. https://www.irrawaddy.com/news/burma/police-arrest-new-zealander-2-burmese-promotion-insulting-buddhism.html.

Lammerts, Christian. 2018. *Buddhist Law in Burma: A history of dhammasattha texts and jurisprudence, 1250–1850*. Honululu: University of Hawai'i Press.

Mandair, Arvind-Pal S. and Markus Dressler. 2011. 'Introduction: Modernity, religion-making, and the postsecular', in *Secularism and Religion-Making*, Markus Dressler and Arvind-Pal S. Mandair, eds, 3–36. Oxford: Oxford University Press.

Mann, Zarni. 2014. 'NLD member denied bail at religious offence trial', 17 December 2014. http://www.irrawaddy.com/news/burma/nld-member-denied-bail-religious-offence-trial.html.

Mann, Zarni. 2015. '2 years hard labor for Htin Lin Oo in religious offense case.' http://www.irrawaddy.com/news/burma/2-years-hard-labor-for-htin-lin-oo-in-religious-offense-case.html.

Penal Code. 1861. Available at Burma Library, http://www.burmalibrary.org/show.php?cat=1860.

Phyo Win Latt. 2018. 'The book, the riot, and the trial: The Indo Burman Riot of 1938 and its immediate cause.' Paper presented at the 13th International Burma Studies Conference, 3–5 August 2018, Bangkok, Thailand.

Schissler, Matt, Matthew Walton and Phyu Phyu Thi. 2017. 'Reconciling contradictions: Buddhist-Muslim violence, narrative making and memory in Myanmar.' *Journal of Contemporary Asia* 47 (3): 376–95.

Schober, Juliane. 2011. *Modern Buddhist Conjunctures in Myanmar: Cultural Narratives, Colonial Legacies, and Civil Society*. Honululu: University of Hawai'i Press

Schonthal, Benjamin and Matthew J. Walton. 2016. 'The (new) Buddhist nationalisms? Symmetries and specificities in Sri Lanka and Myanmar.' *Contemporary Buddhism* 17 (1): 81–115.

Schontal, Benjamin. 2016. 'Securing the sasana through law: Buddhist constitutionalism and Buddhist interest litigation in Sri Lanka.' *Modern Asian Studies* 50 (6): 1966–2008.

Schroeder, Barbet. 2017. *Venerable W (Original title: Le Vénérable W)*. Switzerland/France.

Sherwell, Philip. 2015. 'Briton jailed in Burma for "insulting" Buddha image named prisoner of conscience by Amnesty', 7 October 2015. http://www.telegraph.co.uk/news/worldnews/asia/burmamyanmar/11916748/Briton-jailed-in-Burma-for-insulting-Buddha-image-named-prisoner-of-conscience-by-Amnesty.html.

Telle, Kari. 2017. 'Faith on trial: Blasphemy and "lawfare" in Indonesia.' *Ethnos*. DOI: 10.1080/00141844.2017.1282973.

Time Magazine, Europe, Middle East and Africa edition, 1 July 2013, 182(1).

Tin Maung Maung Than. 1988. 'The "sangha" and "sasana" in socialist Burma.' *Sojourn: Journal of Social Issues in Southeast Asia* 3 (1): 26–61.

Turner, Alicia. 2014. *Saving Buddhism: The Impermanence of Religion in Colonial Burma*. Honululu: University of Hawai'i Press.

United Nations. 2007. 'Report of the Special Rapporteur on the situation of human rights in Myanmar, Paulo Sérgio Pinheiro.' A/HRC/6/14, 7 December 2007.

Walton, Matthew J. and Aung Tun. 2016. 'What the State Sangha Committee actually said about Ma Ba Tha.' *Tea Circle*, 29 July 2016.

Walton, Matthew J., M. McKay and Daw Khin Mar Mar Kyi. 2015. 'Women and Myanmar's "Religious Protection Laws".' *Review of Faith and International Affairs* 13 (4): 36–49.

4
Religious outrage as spectacle: The successful protests against a 'blasphemous' minister

Arild Engelsen Ruud

While in New York the Bangladesh minister for Post and Telecommunications, Latif Siddique, gave an impromptu speech. The people at the meeting were from his own party, the Awami League, and they were from his home district of Tangail. They were his supporters, his people. The minister was relaxed and sitting on the dais he spoke on a range of subjects. A year and a half later he told me that he had felt perfectly at ease; 'it was just *adda*'.[1] '*Adda*' denotes a quintessential Bengali pastime of enjoying informal, often animated conversation with friends (see Chakrabarty 1999).

He was filmed with a mobile phone camera, and no more than a few hours later a cut from the recording was put online and 'went viral'. The most controversial part of his speech was where the minister spoke about the *hajj* (pilgrimage to Mecca) and how he thought it was a great waste of money.[2]

> I am against the Jamaat-e-Islami, but I am even more against the *hajj* and Tablig Jamaat. So much manpower is wasted [*noshto hoye*] in *hajj*. Again [this year] some two million people have gone to Saudi Arabia. But they are not going there to work. They just eat and spend money, and then they return home.

Jamaat-e-Islami is the country's largest Islamist party and historically an enemy of Latif Siddique's party, the Awami League. The Sunni missionary society Tablig Jamaat, on the other hand, is considered moderate; it has a huge following among the pious and largely non-political Muslims in the country.

In his *adda* Latif Siddique then reflected on the reasoning behind the historical institutionalisation of the *hajj*. He suggested it was a means by which the Prophet had secured a means of livelihood for his followers.

> Muhammad son of Abdul thought, 'How are the people on the Arabian Peninsula going to manage?' After all, they were thieves [*dakat*]. So he decided that 'All of my disciples will have to come together once every year.' So they would have a regular income.

The uproar was huge. The video clip created a furore when it hit the news in Bangladesh the following day. Protests came almost immediately, from all over the country. Comments to online news items expressed deep anger. Islamic organisations issued press releases and called for Latif Siddique's resignation, and even for his execution. Facebook feeds were crammed with statements filled with hate.

Among the most visible organisations in this uproar was Hefazat-e-Islam, a rapidly emerging Islamist movement. In joint operations with other Islamist and political organisations, Hefazat organised street protests in most towns and cities, drawing thousands – in some cases tens of thousands – of protesters. The protesters condemned his 'blasphemy'. They demanded Latif Siddique's resignation and his hanging; they also demanded laws against blasphemy to be enacted. The minister's effigy was burnt, and he became the subject of almost 70 legal cases.[3] An order was issued for his arrest, and within three days he was dismissed from his cabinet position. He was also stripped of his primary membership in the ruling party, and there were demands from within the party to annul his election to parliament.

Blasphemy is a religious offence, and the justification for protest is religious sensibility. In view of the suddenness and intensity of the protests against Latif Siddique, and following a certain literature on the subject of protest, I argue for an understanding that takes the religious justification seriously while also incorporating the larger cultural and political context as crucial to the anger and commitment of the young Islamist protesters.

Latif Siddique was a controversial figure; for some he confirmed all popular misgivings about government ministers and ruling party leaders. He was known to be fond of alcohol and unashamed about it, placing him squarely with 'the secularists' in the country's great ideological divide. He and his brother, Kader Siddique, were among the 'godfather' politicians of Bangladesh who bolstered their position with muscular forms of politics (Michelutti et al. 2018). People who knew Latif personally described him as 'foul mouthed'; he could also be brutal. Quite recently he had physically beaten a government official, giving rise to a minor scandal (*bdnews24* 2014).

There were many known complaints of irregularities and corruption against Siddique, some of which had been reported in the newspapers. Some allegations suggested that he had misappropriated government funds or spent them 'in irregular ways', as one newspaper report phrased it (*Prothom Alo* 011014c). However, no action had been taken against him, despite his having many detractors within the party. Indeed his lawyer claimed that most of the 70 cases against him were filed by rivals within the party.[4] One report stated that his adverse comments on the *hajj* had unleashed some of the tensions within the party. Certain voices within the party felt that his countless excesses showed Siddique to be now 'out of control' (*lagamhin*, unbridled).

After about a month in India, Latif Siddique returned to Bangladesh and was immediately arrested. He spent the next ten months in prison, although in the relatively comfortable surroundings of a hospital. While in prison, according to intelligence reports (*Dhaka Tribune* 2014), a bounty of 500,000 taka (£4500) was placed on his head. When he was released, in the late summer of 2015, Siddique apologised to the nation and resigned from parliament (*Daily Star* 2015). Today he lives a quiet life, dividing his time between his home district of Tangail and the capital Dhaka.

In order to understand the suddenness and scale of this case of protestations against blasphemous utterances, and hence their potential danger to the government, we need to understand what it was that motivated the participants. Clearly Latif Siddique's statements were found offensive to religious sentiments and this is, as we shall see and not unexpectedly, central to objections that were voiced. We will find religious hurt central both to statements made by Islamist leaders and to how participants later talked about their motives. And yet, in both these sets of information, there was another strand that referred more to contemporary issues, the nature of the political party Siddique represented and the ruling elite to which he belonged. This strand of criticism raised demands that were distinctly political or even populist in nature.

A useful starting point is the energetic and angry street protests that constituted both the high point and in some ways the end point of this burst of anti-blasphemy mobilisation. To explore this I turn to the literature that enables us to analyse protest marches as performances.

Religious hurt and street theatre

Roland Barthes's take on 'mythologies' offers tools to understand street protests as forms of public display or spectacle (Barthes 1993). In his analysis of wrestling, this 'sport' becomes a 'spectacle of excess' in which its grandiloquence and unsubtle gestures constitute 'an open-air spectacle'. Wrestling's excesses draw the onlooker's attention to the spectacle, focusing attention with dramatic gestures and shouting.

Wrestling, in other words, is a performance. In a study on blasphemy, Lawton criticises Barthes for not acknowledging the potential political content of a wrestling match (Lawton 1993). He points out that in American wrestling – as opposed to the French style of wrestling analysed by Barthes – the political element is sometimes clearly in evidence. In a sense Barthes's essay appears 'curiously resistant to the potential for propaganda'. Its shortfall, Lawton feels, points to the quite radical lack of context in Barthes's essay. The problem is that Barthes presupposes timeless archetypes as if wrestling was some form of *commedia dell'arte* with stock figures in interaction (Lawton 1993, 197).

To Lawton, in contrast, the performance is always unique: its meaning derives from the context in which it takes place, as in the case of blasphemy accusations. He also points out that the complicity between audience and performers always embraces local knowledge. He thus cautions us against treating spectacle events as general phenomena; if we do, they risk becoming over-idealised and unmediated.

Protest marches against alleged acts of blasphemy are not wrestling matches. They are social events that follow a particular script in order for them to have meaning for the participants and the audience. And yet protest marches are not entirely without script, as even American wrestling matches also follow a certain formula and choreography.

In Bangla a protest march is known as a *michil*; it is a well-known stock feature of Bangladeshi and South Asian politics, along with the *gherao*, the *dharna*, the *rel roko* and other forms of 'street theatre' (Hansen 2004, 25). A successful event, writes Annette Hill, is one where people who witness it recognise it as the performance of authority and domination (Hill 2015). A *michil*'s set stock of elements includes the procession, banners, angry shouting and thumping of fists and the chanting of slogans. There will be a caller, someone with a strong voice and possibly a microphone who can shout slogans, with other activists chiming in. The activists often repeat only short sentences or words. In Bangla and other South Asian languages only a small set of rhythms is used. These rhythms are well-known and familiar; they are used by all parties and they easily catch on.

In addition to being ritualised, a *michil* is also potentially uncontrollable. It is scripted yet unpredictable. In *Staging Politics* Strauss and O'Brien suggest 'theatre' as a term for the open-ended performance that stages power – in contrast to more ritualistic state performances that are of less consequence except to underline state authority (Strauss and O'Brien 2007). By pointing to how such a performance is open-ended, O'Brien and Strauss also stress the potential for change embedded within it. They underline how slippage and misunderstandings enter and influence both the development of the actions and their interpretations.

The protests against Latif Siddique were intense, high profile and very successful. They were forceful enough to topple a senior member of the cabinet and of the ruling party within days, which alone is remarkable. These protests were scripted, but also mediated and contextualised by participants; they were choreographed yet prone to slippage in a political culture characterised in the immediate past by violent encounters.

Moreover, the literature on South Asia on protests and feelings associated with protest is large and nuanced; it allows an interpretation of a severalty of motives with the participant. I take as an axiomatic point of departure the fact that protests cannot be seen as a semiotically uniform activity, nor indeed that the activist protesters possess a uniform mind or single purpose. The rationale and motivation of the performance is complex, requiring us to investigate the immediate political context in which this particular performance was meaningful and justified. Thomas Blom Hansen's much-cited 'Recuperating Masculinity' was an early step towards a comprehension of political mobilisation. In it he suggested that communal identities are not brought about by manipulation, but should rather be understood as separate but real 'forms of subjectivity' (Hansen 1996, 149). This proposal led to a series of in-depth studies of mobilised feelings and an investigation into the emotional life of religious hurt in South Asia (e.g. Blom and Jaoul 2008; Guru 2011). Blom and Jaoul point out that in South Asia protesters can be understood to demonstrate outrage through a specific repertoire of action – a repertoire that dramatises and legitimises an 'experience of indignation' (Blom and Jaoul 2008, 2).

In line with this sense of blurred distinctions between the emotional and the orchestrated, Blom and Jaoul acknowledge that blasphemy accusations – 'a prototypical form of outrage' – may constitute what they characterise as a 'smoke-screen' that hides other concerns and struggles (Blom and Jaoul 2008, 10). Nosheen Ali's investigation of the Shia mobilisation against offensive textbooks in Pakistan's Northern Areas in the mid-2000s (Ali 2008) suggests, for instance, that the 'explosive proportions' of those protests reflected at a deeper level the contestation of a long-standing regional subordination and denial of citizenship. In her article on the Danish cartoon riots in Lahore, Blom again recognises the political and social context as the circumstance in which blasphemy accusations legitimise protest and riots. Although one may take exception to the term 'smoke-screen', and its suggestion that the up-front context is irrelevant, it is easy to follow her fine-grained analysis when she asserts that the rioters 'actually found a socially and politically legitimate opportunity to assert a long-felt and multifaceted anger through their protests' (Blom 2008). Similarly, Ali Riaz's study of the protests against Taslima Nasreen in Bangladesh in 1994 stresses how the state contributes to the construction of communities of outrage through its framing and responses (Riaz 2008). His contribution underlines the need to 'bring the state back in' – without, one might add, leaving everything else out.

This larger political context for the protesters does not nullify a religious motivation and sense of hurt, but allows instead for the ambivalence protesters experience with regard to the protest. This is found, for instance, in Björkman's study of the 'ostentatious crowd' (Björkman 2015). Here protesters apparently engaged in a demonstration against an injustice reveal complex motivations for joining; these may include an expectation of being paid and sometimes fed, and in most cases because they have been asked to do so by some patron. The manner in which they self-reflect on their participation makes Björkman use the term 'participant-audience' to characterise them (Björkman 2015, 143).

The literature helps us read the multifaceted nature of the street protests against the 'blasphemous' minister in Bangladesh in 2014 as an expression of protest against a 'blasphemer' as well as a performance to express objection to a wider political landscape. This form of political 'street theatre' expressed outrage at the insult and claimed public space to do so, while the potential for danger that slippages might entail in a historically violent political culture (Klem and Suykens 2018) only enhanced the 'true' nature of the outrage.

Before moving on to the testimonies, however, I will briefly sketch the immediate past cultural and political context in which the protests took place. The argument is that the protests against the blasphemer only make sense in this wider context, and that the conscious and performed outrage against Latif Siddique's blasphemous statements was a protest against the wider injustices the postcolonial subject experiences.

Setting the stage

Just as the Indian state never quite managed to counter its image of being always a bit high-caste Hindu because of its reliance on the Mahatma's legacy and the class of people from which it drew its leaders (see Williams and Wanchoo 2008), the postcolonial and post-independence state in Bangladesh has often striven to balance the secular tendencies of the educated elite that constituted its leadership against the more tradition-bound and culturally conservative ideas of the larger population (see Riaz 2016; Riaz and Fair 2011). On the one hand was the religiously based ideal of the nation, in which Islam, the Prophet, Islamic learning and Muslim culture should rule and in effect have more space than the current situation; on the other was the so-called secular ideal of a nation with modern schooling, a dogma-free government and progressive social values. The dispute has consumed much of the country's political energy over the decades of its modern history (Lewis 2011), even if to varying degrees. An intensification of the dispute took place as the historically more secular Awami League came to power after a convincing election win in 2008 (Jahan and Shahan 2014). It soon escalated into an at times violent confrontation between what has been called an 'assertive secularism' (Islam and Islam 2018) and an increasingly confident Islamist movement.

There were three stages to this escalation. The first was set by the Awami League government's decision in 2009 to prosecute war criminals of the 1971 liberation war. This was an old and sore point for many. Individuals suspected of having committed atrocities during the liberation war were still around, with a number of them enjoying influential positions in large enterprises, banks and political parties. A War Crimes Tribunal was established and those accused were arrested – although some managed to flee the country.

The second stage was set when a prominent Islamist leader was convicted of war crimes and sentenced to life imprisonment in February 2013. As he was escorted out of the court building into a waiting police car he made a V-sign with his hand, indicating that he was convinced his sentence would be overturned as soon as the Awami League government was out of power. Protests erupted immediately and somewhat unexpectedly, calling for him to be sentenced to death instead. The slogan *'fanshi chai!'* ('We want him hanged!') drew an increasingly large crowd of people who considered themselves leftist, progressive or secular to assemble around the Shahbag crossing near Dhaka University (De 2017). The protesters quickly numbered more than 100,000. The government soon altered the relevant law and the Islamist was sentenced to death and later executed. In the meantime others had also been sentenced to death and executed.

The Shahbag mobilisation represented an energised and buoyant reclaiming of public space by the country's secular and progressive forces. It accentuated a claim of embodying the legitimate interpretation of the nation's true values. The mobilisation drew on the whole plethora of signs and symbols of the tradition of a progressive society that wears its religious cloak lightly, including impromptu street dramas, music recitals, painting exhibitions and poetry readings. Some of the art exhibited included papier-maché figures that portrayed the stereotypical Islamist with his henna-dyed beard as an ogre and figurines celebrating Hindu cultural influences. It was possibly the largest show of force from the secular left in the country's independent history.

The third stage was the reaction, only months later. In early May 2013 Hefazat organised a massive demonstration (Bouisson 2013) in Dhaka in favour of its list of demands, all anathema to the secularists. These demands included an end to the government's secular educational policy and opposition to girls' education, a law against defamation of Islam, death penalty for those who defame the Prophet, action against atheist bloggers, that Ahmadiyyas be declared non-Muslim and that Islamic education be made compulsory for all. They also demanded that the foreign culture of free mixing of the sexes be stopped, which by many was interpreted (and probably meant) as an interdiction against working women.

Hefazat was established in 2010 as an umbrella association for the *qawmi* madrassas in the country – that is, the largely private Muslim schools not regulated by the state's educational policy. It is estimated that there are some 15,000 *qawmi* madrassas in Bangladesh, attended by some four million pupils. In terms of doctrine the *qawmi* madrassas are Deobandi, and they are known to be socially and culturally conservative (Riaz 2007).

The Dhaka protests were impressive. The central parts of the city practically swarmed with boys and young men in white dress and skullcap. Their numbers were such that they not only blocked traffic, but literally filled central areas of the city. By the evening many had left, and the 50–70,000 who remained were literally flushed out in a large-scale police operation at night.[5] By the morning the city had been emptied of protesters and major Hefazat leaders were arrested.

Nonetheless, the government was clearly concerned at the scale of the mobilisation and appeared somewhat rattled only months before the parliamentary elections (Islam 2016). The mobilisation had shown the potential power of an agenda that was evidently attractive to many voters.

Large-scale surveys have later confirmed that the conservative – and at times reactionary – sentiments that tie religion to politics are widespread in Bangladesh, and that many supported the actions, if not the methods, of the terrorists (Riaz and Aziz 2017; Fair et al. 2017). We have analysed this elsewhere as a political sentiment comparable to the radical right in Europe (Ruud and Hasan, forthcoming). In 2013 the historically secular Awami League government realised that only the demographically restricted segment of the urban educated opposed the punishment of alleged blasphemers. To defuse the situation, party leader and Prime Minister Sheikh Hasina emphasised her religious devotion on several occasions and distanced herself from the atheists (*NDTV* 2013; Islam 2016, 4; Graham-Harrison and Hammadi 2016). Bloggers were told to respect religious beliefs and some of the higher profiled bloggers critical of Islam were arrested (Hasan 2014; Lorch 2018).

A parallel development was the brutal murder of individual bloggers by jihadists. These murders had started a year before, in 2012, but after the Shahbag movement got under way, prominent Shahbag voices were also targeted. The murders were bloody and spectacular; victims were hacked with machetes and left to bleed to death. The perpetrators, where caught, mostly belonged to fringe jihadist groups. The importance of this development in our context is that accusations of being atheist (*nastik*) were used to justify some of the murders, and that the term gained new currency as a form of abuse that legitimised extreme measures (Riaz and Aziz 2017).

The dispute over the 'true' nature of the Bangladeshi state was confounded by a parallel struggle over political power. The opposition party, Bangladesh Nationalist Party (BNP), and its ally, Jamaat-e-Islami, engaged in a long-drawn-out campaign of general strikes and protest movements. These lasted from the 2013 spring of unrest through the January 2014 election and until only months before Latif Siddique made his infamous speech. During the heat of the struggle the opposition leader Khaleda Zia also described the bloggers as 'atheist' (Islam 2016). The aim of the unrest was to alter the election rules. Violent protests involving bombs, bus burning and confrontations with the police took place. Although an uneasy peace had returned to the country by the time of Latif Siddique's speech, the larger issue of a dispute over the nature of the Bangladeshi state remained unresolved.

The online protests and press statements

An unsigned post on Hefazat Barta's page on 30 September 2014, two days after the film of Latif Siddique had gone viral, called people to join a protest march that was being organised in Dhaka. The purpose of the protest march was to demand the 'public hanging' of Latif, who was called 'a public enemy of Islam'. A cartoon showed him with cockroaches and maggots emerging from his mouth and the words *'fanshi chai'* ('We want him hanged') stamped across his forehead (*Hefazat Barta* 2014).[6]

The demand 'We want him hanged!' echoed the one cried at Shahbag by the secularists a year and a half earlier. It is a cry meant to convey anger and pain at a deep insult, but also a cry for a very real execution.

Hefazat Barta was one of the most vocal sites. This was a blog that catered mainly to the younger generations of its supporters of Hefazat. Although these madrassa students had previously been known as somewhat lagging in their familiarity with the online world, located as they often were in rural areas with poor connectivity, they proved quick to catch up. Facebook also proved popular, in particular Basherkella (Bamboo Fortress) which functioned as a blog for Shibir.[7] By the time of the Latif Siddique controversy the Hefazatis were adept on social media (Rahman 2018).

The cartoon of Latif Siddique with cockroaches and maggots was part of a post that included a statement by a Hefazat leader; it also laid out the line of argument used in those heated days. The leader underlined that the *hajj* was one of the five pillars of Islam, and that to repudiate *hajj* was equal to repudiating Islam. To repudiate Islam was to become an apostate (*murtad*). In addition, Latif Siddique's derogatory comments on the Prophet also indicated the final stage of becoming a non-believer. The leader behind the statement held that 'For the *ummah* the Prophet Muhammad (pbuh) is as precious as a piece of the heart'.[8] The *ummah* is, of course, the international community of Muslim believers, arguably larger than the nation (Hasan 2014). The punishment for an apostate, according to the Koran and the Hadith, is the death penalty, he maintained.

Non-believer and apostate here constitute the same thing. The General Secretary of Hefazat, Allama Hafez Junayed Babunagari, in a separate statement also accused Latif Siddique of being an apostate; he urged the government to sack him and mete out 'exemplary punishment' (Hefazat Islam Bangladesh 2014). Babunagari insisted that Latif Siddique had insulted the Prophet, drawing on the terminology of the

Penal Code, calling him an 'insulter' (*obomanonakari*) of the Prophet and of Islam and demanding that he be given the maximum punishment, i.e. death. Babunagari also called Latif Siddique 'an aggressive atheist' (*ugro nastik*), using that deeply negative term. The term was also used by others in public statements and on the banners of the demonstrators.

Babunagari then declared that it would be the fulfilment of the sacred duty (*imani dahitvo palon*) to ensure that Latif Siddique be given an exemplary harsh punishment. He also stated that he was disappointed by the fact that defamation of Bangabandhu (Mujibur Rahman, honoured as 'Father of the Nation') or the Prime Minister may result in seven years in prison, but no similar punishment existed for insulters of the Prophet, 'the heart pulse' of 'crores and crores' of Muslims (one *crore* is ten million). The government would have to 'act on this insult (*opoman*) to Islam, Allah and the Prophet' or it would be 'partner to the crime' (*eki oporadhe oporadhi*).

The threats to the government were honed to suggest the depth of feelings that had been hurt. Behind the formulations was a threat of uncontrolled anger. The one and a half billion strong Muslim *ummah* had been 'hurt in their hearts', Babunagari wrote, warning that with one and a half billion people insulted and outraged, something bad could happen and 'no one could stay safe'. Sentence has been passed on Latif Siddique already, Babunagari seemed to say, and it was up to the government to carry it out. But if it failed to do so, the government itself would be the target of the uncontrolled anger that followed from insulting Islam (see also chapters 2 and 8). The Secretary General then repeated an ultimatum given the day before, and pointed out that 24 of the 72 hours had already passed.

It was in this setting that street protests were organised throughout the country, within days of the filmed speech being publicly known. Slogans and banners mirrored the press release statements of the previous day, and claiming that Siddique's comments amounted to '*dhormo obomanoni*' (disrespect of religion) and demanding that he should receive '*sorboccho shasti*' (the highest punishment, i.e. death). In several places effigies of Latif Siddique were burnt.

The statements by Babunagari and others expressed that religious sentiments had been hurt and that this had led to anger among Muslims. Any violence would only be an expression of the uncontrollable anger felt by ordinary Muslims when trampled on by the likes of the 'blaspheming' minister. The statements went further, however, and suggested a distance between the ordinary Muslim and the government. They drew a distinction between the ordinary Muslims and the community of believers on the one hand and the government and elite on the other, in an altogether familiar populist way (e.g. Mudde 2004). To suggest that the government put the Father of the Nation above the Prophet, indicated that the government did not share in the emotional world of pious Muslims, that it was irreligious. The demand that the death penalty be executed immediately was also suggestive of populism's preference for simple and quick solutions. These elements point beyond religion as a sole or even main motivation for the protests. In the following section we will move on to consider the protesters themselves and how they talked about and justified their protests.

The protesters

'We went to express our anger,' said Taher, a Shibir activist who had taken part in the protest march in Dhaka.[9] Shibir is the student wing of the Jamaat-e-Islami and Shibir activists have often been found at the forefront of demonstrations and violent clashes. I met Taher, along with 21 other younger, university-educated Islamists and Shibir activists for interviews over a few weeks in Dhaka in April 2016. Five of them had taken part in protest marches against Latif Siddique; the rest had previously taken part in similar protests. All of them related to the Latif Siddique case with strong feelings. 'Latif Siddique is an apostate,' said Taher. 'We demanded that he be punished. Apostasy is forbidden in Islam.' He went on to say that he knew the protest might be dangerous, but there was no choice. The offence was too serious to ignore. 'How could we not protest?'

The kind of statements that Latif Siddique had made were 'insufferable' [*sojjo kora jaye na*], declared Monem, a young, college-educated former Shibir activist. He felt it was necessary for the Muslim *ummah* (the Muslim community of believers) that the crime be punished. The aim of the protest march he had participated in was not just to vent their outrage: it was also to redress the crime, to force the government to punish Latif Siddique.

'We were called through sms and on Facebook. And my friends rang me,' Monem explained. Organisations such as the Islamist ones are generally known to be good at mobilising at short notice. In this case it had not been too difficult: their members had seen the video and were expecting a call. The cadre of Islamist organisations are dedicated and willing to engage for the cause, and Latif Siddique's statements were widely known and condemned. As with outbreaks of protest all over South Asia, such demonstrations were not spontaneous (Brass 2003; Björkman 2014), but they were also not long in planning.

A *michil* can still be intimidating to onlookers, as is its intention. The participants express a depth of outrage and anger that is barely contained. Violence is a prominent feature of Bangladeshi politics, often precipitated by the anger expressed in *michils*, and the violence of the preceding election year was still fresh in the memory. Many of the Shibir activists I interviewed had been active during those months of almost continuous violent outpourings, both before and after the January 2014 election. Rights organisations had counted the number of deaths in hundreds (HRW 2014), and a far larger number of people were injured and hospitalised as a consequence of the violence.

As pointed out above, a crucial aspect of the *michil* is the possibility of the unexpected, of slippage. Sometimes *michils* do turn violent and even deadly, as had often been the case in the election unrest only months earlier. Things can easily get out of hand. An agitated protester throws a stone, or even a Molotov cocktail, at the police, or a nervous police officer overreacts by beating or pushing some of the protesters. 'When we shout the slogans we are very excited,' said Monem. Sometimes participants have travelled considerable distances to be part of the protests, and the protest march itself can be a long and tiresome walk. *Michils* mostly take place during daytime, when they can be filmed, in the heat and bustle of city streets, and protesters experience a mixture of exhaustion, excitement and boredom. Agitated protesters, often facing armed police, are also stressed, a factor with which organisers struggle. '[A *michil*] is always dangerous,' Arif observed. A junior Shibir activist from a village background, he had only recently joined the organisation. It is not unlikely that he had been taken aback by the danger, although he seemed to take it in his stride.

Nonetheless, he was right. *Michils* can be violent and unpredictable. Very often thugs from the Chhatra League, the activist student front that supports the Awami League (for student politics, see Ruud 2010; Andersen 2013; Suykens and Islam 2013) join in, and demonstrations often spiral out of control (Verkaaik 2004). Seven of the 22 Shibir activists I spoke with had been hospitalised after similar incidents; five had been arrested. One of those who had taken part, Julfikar, had been in several previous *michils*, and had taken an active part in Shibir activities over several years while at college.

> I went to the place where I was told to go. Some of my friends were there. Then we went by rickshaw to Bangla Motor [in central Dhaka]. From there we walked. We did not have banners [but there was one up in front of the procession]. We were all in white kurta.

There were many hundred, many thousand. Shouting slogans we went to Motijheel [the Dhaka business centre]. The police was standing along both sides. And armoured cars at intersections. We shouted slogans, very fiercely. Hang him! Hang him! Like that. I am never afraid that the police will shoot. If I die, I die, and it is the will of Allah.

They had discussed among themselves whether to throw stones at the police or some passing car, but agreed not to. Another Shibir activist who had taken part in the demonstrations that day and who went by the name Alam-bhai, spoke loudly about his merits as a protester. When I asked him if he had ever torched buses, he said 'No, no. I never did that.' But when I asked about throwing bricks at the police or Chhatra League activists, he said 'Oh yes, often! The police would chase us but we always got away.' (He later acknowledged, however, that he had at some point been arrested, albeit at a different protest march.)

It is part of the choreographed ritual to confront the police. In turn, the police are often fidgety, particularly when it is a question of politically contentious issues. The police may have their orders and be willing to withdraw – but they may also have orders to the contrary.[10] The more distant the protesters are from the government, such as the Islamists participating in Latif Siddique protests, the greater the risk of slippage and violence. Escalation into riot was a distinct possibility; in a number of cases the protests against Latif Siddique did get out of control and ended in clashes with the police and injuries (*Prothom Alo* 2014a and 2014b).

The context of the postcolony

When I talked to Taher, the Shibir activist, about him being part of the demonstrations against Latif Siddique, I asked him if he realised that it could be dangerous and that he could be hurt. 'Of course!' he exclaimed, adding by way of explanation, 'The police is protecting the corrupt government and they hate us'. For Taher and the other young Islamists, it was not just about Latif Siddique: it was about the system. Latif Siddique was the symbol and symptom of a corrupt and self-serving government. Latif Siddique's blasphemy was upsetting, but the blaspheming minister represented, to Taher, a much larger whole. He was one of a clique of people who controlled the country, who were responsible for its poor governance and the corruption that held it back, preventing it from being another Malaysia. 'They will do anything to stop us!' he declared.

His anger was directed at the government in general and, in a wider sense, the non-religious interpretation of Bangladesh. His views tallied with those of others, including Julfikar, who was the most explicit. They felt that the leaders of the country had inflicted much harm upon it, and they harboured a deep sense of injustice being done to the country by leaders whom they saw as self-serving and corrupt. 'If the costs of a road is ten crore, they will take five. At least. That is why we have such [bad] roads. There is no development!' For Julfikar, Taher and others the ideal was Malaysia, ruled by the iron-fisted Prime Minister Mahathir for many years. Mahathir was considered by them to be a hero for the way in which he had turned Malaysia into a modern country. Another ideal was Turkey under Erdogan. Interestingly, Saudi Arabia was less of an ideal state; it was dismissed by Alam-bhai, another Shibir activist, as being 'not a suitable model for Bangladesh'.

The main reason cited for supporting Jamaat was not about Islam and the Muslim identity of the country: it was about governance and corruption. Dissatisfaction with the situation in the country – and in particular with what they perceived as a negative political culture – was cited as a major reason for supporting Jamaat. The young men pointed to poorly finished public works, corruption scandals and increasing suppression of opposition activities. The huge heist of 80 million dollars was on most people's lips in April 2016, and many tended to see conspiracies and political involvement behind it. Some pointed at the Prime Minister's son and special advisor on information technology. 'Who else,' demanded Julfikar, 'could manage such a transaction?'

The dissatisfaction also fed on a very general sense of the injustice being done to the country by politicians, and a belief that the ills from which the country suffers are largely due to politicians as a class. In this perspective Jamaat leaders were held up as exemplary, because they are believed to be different from other politicians or not even politicians at all. Taher held that:

> This Awami League government is very corrupt. And the BNP is corrupt. Only Jamaat is not corrupt. Jamaat will give Bangladesh better governance and it is not corrupt. This government is very corrupt. You see what happens when they build bridges or schools or hospitals? The costs go up and up. Two times, three times [compared to the original estimate]. Where does the extra money go? The government is corrupt and suppressive. It is not democratic. Jamaat will be much better. Jamaatis do not take bribes [*taka mare na*].

It is a common perception in Bangladesh that corruption (*ghush, taka mara*) is what is holding the country back. (There are other popular explanations for this too, to do with the size of the population, level of education, amount of natural resources, etc., but corruption is a particularly popular explanation that gains much sustenance from the media and civil society groups.) Corruption is filling the pockets of the political class and the rich in unfair ways, taking money and opportunity away from the majority, from the nation, from the ordinary people (*shadharon manush*). Moreover, corruption and malgovernance are seen to go hand in hand; where there is corruption, there is also malgovernance. In other words Julfikar, Taher and several of the others held the view that without politicians there would be no corruption and better governance. Jamaatis would rule and have the ministers, but it would leave administration to competent bureaucrats. The ills that plague the country are believed to be due to self-serving leaders at the top who have corrupted the entire state administration. In this depoliticised vision of society, disinterested religious scholars would become leaders and would rule for the common good, using disinterested meritorious technocrats to implement their common good policies.

The idea that Taher proposed is that all ills that have befallen Bangladesh are due to the Awami League and its leader; they have pulled the country in the direction of self-serving interests and egoism, and this somehow has to do with the idea of secularism. It had become a country 'without belief', Taher maintained (in English).

Moreover, the sense of injustice that the Western world did not respect the Muslim world was strong. Two of the former Shibir activist interviewees, Monem and Babul, both of whom had taken part in the protests against Latif Siddique, pointed to the Universal Islamic Declaration of Human Rights and the Cairo Declaration of Human Rights in Islam to underline the need to stand up against a Westernised understanding of what it means to be a citizen in the modern world. 'But Awami League does what India wants' or it follows the dictates of the United States. Even if Latif Siddique was understood to be worse than the rest of the Awami League leadership, he remained but a symptom of a widespread anti-Islamic attitude in the government and the ruling party.

With his allegedly blasphemous utterances, Latif Siddique became an easy target for pent-up frustrations with the governance of the country and what many saw as reprehensible values associated with what they understood to be a degenerate, Westernised culture of egoism. Latif Siddique represented that Westernised behaviour of those who drank and swore, who pursued political power and influence without respect for fellow humans, tradition or religion, or any sense of service to the nation. Latif Siddique came to represent all that was wrong with the political class in the eyes of the young Islamists. 'Latif Siddique is a very bad man,' said Julfikar. 'He should never have been minister.'

Blasphemy accusations in their context

With the establishment of a War Crimes Tribunal and the sentencing and later execution of war criminals, the government had claimed the right of moral judgement. That right had been effectively countered by the Hefazat's ability to shift the focus away from the atrocities committed in 1971 to alleged disrespect shown towards Muslims and Islam by contemporary bloggers and by a cabinet minister, Latif Siddique.

In postcolonial states, including those in South Asia, the 'twilight zone' of multiple, indeterminate configurations of power and authority from the colonial era persisted to create what Finn Stepputat and Thomas Blom Hansen have called 'always uneven and extraordinarily dispersed' forms of postcolonial government (Stepputat and Hansen 2006, 304). The sovereignty of the state over its populace is challenged by a plethora of competing authorities – including outlaws and multinational companies (Harriss-White and Michelutti, forthcoming). The fragmentation of authority that Gayer finds in Karachi (Gayer 2014) underlines how brittle and uneven state authority is in South Asia. In the plethora of authorities existing in contemporary Bangladesh, Hefazat rose quickly to a position where it could claim to be one.

The precariousness of the moral authority of the Awami League government meant the Hefazat could wrest it from them. It was in this context of an acrimonious conflict between the Islamist interpretation and the secular interpretation, in which the first had been weakened, that Latif Siddique made his comments. In so doing he created an opportunity for the Islamists to retaliate by accusing him of blasphemy and threatening to implicate the rest of the ruling party. And it was in this context that the protests were seen by the participant-audience themselves and must be interpreted.

Notes

1. Interview with Latif Siddique, Dhaka, April 2015.
2. https://www.youtube.com/watch?v=33TWMpq3JYg.
3. Interviews with Latif Siddique and his lawyer, Jyotirmaya Barua.

4. Another controversial remark by Latif Siddique in the same context concerned the Prime Minister's son and advisor, Sajeeb Wajed, popularly known as Joy, and this may have motivated some of the cases from intra-party rivals. But because the papers are kept in the original court, even his lawyer has not been privy to the full details.
5. Reports vary as to the number of deaths, from less than 50 to several hundred.
6. The blog was available through Facebook but was later deleted.
7. Basherkella (Bamboo Fortress) was the stronghold of Titu Mir, famed as an Islamic teacher who led a revolt against the British in mid-nineteenth-century colonial Bengal.
8. In Bangla '*ummoter kolijar tukra*' literally means a piece of the liver, but represents that without which one cannot live.
9. There are theological and political differences between the Hefazat, which organised many or most of the protest marches against Latif Siddique, and the Jamaat-e-Islami, to which these 22 interlocutors felt allegiance. In the case of the protests against Latif Siddique's remarks, however, those differences were of less consequence.
10. Interview, Barisal police officer, April 2014.

References

Ali, Nosheen. 2008. 'Outrageous state, sectarianized citizens: Deconstructing the "textbook controversy" in the northern areas, Pakistan.' *South Asia Multidisciplinary Academic Journal* [online] 2.

Andersen, Morten Koch. 2013. 'The politics of politics: Youth mobilization, aspirations and the threat of violence at Dhaka University.' PhD dissertation, University of Copenhagen.

bdnews24.com. 2014. 'Minister allegedly beats PDB engineer.' https://bdnews24.com/bangladesh/2014/03/29/minister-allegedly-beats-pdb-engineer. Accessed 26 June 2019.

Barthes, Roland. 1993. *Mythologies*. Selected and translated from the French by Annette Lavers. London: Vintage.

Björkman, Lisa. 2014. '"You can't buy a vote": Meanings of money in a Mumbai election.' *American Ethnologist* 41 (4): 617–34.

Björkman, Lisa. 2015. 'The ostentatious crowd: Public protest as mass-political street theatre in Mumbai.' *Critique of Anthropology* 35 (2): 142–65.

Blom, Amélie. 2008. 'The 2006 anti-"Danish cartoons" riot in Lahore: Outrage and the emotional landscape of Pakistani politics', *South Asia Multidisciplinary Academic Journal* [online] 2.

Blom, Amélie and Nicolas Jaoul. 2008. 'Introduction: The moral and affectual dimension of collective action in South Asia.' *South Asia Multidisciplinary Academic Journal* [online] 2.

Bouissou, Julien. 2013. 'Bangladesh's radical Muslims uniting behind Hefazat-e-Islam.' *The Guardian*, 30 July 2013. https://www.theguardian.com/world/2013/jul/30/bangladesh-hefazat-e-islam-shah-ahmad-shafi. Accessed 21 October 2017.

Brass, Paul. 2003. *The Production of Hindu-Muslim Violence in Contemporary India*. Seattle: University of Washington Press.

Chakrabarty, Dipesh. 1999. 'Adda, Calcutta: Dwelling in modernity.' *Public Culture* 11 (1): 109–45.

Daily Star. 2015. 'Bangladesh lawmaker Latif Siddique resigns.' 2 September. https://www.thedailystar.net/backpage/latif-quits-parliament-136390. Accessed 26 June 2019.

De, Sanchari. 2017. 'Memory, imagination and political mobilization: The case of Pro-Shahbag bloggers.' Thesis submitted to Jadavpur University for the degree of Doctor of Philosophy (Arts).

Dhaka Tribune. 2014. 'Report: Hefazat sets Tk5 lakh bounty on Latif Siddique's head.' 3 November. https://www.dhakatribune.com/uncategorized/2014/11/03/report-hefazat-sets-tk5-lakh-bounty-on-latif-siddiques-head. Accessed 26 June 2019.

Fair, C. Christine and Abdallah Wahid. 2017. 'Islamist militancy in Bangladesh: Public awareness and attitudes.' *RESOLVE Network Research Brief* 4. Washington DC: Resolve Network.

Fair, C. Christine, Ali Hamza and Rebecca Heller. 2017. 'Who supports suicide terrorism in Bangladesh? What the data say.' *Politics and Religion* 10: 622–61.

Gayer, Laurent. 2014. *Karachi: Ordered Disorder and the Struggle for the City*. New Delhi: Hurst & Co.

Graham-Harrison, Emma and Saad Hammadi. 2016. 'Inside Bangladesh's killing fields: Bloggers and outsiders targeted by fanatics.' *The Guardian*, 12 June. https://www.theguardian.com/world/2016/jun/11/bangladesh-murders-bloggers-foreigners-religion. Accessed 21 October 2017.

Guru, Gopal (ed,). 2011. *Humiliation: Claims and Context*. New Delhi, Oxford University Press.
Hansen, Thomas Blom. 1996. 'Recuperating masculinity: Hindu nationalism violence and the exorcism of the Muslim other.' *Critique of Anthropology* 16 (2): 137–72.
Hansen, Thomas Blom. 2004. 'Politics as permanent performance: The production of political authority in the locality', in *The Politics of Cultural Mobilization in India*, John Zavos, Andrew Wyatt and Vernon Hewitt, eds, 19–36. New Delhi: Oxford University Press.
Harriss-White, Barbara and Lucia Michelutti, eds, Forthcoming 2019. *The Wild East: Criminal Political Economies across South Asia*. London: UCL Press.
Hasan, Mubashar. 2014. 'Transnational networks, political Islam, and the concept of Ummah in Bangladesh', in *Being Muslim in South Asia: Diversity and Daily Life*, Robin Jeffrey and Ronojoy Sen, eds, 224–48. New Delhi: Oxford University Press.
Hefazat Barta. 2014. Blog available through Facebook, 30 September 2014. Accessed 14 April 2015, later deleted.
Hefazat Islam Bangladesh. 2014. Statement by Hefazat Islam demanding the sacking and punishment of Latif Siddique. Junaid Babunagari, General Secretary of Hefazat Islam, 30 September 2014.
Hill, Annette. 2015. 'Spectacle of excess: The passion work of professional wrestlers, fans and anti-fans.' *European Journal of Cultural Studies* 18 (2): 174–89.
HRW. 2014. 'Democracy in the crossfire: Opposition violence and government abuses in the 2014 pre- and post-election period in Bangladesh.' hrw.org/report/2014/04/29/democracy-crossfire/opposition-violence-and-government-abuses-2014-pre-and-post. Accessed 15 April 2017, later deleted.
Islam, Md Nazrul and Md Saidul Islam. 2018. 'Islam, politics and secularism in Bangladesh: Contesting the dominant narratives.' *Social Sciences* 7 (37): 1–18.
Islam, S. Nazrul. 2016. *Governance for Development: Political and Administrative Reforms in Bangladesh*. Houndmills, Basingstoke: Palgrave Macmillan.
Jahan, Ferdous and Asif M. Shahan. 2014. 'Power and influence of Islam-based political parties in Bangladesh: Perception versus reality.' *Journal of African and Asian Affairs* 49 (4): 426–41.
Klem, B. and B. Suykens. 2018. 'the politics of order and disturbance: Public authority, sovereignty and violent contestation in South Asia.' *Modern Asian Studies* 52 (3): 753–83.
Lawton, David. 1993. *Blasphemy*. Harvester, NY: Wheatsheaf.
Lewis, David. 2011. *Bangladesh: Politics, Economy and Civil Society*. Cambridge: Cambridge University Press.
Lorch, Jasmin. 2018. 'Islamization by secular ruling parties: The case of Bangladesh.' *Politics and Religion* 12: 257–82.
Michelutti, Lucia, Ashraf Hoque, Nicholas Martin, David Picherit, Paul Rollier, Arild E. Ruud and Clarinda Still. 2018. *Mafia Raj: The Rule of Bosses in South Asia*. Stanford: Stanford University Press.
Mudde, Cas. 2004. 'The populist zeitgeist.' *Government and Opposition* 39 (4): 542–63.
NDTV. 2013. 'Bangladesh PM Sheikh Hasina pledges to punish online insults against Islam.' 31 March 2013. ndtv.com/world-news/bangladesh-pm-sheikh-hasina-pledges-to-punish-online-insults-against-islam-517688. Accessed 15 March 2016.
Prothom Alo. 2014a. 'Lotifer bicar dabir manobbondhoen pulisher guli.' 1 October 2014. https://www.prothomalo.com/bangladesh/article/335197. Accessed 26 June 2019.
Prothom Alo. 2014b. 'Lotifer bicar dabir michil pulish badha, songhorshe ahot 15.' 1 October 2014. https://tinyurl.com/y5ovsrbr. Accessed 26 June 2019.
Prothom Alo. 2014c. 'Lotif siddiki bad porchen?' 1 October 2014. https://tinyurl.com/y67s6esx. Accessed 26 June 2019.
Rahman, Md. Mizanur. 2018. 'The making of an Islamist public sphere in Bangladesh.' *Asian Journal of Comparative Politics*. https://doi.org/10.1177/2057891118811952.
Riaz, Ali. 2007. *Islamist Militancy in Bangladesh: A Complex Web*. London: Routledge.
Riaz, Ali. 2008. 'Constructing outraged communities and state responses: The Taslima Nasreen saga in 1994 and 2007', *South Asia Multidisciplinary Academic Journal* [online] 2.
Riaz, Ali. 2016. 'Bangladesh: Islamist militancy, democracy deficit and where to next?', *Al Jazeera Centre for Studies*, 28 June. studies.aljazeera.net/en/reports/2016/06/bangladesh-islamist-militancy-democracy-deficit-160628100147561.html. Accessed 15 March 2016.
Riaz, Ali and C. Christine Fair, eds, 2011. *Political Islam and Governance in Bangladesh*. London: Routledge.
Riaz, Ali and Syeda Salina Aziz. 2017. 'Democracy and sharia in Bangladesh: Surveying support.' *RESOLVE Network Research Brief* 3. Washington DC.

Ruud, Arild Engelsen. 2010. 'To create a crowd: Student leaders in Dhaka', in P. G. Price and A. E. Ruud, eds, *Power and Influence in India: Bosses, Lords and Captains*, 70–95. London: Routledge.

Ruud, Arild Engelsen and Mubashar Hasan, forthcoming. 'Radical right Islamists in a Muslim majority country: A counter-intuitive argument.'

Stepputat, Finn and Thomas Blom Hansen. 2006. 'Sovereignty revisited.' *Annual Review of Anthropology* 35: 295–315.

Strauss, Julia C. and D. Cruise O'Brien, eds, 2007. *Staging Politics: Power and Performance in Asia and Africa*. London: I. B. Tauris.

Suykens, Bert and Aynul Islam. 2013. 'Hartal as a complex political performance: General strikes and the organisation of (local) power in Bangladesh.' *Contributions to Indian Sociology* 47: 61–83.

Verkaaik, Oskar. 2004. *Migrants and Militants: Fun and Urban Violence in Pakistan*. Princeton: Princeton University Press.

Waite, Gary K. 2003. *Heresy, Magic, and Witchcraft in Early Modern Europe*. Basingstoke: Palgrave Macmillan.

Williams, Mukesh and Rohit Wanchoo. 2008. *Representing India: Literatures, Politics and Identities*. New Delhi: Oxford University Press.

5
Affective digital images: Shiva in the Kaaba and the smartphone revolution

Kathinka Frøystad

In 2014 digital images of Lord Shiva presiding over the Kaaba in Mecca caused uproar in several Indian localities. So did morphed digital images of *hajj* pilgrims circumambulating a Shiva lingam instead of the Kaaba. Along with a handful of similar pictures, these images brought to life a previously marginal Hindu nationalist imagination of the Kaaba's origin as an ancient Hindu temple. The outcome was almost predictable. Muslim organisations instigated violent protests in places marked by recent interreligious tension, in this case Ahmedabad, Thane and Malegaon – and later even in Bangladesh. The authorities did their utmost to curb further circulation of these images. And whenever those who had uploaded and circulated them could be identified, they were charged for having violated the legal sections aiming to promote interreligious harmony and protect the public order.

How do we analyse this turn of events? One dimension to be considered is clearly the political ascent of Hindu nationalism. In May 2014 the Bharatiya Janata Party (BJP) came to power in a landslide victory that catapulted Narendra Modi, the controversial ex-Chief Minister of Gujarat, to power as Prime Minister. In the years that followed, a number of moves were made to strengthen the hegemony of Hindus. One element was to reinforce the effort to bring under Hindu control the mosques and buildings believed to have been constructed atop ancient Hindu temples during the Mughal era. Besides the Babri mosque in Ayodhya (which was demolished in 1992) and the Gyanvapi mosque in Varanasi (Benares), certain people even claimed that the famous Taj Mahal in Agra had originally been a Shiva temple – a claim submitted to the courts but promptly dismissed. The sudden proliferation of digital images suggesting that the

Kaaba itself had a similar origin was undoubtedly related to the latter claim, though it could hardly be followed by action given the Kaaba's location in a faraway land.

Although the political ascent of Hindu nationalism is crucial for understanding the appearance of the 'Shiva in the Kaaba' images, this chapter foregrounds the technological dimension of this controversy rather than its ideological and political ones. Starting from the easily overlooked fact that all the 'Shiva in the Kaaba' images that motivated violent protest were digital images circulating on social media, I ask the following: What role did the smartphone revolution play in this turn of events? Why were the protests motivated by digital visualisations of the 'Shiva in the Kaaba' narrative rather than by its textual predecessors? And, more generally, how does the digitalisation of religious images contribute to the rise of religious offence controversies? In order to give these questions the attention they deserve, I develop an analytical lens that pays particular attention to technological mediation, affect and the 'work' of religious images.

Besides detailing the 'Shiva in the Kaaba' controversy, I use it as an empirical stepping stone for examining some of the understudied effects of the digital revolution on a region as heterogeneous as South Asia. I argue that the combination of rapidly decreasing internet rates and growing smartphone connectivity since around 2010 has turned the production, manipulation and circulation of visual images into a cherished leisure activity for youngsters far beyond the 'troll armies' that attract attention in the news media. In societies characterised by 'split publics' (cf. Rajagopal 2001, 2009), image circulation may produce radically contradictory affects in contexts marked by political tension and anxiety. In this way blasphemy controversies frequently grow out of micro-events that may be strikingly unrelated to religio-political controversies at the outset. A speculative theory, pun or joke of the kind that can be safely shared with like-minded people (see Frøystad 2013 for an example) can trigger unpredictable chains of events when converted to an image and uploaded on a Facebook wall for everyone to see. This is how enthusiastic smartphone novices, with limited awareness of the technical properties and security settings of the apps they use, frequently become unwitting trespassers of the law. They thus multiply the number of potential controversies that can be taken to court or politicised by means of protests or violence.

To tease out these dynamics, I begin by describing the smartphone revolution in the north Indian city of Kanpur, Uttar Pradesh, where I have conducted intermittent research for 26 years, as well as the Latourian lens through which I approach it. Next I examine what digital religious images (of which contested ones are a variant) 'did' for low-class Hindu Facebook novices in this city during the 2013–17 period, and spell out the analytical prisms I employ to bring out its real-making effects. The final section returns to the digital 'Shiva in the Kaaba' images that in this period attracted blasphemy accusations – the historical trajectory of which shows that it was not its ideological content in itself, but rather the digital multiplication of its visualised forms that generated controversy. Evidently the medium has now become the message in ways that Marshall McLuhan could hardly have foreseen (McLuhan 1964), and it is about time that the scholarship of religious offence controversies takes notice.

Digital divides and smartphone affordances

Each time I consult the figures for online connectivity in India, the numbers have increased. By early 2017 the country had 432 million internet users (Chopra 2017) of whom 300 million were smartphone owners (IANS/Tech2 2017), a tally second only to China. To convey a sense of how the smartphone revolution related to previous revolutions within information and communication technology (hereafter ICT), let me recount the changes I have observed in Kanpur since my initial fieldwork in this city in 1992. Back then there was little except landline phones (as we now call them) and so-called ISD-STD-PCO booths from which one could make local, long-distance and international phone calls. Long-distance calls were costly; one could only make them late at night, when the pulse rate was favourable. In the late 1990s the first mobile phones and public internet booths emerged in the well-heeled part of town, primarily with men in the 16–30 age group as customers. By the early 2000s, when mobile handsets began to grow smaller and talk time less expensive, middle-aged housewives and humble vegetable vendors could also be seen using mobile phones, the make of their handset reflecting their socio-economic standing. In 2008 smartphones began to appear, following a similar trajectory from the well-heeled to the modestly salaried, from men to women, and from youngsters to older generations.

By 2016 even some of my poor interlocutors owned smartphones. I often saw skinny youngsters stepping out of their one-room family homes, smartphone in hand, even though their homes contained little else apart from a wooden cot, a fridge, a few plastic chairs and occasionally a television. Few of them had computer experience, and their smartphones were often their very first introduction to the internet. For many of them the internet *was* social media, to the extent that searching for something on the internet amounted to ascertaining whether it had a Facebook page and, if so, 'liking' it. The much-discussed digital divide is thus neither singular nor static, but is best conceptualised as a series of moving frontiers that occasionally overtake one another. Many of those who acquired smartphones after 2013 had little prior exposure to computers or the internet, which is not inconsequential to the rapid proliferation of controversial images.

The hope that internet connectivity would usher in development by ensuring access to information, deepen democratisation and enable long-distance education for non-elite youngsters, as reflected in the ICT4D (ICT for development) campaign, was perhaps utopian, as William Mazzarella has observed (Mazzarella 2010). Reporting from rural West Bengal, where many villagers had acquired inexpensive, Chinese-made smartphones by 2012, Sirpa Tenhunen states that, besides making phone calls, her respondents primarily used their smartphones for 'listening to music, taking and storing photos, and watching movies' (Tenhunen 2014, 40). Only four of her interlocutors had used them to look up information. Seconding her impressions four years later, Satendra Kumar states that young villagers in Uttar Pradesh primarily used their smartphones to 'chat, play games or watch porn' (Kumar 2016, 28). Indeed, Kumar observes, they now downplay interaction with local peer groups and village elders in order to communicate with relatives, caste fellows and co-religionists 'beyond the boundaries of the village and the nation state' (Kumar 2016, 28) – the outcome of which is a profound transformation of social relations.

All these observations were easily recognisable in Kanpur. Even more striking in my own fieldwork, however, was the frequent circulation of digital religious images. Besides sharing religious images as festive greetings, many of the working-class Hindu smartphone owners I came to know seemed to like, comment and share religious images as a mode of devotion in their own right. Before detailing this modality of digital devotion, let me spell out the Latourian framework I draw on to tease out its technological and material underpinnings.

One of the seminal points of Bruno Latour's social theory is that contemporary societies are so intertwined with their material surroundings that it hardly makes sense to analyse social formations as consisting uniquely of humans. To bring this point across, he famously refers to the dispute in the United States between the National Rifle Association (NRA) and those who want to curb the sale of guns. Whereas the latter argue that 'guns kill people', the NRA argues that, on the contrary, 'people kill people'. According to Latour both positions are equally wrong. In his view, it is the combination of man + gun that kills people. The gun, Latour argues, is not a tool that enables the man to fulfil a pre-given goal: his goal becomes radically transformed by his possession of a gun. The gun *affords* a certain action. The analytical implication is that, rather than conceptualising society in terms of collectivities of human 'subjects' who relate to the material and technological domain as 'objects' or 'tools', social formations must be reconceptualised as collectivities of humans and materiality in a way that makes agency composite and symmetrically distributed.

A diachronic version of this perspective brings into view how each social collective (or 'assemblage', as Latour began to call them later on, cf. Latour 2005) activates a whole series of past collectivities. To exemplify this nesting, he envisions a driver who applies the breaks when approaching a speed bump (not to protect school children, but to protect his car, which illustrates the goal change), which in turn is 'full of engineers and chancellors and lawmakers, commingling their wills and their story lines with those of gravel, concrete, paint, and standard calculations' (Latour 1999, 190). Though I have serious reservations against following Latour all the way in reassembling the social (cf. Latour 2005), his attentiveness to material and technological affordances forms an indispensable theoretical backdrop for the emergence of the digital devotion that occasionally yielded controversial images such as those of Lord Shiva in the Kaaba.

Digital devotion from computers to smartphones

Describing how people use smartphones to circulate religious texts and images necessitates ethnographic specificity, since this is something that people do in a variety of ways. The ethnographic experience that shapes my thinking derives from the annual field visits I made to the industrial city of Kanpur, Uttar Pradesh, in the 2013–17 period, interspersed with frequent social media contact and phone calls in between. My original aim was to examine the cosmopolitan effects of ritual engagement across religious boundaries, and for reasons explained elsewhere (Frøystad 2016) I began my fieldwork in a Kali temple located in a low-income neighbourhood in the outskirts of the city. Interestingly, when I asked the devotees about their relation to other ritual spaces, they would often pull out their smartphones to show me the additional religious sites, deities and saints they valued.

At this point the questions inevitably turned around in such a way that my interlocutors began to interview me, the anthropologist. Had I seen *this* temple, in front of which they stood smiling in the selfie on their smartphone screen? Had I ever seen *this* particular form (*rup*) of the goddess? And what about Sri Hanuman, Lord Shiva, Sri Ganesha – or saints such as Sai Baba and Gogaji – did I appreciate them too? *Jay ho* (hail)! And so my interest in digital devotion began. This serendipitous topic, which enriched my field research and provided a sense of continuity in between my field visits, may also shed light on the ever-expanding archive of digital 'stuff' from which blasphemy accusations increasingly arise.

As I exchanged contact information with my interlocutors on Facebook, WhatsApp, Messenger and Hike (an Indian chat service), deity images began to pour into my inboxes and onto my Facebook wall. The images ranged from visual images of gods and goddesses spanning from photographed *murtis* (consecrated deity statues) located in famous temples to cartoon-style animations and images resembling calendar and poster art. On Facebook, senders would typically accompany their images with some words of their own, such as *jay mata di* or *jay jay maa* (both meaning hail/victory to the divine mother), *jay sri ram* (hail Lord Ram), *jay bhole nath, bam bam bhole* (hail Lord Shiva) or merely *adesh*, a respectful greeting. On WhatsApp and Messenger, exchanges were generally longer and more specialised. Here those sufficiently well-versed in reading, writing and using the copy–paste function created groups that brought Kali devotees together across the Hindi-speaking region, where they shared images and edifying messages interspersed with videos or audio recordings. Within a remarkably short time, the exchange of religious images and greetings on social media had developed into a cherished 'timepass' (in the sense of Jeffrey 2010). Not only did such messages serve as pleasantries that lubricated and expanded what Mark Granovetter famously referred to as 'weak ties' (Granovetter 1973); they were also held to be meritorious in their own right.

The contrast to desktop digital devotion was striking. Computer-mediated religious engagement had consisted of visiting the home pages of various religious organisations, some of which offered online *puja* (worship), or of sending religious email greetings, usually in the shape of beautifully designed electronic greeting cards. Most of those who used these services owned their own computers, which generally meant that they hailed from the middle class or elite. Though many people of lesser means could certainly approach a cybercafé or a hole-in-the-wall computer, religious information, online *pujas* or religious greetings were not among the activities they prioritised on public computers.

The contrast to the limited Hindu digital devotion that had evolved on regular mobile phones was equally striking. Though many Hindus had certainly used text messaging when sending religious greetings to close relatives and friends in connection with the main religious festivals, the lack of possibility for image transmission gave text messaging a limited appeal. For people of other religious communities this may have been different. As Paul Rollier points out, Islamic texting had been common among young working-class Muslims in Lahore (Rollier 2010). Interestingly, their messages typically ended by postulating the religious merit of forwarding which, besides giving religious texting a chain-letter characteristic, enabled the senders to 'do a charitable action whilst being almost entirely passive' (Rollier 2010, 421).

Similar forms of Islamic texting may well have been prevalent in India as well. In my experience, however, Indians generally held texting to be a cumbersome means of communication, due not least to the amount of bulk messages each mobile user normally received. Multimedia messaging (MMS) could possibly have become a game changer. Yet before the MMS technology became sufficiently speedy and competitive in terms of expenses, it was overtaken by the smartphone revolution and competitive mobile internet plans. For the working-class Kali devotees I associated with in Kanpur, it was thus the smartphone revolution that initiated the digital devotion that occasionally 'spilled out' to the wrong kind of recipients – some of whom could react with anger.

On Facebook, which was the first social media application these devotees began to use, posts with deity images were often tagged to show up on the walls of all tagged friends – smartphone neophytes displaying little awareness back then about the possibility of disabling the auto-display of tagged posts on their walls. Consequently, inexperienced Facebook users were probably more prone than anyone else throughout history to display devotional images that someone or the other could find objectionable – at the same time as they could easily be traced should someone claim that it hurt their religious sentiments.

WhatsApp was another social media favourite. Here the communication took shape as person-to-person or group messages that were invisible to outsiders. In this way WhatsApp communication came across as more private, making it feel less risky. Interestingly, what appeared as safe for the users soon developed into a severe problem for the authorities. Whenever conflicts arose over controversial posts such as the 'Shiva in the Kaaba' images, they found it far more difficult to trace their trajectories and curb their circulation on WhatsApp than on Facebook (see e.g. AFP 2018). Much of the research on social media in India has consequently come to revolve around WhatsApp's role in affording a virtually unfettered circulation of political propaganda and fake news (see e.g. Chakrabarti, Stengel and Solanki 2018). Yet problem-oriented perspectives such as this are not well suited to bring out the immense attraction and real-making effect of smartphone-mediated digital devotion on people new to the world of online activities.

Real-making, genre novelty and contradictory affect

As a close-up example of the attraction that gave rise to smartphone-mediated digital devotion, I turn to 35-year-old 'Sarangdev' (a pseudonym), a male domestic cook who hailed from a backward but non-Dalit community. Married with a daughter aged four, Sarangdev lived in the servant quarters of his employer, from where he came running to the Kali temple at least once a day to pay respect to the goddess and polish the brass lion facing her shrine as a mode of *seva* (voluntary service). Sarangdev could only complete eight years of schooling before poverty forced him to fend for himself. Nevertheless, he read and wrote Hindi with ease, was fully familiar with the Roman alphabet (though not with English) and could even spell his way through a little Urdu.

Sarangdev's smartphone was a hand-me-down handset donated by his employer. By the time I came to know him, man and phone were inseparable – something that was virtually a requirement, as his employer could phone him at any time to detail the orders for the day. The phone was an early smartphone model whose lower half was a fixed keyboard and the upper half a screen. Though outmoded and covered with scratches, it was fully operable. When I first met Sarangdev in 2013, he was taking his very first steps into the world of email, Twitter, Facebook, Messenger and WhatsApp, though he soon downplayed the former two. It was evident that he found social media exciting. Besides enabling a remarkable network expansion by 'friending' random people as well as friends of friends of friends, how did social media expand his religious engagement?

The initial thing to note was Sarangdev's preference for the goddess Kali as his profile photo. Of his 29 profile photos until late 2016, 15 were images of Kali. There were also three of Lord Shiva, four of Sarangdev himself (none of which were used for long), one of a chubby baby boy and five of a historical person whom he admires as a caste hero. Why all the deities? Though he by no means treated these deity images as consecrated or animate (*zinda, jagrat*), they clearly strengthened his identification with them, provided a novel way of showing them respect by ensuring remembrance innumerable times through the day, and offered a strong sense of protection. All this was crucial to Sarangdev, whose relationship with Kali was so close that she frequently entered his body during worship. A Goffmanian interpretation (1969) would also illuminate his potential desire to hide his visual appearance, so far removed from the fair-skinned, straight-nosed ideal of masculinity that it could well hamper his digital network expansion. Anonymity could moreover be useful when he explored Facebook groups such as *Desi larki ki chudai* (fucking village belles) and the cross-dresser group *Shemale India*, both of which were taken down shortly afterwards. As I gently taught Sarangdev to protect his social media privacy,[1] I lost track of his underworld activities. However, the mutual trust we developed in this period made him add me to so many of his social media groups and networks that I obtained a reasonably good impression of how digital devotion can border on the transgressive and offensive should it 'overflow' to the wrong audience.

A typical Facebook exchange among digital neophytes in 2013–14 would begin when someone posted an image of a Hindu deity. To optimise the response, all Facebook friends would be tagged, which made the image appear on *their* Facebook walls as well, unless they had activated their tagging protection. Being tagged served as an invitation, if not an imperative, to respond. When a deity appears on your wall, what could be more suitable than responding with a greeting or salutation? In this way, a Kali image on Facebook typically generated a long thread of invocations such as *jay maa* or *jay mata di* (hail the mother), occasionally interspersed with emoticons such as flowers or joined palms, additional Kali images or merely a respectful ॐ (*aum*) or three.

A randomly chosen thread on Sarangdev's wall in this period had no less than 74 people tagged, meaning that it appeared on up to 74 Facebook walls simultaneously. If each tagged person had 150 Facebook friends, as Sarangdev did at the time, this deity image would be visible to 11,100 people. This was normally unproblematic, but could also spell trouble if the image was daring and the electronic network of friends through which it spread was heterogeneous in terms of religious sensitivities. Even though controversial messages were by no means a novelty in the digital world (see Rollier 2010, 422 for a poignant sms example), Facebook made them circulate far wider and faster while keeping track of their trajectory.

To understand what digital deity images meant to those who shared and commented upon them, a necessary beginning is to reject the distinction between the virtual and the real (cf. Boelstoff 2016). Instead I draw on insights from the visual turn within the anthropology of religion. One of its main representatives is Birgit Meyer, who accentuates how form shapes content and 'tunes' the senses (Meyer 2015). For her Pentecostal informants in Ghana, video films depicting the dualism of God and Satan picture the invisible by revealing 'what happens in the spiritual realm' (Meyer 2015, 328). Similarly, Christopher Pinney (2004) discusses the conceptual slippage that makes Hindus refer to visual deity images as 'photos'. This slippage is key. Just as a photograph depicts the form of a person of flesh and blood, so a deity image depicts the true form (*rup*) of the deity, which is the form(s) the deity is believed to have had in its most representative moments. In this sense Hindu deity images picture the invisible just as much as the Ghanaian films discussed by Meyer, though the emphasis is on form rather than action. In contrast to animated deity figures (*murtis*) used for worship, digital deity images were almost always anthropomorphic, and were rather detailed at that. There was thus a productive interference in which consecrated *murtis embodied* deities despite having variable physical resemblance to them, whereas deity images *revealed* the deity's form without necessarily being animated by it.

My use of 'necessarily' in the previous sentence alludes to the situations in which even deity images are believed to be alive. Such situations typically occur when people encounter new mediations for the first time. Take the late 1980s, for instance, when Hindu gods appeared on television for the first time. Hardly a scholar of Hindu nationalism has missed pointing out how the *Ramayana* serial in 1986–9 made viewers garland their television screens and bow respectfully to the characters appearing on them. In 2014 I witnessed similar reactions to a Kali app I had installed on my smartphone. When one opens it, a beautiful Kali image appears on the screen accompanied by a devotional song. By pressing certain buttons one can throw flowers at her, blow a conch shell, ring the temple bell and circumambulate the *arati* tray with digital flames. Almost instinctively, Sarangdev and several others who saw it for the first time joined their palms together and bowed their heads deeply in front of my smartphone screen before their curiosity about its digital format took over.

Deity images in new genres or mediations tended to generate a pronounced 'wow effect' – a sudden sense of wonder resulting from the dizzying possibility that the deity might be, just *might* be, present within the image since s/he had not been known to appear in exactly *this* particular way before. Though such moments were rare and their impact short-lived, they help to explain the fascination with novel mediations, genres and forms. Pinney's conclusion that people only care about efficacy but not form (Pinney 2004) thus merits some qualification. I would rather suggest that a novel and surprising form brings a deity to life, albeit too momentarily to influence its efficacy.

Let me exemplify the genres that gave rise to this sense of wonder during the initial years of my 2013–17 fieldwork, and which brought about a pronounced impulse to greet it, respond, 'like', comment, share or forward. One was the cartoon-like images of male deities with swelling muscles and deadly weapons, a masculinisation that dates back to the changing iconography of Lord Rama in the 1980s (Kapur 1993) and that has continued since with Lord Hanuman and Lord Shiva. Another genre was GIF animations, which had a particularly strong miraculous allure – such as when Baby Krishna suddenly blinked or the water in the background began to sparkle. A third genre was video animations, which in 2016 included a youthful-looking Durga wishing her viewers 'Happy Navratri' in a childlike voice. When such images popped up on people's smartphone screens for the first time, it was virtually impossible not to miss a heartbeat and press 'like' or 'share' almost instantly.

Yet there were also images that generated less benign wow effects. Sarangdev, for instance, shared several sexualised deity images. One was a pop-art image of Kali squatting naked on Shiva's chest with erect nipples, gazing seductively at the viewer. Sarangdev was so enthralled by this image that he used it as a profile picture for several months. Another was a neo-Tantric depiction of Shiva's intervention in Kali's destructive dance that culminated with intercourse. A third favourite of Sarangdev's consisted of an unusually penis-shaped Shiv *ling* photoshopped next to a photo of the red, yoni-shaped spring of the Kamakhya temple in Guwahati. The wow effect generated by these images did not prompt 'likes' or sharing; they rather generated a momentary eye-popping sensation followed by restraint.

Though I never saw negative reactions to Savangdev's sexualised deity images, similar images could certainly invoke anger elsewhere on Facebook. In 2016, for instance, the Facebook page Old Indian Photos published an image of a late eighteenth-century painting of Lord Krishna squatting naked in between the legs of an equally naked Radha, seemingly ready to plunge into her at any moment. Within a matter of hours critical remarks appeared in English as well as Hindi, ranging from swearwords (including *madarchod*, motherfucker) to demands that the image be removed and threats of First Information Reports (FIRs) that initiate legal proceedings. At this point we begin to see how the fascination for ever-new genres and forms can appear immensely alluring for some, but provoke anger and upset among others.

Crucially, neither wow effects nor the converse sense of offence are mere emotions. As pointed out by scholars who have helped to bring the theory of affect to the centrestage of contemporary theorising (see chapter 1), such wow effects are emotions that involve a strong impulse to act, often in ways that bypass critical reflection. One of the central features of the contemporary moment is the ease and speed with which people can respond to something immediately, whether with 'likes', praise or passionate anger. With the smartphone revolution, India – where political passions are hardly novel – leaped into an intensified age of affect.

Let us now see how the dynamics I have outlined thus far can help us to understand why the 'Shiva in the Kaaba' narrative only generated fury once it was visualised and hit the Facebook fan.

Shiva in the Kaaba

I was in the middle of fieldwork when news reports about social unrest motivated by photoshopped digital images of the Kaaba began to appear. These reports did not merely trigger my attention due to my interest in religious offence controversies: there was also a field-specific reason. I had just heard two Brahmin priests claiming that Lord Shiva is entrapped inside the Kaaba. According to the priests, people who managed to get close enough to the black stone of the Kaaba to lean their ear towards it would be able to hear a feeble voice begging '*Mujhe dudh pilao, mujhe dudh pilao*' (please give me milk). The Kaaba, the priests maintained, had been an ancient Shiva temple prior to the birth of Islam; now Lord Shiva was stuck inside with nobody around who knew how to worship him properly, such as giving him milk to drink. Though the priests continued that all it would take to liberate him would be a sprinkle of water from the sacred River Ganga, they feared that such an act could well destroy the entire religion (*islam ko tor dena*). This was evidently not a desirable option, as both had considerable respect for Islam as an alternative path to Truth – one they even occasionally consulted themselves (cf. Frøystad 2016).

Since I had just heard my priest interlocutors talking about the Hindu origin of the Kaaba, the news stories about controversial Kaaba images provided an excellent opportunity to 'follow the loops', as the late anthropologist Fredrik Barth used to say (Barth 1992, 25; Barth 1993, 249). In my case this made it necessary to trace the unusual chronology and geographical trajectory of the 'Shiva in the Kaaba' narrative. Interestingly this narrative appears to be rooted in a religious speculation among medieval Muslims which was later transformed and repackaged as a 'fact' by Hindu nationalist thinkers.

From medieval Muslim speculation to Hindutva 'fact'

One of the questions that puzzled Muslim intellectuals in medieval India pertained to how Hindu idolatry related to the pre-Islamic idols that existed in the Kaaba before the Prophet destroyed them to enforce monotheism in AD 630 (cf. Armstrong 2002, 23). Two of the theories that emerged are recounted by the Islamic studies scholar Yohanan Friedmann (Friedmann 1975). One held that idolatry was of Indian origin: during the flood in the time of Noah idols floated from India to Arabia, where a *jinn* directed Amar Ibn Luhay to pick them up and encourage their worship. Another theory held that, in the pre-Islamic era, Hindus used to travel to Mecca and Egypt to pay respect to these idols (Friedmann paraphrasing Ferishta 1910, 402). The latter theory was promoted in a chronicle of the rise of Muslim power in India authored by the Persian medieval historian Mohamed Qasim Ferishta (1560–1620).[2] It may well have been the translation of Ferishta's chronicle into English – a task undertaken by the British army colonel John Briggs in the 1820s (cf. Mabbett 1968) and republished in the early twentieth century – which exposed the Hindu elite that emerged during colonial rule to the theory that pre-Islamic Mecca had once been a centre for Hindu pilgrimage.

Exactly how and when the narrative about Hindu pilgrimage to pre-Islamic Mecca entered Hindu circles will have to be established by future research. Yet this was evidently one of the narratives that were tossed about in the tumultuous fight for Independence in an attempt to provide historical anchors for new political imaginaries. For certain Hindu nationalists, the idea that the pre-Islamic idols in the Kaaba had been Hindu was an attractive one, since it encouraged the imagination of an ancient Hindu golden era that could now be brought back to life. Writing in 1942, Babarao Savarkar (1879–1945) drew on such a narrative to argue that the entire Eurasian continent from Arabia to northern Europe, perhaps even the United States, had been Hindu prior to the advent of Islam and Christianity.

Interestingly, Savarkar's source for the claim about Mecca's Hindu past was one Major Bill Ford, who allegedly had learned it from 'Hindus in India' around a century earlier (Savarkar 2016, 30). If so, the theory about Mecca having had a Hindu origin had circulated among Hindus at least since the 1840s, increasing the likelihood that Brigg's Ferishta translation of 1829 had a vital role to play. Parenthetically we may also note the difference between Babarao Savarkar and his more famous brother Veer Savarkar (1883–1966). Whereas Veer had treated Muslims with suspicion since their 'holyland' (as he termed it in a frequently cited passage) was located outside India (cf. Savarkar 1989, 113), Babarao rather implied that their holy land had a Hindu past, with both Islam and Christianity being breakaway offshoots from Hinduism. But although the narrative about pre-Islamic Mecca as a pilgrim destination for Indian Hindus was acquiring some credence in Hindu nationalist circles, the version that claimed Lord Shiva to have been the main deity of pre-Islamic Kaaba appears to be a later elaboration.

It was Purushottam Nagesh Oak (1917–2007) who expounded the theory about the Kaaba's past as a Shiva temple so successfully that it attained persuasive power for generations to come. Oak, who participated in Subhash Chandra Bose's armed combat against the British colonisers and ended up as a journalist, argued that, though the fight against the British was won in 1947, 'Britannia still rules the brainwaves of India's rulers' (Oak 2010, 40). And thus began his mission. In 1964 he established the Institute for Rewriting Indian History, which in turn launched *The Annual Research Journal*) to disseminate its reinterpretations (Tilak 2007).

His argument that the Kaaba was an ancient Shiva temple is part of a broader argument about a Vedic golden age not unlike the one formulated by Babarao Savarkar. If only the age of history were pushed back from 5,000 to 20 million years, Oak argues, we would realise that virtually all the cultures and religions found across the world have sprouted from a single Vedic past (cf. Oak 1977), although foreign rulers and historians have done their best to conceal the fact. Oak's mission was to substantiate this claim, which he attempted to do by highlighting etymological and architectural similarities underlying differences in religion, geography and civilisations, claiming such similarities as proof of Vedic diffusion. While academics routinely dismiss him as a pseudo-historian, the question that interests me here is not how readers could believe him, but why his theories came to gain such an influence several decades later. To understand this will require a closer look at Oak's argument and the ways in which it came to be mediated.

Oak's claim that the Kaaba was an ancient Shiva temple makes its point of departure in the view that pre-Islamic Arabia was part of King Vikramaditya's empire, one that academics generally treat as a legend. He states that the inhabitants of Arabia – or Aravasthan, as Oak speculates that King Vikramaditya may have called it – spoke Sanskrit and used an Indic script, that the name Arabia derives from a Sanskrit word for horse, *arava*,[3] and that the name 'Mecca' is a corruption of the Sanskrit word for a sacrificial fire (*makha*), which makes him interpret Mecca's name as 'the place which had an important fire temple' (Oak 2008, 231).

Oak draws on the background of pre-Islamic Mecca as a venue for a grand annual fair to claim that Mecca was the Varanasi (Benares) of the East: a place where the learned assembled to discuss important matters and the general public gathered in pursuit of spiritual bliss. And just as in Varanasi, Oak continues, the main shrine of Mecca was a Shiva temple centring around a 'Mahadeva emblem' (Oak 2008, 233), which is the expression he prefers for a Shiv ling.

The Shiva shrine in Mecca was, of course, the Kaaba, which Oak claims to have derived its name from an Arabic corruption of the Sanskrit term for sanctum sanctorum, *garbha griha* (Oak 2010, 233). Back then, Oak continues, the Mahadeva emblem was surrounded by 360 deity images, two of which represented Saturn and the Moon, both still revered by Hindus. Inside the walls of the Kaaba, Oak further speculates that there are inscriptions from the *Bhagavad Gita*, though nobody is allowed inside to see (Oak 2010, 233). Moving on, Oak turns to ritual parallels. Just as Muslims circumambulate the Kaaba, Hindus do *parikrama* around temples and wedding fires; just as *hajj* pilgrims dress in white and shave their heads, Vaidik practices used to prescribe head-shaving and seamless white clothing prior to temple entry (Oak 2008, 241).

As far as Lord Shiva is concerned, the most evident parallel emphasised by Oak is the crescent moon, which besides being an emblem of Islam is commonly included in visual representations of Shiva. Turning to linguistic similarities, Oak claims that the word *Shabibarat* (or *Shab-e-Barat*, the annual night of salvation in Islam) must be a corruption of either Shiva *vrata* (fasting for Shiva) or Shivratra (the night of Shiva), thus hinting that the Islamic ritual to which it refers is a derivation of Shiva worship (Oak 2010, 233). Moving on, he claims that 'Shia' is a corruption of 'Shiva'. This makes him argue that the Shia/Shunni divide is but an Islamic version of the divide between Shaivites and Vaishnavites (Oak 2003, 640). The word 'Islam', he further claims, derives from the Sanskrit word *ishalayam*, which means 'the abode of God' (Oak 2010, 660). Oak's overall message is unmistakable: the Kaaba is an ancient Shiva temple, Islam is a breakaway offshoot of Hinduism and the rupture attempted by Prophet Muhammad is hopelessly incomplete.

Oak's attempt to document that the Kaaba was a former Shiva temple would probably have been forgotten today were it not for the growth of the Hindu nationalist movement from the 1990s onwards. In this period Hindutva-friendly publishers such as the Hindi Sahitya Sadan began to republish Oak's books and issue new compilations of his articles – in English and Hindi alike. Writings that had long been out of print were now made available to a new generation. Some of Oak's new readers were so enthralled by his arguments that they began to quote him extensively in online discussions that united Indian computer users with diaspora Indians across the world. However, the loop I am tracing is not yet complete. Equally important were the contributions of Stephen Knapp and Sri Sri Ravi Shankar.

From India to the US and back

Born in Massachusetts, Stephen Knapp read the *Bhagavad Gita* as a young man. He has spent most of his time since then spreading the gospels of Krishna consciousness and Vedic pre-eminence. Author of at least 28 books, his *Proof of Vedic Culture's Global Existence* (2000) expands Oak's overall argument. This is what he says about the Kaaba:

> So, he [Prophet Mohammed] destroyed all 360 images in the Kaba and kept only Allah, along with the Shiva *linga*, which has become known as the Ashwet, or black stone (Knapp 2000, 34).

A few pages on, he is less assertive but nonetheless suggestive:

> It is also said that the Black Stone (Sangay Aswad) is originally a representation of Shiva, Mahadeva, in the form of a Shiva *lingam*. Shiva is also known as Makkeshwar, to which the name Makka or Mecca refers. This *linga* stone was retained by Mohammed as a formless symbol of the Divinity, although its pedestal has been lost. ... It is an ovoid shape, about 11 inches wide and 15 inches high. This is the typical shape and color similar to the black Shiva-*lingas* that are popular in India today (Knapp 2000, 147).

Though Knapp is less detailed than Oak and argues with less certainty, he acknowledges the inspiration from Oak in the preface. He also gives credit to a book titled *World-Wide Hinduculture and Vaishnava Bhakti* (1997) by one Dr S. Venugopalacharya.[4] Though Knapp's book is without formal references and footnotes, it does have a bibliography titled 'references' at the end along with an index and a Sanskrit glossary. Combined with its fluent and self-assured style of writing, this can easily make it pass as research to an academically untrained reader. One of them was Sri Sri Ravi Shankar, who contributed to popularise the narrative about the alleged Shaivite past of the Kaaba, though he later was to regret this move.

Founder of the Art of Living movement, Sri Sri Ravi Shankar has been one of India's highest-profile gurus since the early 1990s. In *Hinduism and Islam: The Common Thread* (2002), Sri Sri (as many of his followers fondly call him) drew heavily on Knapp to argue that, rather than fighting one another, India's Hindus and Muslims must acknowledge the many religious traits that unite them. Though Sri Sri was less explicit than Oak, Venugopalacharya and Knapp in asserting the Kaaba's past as a Shiva temple, his attention to simile was nonetheless suggestive:

> Though Islam prohibits idol worship, Muslims revere the black stone in Kaaba which is held sacred and holy. The black stone in the Kaaba is called *Hajre Aswad* from the Sanskrit word *Sanghey Ashweta* (non-white stone). The Shivalinga is also called Sanghey Ashweta ... Another holy tradition at the Kaaba is that just as every Shiva temple has a sacred water spring that represents the holy river Ganga, there is a *Zam Zam* spring near the Kaaba (Shankar 2002, location 196–7 on Kindle).

Sri Sri Ravi Shankar was about to complete this book when the Godhra incident precipitated large-scale Hindu–Muslim riots in Gujarat in 2002. Believing his book manuscript to be of potential help in preventing further escalation, Sri Sri decided to speed up publication (Ved 2002) without double-checking his sources. For the same reason, he also made public appearances in which he made his conviction about the Kaaba's Shaivite past more explicit. Some of the talks were videotaped and uploaded on the internet. This was not to the liking of his Muslim counterpart, the high-profile televangelist Zakir Naik. In a public debate in Bangalore, televised for Naik's Peace TV channel in 2006, Naik made Sri Sri Ravi Shankar admit his mistake of relying on flimsy sources.[5] According to a transcript, this is what Sri Sri told Zakir Naik and his followers in front of the television cameras:

> I know there are some mistakes in that book ... [T]his Book was printed in an emergency, in urgency, when there was riots in Gujarat. I wanted this book to immediately go. I did not go to big scholars because I do not know much about Qur'an. I myself not a big scholar but the intention he caught behind that is to bring people together (Punj n.d.; grammar and synthax as in the transcription).

Though Naik refrained from initiating legal proceedings, Sri Sri Ravi Shankar resolved not to issue a second edition of the book, though Amazon still provides electronic versions for Kindle.

While Sri Sri Ravi Shankar could easily decide against republication of *Hinduism and Islam*, the television show recordings began to live a life on their own. As soon as one online link was taken down, others appeared; as soon as a YouTube version was removed, it was re-uploaded by a new, anonymous user. The 'Shiva in the Kaaba' narrative had now entered the complex world of electronic communication, but it was nevertheless still only a text or verbal narrative. Let us now examine how it was brought to life visually – something that not only altered its pattern of circulation, but also paved the way for a reinterpretation of meaning.

From narratives to digital visual images

By 2006 the speculative theory that apparently originated in medieval India and was elaborated by the 'one-man brigade' P. N. Oak (as his obituarist Shrinivas Tilak puts it) was freely available in at least four books and a videotaped lecture by one of India's most popular gurus. This made it reach a far broader audience than before, and it was debated by many in blogs and online discussion fora: 'Wow, have you heard? Is it really so? Look what P. N. Oak's research shows!' Evidently the 'news' about the Kaaba as an ancient Shiva temple generated a wow effect of the kind that afforded rapid recirculation, suggesting the possibility of a bottom-up rewriting of history to complement the top-down rewriting studied by several scholars (e.g. Flåten 2017).

Computer-savvy techies who were swayed by this narrative moved on to produce video versions. By 2016 at least 20 assemblages of photos, film clips and accompanying text circulated online, all attempting to illustrate Oak's main points with authoritative voice-over explanation in English, Hindi and other Indian languages, occasionally with subtitles. One of them included a snippet of Sri Sri Ravi Shankar's talk, images of Shiva and an alleged image of a poem that praises Lord Shiva and allegedly was composed by the Prophet's uncle. The latter image was superimposed over an image of the Kaaba and compellingly soundtracked by a Shiva *bhajan* (devotional hymn).

Though the location of these videos at a YouTube server made it challenging for the Indian authorities to remove them, their frequent disappearances and reappearances suggest that the authorities did make occasional attempts to curb their circulation. In October 2016 a web page referred to at the end of one of these videos was suddenly empty save for the following sentence: 'I have the right to write about my religion and religious scriptures', indicating that the owner had been ordered to remove the content. In June 2017, however, the page was up and running again, now with speculations that the birth of Prophet Muhammad had been predicted in the *Bhavishyapurana* scripture – and so suggesting a Hindu incorporation of Islam that surpasses even those formulated by P. N. Oak. In 2018 these speculations were removed again, though similar claims may also be found on Wikipedia.

As the narrative about Kaaba's alleged past as a Shiva temple spread across the internet, it increasingly acquired new content. Additional 'proof' was added, whereas the argument about the Kaaba *having been* a Shiva temple in the pre-Islamic era was replaced by arguments that the Kaaba *remains* a Shiva temple. Some even claimed that the deity himself still resides there, or alternatively is trapped inside, as in the version I encountered in Kanpur in 2014. These slippages owe a lot to the transformation from text or oral narrative to still images. The images had no past, present or future tense[6] and were typically posted without accompanying explanations, making them more open to interpretation. The video versions played no such role. Not only were they closer to the narrative form that located Lord Shiva's alleged reign over the Kaaba safely to a distant past, but videos in this period were also far more expensive to transmit. Besides, they did not cross language boundaries as easily.

On smartphone screens across many localities, images of Hindu deities presiding over the Kaaba began to crop up on Facebook walls and in WhatsApp groups. Seeing a Lord Shiva towering over the epicentre of Islam, just as he towered over Mount Kailash or Kashi (Varanasi), was virtually destined to create a wow effect among his devotees. Wow, is he really *that* powerful? As explained above, the instinctive reaction was a 'like' followed by a *jay bhole nath* or *har har mahadev* salutation and an immediate share or forward.

Reaching the wrong recipients

There were at least five different images that evoked the narrative about the Kaaba's past as a Shiva temple or suggested the incorporation of Islam in Hinduism in other ways. The first was the aforementioned image of Lord Shiva towering above the Kaaba, circumambulated by white-clad *hajj* pilgrims. The second depicted a giant black Shiv ling replacing the Kaaba, against the background of Lord Shiva sitting in front of Mount Kailash. The third image, which my acquaintance Sarangdev found so appealing that he used it as a WhatsApp profile picture for several months, depicted a giant Lord Shiva in his destructive Mahakaal form (*rup*): black, muscular and bearing deadly weapons in each of his six arms. Below him were five white-clad male worshippers and four or five women covered in black veils. Whether the women were respectfully veiled Hindu worshippers or *burqa*-clad Muslim women was impossible to see in Sarangdev's low-resolution version of this image, which created an uncanny ambiguity. The fourth picture was the one I learned about from the newspapers in 2014: an image of Goddess Maa Ambe superimposed upon an image of the Kaaba that presumably was fairly similar to the Shiva images. I did not get to see this because it was taken down from the internet by the time the controversy hit the news.

In 2016 I also came across a fifth image that projects Lord Shiva as the Paramatma who unites all religions, including Christianity and Islam – the latter represented by a man with a red fez standing in front of the Kaaba.[7] By visualising and de-temporalising Oak's claim about the Kaaba being an ancient Shiva temple and, by extension, the idea of Islam as being encompassed by, and thus subordinate to, Hinduism,[8] such images were almost guaranteed to offend Muslims, for whom the imagination of any power supreme to Allah represents heresy. If this offence occurs at a time and place where a simmering discontent awaits its moment of crystallisation (cf. chapter 1), the following scenario is likely.

Imagine being a young Muslim guy on your way back from school, work or the market in 2014. You are waiting for the bus, for a colleague to get ready or for your mother to finish shopping. While waiting you get a chance to check your phone to see what your friends are doing. Keeping the costs in check, you refrain from watching videos, but you can still use WhatsApp and Facebook with text and still images without worrying too much about the costs. Scrolling over your Facebook notifications, you see birthday greetings, a white puppy with photoshopped sunglasses, selfies and skinny youngsters posing macho-style in front of glitzy cars, and suddenly .... whaaat? This is surely from the Mecca during *hajj*, but what is the Hindu god Shiva doing in this photo? Who posted this? How dare he? This is just not allowed! *Tu sala* ... ..hey, *dekho* just look what this *madarchod* (motherfucker) just did! This is how many a contemporary offence controversy appears to begin. Udupa describes a similar reaction to a morphed video of violence against Muslims in Myanmar (Udupa 2017), and judging from the reactions to controversial images I have encountered in numerous Facebook groups since 2013, it is not far off the mark.

The common argument that controversies that motivate inter-religious violence are engineered by politicians in hope of electoral benefits (cf. Brass 2003; Wilkinson 2004) merits a complementary perspective that pays more heed to 'micro affects' of the kind described above. Following the long series of technological revolutions that recently reached the smartphone stage, the 'resource pool' of images that can be acted upon by community leaders has grown exponentially. To explain the *rise* of religious offence controversies throughout South Asia, it is not enough to pay attention to why leaders organise protests or initiate legal action; we must also turn attention to the growing production and circulation of images.

To my knowledge, neither Oak, Venugopalacharya, Knapp nor Sri Sri Ravi Shankar have been taken to court for insinuating that the Kaaba once was an ancient Shiva temple. Nor have their writings motivated political action beyond Zakir Naik's public face-off – let alone violence of any kind. But the digital images these arguments inspired became subject to several heated controversies. The first spate of violence I learned about during fieldwork occurred in Gujarat in September 2014, just as the Navratri festival was about to begin. In Vadodara a photoshopped image of Maa Ambe superimposed on the Kaaba was posted on social media and provoked people to pelt stones on the house of the poster. According to a local newspaper, 'groups from both communities torched vehicles and shops' in the evening, forcing the police to use tear gas and call in firefighters to regain control *(Ahmedabad Mirror* 2014). Despite this the violence spread. The next day NDTV reported that 140 people had been arrested and that mobile internet would remain closed for another two days (Bhan 2014). Without additional information, it is impossible to say whether the precipitating image had been designed and uploaded to visualise her greatness or to make a simmering conflict escalate.

Whatever the truth may be, the anger it provoked must be seen in relation to the prior interreligious tension in the city. The preceding months had been characterised by the provocative 'love jihad' and *'ghar vapasi'* campaigns of Hindu right-wing organisations,[9] followed by a warning by the Vishva Hindu Parishad (VHP) to Muslims against entering the *garba* (dance) stalls during the Navarati festival (*Milli Gazette* 2014). One year later a Shiva idol was damaged (*Express News Service* 2015), which suggests how contested digital images can become part of an antagonistic logic of revenge. Yet to postulate that controversial digital images only are designed and uploaded to provoke protest and violence would be to overlook the sensory dimension that makes them circulate until they suddenly hit the wall of offence.

As I began to dig deeper, I learned that this was not the first time photoshopped images of Hindu deities superimposed on the Kaaba had provoked accusations of offence. In June 2014 derogatory images of the Kaaba and the Koran had circulated on social media in the Maharashtrian districts of Thane and Malegaon. Here too the protests had developed in a context of political tension. On 2 June an IT professional had been murdered for uploading images that allegedly offended the Hindu Maratha community, including images of the legendary seventeenth-century king Shivaji and Bal Thackeray, founder of the right-wing Shiv Sena party. In these cases, however, the police had been quick to follow the demand from a Minority Commission member of initiating legal proceedings for having violated section 295-A of the Indian Penal Code and section 66 of the controversial IT Act before the protests got out of hand (*Beyond Headlines* 2014).

Images of the Kaaba as a Hindu temple have also created international ripples. In March 2015 an Indian citizen was detained in Saudi Arabia for having posted a morphed photo on his Facebook page showing the Grand Mosque in Mecca as a temple complete with Hindu deities superimposed over the Kaaba (Variyar 2015; Wahab 2015). In Saudi Arabia such an act is punishable with up to five years in jail and a fine, and though the offender claimed the image to have been uploaded automatically after he had merely 'liked' it, he was promptly detained. Then in October 2016 the 'Shiva in the Kaaba' image appeared on a Facebook page in the Brahmanbaria district of Bangladesh, where protesters retaliated by vandalising at least 12 temples and ransacking hundreds of Hindu-owned houses along with assailants looking for loot.

In Bangladesh the 'Shiva in the Kaaba' image had turned up in a political context increasingly intolerant of expressions that criticised or ridiculed Islam, and in which several atheist bloggers and cartoonists had been brutally murdered. While this event unleashed a predictable whodunit journalism (cf. Udupa 2017, 194) that terminated with an illiterate Hindu fisherman whose Facebook account had been misused (Associated Press 2016; Editor 2016; Rabbi and Sakhawat 2016), I find it more productive to interpret such cases as arising from contexts of simmering tension that awaits its next crystallisation opportunity. Such an opportunity is increasingly easy to find due to the ever-growing stock of controversial images being uploaded on social media across the world, for reasons that may not necessarily have anything to do with politics.

Concluding remarks

As the smartphone revolution sweeps across one community after the other, while gradually trickling down, the affective potential of digital images and videos will expectedly weaken. Wow effects are by their nature transitory. Offended skins thicken. But as the years of photoshopped deity images, provocative cartoons and controversial videos come to an end, new technological possibilities are bound to appear. Ever since Pokémon Go was launched in July 2016, I have anticipated the next techno-mediated chapter of the 'Shiva in the Kaaba' narrative. What if a Hindutva game developer were to position a digital Shiva inside the Kaaba? Or, conversely, what if someone makes a hologram of Durga wearing a Lady Gaga-style beef dress? Morbid as these fantasies are, it feels safe to prophesise that the age of blasphemy accusations is not quite over yet.

Drawing on cases of violent protests motivated by morphed images of the Kaaba, I have argued that neither the design of such images nor their initial circulation is necessarily done with malicious intent. Sometimes their circulation is rather afforded by a peculiar combination of the technical properties of the medium and the ways in which pious Hindus relate to deity images. Considering the number of speculative religious narratives, rumours or texts that can be visualised, digitalised or technologically mediated in other ways, the past is a veritable repository of potential future offence controversies.

Emphasising the importance of smartphone affordances, the reality effect of daring digital deity images and the contrastive affect they can generate in publics as divided as the Indian one is not intended to shift attention away from those who politicise controversial images by taking them to court or organise passionate protests against them. It is, however, intended as an effort to understand the hyper-mediatised context in which they now operate. If a picture is worth a thousand words, a digital image is worth a million – and it is about time we begin to reflect more deeply on what such digital images can do.

Notes

1. Following a series of image removals, blockings and profile takedowns, he eventually developed the habit of alternating between several profiles, all with slightly different names and deity images as profile photos. Since he had at least five different SIM cards, he was also able to do this on WhatsApp and Hike, where user profiles follow phone numbers.
2. I am indebted to Dr Ronie, lecturer at Parciack at Tel Aviv University for making me aware of these works.
3. Some of Oak's critics erroneously claim that the Sanskrit word for horse is *ashvaḥ*, not *arava*. Yet there is indeed a Sanskrit word that could be Oak's horse, namely *aravan*, which means steed and horse. Ute Hüsken, Professor of Sanskrit at Heidelberg University, kindly pointed this out when reading an earlier version of this chapter in preparation for her afterword.
4. Venugopalacharya's book, now accessible online, is a motley collection of unclear photocopies and typewritten pages seemingly collected over a number of years. The author describes himself as a life-long member of the Institute for Rewriting History (omitting the word 'Indian'), which suggests that he was in close touch with Oak.
5. Interestingly, all online versions of the television show have edited Sri Sri Ravi Shankar away. This must have been done by the Peace TV personnel, partly to ensure that the content remained

within the limits of Indian law, but also to ensure its legality in the many Muslim-dominated countries where Naik's online talks are seen. A transcript of the discussion between Naik and Sri Sri Ravi Shankar is nevertheless available online.
6. Images of the past, however, were often used to convey temporal sequences of action, as epitomised by medieval European church art and depictions of royal Indic battles. Today depictions of action are typically relegated to comic strips or moving images, leaving them astonishingly rare within the frame of a single still image.
7. This image was posted in a Facebook group named 'Kaaba is a Shiva temple' by a follower of the Brahma Kumari movement, but I have not been able to ascertain who made it or how old it is.
8. In making this argument I draw on Louis Dumont's notion of encompassment (rather than on the notion of inclusivism put forward by Wilhelm Halbfass and Paul Hacker), since encompassment better brings out how inclusion implies subordination.
9. The *love jihad* campaign, aimed to prevent Muslim men from 'luring' Hindu girls into marriage to increase the Muslim fold, often ended up as vigilante attacks against interreligious couples. The *ghar vapasi* campaign sought to 'reconvert' Muslims and others whose ancestors were known or believed to have converted from Hinduism by means of the purifying *shuddhikaran* ritual.

References

AFP. 2018. 'India issues fresh warning to WhatsApp over lynching deaths.' *Khaleej Times*, 20 July 2018. https://www.khaleejtimes.com/international/india/india-issues-fresh-warning-to-whatsapp-over-lynching-deaths. Accessed 30 August 2018.

Ahmedabad Mirror. 2014. 'Communal tension in Vadodara, shops torched.' *Ahmedabad Mirror*, 26 September 2014. http://ahmedabadmirror.indiatimes.com/ahmedabad/crime/Communal-tension-in-Vadodara-shops-torched/articleshow/43458135.cms. Accessed 30 August 2018.

Armstrong, Karen. 2002. *Islam: A Short History*. New York: Modern Library Chronicles. Original edition, 2000.

Associated Press. 2016. 'Hundreds attack Hindu homes and temples in Bangladesh.' *New York Post*, 31 October 2016. https://nypost.com/2016/10/31/hundreds-attack-hindu-homes-and-temples-in-bangladesh/. Accessed 30 August 2018.

Barth, Fredrik. 1992. 'Toward greater naturalism in conceptualizing societies', in *Conceptualizing Society*, Adam Kuper, ed, 17–33. London: Routledge.

Barth, Fredrik. 1993. *Balinese Worlds*. Chicago: The University of Chicago Press.

Beyond Headlines. 2014. 'Two FIRs registered in Maharashtra for uploading of offensive images of Holy KABA on Facebook.' *Beyond Headlines*, 21 June 2014. http://beyondheadlines.in/2014/06/two-firs-registered-in-maharashtra-for-uploading-of-offensive-images-of-holy-kaba-on-facebook/. Accessed 30 August 2018.

Bhan, Rohit. 2014. 'Vadodara tense after communal clashes, 140 arrested.' *NDTV*, 29 September 2014. http://www.ndtv.com/cheat-sheet/vadodara-tense-after-communal-clashes-140-arrested-672500. Accessed 30 August 2018.

Boelstoff, Tom. 2016. 'For whom the ontology turns: Theorizing the digital real.' *Current Anthropology* 57(4): 387–407.

Brass, Paul. 2003. *The Production of Hindu–Muslim Violence in Contemporary India*. Seattle: The University of Washington Press.

Chakrabarti, Santanu, Lucile Stengel and Sapna Solanki. 2018. 'Duty, identity, credibility: Fake news and the ordinary citizen in India.' *BBC News*. http://downloads.bbc.co.uk/mediacentre/duty-identity-credibility.pdf. Accessed 13 June 2019.

Chopra, Arushi. 2017. 'Number of Internet users in India could cross 450 million by June: Report.' *LiveMint*, 1 March 2017. http://www.livemint.com/Industry/QWzIOYEsfQJknXhC3HiuVI/Number-of-Internet-users-in-India-could-cross-450-million-by.html. Accessed 30 August 2018.

Editor. 2016. 'Enraged by a blasphemous FB post, Muslim mob demolishes 10 Hindu temples in Bangladesh.' *NewsIn.Asia* 2016. http://newsin.asia/enraged-blasphemous-fb-post-muslim-mob-demolishes-10-hindu-temples-bangladesh/. Accessed 30 August 2018.

Express News Service. 2015. 'Stone-pelting in Vadodara after Shiva idol found damaged.' *Indian Express*, 8 June 2015. http://indianexpress.com/article/cities/ahmedabad/stone-pelting-in-vadodara-after-shiva-idol-found-damaged/. Accessed 30 August 2018.

Ferishta, Mahomed Kasim (trans. John Briggs). 1910. *History of the Rise of the Mahomedan Power in India till the year A.D. 1612, Vol. IV*. Calcutta: R. Cambray & Co.
Flåten, Lars Tore. 2017. *Hindu Nationalism, History and Identity in India: Narrating a Hindu Past under the BJP*. Oxon: Routledge.
Friedmann, Yonahan. 1975. 'Medieval Muslim views of Indian religions', *Journal of the American Oriental Society* 92(2): 214–21.
Frøystad, Kathinka. 2013. 'Cosmopolitanism or iatrogenesis? Reflections on religious plurality, censorship and disciplinary orientations', in *Navigating Social Exclusion and Inclusion in Contemporary India and Beyond: Structures, Agents, Practices*, Uwe Skoda, Kenneth Bo Nielsen and Marianne Qvortrup Figiber, eds, 19–40. London: Anthem Press.
Frøystad, Kathinka. 2016. 'Alter-politics reconsidered: From diffferent worlds to osmotic worlding', in *Critical Anthropological Engagements in Human Alterity and Difference*, Bjørn Enge Bertelsen and Synnøve Bendixsen, eds, 229–52. New York: Palgrave Macmillan.
Goffman, Erving. 1969. *The Presentation of Self in Everyday Life*. London: Penguin.
Granovetter, Mark. 1973. 'The strength of weak ties.' *American Journal of Sociology* 78 (6): 1360–80.
IANS/Tech2. 2017. 'Number of smartphone users crosses 300 million as shipments grew 18 percent.' *FirstPost*, 25 January 2017. http://tech.firstpost.com/news-analysis/number-of-smartphone-users-crosses-300-million-in-india-as-shipments-grew-18-percent-359075.html. Accessed 26 May 2017.
Jeffrey, Craig. 2010. *Timepass: Youth, Class and the Politics of Waiting in North India*. Stanford: Stanford University Press.
Kapur, Anuradha. 1993. 'Deity to crusader: The changing iconography of Ram', in *Hindus and Others*, Gyanendra Pandey, ed, 74–109. New Delhi: Viking.
Knapp, Stephen. 2000. *Proof of Vedic Culture's Global Existence*. Charleston, SC: Booksurge.
Kumar, Satendra. 2016. 'Emergence of new sociality and communal violence.' *Seminar* 2016 (682): 26–9.
Latour, Bruno. 1999. *Pandora's Hope: Essays on the Reality of Science Studies*. Cambridge, MA: Harvard University Press.
Latour, Bruno. 2005. *Reassembling the Social: An Introduction to Actor–Network Theory*. Oxford: Oxford University Press.
Mabbett, Ian William. 1968. 'History of the rise of Mohamedan power in India (review).' *Journal of Southeast Asian History* 9 (1): 184–5.
Mazzarella, William. 2010. 'Beautiful balloon: The digital divide and the charisma of new media in India.' *American Ethnologist* 37 (4): 783–804.
McLuhan, Marshall. 1964. *Understanding Media: The Extension of Man*. New York: McGraw Hill.
Meyer, Birgit. 2015. 'Picturing the invisible: Visual culture and the study of religion.' *Method and Theory in the Study of Religion* 27 (4–5): 333–60.
Milli Gazette. 2014. 'Police–VHP violence in Vadodara.' *The Milli Gazette*, 15 October 2014. http://www.milligazette.com/news/11090-police-vhp-violence-in-vadodaras. Accessed 30 August 2018.
Oak, P. N. 1977. 'Synopsis of the lecture delivered at the School of Oriental and African Studies, London.' *SatyaShodh.com*. http://satyashodh.com/oakatsoas.htm. Accessed 30 August 2018.
Oak, P. N. 2003. *World Vedic Heritage: A History of Histories*. New Delhi: Hindi Sahitya Sadan. Original edition, 1984.
Oak, P. N. 2008. *Some Blunders of Indian Historical Research*. New Delhi: Hindi Sahitya Sadan.
Oak, P. N. 2010. *Some Missing Chapters of World History*. Delhi: Hindi Sahitya Sadan.
Pinney, Christopher. 2004. *Photos of the Gods: The Printed Image and Political Struggle in India*. London: Reaktion.
Punj, Nindi. n.d. 'The true call', https://archive.org/details/RaviShankarZakirNaikDebateTranscriptComplete. Accessed 13 June 2019.
Rabbi, Arifur Rahman and Adil Sakhawat. 2016. 'Rasraj remanded, his phone to be tested.' *Dhaka Tribune*, 4 November 2016. http://www.dhakatribune.com/bangladesh/crime/2016/11/04/new-jmb-planned-big-attack-dhaka-2/. Accessed 30 August 2018.
Rajagopal, Arvind. 2001. *Politics after Television: Hindu Nationalism and the Reshaping of the Public in India*. Cambridge: Cambridge University Press.
Rajagopal, Arvind. 2009. 'A "split" public in the making and unmaking of the Ram janmabhumi campaign', in *The Indian Public Sphere: Readings in Media History*, Arvind Rajagopal, ed, 207–227. New Delhi: Oxford University Press.

Rollier, Paul. 2010. 'Texting Islam: Text messages and religiosity among young Pakistanis.' *Contemporary South Asia* 18 (4): 413–26.

Savarkar, Babarao. 2016. *Jesus the Christ was a Tamil Hindu*. Pune: Anugraha Publications. Original edition, 1946.

Savarkar, Veer. 1989. *Hindutva: Who is a Hindu*. New Delhi: Bharati Sahitya Sadan. Original edition, 1923.

Shankar, Sri Sri Ravi. 2002. *Hinduism and Islam: The Common Thread*. Santa Barbara: Art of Living Foundation, USA.

Tenhunen, Sirpa. 2014. 'Gender, intersectionality and smartphones in rural West Bengal', in *Women, Gender and Everyday Social Transformation in India*, Kenneth Bo Nielsen and Anne Waldrop, eds, 33–45. London: Anthem Press.

Tilak, Shrinivas. 2007. 'P. N. Oak (1917–2007): The lone fighter, etymologist, and historian.' http://creative.sulekha.com/p-n-oak-1917-2007-the-lone-fighter-etymologist-and-historian_318699_blog. Accessed 30 August 2018.

Udupa, Sahana. 2017. 'Viral video: Mobile media, riot and religious politics', in *Media as Politics in South Asia*, Sahana Udupa and Stephen D. McDowell, eds, 190–205. London: Routledge.

Variyar, Mugdha. 2015. 'Saudi Arabia arrests Indian for "liking" Facebook photo showing Mecca shrine as Hindu temple.' *International Business Times*, 5 March 2015. http://www.ibtimes.co.in/saudi-arabia-indian-arrested-liking-photo-that-showed-mecca-mosque-hindu-temple-625278. Accessed 30 August 2018.

Ved, Mahendra. 2002. 'Spiritual meet regrets Gujarat violence'. *Times of India*, 3 March 2002. http://timesofindia.indiatimes.com/india/Spiritual-meet-regrets-Gujarat-violence/articleshow/2602641.cms. Accessed 30 August 2018.

Venugopalacharya, Dr S. 1997. *World-Wide Hinduculture and Vaishnava Bhakti*. Mandya: Dr S. Venugopalacharya.

Wahab, Siraj. 2015. 'Indian national arrested for blasphemous Facebook post.' *Arab News*, 5 March 2015. http://www.arabnews.com/saudi-arabia/news/713876. Accessed 30 August 2018.

Wilkinson, Stephen I. 2004. *Votes and Violence: Electoral Competition and Ethnic Riots in India*. Cambridge: Cambridge University Press.

6
'Durga did not kill Mahishasur': Hindus, Adivasis and Hindutva

Moumita Sen

The relationship of Hinduism with blasphemy, a concept germinating in Abrahamic religions, is a tendentious one. India, a Hindu majority country, has not seen as many killings in the name of blasphemy as have occurred in Pakistan or Bangladesh, for example. Scholars claim that polytropy (Carrithers 2000), cosmopolitanism, ritual crossings, syncretism and tolerance (Van der Veer 1994) are common features of Hinduism, which leads to more religious tolerance. The treatment of religious difference among Hindus has been seen more in terms of 'many panths' (sects) rather than that of complete otherness. Yet scholars have also argued that the tendency of Hinduism to include other religious figures and worldviews within itself – what Paul Hacker has called 'inclusivism' – is in effect a form of subordination (Quoted by Halbfass 1988, 411). Christophe Jaffrelot has argued that this popular understanding of an essentially tolerant and syncretic Hinduism is related to the growth of the now formidable forces of Hindu nationalism (Jaffrelot 1993). Through a process he calls 'strategic syncretism', he shows the ideology of Hindu nationalism was built through the process of Hindu reformation in the nineteenth century.

Acts of vandalism and violent censorship have long been a part of the Hindu right wing (Kaur and Mazzarella 2009). But since the election of Narendra Modi in 2014, and the coming to power of the Bharatiya Janata Party [BJP from now on] (as part of the National Democratic Alliance), the language and politics of blasphemy have featured prominently in national media debates. Lynching of Muslim men in the name of cow vigilantism and cattle protection (Venu 2017), talks of rebuilding the contentious Ram Mandir (PTI 2017) and the witch-hunting of intellectuals as 'anti-nationals' (Bhattacharjee 2017) have been standing topics in the national media from a year or so after the BJP came into power in 2014. The rights and freedoms of minority groups such as Muslims, oppressed castes, indigenous groups and women have been the most threatened by the ideology of Hindutva, or Hindu nationalism.

This chapter will follow a controversial ritual which – instead of being silenced by the repressive acts of censorship – was repeatedly discussed and performed by various groups with differing political interests in public spaces. This led almost to its neutralisation in one case. At the heart of this chapter is a contentious religio-political ritual of a minority indigenous group, the Asurs of Eastern India, who claim to have traditionally worshipped Mahishasur – a figure considered evil and demonic in Hindu mythology. This ritual aroused the anger of the Hindu right wing and was labelled as blasphemous, generating significant controversy and debates in the national media. Yet activists in India's villages and metropolises deliberately repeated the 'blasphemous' discourse in the public sphere instead of being silenced by the hooliganism, legal action and police brutality levied against them by factions of the BJP.

The figure of Mahishasur grew more affective as a champion of minority rights with the growing intensity of the acts of violent censorship. Several scholars, especially those working towards the rights of caste minorities in different parts of India and different regional languages, began to trace the forgotten history of Mahishasur as a deity among the caste minorities of India (Ranjan 2016).[1] The act of reimagining the iconography of the 'demon' into a deity or venerable ancestor, as well as that of commemorating or worshipping him, is a part of a concerted effort among caste minority intellectuals and activists to build a counterculture among caste minorities. This movement seeks to resist the efforts of Hindu nationalism, seen by these indigenous activists and intellectuals to be as much a matter of 'culture' as it is of politics and spreading among indigenous people by hinduising their everyday religiosity (cf. Shah 2014). In this sense the Mahishasur movement contains elements of ethnicisation in its attempts to reform the religiosity of their people, return to 'authentic' practices and purify an identity in order to create a stronger position from which to bargain for economic and political rights with the postcolonial state. By 2017, one year after the blasphemy controversy around the Asur ritual in the national media had died down, disparate activists and groups under the Mahishasur banner had coalesced into a pan-Indian network called the 'Mahishasur movement' (Sen 2019).

This response to violent censorship of cultural practices points us to Michel Foucault's understanding of repressive acts as productive and not simply repressive (Foucault 1984, 305–7). In their analysis of the Foucauldian theory, Kaur and Mazzarella write:

> But censorship can also be understood as a generative technology of truth. Far from only silencing, censorship can be read as a relentless proliferation of discourses on normative modes of desiring, of acting, of being in the world. Censorship, then, would be not so much a desperate rearguard action as a productive part of the apparatus of modern governmentality (2009, 5).

Christopher Pinney complicates this picture by placing this paradox in the historical context of censorship in colonial India. He argues that the legal discourse around image practices had an iatrogenetic effect on their production (Pinney 2009). In other words, the law created a proliferation of that which it chose to hinder.

Addressing these positions, chapter 1 acknowledges that while the understanding of censorship as productive explains its paradoxical effects, it believes such censorship to be too 'mechanistic' in the way law is situated in offence politics. The case that I analyse in this chapter operates primarily within the neoliberal media and the shadow of law, while never being under the consideration of the judiciary. Yet it disturbs the notion of iatrogenesis and the broader understanding of censorship as generative technology of truth from another perspective. The Foucauldian scheme sets off a binary between the censored image/utterance/performance as 'lively, inventive, poetic' (Kaur and Mazzarella 2009, 5), in comparison to which the censor is seen as a brutish anti-intellectual (Boyer 2003).

However, what happens when the dominant ideology is also an important interlocutor in the rhizomatic proliferation of the transgressive discourses around the image/utterance/performance that arise because of violent censorship, albeit in different forms? This chapter locates one act of violent censorship and follows the numerous discourses it generates. It lays out the complex political spectrum of modern governmentality, in which Hindu nationalism and discourses of ethnicisation among caste minorities are poised at extreme ends and all normative discourses around 'modes of desiring, of acting, of being in the world' are refracted through representation in different channels of the neoliberal media. As we follow this case from the well-lit theatre stage of national media debates through the little-known streets of suburban Kolkata and finally into the 'remote' villages of Jharkhand, we see the transgressive phenomenon of 'demon-worship' was hindered not in the act of censorship, but within the networks of proliferation among lay Hindus that resulted from the act of violent censorship. In other words, this mode of theorising imagines the transgressive to thrive in the proliferation paradoxically generated by the act of repression. Yet this case shows how the proliferation of the discourse, because of the ideological positions of the interlocutors, is precisely what allows its containment, to a certain extent.

The complex political spectrum is laid out in several parts. I begin by exploring the national media debate around the series of blasphemy accusations made in the Indian Parliament. Second, I lay out the particular context of the Durga *puja* of Kolkata as an industry thriving on creative transgressions, media attention and spectacular novelties. Third, I show how Bengali Hindus of Kolkata interpreted the 'blasphemous' discourse of the alleged demon-worship. In this connection I lay out the relationship between the political discourse of Hindutva and the dominant ideology of Brahminical (priestly caste) Hinduism among lay Hindus. Finally, I show the dissonance between individual activists and lay indigenous citizens and the burgeoning politics of ethnicisation among Bahujan ('Backward Caste' in the Indian Constitution) and indigenous activists in the Mahishasur movement, which resulted from this blasphemy accusation. In the final sections I revisit the question of the generative effects of censorship by situating it in a polyphonic, complex, political field.

The Minister and her Goddess: The politics of blasphemy

Durga is arguably the most important goddess in the pan-Indian Hindu pantheon. Every autumn in many parts of India she is worshipped for nine nights (Navaratri) as the slayer of the demon Mahishasur. The hegemonic mythological story that most Savarna[2] Hindus grow up listening to, reading, and watching, particularly in Bengal, unfolds like this. The powerful demon Mahishasur had penanced Brahma to earn a boon that no man could kill him. Armed with this boon, he started conquering the abode of the gods, creating much havoc in the heavens. Since none of the male gods could kill him because of Brahma's boon, they decided to create a goddess to do the job instead. They invested their martial skills, powers and weapons in creating a ten-armed goddess, Durga, who fought, defeated and eventually killed Mahishasur in an armed combat. The period in which she fought and defeated Mahishasur, among other demons, is celebrated as Navaratri by Hindus all over South Asia and the South Asian diaspora, albeit in various forms.

In Bengal, Durga is worshipped during Navaratri as a ten-armed goddess flanked by her 'children' – the goddesses Lakshmi and Saraswati, and the gods Ganesh and Kartik. Her standard iconography shows the goddess fixed at the climax of the battle-scene with Mahishasur – at the precise moment when her trident pierced his chest and killed him. The *murti* (model) of Durga is an image complex comprising several attendant deities, their mounts, a buffalo that Mahishasur disguised as Durga's lion mount and the agonising, dying Mahishasur. When the priests and lay devotees worship this image, all these deities, including Mahishasur, receive veneration of different kinds.

The importance of the icon of Durga in the Hindu majority country is enhanced by the fact that the religio-political embodiment of the nation or Bharat Mata (Mother India) is modelled on Durga (Kovacs 2004). The icon of Durga has been used politically to deify female political leaders such as Indira Gandhi, Mamata Banerjee and Jayalalithaa (Sen 2018).

However, the demon Mahishasur – the 'evil' one slain by Durga – has also been worshipped and commemorated publicly as a standalone figure in villages and cities in India during Navaratri since 2011. While the term *asur* means 'demon' to most Indians in their vernacular languages, the Asurs, tellingly, are an Adivasi community (listed as 'Scheduled Tribe' in the Indian Constitution) from different districts of eastern India. The Adivasi believe that Mahishasur, their hero, king and venerable ancestor, was tricked and killed by the fair-skinned, bejewelled goddess of the Aryans or Brahmins.

Mahishasur *puja* (worship) or Mahishasur Smaran Divas (commemoration day) is a provocative, proliferating religio-political festival in which several minority groups, such as the Asurs, publicly worship the demon instead of the goddess Durga during Navaratri in metropolitan universities and villages of eastern and central India. This event of demon-worship has been labelled as 'blasphemy' by Hindu nationalists in the public sphere and the Indian Parliament (ANI 2016, 25 February); in turn some opposition parties have called the accusation of blasphemy itself 'blasphemous'.[3] The use of the English term 'blasphemy' in all these debates and discussions points to the foreign nature of this concept in relation to the popular vernacular terminology associated with Hinduism.

One such event of Mahishasur worship on the campus of Jawaharlal Nehru University (JNU) in Delhi led to violent struggles between student political bodies representing minority rights and those belonging to the Hindu nationalist party. In JNU, this debate over memorialising

Mahishasur has its roots in a controversy over images in *Forward Press* magazine (Lal 2014) which depicted Durga in a sexual position with Mahishasur, deemed blasphemous by the right-wing student bodies. Around the same time a political meeting was assembled on campus to protest against the allegedly extra-judicial hanging of Afzal Guru – a Kashmiri political activist accused of, and sentenced for, terrorism.

A formal police report was registered at the behest of a minister from the ruling BJP. In this report, the students were accused of beef consumption,[4] 'Mahishasur worship' and sedition for their alleged support of the secession of Kashmir.[5] On 9 February 2016 the student union president of JNU was arrested by the Delhi police on charges of sedition, following which two other students from a left-wing party were also arrested. In popular media reportage, meanwhile, these students of JNU were hauled over the coals for being 'anti-national' – a term that is gaining more significance in the popular media.

On 24 February 2016 Smriti Irani, the education minister of India at the time, made an impassioned speech in the Indian Parliament denouncing the 'Mahishasur Martyrdom Day' celebrated by Dalit (listed as 'Scheduled Caste' in the Indian Constitution) activists in the Jawaharlal University (JNU) campus. She declared:

> What is Mahishasur martyrdom day, madam speaker? Our government has been accused [of opposing the right to freedom of speech and expression] … and I miss today Sugata Bose and Saugata Roy in this house, champions of free speech … because I want to know if they will dare to discuss this topic I am about to enunciate this house in the streets of Kolkata? I dare them this. [This is] a statement made by the SC, ST, OBC and minority students of JNU and what do they condemn? … This pamphlet highlights what the communist leaders call Mahishasur martyrdom day! And may my God forgive me for reading this:
>
> 'Durga *Puja* is the most controversial racial festival, where a fair-skinned beautiful goddess Durga is depicted brutally killing a dark-skinned native called Mahishasur. Mahishasur, a brave, self-respecting leader, tricked into marriage by Aryans. They hired a sex worker called Durga, who enticed Mahishasur into marriage and killed him after nine nights of honeymooning during sleep.'
>
> Freedom of speech ladies and gentlemen! Who wants to have this discussion on the streets of Kolkata? I want to know.
>
> These are students? What is this depraved mentality? I have no answers for it! Some say they are just children, let them speak.

But how does this depravity get seeded into the minds of our children? I have said repeatedly: don't turn education into a battlefield! But no one listened to me. Today I am compelled to say this, Madam speaker: are these just slogans? I seek to quote a European philosopher, Roman at that:

'A nation can survive its fools, and even the ambitious. But it cannot survive treason from within. An enemy at the gates is less formidable, for he is known and carries his banner openly. But the traitor moves amongst those within the gate freely, his sly whispers rustling through all the alleys, heard in the very halls of government itself. For the traitor appears not a traitor; he speaks in accents familiar to his victims, and he wears their face and their arguments, he appeals to the baseness that lies deep in the hearts of all men. He rots the soul of a nation, he works secretly and unknown in the night to undermine the pillars of the city, he infects the body politic so that it can no longer resist. A murderer is less to fear.'

Smriti Irani's speech, her outrage and the reverberating exclamations of 'Shame … shame … shame' that one heard in the Parliament (Ranjan 2016) indicates that there is something obviously sacrilegious, shaming and disrespectful about the minority students' assertions. However, it is unclear if the 'shame' lies simply in the fact of 'demon-worship' as blasphemy or in the comparison of the great goddess to a prostitute. Given the relationship between Durga and the nation-goddess, did the rightwing political parties take particular offence to Durga being called a sex worker? Or was it the sexualisation of Hindu deities which generated accusations of blasphemy and obscenity – as in the cases of the Muslim artist M. F. Hussain, charged under the Insult to National Honour Act (Chattopadhyay 2008) and the historian Wendy Doniger (Taylor 2014). In Irani's speech there is a clear line between the violated honour of the female deity and the security of the nation-state. In a broad rhetorical sweep, she connects the idea of blasphemy as an offence to gods and that of treason to the nation. In this instance the affective rhetoric and legal action went hand in hand. This connection between the Hindu goddess and the Hindu nation is not arbitrary in Irani's speech, but part of the larger ideology of Hindu nationalism.

Nor is it accidental that Irani singled out the Kolkata and the Bengali ministers. The city of Kolkata in West Bengal has a deep emotional, social and economic investment in Navaratri or Durga *puja*. Assuming that the Durga-worshipping city of Kolkata would be the most offended by this pamphlet, she particularly called out to Sugata Bose, a Trinamool

Congress Party member who had opposed the BJP's position in the JNU debate, as a 'champion of free speech' and as a Bengali man from Kolkata. Repeatedly she dared two Bengali ministers from the ruling party in West Bengal to have this discussion on the streets of Kolkata.

This brings us back to the argument that censorship or blasphemy accusations cannot be understood as a simple silencing or repression of the provocative act. In fact, blasphemy accusations contain a productive potential which leads to its apparent antithesis: publicity (Kaur and Mazzarella 2009). What happened in Kolkata following this speech almost fulfilled this theory. Irani vehemently asserted that it was deeply provocative or dangerous to discuss the 'blasphemous' Mahishasur martyrdom day in Kolkata. A few months after this blasphemy controversy, as if in response to Smriti Irani's provocative call, a local youth club in Kolkata created a *pandal* (installation to house the goddess in public) based on the theme[6] of Mahishasur *puja*.

This *puja* was not a simple act of 'daring', as Irani put it. Her challenge to the Bengalis of Kolkata, provocative as it may have been for her kind of 'Durga-worshipper', was based on a poor or intentionally misrepresented idea of Durga *puja* in Kolkata. Celebrations of Navaratri are widely divergent in different parts of South Asia (Simmons et al. 2018). Ideals of ritual propriety are different in the Durga *puja* of Kolkata. At least since the 1990s the festival has been transformed into a space where rituals, devotion, art, spectacle, kitsch and all forms of revelry coexist. In order to understand the motivations of the organisers of this 'blasphemous' event in Kolkata that 'dared' to show Mahishasur worship, we need to understand the context of the Durga *puja* of Kolkata better.

The Durga *puja* of Kolkata: Thriving on novelties

Durga *puja* is organised all over West Bengal primarily by local clubs. Each neighbourhood – a loosely demarcated residential unit – has a local club, which is an informal, civic organisation for men of that neighbourhood. These local clubs have several functions, ranging from dispute mitigation to the provision of health care for inhabitants of the neighbourhood; their most visible function in recent years has been the organisation of *pujas*, with Durga *puja* being the most prominent festival. These clubs compete for status, advertising revenues and the attention of powerful ministers by creating spectacular, artistic or even shocking installations in which Durga is worshipped.

The Durga *puja* of Kolkata has always been about status, spectacle and rivalry. Examples from the nineteenth century show that so-called 'Gentoos' (gentleman Hindus) published adverts in British newspapers to attract sahibs to their palaces for Durga *puja* involving great feasts and shows including 'nautch girl' performances (displays by dancing girls) (McDermott 2011, 27). In the decades following the 1950s there have been several examples of popular participation and communal organisation, creative appropriation and the use of the *puja* platform for the popularisation of 'social messages'. Some argue that Kolkata's Durga *puja* is an example of secularisation and democratisation (Simmons et al. 2018).

The Durga *puja* has dramatically changed over the decades since the 1950s. Around the turn of the twenty-first century the format of 'theme' *puja*s took over. The *pandal*, or the temporary shed hosting the goddess in public, would be themed after a contemporaneous event such as 9/11 or an aesthetic form such as the folk art of Bengal; it might also be constructed out of one novel material such as earthen tea cups, chillies, nails, balloons and so on. Around this time the visual language of the Durga *puja* turned from spectacle to art (Guha-Thakurta 2004). Designers and visual artists took over the Durga *puja* industry, forming alliances with – or replacing – traditional artisanal labour. The language of aesthetic finesse thus became a part of popular discourse around Durga *puja*.

I have argued elsewhere that the Durga *puja* of Kolkata is now experiencing another shift: from art to electoral politics (Sen 2018). Entrenched in both electoral politics, media, spectacle and the economy of the state, the nature of Durga *puja* in Kolkata differs from north Indian expressions of Hindu piety. The remarkable permissibility of the Bengali Durga *puja* and the derision it provokes in pious north Indian Hindus is brought out best in comparative studies among the Bengali migrants in a Hindu pilgrimage city such as Benares (Einarsen 2018b)[7].

Before I focus on the particular Mahishasur *puja* of 2016, let me refer to a Mahishasur-related production that preceded this blasphemy controversy. In a Durga *puja* organised by Chetla Agrani Club in south Kolkata in 2012, the artist himself appeared as Mahishasur at the feet of the lissom, sensual Durga. Bhabatosh Sutar, one of the best Durga *puja* artists of contemporary Kolkata, created a winged self-portrait and placed it in the Durga image complex as Mahishasur. This image was not seen as offensive by the viewing publics of Kolkata; instead it went on to win prizes from several juries of artists. Moreover, it was formally collected, preserved and displayed at the Municipality-owned museum for Durga *puja* art (Fig. 6.1).

Figure 6.1 Bhabatosh Sutar's work in Chetla Agrani Club, Kolkata, 2012. Source: author

For the organisers of Durga *puja* – the local clubs of Kolkata – novelty and rivalry are the main motivations. The more media attention they garner, the more prizes they win, and the more industries inundate them with advertising revenue. Neighbourhoods struggle against each other to attract the crowds of the city. What was earlier accomplished by inviting an important artist is now done by pleasing a minister. Anonymity is the worst fate that a Durga *puja* production can meet. If money and effort has been invested, a Durga *puja* must grab its audience's attention by art, by politics or by engineering a media controversy.

Staging the 'unspeakable': The Asur *puja* of FE Block

The club representing the FE Block neighbourhood in Salt Lake (Kolkata), like thousands of other clubs in the city and its suburbs, organises a Durga *puja* every year. But in the Durga *puja* season of 2016 it generated quite a bit of media attention in the city. The theme of the FE Block Durga *puja* was based on Mahishasur *puja*.

The Asurs, as I pointed out earlier, belong to an Adivasi group of roughly 2,000 people. As the representatives of their community told us, they consider themselves to be the direct descendants and devotees of Mahishasur. For most Savarna Hindu Bengalis, the idea of the *asur* is akin to other fictitious characters from mythological narratives, fairy tales and folklore. Like *daitya-danab, brahmadaitya* and *rakshasa* (variants of monsters, ghouls and evil spirits), *asurs* are part of a popular imagination with set iconographic features. Television series portray them as dark-skinned, flat-nosed, bare-bodied men with thick, black, curly hair, fangs and horns. In graphic novels and animated films, *asurs* often appear green.[8] Mahishasur, in particular, has featured in several advertising campaigns that line the streets of Kolkata during the Durga *puja*.

The information that an Adivasi community comprising thousands of people was called '*asur*' was new and rather surprising to many Bengali Hindus, used to thinking of them purely as fictitious characters. In parts of the world dominated by Christian or Muslim faiths, the discovery is comparable to the majority community finding out that an indigenous community is known as 'Satan' or '*Shaytan*'. The more prejudiced Hindu Bengalis, I was told, imagined that these people must have got that name because they are like the ghouls and monsters from folklore and fairy tales who eat raw meat.

In an open field in Salt Lake, the organisers staged a fictional situation where Durga was being worshipped in the palace of a *zamindar* (landlord), surrounded by an Asur village on all sides. In line with the convention of replica architecture that is common in the Durga *puja* of Kolkata, they recreated an imaginary Asur village. The main attraction was the fact that they had invited a family of 'real Asurs' from Sakhuapani village in Jharkhand. Thatched huts made from thermocol, cardboard and other temporary material were labelled 'Asur hut'. Artificial trees and a photographic green backdrop were placed to create the idea of a forest. Clay figures representing male members of the Asur community – much like colonial ethnographic figures – were shown standing, farming and iron-smelting (Fig. 6.2). On one side was a shrine to Shabari, the hunter goddess of the Sabar community[9] – she does not belong to the Asur community, who are not idolaters.

At first glance, it looked like a hastily executed ethnographic exposition or a human zoo, except that the Asur family was nowhere to be seen. When I entered the compound, I found middle-class Bengali revellers in the *puja* taking selfies against this backdrop of a forest with the label 'Asur village' (Fig. 6.3). I was told later that the Asur family perform their traditional music and dance every evening, along with 'demonstrations' of their indigenous crafts and objects of daily use such as utensils, rain covers, bows and arrows etc.

Figure 6.2 Representations of Asur village, FE Block, Kolkata, 2016. Source: author

Figure 6.3 Families taking selfies against the backdrop of the Asur village, FE Block, Kolkata, 2016. Source: author

The FE Block *puja*, like that of every other aspiring club, was designed to grab the attention of the media. Taking on a national level controversy is one way of rising out of anonymity in the Durga *puja* market. Moreover, for several decades there has been an unbroken tradition of using the Durga *puja* platform to address issues of social inequality, including women's empowerment, the perils of addiction, rights of labourers, rebuilding areas stricken by natural disasters and so on. Instead of explicitly mentioning the controversy raised by Smriti Irani, the FE Block club framed their endeavour as an issue of social inequality. The explicitly stated aim of this production was to humanise the *asur* in public imagination.

'Are they *rakshasas*?'[10] 'Do they eat raw meat?' 'Do they have horns?' 'Have they got big ears?' 'Are there still *asurs* in modern India?' Sohomjit Ray (name changed), the man who designed the theme of the *puja*, was asked these questions by the upper middle-class, caste Hindu residents of the FE Block. Ray is an engineer, not an Indologist or an academic by profession, but he is well-versed in the *puranas*. By bringing a group of people belonging to the Asur community from Sakhuapani, he wished to show these neighbours 'who have these ideas, even in this day and age, that Asurs are also one of us'.

Given the popular imagery of *asurs* as green or black skinned, horned and fanged demons, the residents of FE Block did not want to invite such an '*ashubha shakti*' (evil force) to their own courtyards. Ray was also repeatedly told that bringing the worshippers of Mahishasur during the auspicious time of Durga *puja* is *ashubha* or inauspicious.[11] However, as the Mahishasur controversy spread from the capital to Bengal, several newspapers and television channels repeatedly used headlines to make their readers and viewers aware of the fact that the '*asurs*' are, in fact, 'real people' living in villages of Jharkhand.[12]

'Durga did not kill Mahishasur': Bhadralok hermeneutics

When asked about the supposedly blasphemous nature of the worship of Mahishasur, Ray looked at me with a frown and some suspicion. 'So you are working on Durga *puja*? Do you know who killed Mahishasur?' 'Durga,' I answered. 'That's wrong ... there are three chapters (*adhyayas*) in the *Chandipurana*. In the first *adhyaya*, Ma Durga kills Madhu-Kaitabha. In the second *adhyaya*, Mahalakshmi kills Mahishasur with her *kharga* (a sickle-like weapon) and in the third *adhyaya*, Durga kills Mahamahasura.[13] Even in Birendra Krishna's recitation,[14] Mahalakshmi kills Mahishasur, not Durga. So there is no effective documentation in the *puranas* about Durga killing Mahishasur.'

About Mahishasur, he added, 'In Markandeyapurana or any of the *Puranas* ... you know, our ancient texts, there is no mention of Mahishasur as a very harmful *rakshasa*. Instead, *Puranas* says that the term "*mahish*" means *pradhan* [the head of a community]. *Asur* means "brave warrior" or those who are adept at the use of weaponry'. Ray concluded by observing, 'Actually the texts say that Mahishasur was a brave warrior of the Dravidian clan. The religious belief or the *Puranas* of the Asurs state that he was a great leader of their clan. He was tricked to death by a woman.'

According to Ray, there is no 'effective' similarity between the woman who killed Mahishasur and Durga. 'Are you saying Durga did not kill Mahishasur?' I asked again. 'No, Durga did not kill Mahishasur,' Ray confirmed. 'But the *murti* [image] shows that Durga is killing Mahishasur?' I queried, pointing at the Durga *murti* in the *pandal* (Fig. 6.4).

The image, Ray explained, had been ordered three months before the 'theme' had been decided, and thus did not reflect their ideas behind the final 'theme' *pandal*.

A documentary made by the organisers was screening on a loop near the *pandal*. It took the viewers to Sakhuapani village in the neighbouring state of Jharkhand where the Asurs are from. It showed Mahua Asur (name changed) narrating the story of the 'real' Mahishasur, the great non-Aryan king, who was tricked and killed by the fair-skinned Aryan goddess Durga. However, a part of the documentary borrows imagery from popular televised versions of the Durga-Mahishasur narrative to question its scriptural validity. Going into the details of *Chandipurana*, it establishes that Durga did not kill Mahishasur. 'Then in *Chandipurana*,

Figure 6.4 Durga *murti* in the *pandal*, FE Block, Kolkata, 2016. Source: author

who is that mysterious *devi* who actually killed Mahishasur?' the documentary screened at the *pandal* asked.¹⁵

There was a cacophony of discourses at the site of the *pandal*. The Asurs claim Mahishasur as the hero slayed by the duplicitous Durga. The Durga-worshipping organisers, in response, are willing to concede that Mahishasur was not a 'demon', but a brave Dravidian warrior. They also agree that he was wrongly killed by the *devi*; however, that *devi* was not Durga at all.

Meanwhile, at the centre of the *pandal* stands the image being worshipped, which shows Durga killing the muscular, dark Mahishasur with her trident. As ground-breaking as that assertion that Durga did not kill Mahishasur might be, it is difficult to establish it academically. The episodes Ray mentioned closely resemble the narrative structure *Devi Mahatmeya* (DM), *Chandipurana* being its vernacular, oral counterpart. The *Madhyama carita* of the DM narrates the 'slaying of Mahisa' by the goddess (Einarsen 2018a, 5). He writes: 'The myth of the middle episode is said to be the most famous of the DM's three myths and the most important one for the ongoing identity of the goddess as Durga' (Einarsen 2018a, 6). To me, however, testing the academic validity of this hypothesis is less interesting than his intention of establishing this proposition – one at variance with the popular narrative that every Bengali Hindu grows up hearing.

I argue that Ray's position shows the inherent cosmopolitanism of Hindu religiosity in its capacity to cohere and co-opt other traditions at the cost of modifying itself. Hindu religiosity thrives in contradictions, polyphony, polytropy and dynamic narratives. Simply put, Ray's assertion that Durga did not kill Mahishasur achieves this: if Durga did not kill Mahishasur, but Mahishasur was killed anyway, then the Asurs and the Durga-worshipping Bengali Hindus have no conflict at all. The argument is then deflected on to whoever actually killed Mahishasur, or the identity of the 'mysterious, unknown *devi*' from *Chandipurana*. The work of mitigating contentious contradictions, and cohering other narratives into the dominant narrative by tweaking it strategically, can be seen as a laborious act of peacekeeping. In the following section I delve deeper into the 'true meaning of Hinduism' according to Ray, vis-à-vis the blasphemy controversy.

Washing off Mahishasur's blood: Hindutva v. Hindus

'Durga *Puja* is a festival of togetherness; it's the opposite of war' was a concept repeatedly stated in a documentary screened at the venue of the worship; the belief was reiterated in my interviews with the members of the club. 'Intolerance is a result of our ignorance. The rhetoric of intolerance is raised by politicians or those who have vested political interests. Common men, like us, want to highlight this indigenous tribe and their traditional knowledge of iron.' As an engineer himself, Ray was particularly fascinated by this lost art of making iron that could never gather rust as if by magic. The exoticisation and magical nature of this lost craft was extended to the nature, food and lifestyle of the Asurs.

'Smriti Irani,' he emphasised, returning to the issue of intolerance, 'did not know one thing: when we offer *pushpanjali*[16] to the goddess, we also offer flowers to Mahishasur. Everyone there… [points to the Durga *murti*] … they are all thought of as gods! Otherwise why will we offer *pushpanjali* to them?' In other words, according to Ray, Bengali Hindus worship Mahishasur too, alongside the one who slays him – a point that does not readily accord with the popular perception of the 'demon' in popular Bengali Hindu religiosity. The core motivation of staging this 'theme' was Ray's idea of what Hinduism and Durga *puja* are in essence. 'There is no conflict in Hindu religion and Hindu faith,' he says. 'Ma granted *barabhay*[17] (protection and blessing) to Mahishasur at the end of the battle. If you read *Ramayana*, you will see that at the end the valour and spirit of Ravana's army was praised after Rama defeated him. Their spirit was also venerable. Our religious faith rules out conflict.'

Ray's approach seeks to draw a line between his idea of Hinduism and the meaning of Durga *puja*. 'Durga *puja* is a *puja*, but it is also a communal festival, a celebration of togetherness. We wanted to uphold the issue of Asurs in such a platform,' he observes, attributing the incidence of riots, communal disharmony and even the Maoist insurrection in Adivasi belts of India to 'inner feelings' of hatred and violence. Echoing the issue of auspiciousness raised by his neighbours, he reflects, 'What is *ashubha shakti*? It is the hatred within us. We must conquer the *ashubha* with *shubha shakti* or love'. A common trope in the Durga *puja pandals* of Kolkata is morally to polarise actors in 'current affairs', as they are often called, into good and evil, as metaphors of the goddess and the demon respectively.

Madhav Singh (name changed), a club member with connection to the central defence department, was an integral part of the process of collecting charity for the Asurs. When I asked him about the issue of JNU in relation to this *pandal*, he said that irrespective of the validity of Irani's position on this, the JNU students got it all wrong. The JNU 'kids', he said, were definitely twisting the religious practices of the Adivasis for their own political gain. The Adivasis are neither idolatrous nor political. They are poor, simple-minded nature worshippers, according to him. Ray pointed out that the Adivasis were confused at the end of the day; they believed an imaginary figure to be their historical ancestor. But the *Chandipurana* is no mere imaginary story for Ray. He cites it carefully to prove that there is no 'effective documentation', in his words, that Durga killed Mahishasur.

On one hand, the middle-class Bengali organisers of Durga *puja* clearly do not succumb to the ideology of Hindutva. The clever hermeneutical exercise performed by Ray shows how deftly he is willing to reinterpret the narratives from one of the best-known Hindu scriptures in the subcontinent in order to do away with a root cause of conflict. This reflects Asish Nandy's argument about religious violence in India: when acts of religious violence occur, it is not due to the inherent intolerance among common people, but rather to the shrewd manipulation of political leaders, religious fanatics and in general those who might gain materially from disharmony (Nandy, qtd. in Van der Veer 1994, 190).

Of course, the Bahujan activists and intellectuals saw this hermeneutic act as yet another example of 'Brahminical trickery' to include, co-opt and maintain the social hierarchy in the face of any possibility of overhaul. This echoes Peter Van der Veer's rebuttal to Nandy's argument about the inherent tolerance of lay Hindus. As he rightly points out, even those who commit acts of violence in the name of religion repeat these ideals of Hindu tolerance as part of their identity (Van der Veer 1994, 190–1). Because, trickery or not, the attitude of the organisers towards the Asurs is one of the elite civil society extending charity towards the poor, noble savage.

Such a view is pregnant with ideas of anachronism and evolutionist beliefs about society which lead to 'universal taxonomy of primitives' (Skaria 1997, 730) – a perspective in which the goddess of Sabars is placed in the representation of Asur village because 'they are all interlinked'. Their fetishisation of Asur community's dance, their diet, their objects and their lands is symptomatic of the processes through which colonialism produced the primitive (Banerjee 2006). Scholars studying indigeneity across the world have pointed out that this is precisely how indigeneity acquires 'positive meaning' – not through essential properties of its own, but due to perceived lacks in the dominant culture (De la Cadena and Starn 2007, 4).

Mourning among revellers: The Asurs at FE Block, Salt Lake

In a political milieu where Maoist insurgency among Adivasi youth is crucial to the political landscape of India, Bengali civil society sees the Adivasi in two or three possible roles: mostly as savages to be civilised, or 'developed', through a mix of educational and commercial initiatives, but also, particularly by activists and scholars, as 'victims in need of protection' (Chandra 2016, 222). The third possible image is of the desperate, bloodthirsty rebel emerging from thick forests with an AK47. All these images of the Adivasi were invoked in my conversations with the organisers. Yet the demands and desires of the members of the 'Asur family' posed a counterpoint to these stereotyped images.

The Asur family was put up in an unfurnished, newly built top floor of the FE Block clubhouse. When I was led up to them by Ray, I found several of them taking a nap on mattresses on the floor. They quickly sat up as Ray said, 'Will there be a little song and dance tonight also?' Mahua Asur, the leader of the group, emerged from one of the rooms. While tying her hair, she pointed out with a laugh that everyone was tired from the multiple dance performances. Mahua Asur became a visible person in social media after Smriti Irani's diatribe on Mahishasur *puja*. She was the most prominent face of the 'Asura pride', a social movement based on the unique culture and identity of the Asur people.[18]

Back in the clubhouse, grey plastic chairs were arranged in a circle and some of us sat down. Two girls and two women from 'the Asur *paribar*' (family) sat close to Mahua'ji, and we sat opposite. It emerged that they were not so much a single family as a group of distant cousins, neighbours and friends. Mahua'ji seemed prepared for an interview: after all, she had been meeting a variety of journalists from print and electronic media for the last four days in Kolkata. She said she did not want me to record our conversation and whispered something in Asuri to the women around her – presumably a set of instructions. Mahua'ji began talking to us by saying that they are in mourning (in stark contrast to the reverberating beats of *dhak* and the bells of *sandhya arati* [evening prayers] outside). She explained that there is little ritual and external manifestation of this mourning: it is a deeply personal and internalised process of grieving for the death of someone loved. Back in her village, people go about their day's activities, working at home, in the mine or on the farm while they mourn. 'We don't worship dolls,' she said in Hindi. 'If the doll had any real power, wouldn't it stop murder, violence and war happening under its nose?'

At the time of the FE Block *puja*, a report was published from a Bahujan rights platform *Forward Press* (Varghese 2016). It stated that Asurs were being 'tricked again by Durga-worshippers in Kolkata' and that they were being mistreated and forced to worship Durga. However, echoing Ray's statement, Mahua'ji said that none of them had stepped into the *pandal*; they simply walked around it. While their faith had also prevented them from entering the Durga temple that came up to Sakhuapani around 15–20 years ago, Mahua'ji lamented that the youth of the Asur community are now prone to celebrating Dussera. 'The *baniyas* (caste group of merchants) came and started business in the village,' she said. 'They convinced the villagers that if they have a *mela* (festival) during Dussera, more money will come to the village.'

Mahua'ji thinks that the lure of Dussera and *'masti'* (partying, in this context) is slowly creeping into the youth of the village. They are losing their own tradition and heritage, she said. This is in keeping with Amita Baviskar's study among the Bhilala Adivasis in western India, where the cultural wing of Hindutva politics or the Rashtriya Swayamsevak Sangha (RSS) has undertaken several waves of Hinduisation. They lined the area with temples to Hindu deities and several local religious practices now incorporate Hindu elements (Baviskar 2005, 282).

This ideal of a monolithic Hinduism has become so entrenched that some of the Adivasis joined the Hindutva movement against Muslims as the ultimate other. In the wake of a rejuvenated politics of ethnicisation, one can understand Mahua'ji's assertion as a resistance to Hinduisation by reconverting the Asur youth back to their traditional practices. Participation and propagation of Mahishasur *puja* appears to be one such act.

Yet Mahua'ji also stated unequivocally that politics play no part in Mahishasur *puja*. She is affiliated to no Adivasi or Dalit political organisation. This is a common assertion in India because politics is popularly perceived as 'dirty' and politicians as criminal (Ruud 2001). However, the purpose of her visit to Kolkata during Durga *puja* was clear. Mahua'ji wanted to eradicate the prejudice in the minds of urban Hindus about her people being demons with horns and teeth. She wanted to 'let them know that we are also human beings, just like them'. At this point, some Marwari children came with an adult to meet the Asurs. Mahua'ji told them stories about her village, her people and about Mahishasur. 'We are just like you? Aren't we? Will you tell your friends at school?' she smiled and asked, leaning over to meet the little boy's gaze. He nodded awkwardly.

Soon they started showing us objects they had brought with them from the village as if it were a practised performance. Out came a beautiful vessel made of leaves that could preserve the temperature of food, then a cover fashioned from similar leaves, used by the Asurs as umbrellas. This performance can be understood as a move towards ethnicisation; a mode in which one clearly emphasises their cultural difference to resist the dominant culture's attempts to incorporate and homogenise it. Pointing to the growing visibility of the discourse of indignity in India, Baviskar shows how the new politics of Adivasi identity in India recreate colonial notions of hunter-gatherers wearing loin cloths (Baviskar 2005). This creates two problems: first, it appears completely to separate the rural poor of India from the Adivasis in cultural terms. Second, it obfuscates the fact that not all Adivasis live in secluded rural societies. In fact, several Adivasis live in towns and cities, even as Mahua'ji did.

Rukmini Asur, aged 23, had accompanied her 'aunt' Mahua'ji to Kolkata. Her assertions of identity vis-à-vis indigeneity were very different from Mahua'ji's. She did not see herself as part of the 'Asura pride' movement, or even think of herself as 'tribal'. According to her, she belonged to the 'Asur caste', not to a 'tribe'. In school she considered her first language to be Hindi and her second language Sanskrit. When asked what she spoke at home, she replied 'Asuri'. Even though Rukmini had never watched television in her life, she thoroughly enjoyed cricket and Bollywood, perhaps the most effective conduit of the culture of *masti* in India. With solar energy, it was now possible for her and her friends to use mobile telephones in Dipakujam, her village in the Gumla district.

This was Rukmini's first time away from the village. She mentioned the School Service Commission, which requires candidates to pass a state-level competitive examination before they are eligible to apply for the position of a schoolteacher at a public or *sarkari* (governmental) school. Rukmini expressed her apprehension about remaining unemployed, given that public sector jobs are highly competitive. Her position as a young woman of the indigenous community reveals the inner contradictions of the drive towards ethnicisation. Her statement that 'Asur' is her 'caste' shows that she does not consider herself a radical outsider to the Hindu social order; she rather aspires to become a public sector employee. In other words, Rukmini wishes to become a member of social standing in the postcolonial state.[19]

Tensions between difference and sameness have been a hallmark of articulations of indigeneity in postcolonial societies, a situation forcing people to deal with both exclusions and forced exclusions (De la Cadena and Starn 2007, 5). During this *puja* an article appeared about FE Block in *Forward Press* condemning the fact that Bengali Hindus 'tricked' the Asurs again, much as Mahishasur was tricked by Durga. However, my interviews with the organisers or the Asurs do not corroborate any idea of simple deceit. Turning individuals into exhibits in a hastily made ethnographic zoo or into helpless recipients of charity is surely a lot more than deceit. But 'Brahminical trickery' or not, the Asurs were clearly not being forced into any ritual participation ostentatiously. They were in that club by will, with a clear purpose and message of their own. In that sense, they were collaborating with the Bengali elite Hindus – if such negotiations of self-interest between a dominant social group and a disempowered minority can be called 'collaboration'.

A year after this meeting, when I visited Rukmini and Mahua'ji in their villages in Jharkhand, both of them reported that the FE Block club had taken financial responsibility for the education of both the young women who had travelled to Kolkata. Thanks to their support, Rukmini was soon going to start working as a teacher in Ranchi, the capital city of Jharkhand. However, Mahua'ji's alliances with the FE Block club meant that other indigenous activists ostracised her from the Mahishasur movement. In my interviews with 'Backward Caste' and other indigenous activists in Delhi, Kolkata and villages of West Bengal, I was repeatedly told that Mahua'ji had 'turned her back on the struggle', 'sold out' or 'been co-opted by the system' (Interviews with activists, New Delhi, Kolkata, Purulia town, 2016–18). For Mahua'ji, who still did not regret her trip to Kolkata, the question of basic rights such as education, health and so on remained as important, if not more so, than questions of 'politics'.

Since the 'Prose of Counter-insurgency' (Guha 1994), the dominant mode of understanding Adivasi resistance has been in opposition to the postcolonial state. Uday Chandra has argued that Adivasi politics 'can be best understood as the negotiation, not negation of modern state power' (Chandra 2016, 223). In a situation where the state is omnipresent and the only player on the scene, he argues that the Adivasi must rework the terms of engagement with the state. It is not the trope of the subaltern rising against the colonial overlord; neither is it the one where activists save their rivers for them. It is rather 'resistance-as-negotiation' (Chandra 2016, 227).

We see in the negotiation between the organisers of FE Block and Mahua Asur an emerging face of Adivasi rights campaigns. Appropriating the language of ethnomuseology employed by the colonial and the postcolonial state, the Asurs display their possessions with pride. For Mahua'ji, the trip to FE Block had been part of her larger campaign to humanise Asurs in popular imagination. She hoped that this would bring electricity, running water and a working school to the village. In Rukmini, we see the youth in which Mahua'ji is disappointed: the youth that is interested in what Baviskar calls '*bazaariya* modernity' (Baviskar 2005), *masti* (partying) and the will to assimilate in the postcolonial state. Yet what Mahua'ji nevertheless shares with Rukmini is the need for development in their village where there is no electricity, school or hospital, the men suffer from chronic alcoholism and the neoliberal state is only interested in the bauxite mines.

Back in the clubhouse, after more tea, more stories, more upper middle-class women (dressed meticulously for the final day of *puja*) peeping into the hall and hundreds of photographs taken by a stream of visitors from the neighbourhood, Mahua'ji asked me to bring out my camera and my recorder. She wanted to sing their folk songs about Mahishasur for us. She asked Rukmini, Budhmanya and her sisters to sit around her. And together they began to sing a ditty to the brave king Mahishasur – about how he ruled, how he fought and how he fell. They sang with their eyes closed in front of the blinking red lights of our cameras, phones and recorders. For once, the pulsating *dhak* and the droning *shanai* from the *pandal* downstairs faded as the poignant melody of the song echoed through the hall.

When they had finished, the Marwari man came up to me and said, 'Do you use WhatsApp? Please send me your video, your camera is HD quality no? I want to put it up on Facebook!' Clearly, despite the divergent and, to some, blasphemous politics of the Asur people, they had seamlessly become part of the world of novelties that the Durga *puja* festival lays out annually for zealous visual consumption.

Blasphemy or inclusivity: Ripples from the centre to the margins

In this chapter I present two versions of Hinduism. The more overtly political version is striving to create a homogenous tradition that is in conflict with other religious traditions; the other is marked by a tendency to include the other unto itself. The Asurs, with their conflicting agenda of assimilation and ethnicisation, are negotiating both these versions of dominant Hinduism.

The growing ideals of ethnicisation, as we see in the 'Asura pride' movement, have led to public celebrations of a hitherto remote, rural tradition in the heart of the nation. The social movements, with their multifaceted goals of political and cultural resistance, had directly provoked the BJP, leading to allegations of blasphemy from the Hindu right wing and their sympathisers. As this attempt to homogenise Hinduism into a monolithic system has not yet succeeded, however, the minister's provocative speech failed to create the kind of outrage that would lead to a complete repression or silencing. What we saw instead was an attempt to create both peace and publicity by precisely negotiating and reclaiming that which was deemed unsayable.

Smriti Irani's challenge to Bengalis to discuss the issue of Mahishasur *puja* in the streets of Kolkata was clearly met by this small neighbourhood. Unlike most major clubs in the city these days, it was not clear whether the smaller FE Block club was patronised by any particular political party. While some of them may well be BJP sympathisers, the members of the FE Block *puja* appear to hold allegiance to different political parties. However, their version of what constitutes Hinduism or goddess worship is strikingly different from what Smriti Irani assumed.

It is not a completely unfounded idea that lay Bengali Hindus know and accept the fact that their gods and goddesses are somebody else's demons.[20] The best example of this appears in the nationalist poet Michael Madhusudan Dutta's rewriting of the epic *Ramayana*, which identifies Ravana as a tragic hero and Rama as a shrewd, manipulative villain. Michael is not only a much-loved poet: he is also seen by Bengalis as a true patriot. Moreover, an excerpt showing the tragic portrayal of Ravana's virtue vis-à-vis Ram's Machiavellian persona from the *Meghnad Badh* epic is part of the secondary school curriculum in West Bengal.

This acceptance, and even celebration, of contradictory versions of mythology is by no means peculiar to Bengal. Several instances of traditions that contradict the type of Hinduism practised in the north Indian Hindi heartland abound in other regions. For example, Sitaram Yechuri, the Communist Party of India (Marxist) leader, pointed out in Parliament as a response to Irani's diatribe that Malayalis's major festival Onam celebrates the return of the valiant *asur* Mahabali, tricked into submission and death by Vishnu disguised as a Brahmin *vamana* (dwarf) (Vincent 2016).

Both the academic scholarship and popular practices of Hinduism have repeatedly shown that it is practised in diverse, regional, esoteric and sometimes even contradictory versions. Yet the challenge of Hindu nationalism has been to establish the opposite: that there is a unified, monolithic, grand narrative of Hinduism. They have tried to accomplish this in terms of the televised epics (Rajagopal 2001), Advani's *rath yatra* (Davis 1996) or the mobilisation of other religio-political symbols during Ayodhya (Van der Veer 1992; Panikkar 1993) and after. In a similar vein the Akshardham temple complexes in different parts of north India, completed in the 2000s, were seen as an attempt not only to create 'the

Vatican of Hinduism', but also to 'narrate the nation' (Singh 2010, 52) as a story of Hindu civilisation.

Smriti Irani's passionate speech addressed an abstract, pan-Indian Hindu offended by the twin blasphemies of demon-worship and sexualisation of the goddess. But neither the sexualisation of the goddess nor the divergent practice of Mahishasur *puja* created any ruckus in Kolkata. Even though several major national and local newspapers reported this event, it did not even attract the kind of massive crowd that any medium-scale club boasts of in Kolkata. The acceptance of this event was partly because the larger narrative of Hindu nationalism is incommensurate in the regional context of the east and the south of India. These regions are not only characterised by linguistic and cultural diversity; they also have their regional version of both Hinduism and cultural nationalism.

However, this does not mean that the regional version of cultural nationalism does not derive from their predominantly Hindu identity. As we saw in the case of the FE Block Durga *puja*, Ray repeatedly claimed that 'there is no contradiction in Hinduism'. In the end Ravana surrenders to Ram; Durga offers *barabhay* (security and blessing) to Mahishasur. The resolution of this contradiction means the co-option of divergent practices under the dominant narrative of Brahminical Hinduism. From his study of pre-modern Hinduism, Hacker uses the term 'inclusivism' to identify this tendency. He defines inclusivism in this way:

> [Inclusivism is] the practice of claiming for, and thus including in one's own religion or world-view, what belongs in reality to another foreign or competing system. It is a subordinating identification of the other ... The other, the foreign is not seen as something that could be added to, or combined with one's own system: instead, it is something a priori contained in it (Quoted by Halbfass 1988, 411).

In this case, we are faced with a variant of Brahminical Hinduism which, as the dominant mode, will extend its toleration to the deviant one even as Durga offers her blessing to the fallen Mahishasur. While Irani's call tries to stir up an affective reaction of offended outrage in the face of a divergent tradition, the strategy of the Durga-worshippers at FE Block has been to claim it as part of their own tradition. Whatever contradiction there may have been has been eradicated by citing Brahminical sources to assert that Durga did not even kill Mahishasur. On the one hand, this can be seen as the labour of peacekeeping. On the other hand, it reinstates the hierarchical relationship that caste minority intellectuals and activists seek to overhaul, in the interest of social justice and at the cost of a political struggle.

Conclusion

This chapter followed a blasphemy controversy from the Indian Parliament to the suburbs of Kolkata that resulted from a nationwide controversy after experiencing its climax on newspaper headlines and airwaves. It follows the ripples of a controversy that travelled from the Indian Parliament to a small neighbourhood in a city and then on to an Adivasi village. This case shows that there is a conflict between the Hindu nationalists and lay Hindus in different parts of the country over the essential understanding of what it means to be Hindu. This conflict becomes crucial in a blasphemy accusation because lay Hindus appear to resist the ideological persuasions of Hindutva.

However, this case study does not reveal a simple antithesis between Hindus and Hindu nationalists. Instead it shows a polyphony of discourses of different groups with varying, sometimes contradictory, political interests. On the one hand this case reflects the agenda of Hindu nationalists: in seeking to create a hegemonic narrative of Hinduism, they were led to accuse the ritual and narrative, framed by Adivasi rights activists, as blasphemy. Meanwhile the elite Bengali Hindus appeared to work with the notion of inclusivism and 'peace-keeping' that so often characterises Hinduism as practised in South Asia and beyond. However, other caste minority rights activists saw this politics of inclusivism not as peacekeeping, but rather as an insidious attempt to suppress dissent so that their place in the caste hierarchy can be maintained. Moreover, individual members of the indigenous community, the most vulnerable group in this debate, used this event as a platform to gain media attention about the lack of infrastructure in their village, their pride in their indigenous way of life and, finally, financial support from the civil society.

And so we return to the Foucauldian scheme of censorship as generative (Kaur and Mazzarella 2009). While this case illustrates the negotiations in modern governmentality, it also breaks the binary between the transgressive word and the anti-intellectual censor by showing the multiplicity of ideological positions and political interests that jostle as the discourse proliferates from the centre of the nation to its margins. The act of censorship from the BJP, itself embroiled in the politics of creating a media spectacle, fails to contain the transgressive demon-worship. The discourse of inclusivism among lay Hindus, which is placed as a contradiction to the act of censorship, ironically comes the closest to containing the transgressive. Yet it fails to contain fully the desire to transgress – and a keen vigilance against these strategies of co-option among indigenous and Bahujan activists – that makes this alleged case of 'demon-worship' overflow every act of containment.

Notes

1. Irrespective of the claims of an unbroken tradition, my research shows that Adivasis (indigenous peoples) of contemporary Jharkhand do not venerate Mahishasur in any obvious way.
2. Savarna (literally, those with a *varna*, i.e. those accepted within the Hindu fold) is a term popularly used in popular discourse, primarily by caste minority activists and their supporters, to identify '*jatis*', meaning communities which are/were not untouchable and which, some of whom despite their non-Brahmin status, have socio-political and economic leverage in everyday life.
3. Ironically the Communist Party of India (Marxist) demanded the arrest of Smriti Irani on charges of 'blasphemy' given the prohibition on inflammatory statements about any religious figure (Shrivastava 2016). The Communist Party of India (Marxist) issued a statement in which it declared: 'Anything inflammatory about any God, Prophet, if any member, especially the Minister is speaking, it will not be taken. We want the minister to be arrested and charged. Anything blasphemous should not be said in this house'.
4. Cow slaughter is prohibited by law in most states in India because of the religious sentiments held by upper caste Hindus about the sacredness of the cow. This makes Muslims' and Dalits' practice of consuming beef volatile and contentious (Chigateri 2011).
5. For details of Kanhaiya Kumar's arrest, see 'The FIR filed by Delhi Police in sedition case' (*Indian Express* 2016).
6. Theme *pandal*: A format of Durga *puja* in Kolkata in which an installation is created on the basis of a single theme – either a concept or a material – in order to display the goddess in public spaces. For a detailed understanding see Tapati Guha-Thakurta's detailed account of artists and designers in the Durga *puja* industry of Kolkata (Guha-Thakurta 2015).
7. Silje Einarsen notes how the Benaresi youth embrace the revelry of the Bengali style '*pandal puja*' while the elders of the community prefer the traditional *Ramlila* (Einarsen 2018b).
8. For examples, see televised Mahalaya programme (https://www.youtube.com/watch?v=AI-ugz0q1_SM) and an animated series on Mahishasur (https://www.youtube.com/watch?v=T-bFcDxuDK3o).
9. The interview revealed that even though this goddess has no relationship to Asurs, the organisers wanted to highlight the interconnectedness of these two groups.
10. "राक्षस or *rakshasa* refers to a range of things: *rakṣasa* (myth.), meaning the member of a non-Aryan, anthropophagous race of India, a *rakshas(a)*; a cannibal; (facet.) a glutton (Biswas 1982, 907).
11. Since I could not find any of these prejudiced neighbours, nor anyone who aired these opinions in public, I could not verify Ray's point. It is possible that he exaggerated people's prejudice to make a case for the philanthropic work that his peers had done to destigmatise an indigenous community.
12. For a journalistic story based on the Asur communities of northern Bengal see 'Meet the Asurs – a marginal tribe that describes Durga as a goddess who enticed Mahishasur' (Pandey and Biswas 2016).
13. It remains unclear to me who this Asur is.
14. Birendra Krishna Bhadra (1905–91), an Indian broadcaster, playwright, actor, reciter and theatre director from Kolkata, is known best for a Sanskrit recitation throughout a two-hour audio programme, *Mahishashura Mardini* (Annihilator/Destroyer of Mahisasur) in 1931. This collection of shlokas and songs was broadcast by All India Radio Calcutta. It is popularly believed that Bhadra reads from *Chandipurana*.
15. https://www.youtube.com/watch?v=q3Ruw1UpNQM.
16. 'To give *pushpanjali*' is a ritual involving the offering of a handful of flowers in devotion or worship. It is typically accompanied by the chanting of mantras, guided by a priest (Biswas 1982, 654).
17. A particular sign made with the fingers, indicating the granting of desire and the assurance of safety (Biswas 1982, 721).
18. She has travelled all over India to speak at Ambedkarite platforms and has visited JNU every year – not only to speak at Mahishasur martyrdom day, but also in academic conferences alongside historians at the Centre for Historical Studies. Together with professors, she has published her thoughts in poetry and prose. She is working on transliterating the lost Asuri script in Devanagari and writing the history of the Asur community at a project housed at the University of Bangalore.

19. This interview was conducted by my partner Knut Aukland, a researcher in the study of religion, specialising in Hinduism and Jainism.
20. Besides, assertions such as '*jato mat tato path*' (as many opinions as there are paths), '*jei Ram, shei Rahim*' (Ram and Rahim are the same) are commonly used by Bengali Hindus when they discuss different traditions of goddess worship in north and south India.

References

ANI. 2016, February 25. 'Opposition reacts sharply to Smriti Irani linking "Mahishasur Martyrdom Day" to JNU row', Diligent Media Corporation. http://www.dnaindia.com/india/report-opposition-reacts-sharply-to-smriti-irani-linking-mahishasur-martyrdom-day-to-jnu-row-2182436. Accessed 1 April 2016.

Banerjee, Prathama. 2006. *Politics of Time: 'Primitives' and History-writing in a Colonial Society*. New York: Oxford University Press.

Baviskar, Amita. 2005. 'Adivasi encounters with Hindu nationalism in MP.' *Economic and Political Weekly*: 5105–13.

Bhattacharjee, Manash Firaq. 2017. 'Hindutva, Delhi University and the violent binaries of nationalism.' *The Wire*, 22 February 2017. https://thewire.in/education/violent-binaries-nationalism-ramjas-abvp. Accessed 2 October 2018.

Biswas, Premankur and Prashant Pandey. 2016. 'Meet the Asurs – a marginal tribe that describes Durga as a goddess who enticed Mahishasur.' *The Indian Express*, 8 December 2016. https://indianexpress.com/article/india/india-news-india/meeting-the-asurs-a-marginal-tribe-in-eastern-india/. Accessed 3 March 2019.

Biswas, Sailendra. 1982. *Samsad Bengali-English Dictionary*. Calcutta: Sahitya Samsad.

Boyer, D., 2003. 'Censorship as a vocation: The institutions, practices, and cultural logic of media control in the German Democratic Republic.' *Comparative Studies in Society and History* 45 (3): 511–45.

Carrithers, Michael. 2000. 'On polytropy: Or the natural condition of spiritual cosmopolitanism in India: The Digambar Jain case.' *Modern Asian Studies* 34 (4): 831–61.

Chandra, Uday. 2016. 'Intimate antagonisms: Adivasis and the state in contemporary India', in *Indigeneity on the Move: Varying Manifestations of a Contested Concept*, Gerharz et al., eds, 221–39. New York: Berghahn Books.

Chatterjee, Partha. 1994. 'Secularism and toleration.' *Economic and Political Weekly* 29: 1768–77.

Chattopadhyay, Swati. 2008. 'Contours of the obscene, architectures of the visible.' *Third Text* 22: 769–85.

Chigateri, Shraddha. 2011. 'Negotiating the "sacred" cow: Cow slaughter and the regulation of difference in India', in *Democracy, Religious Pluralism and the Liberal Dilemma of Accommodation*, Monica Mookherjee, ed, 137–60. Dordrecht: Springer Netherlands.

Davis, Richard H. 1996. 'The iconography of Rama's chariot', in *Contesting the Nation: Religion, Community, and the Politics of Democracy in India*, David Ludden, ed, 27–54. Philadelphia: University of Pennsylvania Press.

De la Cadena, Marisol and Orin Starn. 2007. *Indigenous Experience Today*. Oxford; New York: Berg.

Einarsen, Silje. 2018a. *Doctoral dissertation on Devi Mahatmeya*. Submitted to the University of Aarhus.

Einarsen, Silje. 2018b. 'Navaratri in Benaras: Narrative structures and social realities', in *Nine Nights of the Goddess: The Navaratri Festival in South Asia*, Caleb Simmons et al. eds, 139–56. New York: SUNY Press.

Foucault, Michel. 1984. *The Foucault Reader*. Paul Rabinow, ed, 301–39. New York: Pantheon Books.

Ghosh, Kaushik. 2006. 'Between global flows and local dams: Indigenousness, locality, and the transnational sphere in Jharkhand, India.' *Cultural Anthropology* 21: 501–34.

Guha, Ranajit. 1994. 'The prose of counter-insurgency', in *Culture/Power/History: A Reader in Contemporary Social Theory*, Nicholas B. Dirks, Geoff Eley, Sherry B. Ortner, eds, 336–71. Princeton: Princeton University Press.

Guha-Thakurta, Tapati. 2004. 'From spectacle to "art": The changing aesthetics of Durga *Puja* in contemporary Calcutta.' *Art India*, Vol. 1X: 34–56.

Guha-Thakurta, Tapati. 2015. *In the Name of the Goddess: The Durga Pujas of Contemporary Kolkata*. Kolkata: Primus Books.

Halbfass, Wilhelm. 1988. *India and Europe*. New York: State University of New York Press.

Indian Express. 2016. 'The FIR filed by Delhi Police in sedition case', 17 February 2016. http://indianexpress.com/article/india/india-news-india/kanhaiya-kumar-arrest-the-fir-filed-by-delhi-police-in-sedition-case/#sthash.qmagBVNO.dpuf. Accessed 29 December 2016.

Jaffrelot, Christophe. 1993. 'Hindu nationalism: Strategic syncretism in ideology building.' *Economic and Political Weekly*: 517–24.

Kaur, Raminder and William Mazzarella. 2009. *Censorship in South Asia: Cultural Regulation from Sedition to Seduction*. Bloomington: Indiana University Press.

Kovacs, Anja. 2004. 'You don't understand, we are at war! Refashioning Durga in the service of Hindu nationalism.' *Contemporary South Asia* 13 (4): 373–88.

Lal, Ratnakar. 2014. 'King Mahishasur's Martyrdom', in *Forward Press*, 6–8. New Delhi: Forward Press.

McDermott, Rachel Fell. 2011. *Revelry, Rivalry, and Longing for the Goddesses of Bengal: The Fortunes of Hindu Festivals*. New York: Columbia University Press.

Oskarsson, Patrik. 2010. 'The law of the land contested: Bauxite mining in tribal, central India in an age of economic reform.' PhD dissertation submitted to, and published by, the School of International Development, University of East Anglia.

Panikkar, K. N. 1993. 'Religious symbols and political mobilisation: The agitation for a mandir at Ayodhya.' *Social Scientist* 21: 63–78.

Pinney, Christopher. 2009. 'Iatrogenic religion and culture', in *Censorship in South Asia: Cultural Regulation from Sedition to Seduction*, in Raminder Kaur and William Mazzarella, eds, 29–62. Bloomington: Indiana University Press.

PTI. 2017. 'Will build Grand Ram Temple if BJP wins majority, says Party's UP Chief. ' *The Wire*, 24 January 2017. https://thewire.in/politics/will-build-ram-temple-bjp-majority-up-chief. Accessed 24 February 2017.

Rajagopal, Arvind. 2001. *Politics after Television: Hindu Nationalism and the Reshaping of the Public in India*. Cambridge: Cambridge University Press.

Ranjan, Pramod. 2016. *Mahishasur: A People's Hero*. New Delhi: Forward Press Publications.

Roy, Indrajit. 2015. 'The imaginary of the Mulnibasi in West Bengal', in *The Politics of Caste in West Bengal*, Kenneth Bo Nielsen et al., eds, 169–92. New Delhi: Routledge.

Ruud, Arild Engelsen. 2001. 'Talking dirty about politics: A view from a Bengali village', in *The Everyday State and Society in Modern India*, C. J. Fuller and Veronique Benei, eds, 115–36. New Delhi: Social Science Press.

Sen, Moumita. 2018. 'Politics, religion and art in the Durga *Puja* of West Bengal', in *Nine Nights of the Goddess: The Navaratri Festival in South Asia*, Caleb Simmons et al., eds, 105–20.

Sen, Moumita. 'The Mahishasur Movement online: A precarious network of 'demon-followers', *Journal of Media, Religion, and Digital Culture* 8.1 (2019): 105–31, Special Issue: 'Religious Controversies'.

Shah, Alpa. 2014. 'Religion and the secular left: Subaltern studies, Birsa Munda and Maoists.' *Anthropology of this Century* 9.

Shrivastava, Rahul. 2016. 'Smriti Irani row leaves Rajya Sabha truce over bills in tatters', NDTV.com. http://www.ndtv.com/india-news/fate-of-bills-uncertain-as-government-opposition-fight-over-smriti-irani-comment-1281450. Accessed 7 April 2016.

Simmons, Caleb, Moumita Sen and Hillary Rodrigues eds, 2018. *Nine Nights of the Goddess: The Navaratri Festival in South Asia*. New York: SUNY Press.

Singh, Kavita. 2010. 'The Temple of Eternal Return: Swaminarayan Akshardham complex in Delhi.' *Artibus Asiae* 70: 47–76.

Skaria, Ajay. 1997. 'Shades of wildness tribe, caste, and gender in Western India.' *Journal of Asian Studies* 56: 726–45.

Spivak, Gayatri Chakravorty. 1985. 'Scattered speculations on the question of value.' *Diacritics* 15: 73.

Taylor, McComas. 2014. 'Hindu activism and academic censorship in India.' *South Asia: Journal of South Asian Studies* 37: 717–25.

Van Der Veer, Peter. 1992. 'Ayodhya and Somnath: Eternal shrines, contested histories.' *Social Research* 59 (1): 85–109.

Van der Veer, Peter. 1994. 'Syncretism, multiculturalism and the discourse of tolerance', in *Syncretism/Anti-syncretism: The Politics of Religious Synthesis*, Charles Stewart and Rosalind Shaw, eds, 180–200. London: Routledge.

Varghese, Anil. 2016. 'Attempts made to trick Asurs into worshipping Durga.' *Forward Press*. https://www.forwardpress.in/2016/10/efforts-to-trick-asurs-into-worshipping-durga-repelled/. Accessed 5 October 2016.

Venu, M. K. 2017. 'RSS Chief's call for National Cow Protection Law echoes a familiar pattern.' *The Wire*, 10 April 2017.

Vincent, Pheroze L. 2016. 'Footnote to fabled story on Indira.' *The Telegraph*, 27 February 2016. Kolkata.

7
The languages of truth: Saints, judges and the fraudulent in a Pakistani court

Asad Ali Ahmed

Introduction

'Pretender saint repents', 'Furore over Quranic verses' and 'Daler Mehndi's Song Offends' were the subheadings from a popular feature in *The Friday Times*, Lahore's English language weekly that serves English-speaking liberals.[1] The column entitled 'Nuggets from the Urdu Press' collects, translates and summarises news items from Pakistan's Urdu dailies and innocently disclaims:

> These nuggets are culled from the Urdu press. They are summarised here without comment. True or false, absurd or ridiculous, TFT [*The Friday Times*] takes no responsibility for them.[2]

As far as *The Friday Times* and its predominantly liberal readership were concerned, not only was the Urdu press obsessed with 'blasphemy', but the translation and summarisation of these stories was itself sufficient to demonstrate their absurdity. 'Nuggets' also suggests that these were especially choice examples drawn from rich seams of material, extracted from subterranean currents of irrationality and superstition that coursed through the social body. For the urban[e] liberal readership of *The Friday Times*, these stories index backwardness, the uneducated or insufficiently educated, marking an uneven and inadequate modernity. 'Nuggets' was a popular feature, and I must confess that I, and many others I knew from the English-reading public, enjoyed these purportedly unmediated accounts. The act of reading, the pleasure of encountering and consuming alterity as 'absurd and ridiculous', enables one to inhabit and reinscribe a subject position crucial to the construction of identity and difference, and to the maintenance of social hierarchies where, if broad generalisations are permitted, 'English' marks liberal and cosmopolitan and 'Urdu' indexes conservative, religious and nationalist.[3]

> ### Pretender saint repents
>
> According to daily *Jang*, the *jaali pir* (fake saint) of Nankana Sahib repented of the crime of changing the *kalima* and claiming that he talked to angel Jibrael and the various Prophets of Islam. The people gathered around him and forced him to wed his wife again after he had repented.
>
> From *The Friday Times*, 25–31 May 2001; Vol. XIII (13): 8.

Attitudes towards 'blasphemy' were regarded as the definitive maker of this difference. In a social and religious field marked by considerable variety, certain signs, acts and utterances become marked as dangerous and suspect. Often blasphemy allegations come to public attention through newspaper reports, and many subsequently result in criminal charges.[4] Commenting on the coverage of blasphemy cases, the editor of one national English language daily informed me that it was the paper's editorial policy to give the minimum required coverage to blasphemy – a policy shared with many other English-language papers. In contrast the Urdu press, and in particular the Punjab-based Urdu press, gave substantial and often provocative coverage to such cases. 'It is,' the editor observed, 'as if the English and Urdu presses are coming out of different countries.'[5]

This linguistic, social and political cleavage is something that Rajagopal, in the Indian context, has described as 'split publics' (Rajagopal 2001). While these explicit ideological differences, premised on a language divide, are sharp, I would like to suggest that, irrespective of language, there are commonalities to reportage: presumptions and practices about fact finding; what counts as evidence; the premise of objectivity; and the function and nature of language and communication. While social and political ideologies that mark 'liberal' and 'conservative' as oppositional are often highlighted, it is the shared epistemological practices and language ideologies that traverse professional groups such as journalists and – especially – the judiciary that is the focus of this chapter.[6]

The Friday Times' disclaimer of commentary, and by implication mediation, assumes that processes of translation and summarisation, from Urdu into English, are sufficient to enable the objective evaluation of these stories as 'True or False'.[7] This is indicative of a language ideology in which the function of language is largely understood as communicating statements about the world, statements that can be evaluated as true or false. The addition of 'absurd or ridiculous', however, suggests that the Urdu press and public may inhabit a different world – one of radical epistemological alterity, opaque to rational scrutiny and where these conditions of truth and falsity may not hold: in truth, 'a different country'. This presumption of separate and incommensurable social, moral and epistemological universes, indexed by different languages, is one that I would like to subject to critical scrutiny. I suggest that the production of this presumed incommensurability in part derives from linguistic and textual ideologies that regard translation, inscription and reportage as seamless, transparent and unmediated processes. On the contrary, a focus on these processes may help in understanding how the absurd and ridiculous, the false and the fraudulent – and indeed the blasphemer and apostate – can emerge and crystallise from these mediating practices.

To anticipate, I suggest that the key difference is not the one so apparent between literate Urdu- and English-speaking publics. To be sure they may differ in their moral hierarchies of value, explicit political stances and social ideologies, but professional groups such as journalists and the judiciary have much in common. That is, assumptions and conventions in relation to description, evidence and fact finding are a result of the organising practices, premised and constitutive of a positivist methodology, that shape both the judicial and journalistic professions.[8] Because they are shared, they often go unremarked.

The more significant difference, I suggest, is between these groups and social actors who are principally located in diverse traditions – for example, in the diverse range of thought broadly characterised as 'Sufism'. These alternative traditions have epistemologies, practices and social ideologies at variance in key respects with those central to modern professional social groups such as journalists and judges – a variance that is highlighted in the legal encounter. Journalists and judges, despite obvious differences, share common practices. Both are engaged in transforming narratives and contexts into particular kind of texts – ones that involve fact finding, reporting, inscribing speech and evaluating words and witnesses with respect to credibility. The most pronounced difference, to state the obvious, is that the judiciary seeks to arrive at truth, or at least actionable approximations, that enable legal judgement and the attribution of guilt and innocence.

These shared linguistic and textual ideologies and practices, of journalists and judiciary, are formative of a positivist epistemology and a regime of truth – one that is thrown into relief when encountering epistemological and ontological alterity. In the Pakistani context this often is the encounter with Pirs and Sufis (Rozehnal 2006, 2010; Ewing 1983, 1984a, 1984b, 1997). The latter do not necessarily subscribe to these ideas of language or secular positivist knowledge, and consequently have differing notions of the nexus of language, truth and self (Ewing 1997). They do not share a liberal ontology of the self as monadic and autonomous.

I discovered during fieldwork in 2000–1 that a considerable number of Pirs and Sufis had recently been charged under Pakistan's various blasphemy laws.[9] The most infamous and high-profile case was that of Muhammad Yousaf Ali, who was charged with claiming to be a Prophet – claiming, in fact, to be the Prophet Muhammad. Specifically the charge was that he said 'Ana Muhammad' (I am Muhammad), declared his family members to be *Ahl-e-Bayt* (Family of the Prophet) and some of his *murids* (spiritual devotees) to be *Sahaba-e-Rasul* (Companions of the Prophet).[10] For Muslims, any claim to prophetic revelation or prophetic status is regarded as heresy.[11] Even the use of some religious terms can be contentious, as some people hold that particular terms are exclusively reserved for the Holy Prophet's family and Companions.[12] In addition to the blasphemy charge, Shaykh Yousaf Ali was accused of financial extortion and sexual impropriety – charges that are common with respect to 'Pirs' in Pakistan.[13] In short, his accusers claimed that he was a charismatic religious charlatan and cult leader whose fraudulent claim to be similar to, or to be, the Prophet Muhammad was used to extort financial and sexual favours from his devoted and deluded followers.

The criminal charges against Muhammad Yousaf Ali were instigated in March 1997 by the *Tehrik-e-Khatm-e-Nabuwaat* (Finality of Prophethood Movement) in Lahore, in alliance with a daily newspaper called *Khabrian* (The News). These two groups have been at the forefront of many blasphemy allegations and charges, which often result from a combination of newspaper reports and subsequent mobilisation by various religious organisations. Despite considerable pressure from *Khabrian*, judicial reluctance led to delays. Many judges view blasphemy trials as problem cases, especially as they commonly attract considerable mobilisation by religious, often militant groups, leading to an atmosphere of palpable intimidation during proceedings. This was particularly evident at the time, as only a few years earlier a retired Lahore High Court judge was murdered for acquitting a young Christian.[14] Judges often deploy various stratagems to evade and shift responsibility for hearing these cases.

Consequently, the trial did not begin until three years later, when the Lahore High Court instructed the Sessions Judge of Lahore, Mian Mohammed Jahanghir, to hear the case. In one of those coincidences that affect one's entire fieldwork, the trial happened to start on 3 February 2000, the first day that I visited the courts in Lahore. I had arranged to meet my namesake, Asad Ali, a reporter from an English language daily who covered the 'law beat', there. He had promised to effect introductions with court personnel and familiarise me with the social and legal landscape. We spent an interesting morning at the civil courts exploring the various issues that plague the Pakistani judicial system: nepotism, corruption, the ability of lower court officials to create procedural delays; the inordinate case load that meant that civil cases could be inherited by the next generation; the lack of judges and their inadequate training; and even the spatial layout of the compound and how that created inefficiencies – in short all the characteristics that feature in various internationally and national commissioned reports on the judiciary in Pakistan.

We then shifted to the criminal courts, where we chanced upon a number of journalists who informed us that the blasphemy trial of Yousaf Ali was about to commence. I was somewhat surprised to hear of a case against a Sufi, as hitherto the predominant understanding in Pakistan was that the blasphemy laws were being used against minorities. Milling outside the courtroom were half a dozen journalists from wire services, Urdu papers and a couple of photojournalists. No reporters from the English press were present apart from Asad, who no longer covered the criminal law beat. However, given that he was there, he said he would report the bare facts if the judge had introduced the charges legally, commenting: 'In sensitive issues we do not report unsubstantiated allegations; only when it comes before the court can we state the allegations.' This policy, he explained, was the opposite of *Khabrian*, a paper that he and others believed to have been instrumental in bringing the case to court, publishing sensational and lurid allegations against the accused.

The efforts of Asad and the other journalists to report the facts were hindered, however, as the judge had barred all reporters and the public from entering the courtroom. They found this unusual, as none of them had been denied entry to trials before. But, as I soon discovered, this was part of the trial judge's precautionary and preventative measures to defuse tensions and diminish the scope for potential conflagrations.

These included prohibiting demonstrations within the court compound, discouraging media coverage of the case and insisting that only a court authorised summary of the day's proceedings could be published. More significantly, as far as I was concerned, is that the judge continued to treat the proceedings as if they were *in camera*, thereby barring media and the public from attending.[15]

After the first few hearings, when I managed to enter with the help of lawyers, I too was barred from the courtroom. Despite attempts to negotiate access I was unsuccessful, and therefore had to arrange interviews with the contesting parties to keep track of developments. However, I was soon confronted by one of *Khabrian's* senior editors and trial witness, Mian Abdul Ghaffar. He refused to accept that my research was a legal anthropology of blasphemy accusations and trials, suggesting instead that I was an American spy and informing me that his reporters would keep an eye on my activities.[16] I had subsequently no option but to interview the defendants and rely upon them for primary information. Yousaf Ali declined to meet me, but deputed one of his foremost *murids* (spiritual devotees), Zayd Zaman Hamid, as my principal interlocutor.[17]

As the trial proceeded, I continued to meet with the defence to keep abreast of developments. Being excluded from the court meant that I was unable to follow the witness testimony or legal arguments, relying instead on the transcripts of the proceedings. But these were far from transparent and I had to re-contextualise the transcript, with the defence's help. This led me to ask what framing conventions, acts of translation and methods of inscription had been central to its production, and to what extent were these mediating practices significant. The defence team, and Zayd Hamid in particular, would attempt to clarify the various ambiguities, opaque references and translation errors in the transcript that to my mind depicted Yousaf Ali as evasive, shifting and strange. While Zayd remained optimistic of an acquittal I was not sure that the transcripts warranted such optimism, as his contextual clarifications formed no part of the legal record. As far as the judiciary and the wider reading public were concerned, it was only the judicial record that mattered.

Language and textual ideologies in legal process

In Pakistani courts, proceedings are conducted in a mixture of English, Urdu and the local vernacular – in this instance, Punjabi.[18] Facility in English marks the postcolonial elite and this is reflected in the hierarchies of the court system, where English remains the ranking language.[19]

Command over and fluency in English was – and arguably remains – one of the most important factors in determining suitability for the appellate judiciary. The lower and trial court judges, however, were for the most part primarily Urdu-speaking and their expertise in English varied considerably. Nonetheless, one of the trial judge's most important tasks is to translate witness testimony from the vernacular into a form of postcolonial English legalese. This 'translation' is typed by the stenographer and becomes the official court transcript while another official, the Reader, transcribes the proceedings in Urdu by hand. The English transcript is the record of priority, and it is this to which the judge refers when writing the judgement. The Urdu record can be consulted for additional clarification when necessary.

During the course of a trial the various documents or text-artifacts (Silverstein and Urban 1996, 1–6) that are produced before, or generated by, the court – from the initial First Information Report (FIR) through to the judgement – are collated into what is known as the 'paper book'.[20] When a sentence is appealed the paper book forms the case repository examined by the High Court. Although the High Courts can call witnesses and even re-try a case, it is extremely rare for them to do so. Barring the occasional exception, appeals are decided by hearing counsel's arguments in relation to the textual material generated during the judicial process. The trial judge has therefore to ground and support his decision and argument in relation to these text-artifacts. In cases of language crimes, such as blasphemy, hate speech, defamation and sedition, the record of the trial and the testimony of the witnesses as sedimented in the trial transcripts are the most significant part.[21] This is because conceptually 'blasphemy' is a verbal transgression, and consequently the manner of its inscription into legal documents and subsequent interpretation is of crucial import when it comes to determining culpability – judgement often depended on who was believed.[22]

In many of the blasphemy cases I encountered, including that of Yousaf Ali, the principal allegation arose out of an oral exchange between two individuals – at times there were no other witnesses.[23] Defendants rarely denied that they had been involved in a verbal encounter, but they usually contested either what was said, its interpretation or whether it amounted to a legal offence. From the initial verbal exchange to the judge's final pronouncement, such cases involve meta-linguistic commentary on the utterance, meaning and context of various offending words.

Narration and reporting of cause, event and intention are general features of criminal trials, such as for cases of theft, bodily harm or homicide. But in these cases there is some relation between witness narrative and an independent external material entity, or evidential object.[24] In such cases the statements of the various witnesses can usually be indexed to an external entity, whether this is a stolen object, a physical injury or a dead body. These 'objects' generate their own forms of evidence, forensic or otherwise. By contrast, in linguistic crimes, the 'evidence' is primarily self-referring – the words are the 'objects' under dispute – and there may be no external non-discursive forensic evidence.[25]

These cases thus depend to a far greater degree on the conventions and practices of reporting and inscribing the allegedly offensive utterances. Such cases, I argue, are therefore extraordinarily susceptible and sensitive to conventions and practices that transform an interactional verbal encounter into various forms of documentation. Processes of translation and inscription of witness testimony into a legal text-artifact that records the interactional real-time encounter, the 'transcript', are highly significant. A 'transcript' implies a verbatim record – that is, a precise, neutral and transparent representation. As such it is one of the most critical documents in grounding judgement. But the text-artifact produced by courts in Pakistan, which I will continue to refer to as a 'transcript', is far from a verbatim record (Walker 1986).[26] Nonetheless, the textual and language ideologies of the judiciary understand the transcript as a transparent document – at least to legal professionals.

Regnant ideas about the nature and function of language – that is, both of language ideologies and processes of translation, transcription and documentation, what Silverstein has called 'entextualisation' – are of greater consequence in such trials and demand critical attention (Silverstein and Urban 1996; Philips 1998; Riles 2006).[27] The predominant understanding of language among lawyers and the judiciary is of language as referential. In this context, language is understood primarily as descriptive of an independent reality whose function is to communicate propositional information between speaker and addressee – information that can be evaluated as true or false (Lee 1997; Duranti and Goodwin 1992).[28] In this functional and correspondent conception, language is thought of as exterior to reality, as a representational mirror (Rorty 1980). This propositional conception of language was pivotal to the utilitarian nineteenth-century project of codification, of which the Indian Penal Code is the most celebrated example (Ahmed 2010; Stokes 1959; Clive 1975; Chan et al. 2011).

The crucial relationship between language and legal ideologies that underpin codification I have explored elsewhere.[29] It is, however, important to note that the language ideology that informs legal process can, to use John Austin's terms, be understood as 'constative'. Austin critiqued this view as he recognised that language as a social medium was not simply about description, but also about active social action: that is, we are doing things with words. In opposition to constative he emphasised the performative aspects of language (Austin 1962).[30] Blasphemy, insults, hate speech and various other forms of offensive speech are performative speech-acts that can have consequential effects on the listeners – in Austin's terms, they are perlocutionary. Offensive speech can cause aggrieved sentiments and moral injury, and is therefore registered as a linguistic crime; as such, it is indicative of the limits and aporias to the propositional language ideology that underlies codification.

Blasphemy is a particularly glaring contradiction: not only is it performative and perlocutionary but it is also an offence against religion being tried by a secular criminal court (Ahmed, forthcoming). As many have noted, these transgressive words pose problems for legal professionals during trial as lawyers and judges often hesitate or refuse to repeat the alleged blasphemy for fear of reproducing the offence.[31] If the offending words are repeated, various ritual invocations to contain the baleful effects of such harmful speech are used (chapter 2). Thus while multiple language ideologies may exist in a social and legal setting, the law and its textual practices privilege referentiality.[32]

This language – and legal – ideology, insofar as these conceptions are encoded in laws such as the Indian Penal Code and its derivatives, are articulated to an ontological imaginary where the subject of the law is the rational, autonomous subject with command over language. That is, one is one's self through a particular regime of language, truth and self. One is presumed as simultaneously agentive and as a necessary corollary, also responsible, and hence culpable under criminal law. In court, an individual's credibility and integrity depends on establishing a coherent, consistent and verifiable narrative account.

Standard trial strategy involves undermining witness testimony by trying to ascertain or generate inconsistencies both within a witness's court testimony and between that testimony and earlier statements that form the documentary record (Matoesian 2001). In general, if a witness can be shown to be uncertain, ambiguous or, better still, inconsistent or contradictory, then counsel will consider the witness's testimony and credibility as potentially compromised. In the best-case scenario, the opposition witness would be undermined – or, as lawyers say in Pakistan, the witness's testimony and credibility is 'shattered'. The manner and process through which testimony – what the witness actually says – is 'translated' from the vernacular and 'transcribed' from the interactional real-time trial encounter into a legal text-artifact (the 'transcript') is therefore crucial.[33] I argue that while the legal, linguistic and textual ideologies and their corresponding practices and procedures leads to a valuing of propositional coherence, consistency and transparency, these are undermined by processes of entextualisation in Pakistani criminal courts. I will shortly illustrate this with examples from the trial of Muhammad Yousaf Ali. First, however, I highlight some of the conventions of translation and transcription that can introduce ambiguities, inconsistencies and even contradictions into a witness's testimony.[34] These are potentially problematic in all cases, but have intensified effects when it comes to linguistic crimes.

As translator, the judge is involved in both linguistic and social translation. Linguistic in that he translates from local languages into postcolonial English legalese, where the judge emphasises the referential, propositional and legal dimensions of a witness's statements as his primary objective is to establish the facts. This objective means his translation is rarely word for word: it is not a strict translation. Nor is it always a comparable English sentence that echoes the sense of the original vernacular statement. Often the judge produces a propositional paraphrase, that is, a statement in which emphasis is on distilling factual information from a witness's account.[35] Social translation occurs insofar as his paraphrasing leaves out much contextual and sociological information and inflections, which may be of less consequence when trying to establish causal relationships, a staple of criminal trials, but can be of greater significance when words – their factuality, inflection and interpretation – is what is at issue in the trial.[36] The polyvalent, figurative and social aspects of language – that is, the way in which words index identities, relationships and self-understanding – are either of secondary import or legally irrelevant; at times they complicate the requirements of referential clarity, consistency and causality.

Another problem is that of temporal or sequential punctuation (He 2017). That is, a witness is asked a question and replies in Urdu or Punjabi. The judge then translates the witness's response without necessarily being aware of its valence. His understanding emerges as the line of questioning and responses develop. However, he may or may not return and repair the earlier translation in the light of subsequent information. These sequential punctuations can contribute to disjointedness in the witness's narrative, particularly if the examining counsel changes tack and asks a different set of questions before returning to a previous line of questioning.[37]

A further problem with the transcript is that counsel's questions are usually not recorded. A form of legal short cut has developed in which the question is often folded into the witness's response. Technically this is a form of ellipsis. While at times the question can be inferred from the witness's response, in other instances, it is completely erased. The ellipsis and erasure of questions can be extremely problematic as the referential coherence of the witness's responses to questions can be lost.[38]

These practices of translation, sequential punctuation, erasure and ellipsis in the textual sedimentation of an interactional, real-time examination into a text-artifact can introduce ambiguities, inconsistencies and even contradictions into a witness's testimony. Nonetheless, the ideological and systemic requirement of a seamless coherent account is central for the representation of the examined subject and, critically, to his claims of speaking the truth. If any ambiguities, incoherencies or inconsistencies are left in the account, and I have suggested here that these could arise for a whole series of reasons integral to the production of the legal text, it can sunder the relationship between language, truth and self, and create anxiety regarding the moral probity of the witness.

The singular importance of testimony and the exclusively oral and discursive dimension of the case was recognised by the judge. He began his judgement with the following comment:

> Keeping in view the importance of this case the judgment is being written up in a different style because the evidence of both parties, oral in nature, is being reproduced in verbatim so that the Reader of this judgment should not feel the necessity to think as to what was the evidence on the basis of which the judgment had been passed.[39]

Apart from making manifest his verbatim or referential language ideology, the judge suggests that the general reader can make up his or her own mind on the basis of the text-artifact before them, much as a High Court judge might. The different style to which he alludes is the fact that the judgement includes the transcripts of prosecution and defence witnesses.[40]

Ambiguity and danger

The principal issue, the judge argued, was whether any Muslim could claim to be a Prophet, let alone to be the Prophet Muhammad. He further argued that the evidential requirements of such a case differed from the majority of criminal cases where witness testimony is compared for corrboration. In this case, and by implication blasphemy cases in general, he argued that the nature of the offence is indexed by the outraged feelings of the complainant. Consequently, the testimony of even a single witness would be sufficient for conviction. This favoured the prosecution case, as the defence case rested on the statement of the accused, the inconsistencies they had brought out in the prosecution testimony and a challenge to the legal admissibility of the supplementary evidence. The judge, however, chose for all intents and purposes to ignore the prosecution case and the burden of proof, emphasising instead the accused's statement as sufficient incriminatory evidence:[41]

> Now this aspect is worth examination that as to whether first of all the prosecution is to be taken up or the case against the accused on basis of his statements be examined first. Formally, it is the prosecution who has to prove its case. But here I prefer to take up the statements of the accused to examine his personality.[42]

Although it is not common practice for defendants to take the stand, as it risks inadvertently introducing incriminating corroboratory evidence, Yousaf Ali had testified in his own defence. The defence believed that his erudition and personality would be far superior to those of the prosecution witnesses, and that when the judge heard his explanations the allegations would be revealed as misunderstandings based on ignorance of Sufi thought. However, this strategy proved to be Yousaf Ali's undoing. The judge was able to dispense with the prosecution case, also beset by inconsistencies and ambiguities resulting from these same processes of entextualisation, and focus only on the seeming incoherences and contradictions between the accused's statement and his later responses under questioning. The judge read all the various ambiguities in the 'transcript' as evidence of 'concealment', 'deviousness' and 'double-meanings' on the defendant's part. In short, the defendant was convicted on his own testimony.

The question of whether the judge read the transcripts in bad faith, that is, in an instrumental and manipulative way, is one that can be raised in every case; the idea that judges have been 'bought' is a common charge in Pakistan.[43] It is not, however, my concern to read intent or motivation – this would simply reproduce the positivist methodology as well as a misplaced fidelity to questions of truth and individual culpability. My concern rather is with the forms of linguistic and legal mediation that enable such a reading.

One line of prosecution questioning was to show that Yousaf Ali's wealth was disproportionate to his income. It was alleged that by posing as a 'God-man' he had duped and extorted money from his followers, which he then used to purchase a house in an up-market area of Lahore called 'Defence'. His responses to the prosecution counsel's questions in the 'transcript' are as follows:

> *The residence bearing no 218-Q in the Defence is neither owned by me nor by my wife.* However, I had resided there. It is incorrect that my service was dismissed in the Defence.[44] Volunteers that I had resigned.[45] It is incorrect to suggest that I was dismissed from the services on basis of serious charges. As being the Captain, my Number in Defence services was PSS-11741. Volunteers that my name recorded in Defence services was 'Yousaf Ali Nadeem.' The house known as 'Jannat-e-Tayyaba'(Paradise of the Pure) was situated in 218-Q, the Defence, Lahore. It is incorrect that the said house was got purchased by Muhammad Ali Abubakar (Prosecution Witness). *It is correct that the above mentioned house has been sold. I have not sold this house but it has been sold by its owner. It is correct that the owner of the house was my wife.*[46] (emphasis added).

In the judgement the judge's gloss reads:

> About his residence bearing no 218.Q in the Defence, Lahore, he stated that it is neither owned by him nor by his wife but he had resided there. And about his name recorded in the service record, he stated that it was 'Yousaf Ali Nadeem' and that the house known as 'Jannat-e-Tayyaba' situated at 218-Q Defence, Lahore and later on admitted the owner of the house was his wife ... Meaning thereby he is in the habit of making contradictory statements.[47]

The judge argued that Yousaf Ali had been contradictory – that is, he first denied that he or his wife owned the house only to later admit that his wife had owned the property. Can the apparent contradiction vis-à-vis the ownership of the house be explained by the transcription/extextualisation process rather than disingenuousness on the accused's part?

In this section the first question to the witness can be inferred as, 'Do you own the house bearing 218 Q in Defense?' to which Yousaf Ali responded in the negative. The questioning then shifted to his record in the army. Somewhat later he is asked if the house had been sold and if it belonged to his wife. He responded affirmatively. This is the temporal and sequential punctuation problem I indicated earlier. The judge did not return to modify or clarify the earlier statement in light of the later answers.[48] Second, the erasure of the questions makes it seem that he is contradicting his earlier statement. It is clear the referential work performed by the questions would have made this segment of discourse coherent. The first question asked by counsel referred to a current state of affairs, and the tense is encoded in the accused's response. Since Yousaf Ali's wife no longer owned the house, his answer was correct. The later questions referred to a state of affairs *in the past*, to which he responded that she had been the owner and had sold the house. In short the key questions were of the sequence: Do you or your wife own the house? Has the house been sold? Did you sell it? Did it belong to your wife? To which his replies were No/Yes/No/Yes. This is but one example where the process of transcription has effectively created incoherences and seeming contradictions in the text-artifact. These then are read as signifying the witness's doubtful capacity for speaking the truth.[49]

Some of the key instances in the trial are indicative of these competing understandings of language, of an emphasis on literalness on the one hand and on polyvalence and metaphor on the other. Recall that the principal charge against Yousaf Ali was that he was understood as having claimed to be the Prophet Muhammad through saying 'Ana Muhammad' and that he used terminology, understood by some, as exclusively reserved for the Prophet, his Companions (*sahaba*) and family (*Ahl-e-Bayt*).[50] There were a number of arguments during the trial about the meaning of such terms and the legitimate use of religious terminology.

One seemingly minor but nonetheless significant instance was over Yousaf Ali's self-referential usage of 'faqir'. In the South Asian context 'faqir' generally refers to Sufi ascetics characterised by an attitude of extreme humility and explicitly unconcerned with the norms of public respectability. There is considerable variety and differentiation within the ambit of Sufism. Once when I asked an ascetic, who had also been charged under the blasphemy laws, whether he was a Sufi, he replied that he was a 'faqir'.[51] Elaborating on his view of the differences between faqirs and Sufis, he clearly saw himself as more authentically linked to the divine, as compared to Sufis, through his disregard for 'this-worldly' social norms.[52] By contrast, Yousaf Ali did not regard himself as a faqir, but as a Sufi attuned to the modern world. However, in legal correspondence documents attempting to signal his deference to the court, he had referred to himself as a 'faqir'. The judge noted what he considered to be an inconsistency between the humility associated with this term and what he took to be the self-aggrandisement of Yousaf Ali's repeated use of first person plural pronouns: ' … he repeatedly used the word "we" or "us" for himself, then how such a person can claim as "faqeer"' (*State v. Muhammad Yousaf Ali* 2000, 163).

The judge thus read the various statements in the English transcript as indicative of contradictions which, in his view, were further evidence of Yousaf Ali's duplicity and malign intent. The English transcript is confusing; only by reviewing the Urdu record and having familiarity with Sufi discourse is it possible to understand Yousaf Ali's contextual usage of the term 'faqir'.[53] That is, it signalled his supplicant status vis-à-vis the court, the theological distinctions he drew between faqir and Sufi and his simultaneous abnegation of the self – and therefore, in some contexts, of his usage of the first person plural.

Sufi mystical thought posits quite distinct conceptualisations of the relation between language, self and truth. The goal of a Sufi initiate is to unite with the divine presence through abjuring 'this-worldly' attachments. Crucial then is the overcoming of the self (*nafs*) that is expressive of an ego – an 'I', the existence of which continues to prevent the annhilation (*fana*) of the self and the ultimate goal of subsistence (*baqa*) in the divine. But this self-renunciation is a long and arduous path (*tariqa*); it requires submission to, guidance from and imitation of those further along that path.

Worldly attachments are, in a sense, constitutive of the self (*nafs*); they obscure (veil) one from God's proximity and love. It is only by divesting one's self that one becomes closer to God and one with God. Only love has the capacity to transform one's lower base self (*nafs*), so a key step on this spiritual journey is to cultivate love for, follow the conduct of, and eventually overcome one's self, through the instruction and example of one's spiritual guide (*murshid*). One's guide is in the same relation to the Prophet Muhammad, the perfect man (*insan-i-kamil*), the most beloved of God and manifestation of the divine. The ultimate aim is to overcome and annihilate all that separates a seeker from the ultimate truth and reality of God, encapsulated in the Sufi understanding of the first part of the Muslim confession of faith, the *kalyma shahadah*: 'There is no god but God'. That is, as Chittick puts it: '"No god" negates all false realities, and "but God" affirms the subsistence of the Real' (Chittick 2000, 45). Rumi captures this intricate movement from self to union through love:

> Love is that flame which, when it blazes up,
> Burns away all except the everlasting Beloved.
> It slays 'other than God' with the sword of *no god*.
> Look carefully: After *no god* what remains?

There remains but God, the rest has gone.
Hail, O Love, great burner of all others!
(Mathnavi Book 5, 588–90 cited by Chittick 2000, 84)

With the annhilation of self, one no longer exists apart from the divine reality (Chittick 2000; Ernst 1997; Schimmel 1975). In other words, the first person plural indexes not grandiloquence but self-abnegation. The Sufi is simultaneously nothing and subsisting with the divine – not an 'I', nor perhaps a 'we', but perhaps grammatically ineffable. As such, Sufi subjectivity is complex and difficult to circumscibe within legal conceptions of personhood, which by contrast emphasises an autonomous individual with command over language.

Another instance of these differential linguistic and religious understandings was Mohammed Yousaf Ali's use of *'sahaba'* in relation to some of his *murids*. He had in a speech referred to two of his *murids* as *'sahaba'*, where he was understood by the complainants to mean *'Sahaba-e-Rasul'* (Companions of the Prophet). They took this to mean that Yousaf Ali was indicating that he was the Prophet and they were his Companions, that there was no difference between him and the Prophet Muhammad.

Yousaf Ali, however, differentiated *'sahaba'* from *'Sahaba-e-Rasul'*, but his ambiguous, allusive and rhetorical style also allowed these to overlap and converge. For example, with respect to *'sahaba'* he understood this as referencing steadfast and faithful Muslims, but seemingly with the condition that this steadfastness was conditional on the presence of the Prophet. Second, he said that with due caution one could use the word *'sahabi'* (pl. *sahaba*) as also applicable to the companions of the leaders of the *Ahl-e-Bayt*, which he understood to be various spiritually elevated Sufis. Although in common parlance, *Ahl-e-Bayt* is understood as referring to the Prophet's immediate family, it has also been associated with the Prophet's descendant. Sufis, who regard themselves as proximate to the Prophet, as his spiritual descendants, have also appropriated the term.

Further, given that Yousaf Ali considered himself to be one of these spiritually elevated Sufis, that is, of the *Ahl-e-Bayt*, he may have felt that he could use the term *'sahabi'* for his *murids*. Reading these various statements together, one could infer that he was claiming, as the prosecution alleged, that the Prophet was present and that the *murids* he had introduced were, by inference, *'Sahaba-e-Rasul'*. This reading is possible – especially when examining his statements for literal reference.

One's interpretation depends on how one understands 'presence'. In Sufi discourse the Prophet is considered to be the anthropomorphic form of divine light (*nur-i-muhammadi*). This light may have had a temporal and physical manifestation in seventh-century Arabia, but is originary, immutable and eternal. As such, the Prophet's presence/light is understood to be continually manifest in the world (Chodkiewicz 1993, 61–5; Schimmel 1975, 214–16). All steadfast Muslims, alive to his continuing presence, are consequently 'sahaba' and therefore, in this context, we begin to understand how Yousaf Ali may have used this term.

In his conception, this possibility of proximity to the Prophet (Companionship) was not temporally confined to the historical period of the Prophet's life. '*Sahaba-e-Rasul*', he acknowledged, was a more specific designation that only referenced the historical companions of the Prophet – but in Yousaf Ali's account the historical dimension was secondary to the continued vitality of the Prophet's presence. Given that Yousaf Ali considered that he had overcome his self/ego and achieved *fana fi'r-rasul* (unity with the Prophet), it was not difficult for the prosecution – and eventually the judge, who was exasperated and baffled by his polyvalent language – to conclude that Yousaf Ali was conflating himself with, and identifying himself with, the Prophet.

The defendants' various attempts to explain how terms such as *sahaba* and faqir were polyvalent and had varying contextual uses were understood by the judge as cunning and specious. He read contextual polyvalence as 'double meaning', indicative of dissimulation and duplicity, and advised that: 'If anyone is a true Muslim he should avoid such Islamic terms, which may confuse others' (*State v. Muhammad Yousaf Ali* 2000, 158).

Another argument centred on Yousaf Ali's use of 'Muhammad' as part of his name. The prosecution pointed out discrepancies with official documentation, such as his school and army enrolment records, in which his name was initially recorded as Yousaf Ali and, subsequently, as Yousaf Ali Nadeem.[54] The defendant countered that although he had been named Muhammad Yousaf Ali at birth, 'Muhammad' had not been used in official documentation. He only corrected this omission, given the bureaucratic difficulties involved, after he had left the army.[55] Yousaf Ali further explained that his parents had been part of a Sufi order; they had been informed of his impending birth by their *murshids* (spiritual guides) and by the Holy Prophet, who had appeared in their dreams.[56] Originally his parents had wanted simply to name him 'Muhammad', because of the blessings associated with the name. However, given that the singular use of the name 'Muhammad' is considered culturally unacceptable, they had settled on Mohammed Yousaf Ali.

However, the prosecution argued that Yousaf Ali had only subsequently added 'Muhammad' to his name as he sought to create an identity with the Holy Prophet. The lack of legal proof served only to raise suspicion. This was further fuelled by the prosecution's introduction of a written text, addressed to the Shaykh by one of his *murids*, in which the letter/diacritical symbol (ص) (swaad), which stands for *Sallallahu alayhi wa alihi wasallam* (Peace and blessings on the believers) was used above 'Muhammad'. In Pakistan, the common convention is to use this diacritical symbol only in relation to the Holy Prophet, and this evidence was culturally compelling. However, while increasingly rare, there are those who use this diacritical sign on every instance of the name 'Muhammad' arguing that it signals both respect and intense devotion. That some of Yousaf Ali's followers used this diacritical symbol may suggest that they considered that he had achieved the stage of *fana fi'r-rasul* (unity with the Prophet). His lawyers, however, restricted their argument to the legally pertinent point that the defendant should not, and could not, be held responsible for the myriad actions of his followers.

All these contestations concerning grammar and reference in relation to a distinct Sufi ontology – one that is not bound by positivist categorisations of time, space, causality and self-hood – was compounded by processes of translation and transcription. Pakistani criminal courts, as ostensibly secular, are not used to debating theological and ontological differences. Sufistic discourse, which abounds in metaphor, allusion, paradox and the play of ambiguity, does not translate easily into a juristic discourse with its emphasis on reference, causality and consistency (Ewing 1988). This encounter of ontological and epistemological difference, and its entextualisation, was exemplified in the key and determining episode in the trial – the existence and production of a document understood as a 'spiritual certificate'.

The banality of miracles

Throughout the trial, the defence had denied that Yousaf Ali had claimed *Nabuwaat* (Prophethood). The judge asked them to clarify the nature of Yousaf Ali's claim in writing, whereupon in response to the court's request they produced a one-page laminated document (Exh DL).[57] This document outlined that he had been spiritually awarded the *Caliphiyyat* (Spiritual Deputy/Successor) by the Prophet Muhammad. This claim, while a little unusual, is possible within Sufi discourse (Buehler 1998, 15). This honour, Yousaf Ali explained under questioning, had been confirmed by the *awliya* (Those close to God, that is, Sufis).

The complainant's counsel, the prosecution and subsequently the judge believed that the defence were arguing that this document was a physical 'certificate' miraculously sent by the Prophet and verified by the *awliya* to Yousaf Ali.[58] That is, it had popped out of a computer all by itself and landed, as it were, on the Shaykh's desk.[59] Why did they believe this? And what made it so important for them to disprove their own misperception?

To answer the second question first: the prosecution had to disprove the 'miracle' (*karamat*) of this document's production – for the manner of its production, as they understood it, not only substantiated the claim inscribed on it, that is the claim to *Caliphiyyat*, but also, more scandalously, indicated a claim to prophetic attributes. For the prosecution held that the defence's contention was that the manner of production (miraculous) and the inscription corroborated each other as indexing Yousaf Ali's power, status and similarity to the Holy Prophet, and closeness to God. In short it would indicate *karamah* as opposed to merely *baraka* (spiritual power), which is more commonly associated with Sufis. Miracles are usually, but not exclusively, associated with Prophets.[60]

Yousaf Ali's opponents identified this as a key moment in the trial, one that to them demonstrated Yousaf Ali's fraudulent personality and ridiculous claims to Prophecy. Why did the prosecution believe the defence was claiming this document as a miracle? The 'transcript' is suggestive of the ambiguity that emerged from this encounter.[61] Under cross-examination Yousaf Ali's responses are inscribed as follows:

> I received Certificate Exh DL directly from the Holy Prophet (Peace be Upon Him) but it was verified indirectly by the 'Aolia-e-Karam' through Hazrat Abdullah Shah Ghazi. Volunteers that this Certificate was received spiritually and I cannot tell the details in this regard. I had received the document Exh DL spiritually and I cannot tell its detail that as to whether I received the Document Exh DL, either typed or un-typed. It is correct that document Exh DL is computerized/typed document. I had got this document Ex DL computerized/typed from Islamabad. It is correct that whatsoever is fed to the Computer, it may be returned in the shape of a document. It is correct that there may be a change in feeding of the Computer and receiving of the document if some change is caused therein[62] ... I do not know the writer of the Document Exh DL. I know as to who had typed this document (Exh DL) but I cannot tell his name. It is incorrect that since I do not know the name who typed document (Exh DL) therefore am not telling his name

> ... I have received this document about forty days earlier, in typed form. I have produced this document before the court to satisfy this court.[63]

It would seem that Yousaf Ali is being elusive, if not contradictory, for he says first that he did not know if he had received the certificate as a typed document; then he admits to it being typed; then that he had it typed but did not know who wrote the document. And finally he says that he knew who had typed it, but refused to divulge the name. These referential ambiguities or incoherences were understood by the prosecution as indicative of Yousaf Ali's deviousness.

However, there is another, more prosaic explanation for his responses. This can be accounted for by the division of labour involved in the production of the document and the attempt by Yousaf Ali to give as correct answers as possible without being aware of how the questions developed.[64] To the question of who wrote the document, he responded that he did not know. One of his *murids* (devotees) had written it by hand, but Yousaf Ali was not aware who – hence his answer was correct. This handwritten text was then given to someone else to type up, but he did not know by whom. He did, however, happen to know who had typed it, but refused to reveal this because the prosecution were alleging the document was blasphemous. Given that section 295-C, under which he had been charged, regards even an 'indirect' blasphemy as a crime – and that typing the document could fall within the ambit of 'indirectly' and therefore be blasphemous – Yousaf Ali refused to incriminate the typist.

Throughout this exchange the prosecution and the defence were at cross-purposes. As advised by his counsel, Yousaf Ali gave brief responses while the prosecution, regimented by conventional criminal court procedures, treated it as an evidential document that had to be disproved. First, they had asked about the nature of the claims and who had authorised and verified them. Subsequently, they asked very specific questions about how this document had been produced and communicated. They questioned him at length about which language this honour had been communicated in – whether it was in English, Urdu, Punjabi, Arabic or Persian? They also sought to know who had approved or verified the claim as inscribed. On this occasion Yousaf Ali gave as literally correct but abbreviated answers as the law required, explaining what he knew and did not know about its actual production in the temporal world – that is, whether he knew who had written and typed it.

Yousaf Ali's lack of the specifics on the document's production contributed to the prosecution's conviction that he was alluding to metaphysical forces behind its emergence as a sign of his exalted and elevated spiritual status and powers. Once this exchange between the adversaries – one already characterised by substantial religious differences – was transcribed into a judicial text, the latter's referential opacity was exacerbated by these conventions of translation, ellipsis and, especially, the erasure of the questions. Yousaf Ali's attempt to argue that this spiritual communication from the Prophet had been validated by Sufis through non-verbal signs and experiences was unrecognisable to the court.[65] The prosecution pressed him on which language it had been communicated in and who had verified it. His attempt to explain spiritual authorisation in the documentary forms of the court was understood as a evidentiary legal document – a 'certificate'.

This term has a particular valence in Pakistan where the acquisition, authorisation and control of paper documents is an acute concern (Hull 2012). The judge treated the document as an evidentiary one and argued that none of its claims could be proved. He regarded the idea that the Holy Prophet would communicate in this way as absurd as well 'as ridiculous towards Islam', and concluded:

> After analysing this document, I am forced to say that there is no need to examine the prosecution evidence in presence of this original document, which itself is sufficient to declare Yousaf, accused, as 'KAFIR' AND 'MURTAD'. Now, thereafter I shall not use the words 'Muhammad' and 'Ali' along with his name in the judgment but only Yousaf Kazab (*State v. Muhammad Yousaf Ali*, 2000 165).[66]

Throughout, the prosecution had cast doubt, through the discrepancy with official records, as to whether 'Muhammad' had been considered part of his name. Given that he had been accused of literally claiming to be the Prophet Muhammad, the judge determined that he was using the name in an attempt 'to pose like the Holy Prophet' (157). Noting that the surname 'Nadeem' had been added during his school years, the judge speculated that this was perhaps because the accused was in thrall to one of the most popular film-stars of the seventies, Nadeem Baig (161). This allusion was to the defence a sign of the judge's bad faith, but it might make sense if one counter-poses actor and prophet, impersonator and personification, [dis]simulation and the Real. Consequently, the judge felt he could no longer refer to him with the Prophet's name, nor, indeed, by the name of the Prophet's revered son-in-law Ali, for to do so might be to recognise what he considered as Yousaf Ali's fraudulent claim.

But how else may one understand Yousaf Ali's claims? In his statement to the court he had argued that imitation of the Prophet

Muhammad, to become like *al-insaan al-kamil* (the perfect man), was a legitimate and necessary moral quest. As a young man, disturbed by the multiple and contesting sects and views on Islam in Pakistan, he had turned towards Sufism. However, he had not joined one of the existing Sufi orders, nor followed the spiritual guidance of a *shakyh* (spiritual master). Instead, he was an *uwaysi*. That is, like Uways al-Qarani – a contemporary of the Prophet who, while he never met him, was nevertheless spiritually instructed by him – Yousaf Ali considered himself as a *murid* of the Holy Prophet, the perfect man and embodiment of the divine word. The Prophet was the expression of the Quran, or God's speech.[67]

As a human expression of the divine, 'The Muhammadan Reality' – as expounded in the thought of thirteenth-century mystic, Ibn Arabi (1165–1240) – articulated a potential anthropomorphism between the divine logos and human form.[68] Humans could achieve union with the divine through the annihilation of one's ego (*nafs*) and the opening of one's heart through various practices and the imitation of those who were already on, or had achieved that path – that is, first one's *murshid* and then the Prophet. As such humans can reflect and mirror the divine in a direct and unmediated manner (theophany). In his testimony Yousaf Ali explained how he had founded his own inclusivist Sufi order, the *Silsilah Haqeeqat e Muhammaddiya* (The Muhammadan Reality) – a name that indicates the influence of Ibn Arabi. After 17 years of struggle he felt that he had finally annihilated his self, thereby enabling him to be a mirror, to reflect the perfect man (the Holy Prophet). In court Yousaf Ali said:

> We are blessed to be a follower of the Prophet which, in short, means (we) have been made a mirror and this has been made possible for every human being (106).

Compare this contextual translation of the Urdu record with the judge's more literal version, as in the English transcript:

> We were blessed with the followings of Holy Prophet (Peace be Upon Him), the summary of which is that a mirror was made and it was possible for every human being (106).

Yousaf Ali further explicated his position by quoting from poetry reproduced in a book by the principal complainant in the case:

> The sun is a mirror to the Prophet's majesty
> The moon is a mirror to the Prophet's beauty,

The sky shades the world
The heart is the inner sanctum of focus upon Muhammad
Is it/It is possible that a human become
The Mirror of the Prophet's Excellence?[69]

To answer the question posed in the final couplet, Yousaf Ali had submitted the certificate. But this attempt at translation, by his *murids*, of his claims of mystical experiences and communication through signs (*ayat*) of God – that is, communication beyond language, beyond self – a mirror to the divine was in its linguistic and textual form understood as a propositional and verifiable claim, a mirror of reality. As a truth claim, it could be evaluated and judged. Found to be fraudulent, it was proof to the court not of his self-negation, but of his abominable impersonation.

Shortly after the verdict the newspaper at the forefront of pushing this case, *Khabrain*, serialised the Urdu version of the trial.[70] Each day's serialisation was accompanied by a passport-style photograph of the accused until Yousaf Ali began his own statement, whereupon the image was discarded. On the day subsequent to the serialisation of the final segment of the 'certificate' episode, however, a darkened image of Yousaf Ali appeared. This pictorial representation, clearly considered inadequate, was replaced the following day, with one that was used thereafter.[71]

Due to copyright restrictions I have been unable to reproduce the three images from the *Khabrain* newspaper. I have elected to include a stock image of Hillary Clinton, similarly transformed, to make my point. Clinton was the target of a parallel demonisation in the US during the 2016 elections, from calls of 'lock her up' to allegations she led a paedophile ring.

Figure 7.1a-c Representations of the photographs of Yousaf Ali, as they appeared in the *Khabrain* newspaper. Stock image

The original positive was reversed with a negative, meaning that Yousaf Ali was literally represented as the negation. His metaphorical, allusive and rhetorical language, the protocols of legal language and the processes of entextualisation ensured that he was 'read' as neither using language as a mirror, to describe truthfully, nor to be comprehended as the mirror of the divine. He was then the 'other' to truth and rectitude: the satanic.

Shortly after the verdict a disheartened Zayd Hamid, hoping for a more considered reading of the case, delivered a copy of the case record – that is, the transcripts and judgement – to a respected, secular-liberal commentatator at *The Friday Times*, one with considerable learning of Islam. Much to his surprise and chagrin the commentator supported the judge's verdict and highlighted the various 'contradictions', among which the instances of house ownership and the certificate, discussed above, were prominent. While his secular sensibility led him to refrain from calling Yousaf Ali a blasphemer or apostate, he nonethless described him in liberal equivalent terms – that is, as a religious con-man.[72] To both Urdu and English commentators Muhammad Yousaf Ali was, in varying respects, anathema to their sensibilities.

Without in any way minimising the various differences between religious and liberal sensibilities, as indexed by Urdu and English, I have suggested instead that their shared positivism, across the language divide, merely frames their differences in religious or secular terms. The epistemological and ontological difference of the Sufi, however, is to an alterity that is always already suspect: one liable to be read as false and fraudulent – and/or as absurd and ridiculous.

***

On 11 June 2002 Mohammed Yousaf Ali was shot and killed in Kot Lakhpat jail by another inmate, one belonging to a sectarian religious party. The accused and his accomplices were eventually acquitted.[73]

Notes

1. Daler Mehndi, an Indian Punjabi pop star, released a song entitled '*Nabi [Meh]Buba Nabi*' ('My Beloved Prophet') which included lyrics that were understood as suggesting that Hazrat Ali, the Prophet's son-in-law, was being referred to as a Prophet. A Mumbai-based Indian Muslim group protested, and thereafter some protests also occurred in Pakistan. *The Friday Times*, 25–31 May 2001; Vol. XIII (13): 8–9.
2. 'Nuggets' continues as a feature in *The Friday Times*, but 'True or False' has been removed from the current disclaimer.

3. That English indexed rationality, sophistication and cosmopolitanism for *The Friday Times* was evident from two of their most popular satires. The first was a column purportedly of the musings of former Prime Minister, Nawaz Sharif. It was entitled '*Ittefaq Nama*' which, through Sharif's struggles with the English language, wittily demonstrated that he was a nonsensical figure to be laughed at. ('*Ittefaq*' means 'agreement' and is also the name of the Sharif's families' business group, while '*nama*' means 'collection of stories'; it refers to the classical Persian and Urdu tradition of biography, usually of a leader.) The second satirical column, '*The Diary of a Social Butterfly*', detailed the life of an aspiring cosmopolitan whose failure to command English demonstrated her shallowness.
4. On background to these laws, see Ahmed (2009), Abbas (2013) and Siddique and Hayat (2008).
5. Interview with Zafar Iqbal Mirza (13 May 2001).
6. Language ideology does not simply mean the ideas that social actors hold about language, but also refers to how these ideas, whether explicit or implicit, have pragmatic effects in daily acts of linguistic usage (Schieffelin, Woolard and Kroskrity 1998).
7. One should note *The Friday Times*' formulation is a classically liberal conception of the relation between language and personhood in that it sets up a relation between truth, transparency, objectivity, evaluation and responsibility.
8. This is not to diminish the differences within and between these professions, but only to indicate that despite functional differences they operate with similar epistemological presumptions.
9. At the time I was somewhat surprised to hear of a case against a Sufi, as hitherto the predominant understanding in Pakistan was that the blasphemy laws were being used against religious minorities. This perception has since changed; it is now common for those who defend the blasphemy laws to point out that the majority of cases are against Muslims. In a country where over 97 per cent of the population is Muslim, this is not altogether surprising. Numerically there may be more cases against Muslims, but proportionally there are more cases against the minorities.
10. The allegation echoes one made against the Sufi mystic Husayn ibn Mansur al-Hallaj for his famous ecstatic expression of '*ana'l-Haqq*' (I am the Real) – for which, in popular understanding, he was tried and executed for heresy by the Abbasid ruler in 922. As with many such cases, there were complex social and political factors that were more decisive in bringing a trial than the seeming heresy. On ecstatic expressions (*shath*) by Sufis, see Ernst (1985).
11. This question on the finality of the Prophet has a saliency in Pakistan where the Ahmadis were effectively declared as non-Muslims, through a constitutional amendment, by Pakistan's Parliament in 1974 – purportedly for believing that the founder of their movement, Ghulam Mirza Ahmed (1835–1908), was a Prophet (Ahmed 2010; Qasmi 2015).
12. This increased referential specificity and criminalisation of the use of Islamic religious terminology began with the passing of section 298-A (1980) and intensified with section 298-B (1984), which prohibited the Ahmadi minority from using terms regarded as exclusive to Islam (Ahmed 2010).
13. Similar charges were made against the Sindh-based Pir Riaz Ahmed Gohar Shahi of the *Anjuman Sarfaroshan-e-Islam* [(ASI) Association of Devotees for Islam], who had at least four cases registered against him by the *Khatm-e-Nabuwaat*. By mid-2000 the ASI claimed they had over 27 cases registered against them. Of these I examined legal documents in which 34 individuals had been charged in 10 cases. Pir Gohar Shahi was convicted and sentenced to life imprisonment *in absentia*; he died a natural death abroad a few years later. Another Sufi accused of claiming to be a Prophet was Masood Ahmed Siddiqui of Faisalabad, otherwise known as *Lasani Sarkar* (Peerless Leader). He was exonerated by the police investigation and did not go to trial. Sociologically they were similar, being charismatic leaders of relatively new religious Sufi movements, rather than part of established Sufi orders. Furthermore, unlike many of these traditional Sufi orders, they entered the public domain through publications, newspaper columns and the internet. As such they neglected traditional Sufi circumspection on what can be said publicly, an argument also made against Hallaj by sympathetic Sufis; see also Ernst (2011, 215–18).
14. Justice Arif Iqbal Bhatti was murdered by Ahmed Sher in October 1997 for his part in the acquittal of Salamat and Rehmat Masih (Salamat Masih v. State (1995) 28 P.Cr.L.J. 811 (Lahore) (Pak.)). The trial of Ahmed Sher for Arif Bhatti's murder was never concluded, but he was convicted and sentenced to death for murdering another man accused of blasphemy. See http://tribune.com.pk/story/472495/1990s-blasphemy-acquittal-judges-murder-case-put-in-hibernation/. Accessed 27 June 2017.

15. He never actually legally declared it as *in camera*, and thus barring the public was technically illegal.
16. This was because of my affiliation with a US research university. On the difficulties of conducting fieldwork in highly polarised and conflictual situations, see Verkaaik (2001) and Nordstrom and Robben (1995).
17. Zayd Zaman Hamid subsequently became a controversial media pundit and public figure in Pakistan. At the time he was in his mid-thirties and one of Yousaf Ali's closest *murids*. He ran a security consultancy called *Brasstacks* that offered expertise and advice on Pakistan's security scenario to various clients. Sometime around 2006 he hosted and produced his own television programme on one of Pakistan's new media channels (*NewsOne*), espousing an ultra-nationalist line. His non-sectarian, militaristic and nationalist ideology had great appeal to male urban youth, but angered many others. Liberals criticised him for his ultra-nationalism whereas religious groups associated with the *Khatm-e-Nabuwaat* vilified him for his association with Yousaf Ali.
18. The language of record depends on the court. In subordinate courts, such as magistrates' courts, it is Urdu, whereas in the sessions courts and above, English is used.
19. Although in September 2015 the Supreme Court ruled that Urdu was to become the official language. https://www.dawn.com/news/1205686. Accessed 27 June 2017.
20. Paper books are required in cases of capital punishment.
21. Trial judges may make personal notes during trial, but their main preoccupation is translating for the official record.
22. Etymologically and conceptually, 'blasphemy' has an oral connotation. Etymologically the word combines two roots from the Greek: 'to hurt' and 'to speak', thus 'to harm by speaking'. Historically the meaning of 'blasphemy' varies considerably (Nash 2007; Levy 1993). In many legal contexts it includes non-oral, representational or semiotic offence such as writing, image or gesture.
23. The majority of cases I came across arose from an oral exchange. The second most common type arose from offensive written material whereas the third were cases of sacred words and signs that, to paraphrase Mary Douglas, were often 'signs out of place' – for example, the word 'Allah' imprinted on the sole of a shoe or Quranic text on women's clothes or bedsheets. More recently social media has become a key medium, with international media recently reporting what is believed to be the first death sentence for blasphemous content on social media: http://www.bbc.co.uk/news/technology-40246754 . Accessed 15 June 2017.
24. This is not to deny the material or phatic quality of language, but only to note that unless speech is artefactualised it lacks an externalised physical form that can be used to assess verifiability.
25. On the general lack of scrutiny of linguistic evidence, see Shuy (1993).
26. The idea of an unmediated transcript reflects this particular language ideology of perfect correspondence. The inscription of any interactional real-time encounter necessarily involves textual mediation and hence transformation.
27. Entextualisation refers to the 'coming into being' of a text or text-artifact. Silverstein's notion is more expansive than I am using here, as he understands 'text' to mean any organised internally coherent sign medium (Silverstein and Urban 1996).
28. US courts exhibit similar language ideologies (Haviland 2003), although there may be multiple language ideologies within a courtroom setting (Philips 1998).
29. I have argued elsewhere that the Indian Penal Code was the first major intersection of a particular language and legal ideology – one exemplified by Bentham's utilitarian project of codification (Ahmed n.d.).
30. Austin ultimately dispensed with the dichotomy of constative and performatives that he established for heuristic purposes, recognising that language is inherently performative and emphasising the importance of the 'total speech situation' (Austin 1962; Duranti and Goodwin 1992).
31. As has on occasion also occurred in English courts (Nash 1999, 85; Marsh 1998, 235–7).
32. Oral arguments by counsel in a jury system is perhaps one area of legal proceedings where the rhetorical as opposed to the referential is given space. However, Pakistan does not have a jury-based legal system.
33. For one study of translation in US courtrooms, see Berk-Seligson (1990).
34. My outline of the processes of entextualisation has necessarily been based on other trials I attended, as well as on interviews with legal professionals.

35. A propositional paraphrase also differs from rough translations – that is, where a comparable English sentence echoes the sense of the vernacular statement, which Silverstein terms a 'transduction' (Silverstein 2003).
36. For another account of discrepancy between legal categories and social norms in Pakistan, see Shah (2016, 168–88).
37. This shift in questions is a common tactic by opposing counsel, with the aim of generating inconsistencies and ambiguities.
38. In the Yousaf Ali case the questions were only recorded when he was cross-examined on his opening statement under section 342 of the Criminal Procedure Code (*State v. Muhammad Yousaf Ali* 2000, 76–93).
39. *State v. Muhammad Yousaf Ali* 2000, 1. I have reproduced all quotes from the trial text without grammatical corrections. I have, however, corrected minor spelling mistakes. Page citations are from court authorised text.
40. This text artifact, the judgement, is not the same as the paper book that goes to the appeal court. The latter includes much of the police and legal record prior to the trial, such as the First Information Report (FIR), charge sheet, bail hearings, etc. as well as additional documentary evidence produced by the adversarial parties.
41. This is not common, but possible in Pakistani criminal courts.
42. *State v. Muhammad Yousaf Ali* 2000, 155.
43. The same issues of ambiguity, incoherence and inconsistencies arising from translation and transcription exist in prosecution testimony. It may well be that the judge dispensed with the prosecution case for this reason, which could indicate bad faith on his part. But imputing bad faith is too easy an explanation, repeats legal and positivistic methodologies of ascribing motivation and intention and does not further the analysis. The analytical task I argue is to examine the judge's reasoning, what made it possible and on what basis it was textually justified.
44. Here he is referring to his employment as a Captain in the Pakistan Army. As an ex-army officer he may have been eligible to get a plot in Defence, an area reserved for army personnel, at concessional rates (Siddiqa 2007).
45. Note that information supplied by the witness beyond his direct response to counsel's question is conventionally signalled within the 'transcript' by this shift to indirect discourse. Thus "Volunteers…"
46. *State v. Muhammad Yousaf Ali* 2000, 118. While the Urdu 'transcript' is somewhat clearer than the translated English version, there are issues with reported speech, shift in tense and the lack of quotation marks that make it difficult to follow shifts from first to third person narrative.
47. *State v. Muhammad Yousaf Ali* 2000, 161.
48. The whole process of asking a question, eliciting a response and then translating and transcribing it is quite time-consuming. The excerpt above may have involved up to eight questions and could have taken between 25–50 minutes.
49. One should note that someone completely unaware of the context could also legitimately read the above excerpt, especially the last line, to understand that Yousaf Ali's relationship with his wife had ended – that is, either they had divorced or she was deceased.
50. On Sufi thought of the relations, similarities and distinctions between Prophecy (*nabuwwa*) and sainthood (*walaya*), see Chodkiewicz 1993; Buehler 1998, chapter 1.
51. On the modernist suspicion of faqirs from the colonial to contemporary period, see Ewing 1997; Rozehnal 2006. On the importance of *faqr* (poverty) for the Sufi path to God, see Schimmel 1975, 120–4. Afsar Mohammed notes that various studies of *faqiri* view it as associated with 'the lower end of the Sufi hierarchy of mystical practices' (Afsar 2013, 106–7).
52. Interview with Pir Wazir Ali Quadri (30 October 2000).
53. While the Urdu record is, for the most part, closer to the actual speech of the witness in that it is not transformed into postcolonial English legalese, it also uses its own formulaic phrases, often includes the judge's formulation and interjections and most notably is characterised by non-existent or inconsistent use of quotation marks which leads to problems of voicing and ventriloquism – there are often shifts from first person direct speech to third person indirect, which are hard to track.
54. On the fixing of proper names by modern state systems, see Scott 1998; Torpey 2000.
55. *State v. Muhammad Yousaf Ali* 2000, 121 and 124.
56. That the Holy Prophet may appear in dreams is commonly accepted within Muslim thought (Goldhizer 1912; Gilsenan 2000; Mittermaier 2010).
57. Exh DL stands for Exhibit Defence 'L'.

58. While criminal cases are brought by the state, it does allow private counsel hired by the complainants to assist the prosecution case.
59. Interview with complainant's counsel Mohammed Ismail Qureshi (18 May 2001). See also Qureshi (2000, 8). One should note that the word 'certificate' in Pakistan has an especial valence. Certificates are required in many areas of life – even beggars have them – and much energy is expended in acquiring them. However, they also indicate a discourse of fraudulent production in the public imagination. The prosecution and the *Khabrian* newspaper made great play of this incident to ridicule Yousaf Ali's claim viz. a fraudulent Prophet with a fraudulent 'certificate' purporting to prove his Prophecy.
60. There is a technical theological distinction between prophetic miracles (*mu'jizat*) and miracles in general (*karamah*), which Sufis are capable of performing (Schimmel 1975, 206; Ernst 1997, 68; Chodkiewicz 1993, 32). In common parlance, however, the claim of being able to perform miracles is associated with prophecy.
61. The prosecution questioning of this 'certificate' takes up a number of pages (120–4 and 127–8). Questions concerning the certificate were raised on three successive days (19–21 July 2000).
62. *State v. Muhammad Yousaf Ali* 2000, 122. After this he was questioned at length as to who among the Sufis had verified this.
63. *State v. Muhammad Yousaf Ali* 2000, 124.
64. As detailed to me by Zayd Hamid.
65. On the difficulties of communicating the divine into human language Wadud cites Kenneth Burke: 'Language is intrinsically unfitted to discuss the supernatural literally' (Wadud 1999, 15–16).
66. *Kafir* means unbeliever, *Murtad (murtadd)* means apostate and *Kazab* is an Arabic word translated into Urdu as 'ultimate liar'. *State v. Muhammad Yousaf Ali* 2000, 165.
67. There is a hadith sourced to Aisha, where replying to a query asking her to describe her deceased husband she said that '…his character was the Qur'an' (Ware 2014, 7).
68. Ibn Arabi was, as Chittick notes, one of the most original, influential and subsequently controversial Sufis in Muslim thought. He was targeted in particular by reformist and modernist movements from the latter half of the nineteenth century onwards (Chittick 2005).
69. *State v. Muhammad Yousaf Ali* 2000, 120. The poem is transcribed in Urdu and untranslated in the text.
70. See *Khabrian*, 2 September to 20 October 2000.
71. See *Khabrian*, 2–8 October 2000.
72. *The Friday Times*, 25–31 August 2000; Vol. XII (26): 9.
73. https://tribune.com.pk/story/1010594/absolved-accused-in-yousaf-kazzab-murder-case-acquitted/. Accessed 10 July 2017.

Acknowledgement

I am grateful to Mustafa Samdani and Sohail A. Warraich for their help with the intricacies of translation in relation to Sufi thought and Pakistani law respectively. My thanks to Brinkley Messick, Anita Mir, Nicholas Harkness, Nada Moumtaz and this volume's editors for their comments on various earlier drafts of this chapter.

References

Abbas, Shameem Burney. 2013. *Pakistan's Blasphemy Laws: From Islamic Empires to the Taliban*. Austin: University of Texas Press.
Ahmed, Asad Ali. 2009. 'Specters of Macaulay: Blasphemy, the Indian Penal Code and Pakistan's postcolonial predicament', in *Censorship in South Asia: Cultural Regulation from Sedition to*

Seduction, Raminder Kaur and William Mazzarella, eds, 172–205. Bloomington: Indiana University Press.

Ahmed, Asad Ali. 2010. 'The paradoxes of Ahmadiyya identity: The legal appropriation of Muslimness and the construction of Ahmadiyya difference', in *Beyond Crisis: Re-evaluating Pakistan*, Naveeda Khan, ed, 273–314. New Delhi: Routledge.

Ahmed, Asad Ali Forthcoming. 'Of Panopticons, Pannomions and the Corpo-Real: Bentham and the universalization of blasphemy.'

Austin, John. 1962. *How to Do Things with Words*. Cambridge, MA: Harvard University Press.

Berk-Seligson, Susan. 1990. *The Bilingual Courtroom: Court Interpreters in the Judicial Process*. Chicago: University of Chicago Press.

Buehler, Arthur F. 1998. *Sufi Heirs of the Prophet: The Indian Naqshbandiyya and the Rise of the Mediating Sufi Shaykh*. Columbia: University of South Carolina Press.

Chan, W. C., B. Wright and S. Yeo, eds, 2011. *Codification, Macaulay and the Indian Penal Code: The Legacies and Modern Challenges of Criminal Law Reform*. Farnham: Ashgate.

Chittick, William C. 2000. *Sufism: A Short Introduction*. Oxford: Oneworld Publications.

Chittick, William C. 2005. *Ibn Arabi: Heir to the Prophets*. Oxford: Oneworld Publications.

Chodkiewicz, Michel. 1993. *Seal of the Saints: Prophethood and Sainthood in the Doctrine of Ibn Arabi*. Cambridge: Islamic Texts Society.

Clive, John L. 1975. *Thomas Babington Macaulay: The Shaping of the Historian*. New York: Vintage Books.

Duranti, Allesandro and Charles Goodwin. 1992. 'Rethinking context: An introduction', in *Rethinking Context: Language as an Interactive Phenomenon*, Allesandro Duranti and Charles Goodwin, eds, 1–42. Cambridge: Cambridge University Press.

Ernst, Carl W. 1985. *Words of Ecstasy in Sufism*. Albany: State University of New York Press.

Ernst, Carl W. 2011 (1997). *Sufism: An Introduction to the Mystical Tradition of Islam*. Boston: Shambhala.

Ewing, Kathryn Pratt. 1983. 'The politics of Sufism: Redefining the saints of Pakistan.' *Journal of Asian Studies* 42: 251–65.

Ewing, Kathryn Pratt. 1984a. 'The Sufi as saint, curer, and exorcist in modern Pakistan.' *Contributions to Asian Studies* 18: 106–14.

Ewing, Kathryn Pratt. 1984b. 'Malangs of the Punjab: Intoxication or Adab as the path to God?', in *Moral Conduct and Authority: The Place of Adab in South Asian Islam*, Barbara Metcalf, ed, 357–71. Berkeley: University of California Press.

Ewing, Kathryn Pratt. 1988. 'Ambiguity and Shar'iat', in *Shariat and Ambiguity in South Asian Islam*, Kathryn Pratt Ewing, ed, 1–22. Berkeley: University of California Press.

Ewing, Kathryn Pratt. 1997. *Arguing Sainthood: Modernity, Psychoanalysis, and Islam*. Durham: Duke University Press.

Gilsenan, Michael. 2000. 'Signs of truth: Enchantment, modernity and the dreams of peasant women.' *Journal of the Royal Anthropological Institute* 6 (4): 597–615.

Goldziher, I. 1912. 'The appearance of the Prophet in dreams.' *Journal of the Royal Asiatic Society of Great Britain and Ireland* 44 (2): 503–6.

Haviland, J. B. 2003. 'Ideologies of language: Some reflections on language and US law.' *American Anthropologist* 105 (4): 764–74.

He, Agnes W. 2017. 'Discourse analysis', in *The Handbook of Linguistics*, Mark Aronoff and Janice Rees-Miller, eds, 445–62. Oxford: Blackwell.

Hull, Matthew S. 2012. *Government of Paper: The Materiality of Bureaucracy in Urban Pakistan*. Berkeley: University of California Press.

Lee, Benjamin. 1997. *Talking Heads: Language, Metalanguage, and the Semiotics of Subjectivity*. Durham: Duke University Press.

Levy, Leonard. 1993. *Blasphemy: Verbal Offense against the Sacred, from Moses to Salman Rushdie*. New York: Knopf.

Marsh, Joss. 1998. *Word Crimes: Blasphemy, Culture, and Literature in Nineteenth-century England*. Chicago: University of Chicago.

Matoesian, Gregory M. 2001. *Law and the Language of Identity: Discourse in the William Kennedy Smith Rape Trial*. Oxford: Oxford University Press.

Mittermaier, Amira. 2010. *Dreams that Matter: Egyptian Landscapes of the Imagination*. Berkeley: University of California Press.

Mohammad, Afsar. 2013. *The Festival of Pirs: Popular Islam and Shared Devotion in South India*. Oxford: Oxford University Press.

Nash, David. 1999. *Blasphemy in Modern Britain: 1789 to the Present*. Aldershot: Ashgate.
Nash, David. 2007. *Blasphemy in the Christian World: A History*. Oxford: Oxford University Press.
Nordstrom, Carolyn and Antonious C. G. M. Robben, eds, 1995. *Fieldwork under Fire: Contemporary Studies of Violence and Survival*. Ann Arbor: University of California Press.
Philips, Susan U. 1998. *Ideology in the Language of Judges: How Judges Practice Law, Politics, and Courtroom Control*. New York: Oxford University Press.
Qasmi, Ali Usman. 2015. *The Ahmadis and the Politics of Religious Exclusion in Pakistan*. London: Anthem Press.
Qureshi, Muhammad I. 2000. 'Foreword', in *Judgment of Yusuf Kazzab Blasphemy Case*, Arshad Qureshi, ed, 7–12. Lahore: Al-Maarif.
Qureshi, Muhammad I. 2010 (1994). *Namoos i Rasool aur Qanoon i Tuheen e Rissalat Quran o Sunnat*. Lahore: Al-Faisal Nashran Printers.
Rajagopal, Arvind. 2001. *Politics after Television: Hindu Nationalism and the Reshaping of the Public in India*. Cambridge: Cambridge University Press.
Riles, Annelise. 2006. *Documents: Artifacts of Modern Knowledge*. Ann Arbor: University of Michigan Press.
Rorty, Richard. 1980. *Philosophy and the Mirror of Nature*. Oxford: Blackwell.
Rozehnal, Robert. 2006. 'Faqir or faker? The Pakpattan tragedy and the politics of Sufism in Pakistan.' *Religion* 36 (1): 29–47.
Rozehnal, Robert. 2010. 'Reimagining the Land of the Pure: A Sufi master reclaims Islamic orthodoxy and Pakistani identity', in *Beyond Crisis: Re-evaluating Pakistan*, Naveeda Khan, ed, 118–41. New Delhi: Routledge.
Schieffelin, Bambi B., Kathryn A. Woolard and Paul V. Kroskrity, eds, 1998. *Language Ideologies: Practice and Theory*. New York: Oxford University Press.
Schimmel, Annemarie.1975. *Mystical Dimensions of Islam*. Chapel Hill: University of North Carolina Press.
Scott, James C. 1998. *Seeing like a State: How Certain Schemes to Improve the Human Condition Have Failed*. New Haven: Yale University Press.
Shah, Nafisa. 2016. *Honour and Violence: Gender, Power and Law in Southern Pakistan*. Oxford: Berghahn.
Shuy, Roger W. 1993. *Language Crimes: The Use and Abuse of Language Evidence in the Courtroom*. Cambridge, MA: Blackwell.
Siddiqa, Ayesha. 2007. *Military Inc: Inside Pakistan's Military Economy*. London: Pluto.
Siddique, Osama and Zahra Hayat. 2008. 'Unholy speech and holy laws: Blasphemy laws in Pakistan – Controversial origins, design defects and free speech implications.' *Minnesota Journal of International Law* 17(2): 305–85.
Silverstein, Michael and Greg Urban. 1996. 'The natural history of discourse', in *Natural Histories of Discourse*, Michael Silverstein and Greg Urban, eds, 1–17. Chicago: University of Chicago Press.
Silverstein, Michael. 2003. 'Translation, transduction, transformation: Skating "glossando" on thin semiotic ice', in *Translating Cultures*, Paula G. Rubel and Abraham Rosman, eds, 75–105. New York: Berg.
State v. Muhammad Yousaf Ali. 2000. Case FIR No. 70/97 Millat Park Police Station, Lahore (28/2/97). Decision by Lahore Sessions Court, 5 August 2000.
Stokes, Eric. 1959. *The English Utilitarians in India*. Oxford: Clarendon Press.
Torpey, John. 2000. *The Invention of the Passport: Surveillance, Citizenship and the State*. Cambridge: Cambridge University Press.
Verkaaik, Oscar. 2001. 'The captive state: Corruption, intelligence agencies, and ethnicity in Pakistan', in *States of Imagination: Ethnographic Explorations of the Postcolonial State*, Thomas Blom Hansen, Finn Stepputat, Julia Adams and George Steinmetz, eds, 345–64. Durham: Duke University Press.
Wadud, Amina. 1999. *Qur'an and Woman: Reading the Sacred Text from a Woman's Perspective*. New York: Oxford University Press.
Walker, Anne Graffam. 1986. 'The verbatim record: The myth and the reality', in *Discourse and Institutional Authority: Medicine, Education, and Law* (Vol.19), Sue Fisher and Alexander Dundas Todd, eds, 205–22. Norwood: Ablex Publishing Corp.
Ware, Rudolph. T. 2014. *The Walking Qur'an: Islamic Education, Embodied Knowledge, and History in West Africa*. Chapel Hill: University of North Carolina Press.

8
Blasphemy and the appropriation of vigilante justice in 'hagiohistoric' writing in Pakistan

Jürgen Schaflechner

Introduction

In June 2009 a group of peasant women got into a fight over the usage of a drinking cup in Ittan Walli, a small village in Punjab. The parochial quarrel led to charges of blasphemy against Asia Bibi, a Christian woman involved in the argument. Asia spent eight years on death row until she was acquitted in Pakistan's Supreme Court in October 2018. The course of events triggered the assassination of the governor of Punjab, Salman Taseer, on 4 January 2011, an outspoken supporter of Asia Bibi. His murderer, Malik Muhammad Mumtaz Qadri, was a member of Taseer's own security team and a follower of the Sufi-oriented Barelvi movement.

Much has already been written about these incidents. In this chapter I will broaden the scope of former research by showing how the Sufi-oriented Barelvis spearheaded a campaign that championed Mumtaz Qadri as an Islamic hero (*ghāzī*)[1] and a martyr (*śahīd*). Furthermore, I will analyse texts on Ilmuddin (1908–29) and Amir Cheema (1977–2006), two men who also became famous for assassinating an alleged blasphemer, to show how Qadri's veneration builds on an already sedimented affective history. I will call the textual archives of such and similar veneration 'hagiohistoric', as they intertwine meticulous research with accounts of divine intervention with the goal of naturalising certain moral claims in the present. These texts not only describe the feelings Muslims *ought* to have when encountering blasphemy, but also produce an affective economy in which the extrajudicial killing of an alleged blasphemer is portrayed as a 'natural' reaction. With the help of Sara Ahmed's work (Ahmed 2014), I will argue that the term blasphemer (*gustākh-i rasūl*) gains this affective value through a variety of concealed signs that simultaneously involve local and global power relations.

Setting the scene: Pakistan's blasphemy laws

Pakistan's blasphemy laws have in recent years continued to stir up controversy. While many religious scholars argue that the current laws represent the Quran and the Sunna, and therefore cannot be abolished or amended without committing blasphemy in the act (Sayalvi 2016; Turabi n.d.; Qadri 2012), more liberal interpretations maintain that the ambivalent nature of the laws makes them prone to abuse, and to being used as instruments for personal animosity (Siddique and Hayat 2008; Abbas 2013). The amendments to the Pakistan Penal Code (PPC) in the 1980s may even be described as performative because they deem the act of blasphemy criminal and punishable in the most severe form.

Studies show that blasphemy cases have steadily increased since the 1980s (Siddique and Hayat 2008, 322–7). Quoting the Centre for Social Justice, a 2016 report by the Human Rights Commission of Pakistan states that at least 1,472 people were accused of blasphemy between 1987 and 2016. The biggest portion of this number is made up of Muslims (730) and Ahmadis (501), followed by Christians (205) and Hindus (26).[2] Furthermore the report points out that in 2015 alone, courts found 15 out of 25 acquitted cases to have been fabricated due to personal vendettas. The remaining cases were cleared on the basis of a lack of evidence or due to the accused being declared insane (Pakistan 2016, 96). Liberal Pakistanis take such reports as supporting their stance that the blasphemy laws represent a relic of the past and should therefore be amended or abolished. A serious discussion on the blasphemy decrees and their advantages and disadvantages for Pakistani society, however, has so far been repeatedly thwarted by united protests of the religious right.

The Sufi-oriented Barelvi community has been very active in supporting the blasphemy laws and agitating against any perceived disrespect to the Prophet. While other religious parties also emphasise the necessity of protecting the Prophet's dignity, the Barelvis' veneration of Muhammad is unsurpassed. This renders the Barelvis as central actors when it comes to agitation against perceived blasphemy or any possible amendments to the decrees. According to his own statement, Mumtaz

Qadri was influenced by the sermons of Hanif Qureshi, a Barelvi preacher and nᶜat singer, in his decision to assassinate the governor. Barelvi preachers and writers also played a crucial role in rendering Qadri into a larger than life saintly figure. To grasp this development fully, I first need to introduce the theological and political discourses of the nineteenth and the twentieth centuries that have shaped today's Barelvi community.

Barelvis and the apotheosis of the Prophet Muhammad

The Barelvis are the outcome of a reactionary movement to reformist dynamics in South Asian Islam in the nineteenth century. Today Barelvism is found all over the subcontinent, its members deeming themselves the 'real' Sunnis who practise Islam in a similar way to the Prophet Muhammad (I. Khan 2011, 54). The Barelvi movement dates back to Ahmad Raza Khan (1856–1921) – an interpreter of Islamic law (*muftī*), a religious scholar (*ᶜālim*) and a spiritual guide (*pīr*) (Gugler 2015, 173) – who hailed from Bareilly, a city in what is now the north Indian state of Uttar Pradesh. It is also the city's name which led to the term 'Barelvi' (*barelvī*), by which Raza Khan's followers are widely known today. The community itself prefers to be called 'Sunni', however, to emphasise that they see themselves as the bearers of an original and majoritarian Islam. This claim to represent 'actual' Islam is characteristic of Islamic reform movements of the nineteenth and twentieth centuries in South Asia. Communities such as the Ahl-e-Hadith, the Ahmadiyyas and the Deobandis struggled (and continue to struggle) over which group has the authority to demarcate the main tenets of Islam. These attempts to define the 'actual', the 'real' or the 'proper' centre of a tradition are not particular to Islam, however, nor to the colonial period. Such dynamics are rather a common reaction to the dislocation of established orders and the reshuffling of traditional structures (Schaflechner 2018).

While the East India Company initially supported local power structures and the usage of Persian as the official language, in 1835 the introduction of English and 'Western-style' education as a condition for governmental jobs brought forth a variety of epistemic shifts to the subcontinent (Moj 2015, 6). Christian missionary activity further augmented the impression among South Asian Muslims that Islam was under threat and in dire need of reform. As I will show in the following, this notion is still pertinent in many 'hagiohistoric' writings today.

The establishment of a religious seminary in Deoband, a north Indian town in what is now the state of Uttar Pradesh, was one reaction to such power shifts. The madrassa at Deoband became crucial in founding a network of schools independent of the state which spread reformist ideas in South Asia (Singh 2012). The scholars of the Deoband network (henceforth known as Deobandis) preached a scriptural and reformist Islam based on the Hanafi school of jurisprudence. They were opposed to popular beliefs and practices such as shrine worship and saints' intercessory power on behalf of the faithful.

Reacting to the Deobandis and other even less permissive Islamic groups, such as the Ahl-e-Hadith, Raza Khan united various madrasas, shrines and religious saints (*pīrs*) at the end of the nineteenth century on the basis of their common opposition to these new reform movements (Philippon 2014, 154). Raza Khan became the official leader of the emerging Barelvi community in 1900 (Gugler 2015). He aimed to defend a body of traditional practices – such as ritual journeys to shrines (*ziyārat*) and the singing of devotional songs to the Prophet (*nᶜat*) – which were increasingly criticised by other reformist movements as being backwards.

To counter such allegations, Raza Khan utilised his contacts with religious scholars in the holy cities of Mecca and Medina. During his *hajj* in 1906, he gained official support for his fatwas on the proper veneration of the Prophet Muhammad, which were collected in the book *Ḥussām al Ḥarmīn*. According to Barelvi sources, 33 of these respected *ulama* endorsed Raza Khan and gave weight to his traditionalist teachings (Khan 2011, 55). This support further exacerbated Barelvi criticism of other denominations – especially of the Deoband school.

In Barelvi cosmology, the Prophet is elevated to a position that almost matches that of God (Philippon 2014, 161); unconditional devotion to him is a crucial part of Barelvi religious practice (Gugler 2015, 175). Muhammad is not only the most perfect man (*insān-i kāmil*), but also *nūr* (light), an ever-present light guiding the faithful. This apotheosis sets the Barelvis apart from the Deobandis, who share the Barelvis' respect for the Prophet, but emphasise that Muhammad was a human being. This theological argument is also translated into religious practice. While the Barelvis, for example, lavishly celebrate the Prophet's birthday (*mīlād*), the festival is criticised by the Ahl-e-Hadith and the Deobandis as being polytheistic (Ahmad 2009; Reetz 2006, 125).

The Barelvis' excessive veneration has repeatedly led to tension between these different schools. According to Sumbul Farah, however, it is precisely the theological proximity to Barelvis and Deobandis which causes a violent insistence on certain points of difference (Farah 2013, 279). Diverging opinions on the Prophet's ontological position have caused Barelvis to condemn the Deoband school for their lack of respect and heretical behaviour (Khan 2011, 55).

During his lifetime Raza Khan avoided wider conflict and political engagement with the British colonial power. This separated the Barelvis from other reform groups, such as the Majlis-i Ahrar, the Ahl-e-Hadith, the Deobandis and the Khaksar (Gugler 2015, 174). The Barelvis' anti-political stance, together with the community's inclination towards saint worship and mysticism, helped to create an image of Barelviism as a non-violent Sufi interpretation of Islam. While the Barelvis were apolitical in the days of their establishment, the community has become increasingly politicised over the last few decades.

Philippon argues that this rise of political engagement is linked to a perceived 'talibanisation' of Pakistan's society (Philippon 2014, 156). The Taliban's rigid interpretation of Islam is widely influenced by the Deobandi school, and is thus opposed to Barelvi practices. These differences in theology and religious practice have been successfully used by the Barelvi movement to advertise itself to the Pakistani government and the military as a moderate and state-friendly version of Islam. At a time when the military started its first operation against the Taliban in the Swat Valley in 2007, the administration willingly supported the Barelvis' political ambitions, making them into an important ideological ally for rallying public opinion in support of the military.

This provided momentum for an increasing radicalisation of the Barelvi communities over recent years. The Sunni Tehreek (ST), a Barelvi political party, became one of the main actors in agitation against the Taliban (Philippon 2014, 162–5). Their willingness to show street presence, paired with the Barelvis' emotional elevation of the Prophet, furthermore turned the ST into an important factor when it comes to protesting about perceived insults against Muhammad. However, this readiness to take to the streets – especially in the aftermath of Salman Taseer's support of Asia Bibi – also jeopardised the ST's good relationship with the state and the military. While various Barelvi groups have organised peaceful public protests against Mumtaz Qadri's conviction,[3] some of the Sunni Tehreek's rallies have also turned violent, thus tarnishing the Barelvis' image as a peaceful alternative to the more excessive Deobandi Islam.[4]

The ST, however, was not able to translate agitations around the Prophet's honour into vast amounts of political votes. Only the Tehreek-e Labbaik Pakistan (TLP), a party established in 2015 in the aftermath of Mumtaz Qadri's arrest, was able to turn their street presence into voter behaviour. Formed around Hussain Rizvi, the TLP is supportive of the military and the state; however, it also raises demands to safeguard the honour of the Prophet by strictly implementing the blasphemy laws. In the 2018 general elections the TLP became the fifth largest political party in Pakistan in terms of polled votes. Following the riots after Asia Bibi's acquittal in the Supreme Court, in October 2018, however, the government cracked down on the TLP and its leading figures. At the time of writing in spring 2019, Rizvi was still awaiting his sentence in court.

Lastly, it is important to note that such discussions are often detached from the self-perception of many South Asian Muslims today. Especially in rural areas, many individuals might not assign themselves to any of these sects (see Simpson 2008). That being said, new possibilities in social media also support a tangible fortification of sectarian borders. Furthermore, theological disputes may also disappear in the eye of a common enemy. Taseer's criticism of the blasphemy laws, for example, unified Deobandis and others on the religious right with the Barelvis in their condemnation of the governor. However, those associating with the name 'Barelvi' do not form a homogeneous group. While some Barelvi scholars – such as Tahir-ul Qadri, a preacher and politician, and Illyas Qadri, founder of the organisation Dawat-e Islami – openly spoke out against the extrajudicial murder of Taseer and condemned Mumtaz Qadri's actions, others, as we will see below, fully supported the murderer and elevated the assassin to the status of a saintly figure.

Barelvis call themselves the 'lovers of the Prophet' (ʿāśiq-i rasūl), and for many the true faith (ṣaḥīḥ ʿaqīdah) is linked to the Prophet Muhammad and the ways in which he acted. This may include seemingly mundane acts, such as which foot is put forward first when entering a building or the location of a toilet in a new house (Farah 2013, 270). This role as the *axis mundi* of Barelvi cosmology, however, makes any insult against the Prophet a significant transgression and a capital sin. The emotional investment in the Prophet's dignity (śān) and the commitment to defend his honour renders the Barelvis as the prime agents when it comes to reacting to perceived defamation. Thus I will mainly, but not exclusively, focus on Barelvi voices when portraying the circumstances around Salman Taseer's assassination.

Asia Bibi's transgression

On 14 June 2009 Asia Noreen Bibi, a Christian woman from a lower caste, drank from a well in the village of Ittan Wali in the Sheikhupura district of Punjab. She used a cup which did not belong to her and thereby infuriated the local Muslim women, who claimed that Asia had made the water '*ḥarām*' (forbidden). A fight broke out among the women, during which Asia allegedly insulted the Prophet Muhammad by saying, 'What did your prophet ever do to save mankind?' (Bibi and Tollet 2012, 21). A few days later the local mullah, Qari Muhammad Salim, arrived with a few men at Asia Bibi's house and demanded that she be punished. Asia's family informed the police, who took Asia Bibi into custody – for her own safety, as it is claimed. On 8 November 2010 she was convicted of blasphemy and sentenced to death. This decision was suspended by the Supreme Court on 31 October 2018.

This incident opened a rift in Pakistan's political landscape due to its wide-reaching media coverage. Many national liberal thinkers, scholars and politicians came to Asia Bibi's aid, interpreting her case as yet another proof of the inhumane blasphemy laws. International human rights organisations and Christian groups also demanded mercy for Asia Bibi. Pakistan's liberal media condemned the contentious laws as man-made and forced upon the nation by a military dictator. The religious right was united in their own outrage. They saw the incident as a litmus test for the state of morals in the Islamic Republic which, according to them, had been put into question by a 'loose' Christian woman (Turabi n.d., 31f.). Barelvi political parties, such as the Jamaat Ulema-e Pakistan and the Sunni Tehreek, took to the streets and openly called for Asia's death. Maulana Yousuf Qureshi, a Deoband scholar and an active member of the Jamaat-e-Islami, offered a bounty of Rs. 500,000 (around €4,500) to anyone who successfully killed Asia Bibi.[5] The village quarrel in Ittan Wali escalated into a nationwide debate in which a Christian woman's fate was perceived as a symbol for the current state of the nation.

Salman Taseer, governor of the Punjab province at the time, was at the forefront of the liberal struggle for Asia Bibi's rights. On 20 November 2010 he visited Asia Bibi in jail and, in an event clearly geared towards media coverage, openly supported her plea for mercy. The following is an excerpt from his statement that day.

> I want to start in the name of Allah, who is great and merciful. I came here to meet with Asia Bibi, who has been in jail for 1½ years now. She has been given a punishment which I consider extremely strict and oppressive. She appealed to the President of Pakistan, Mr. Asif Ali Zardari, that she may be pardoned for her punishment. And hopefully Mr. President will pardon her on the basis

of humanity and sympathy. In Muhammad Ali Jinnah's Pakistan, there was no such law, and a law with such an oppressive punishment could have never been possible. In our religion, we need to protect the minorities. The white stripe in our flag is there to show that the minorities are recognised in our country. I think that the punishment that she has gotten is a punishment against humanity, and so, in my role as the Governor of the Punjab, I have received her appeal which I will bring to the President in hope that he will pardon her for her mistake ... This has nothing to do with religion; I speak from the framework of humanity. I don't want to drag religion into this. Muhammad Ali Jinnah's Pakistan is an enlightened Pakistan and a progressive Pakistan. Hopefully we will pull Pakistan into this direction. We are the heirs of Muhammad Ali Jinnah, the heirs of Zulfikar Ali Bhutto Shaheed, and the heirs of Benazir Shaheed Bhutto; we want to see an enlightened and progressive Pakistan.[6]

Taseer's comments reveal his attempt publicly to negotiate Asia Bibi's case in Pakistan. First and foremost, he aimed to lift the discussion from a religious plane in order to re-frame it into a wider narrative of enlightenment and national progress. Humanity, in his interpretation, trumps religion: this makes the incarceration of Asia Bibi and her death sentence reactionary and regressive. Taseer thereby bifurcated the discourse into a progressive, humane and enlightened side (the liberal Pakistanis) versus an oppressive, inhumane and backward side (the religious right). In his narrative, society's reaction to Asia Bibi's case separated humanity from inhumanity. Even though he attempted to leave religion out of the equation, Taseer's statement was taken as an insult and immediately attacked by many members of Pakistani *ulama*.

In the days following the press conference, Taseer kept publicly calling for a revision to the blasphemy decrees; at one point he termed them a 'black law' (*kālā qānūn*). For several members of the Pakistani *ulama*, this statement was in itself already blasphemous and many began to issue fatwas against the politician.[7] Responding in a BBC Urdu interview to the question of whether these rulings would worry him, Taseer again ridiculed the *ulama* when he answered, 'Do you think I care about the fatwas of these ignorant (*jāhil*) maulvis? These people have even issued rulings against the kite festival (*basant*)'.[8] This open and bold confrontation provoked violent reactions from Pakistan's right.

Villainising Salman Taseer

To counter Taseer's campaign in support of Asia Bibi, parts of the *ulama* framed the governor as a blasphemer (*gustākh-i rasūl*) and an enemy of Islam. Attacks on his private life became frequent, and were clearly aimed to portray Taseer as a flawed character. Some religious scholars even declared the governor *vājib-al qatl* – literally meaning 'ought to be killed' – and thus sanctioned Taseer's death months ahead of his assassination. The phrase *vājib-al qatl* is consistently used in such incidents by the religious right in Pakistan; it implies that the accused has committed a crime so grave that their murder is no longer against Islamic law. Declaring somebody *vājib-al qatl* publicly is a serious matter, as it invites vigilante justice and legitimises extrajudicial killings.

The pronouncement of *vājib-al qatl* also reveals a direct link to power. In other words it shows how certain sections of the *ulama* consider themselves to be sovereign actors who are above the state law and able to dictate life and death. Unfortunately, declarations of *vājib-al qatl* are, to a certain extent, also supported by the ambivalences of section 295-C of the PPC – particularly through the absence of an intention requirement (see chapter 1). The inconsistency in the clause allows the *ulama* to frame their invocations to murder as patriotism and as an attempt to uphold the law in the face of an impotent state. Qadri repeated this point in court when he justified his actions as a natural development that occurred resulting from the state's reluctance to persecute and execute blasphemers such as Taseer (Khosa, Alam and Khan 2015, 5).

Religious scholars of various denominations had a hand in declaring Salman Taseer *vājib-al qatl* and subsequently created an atmosphere which led to the governor's assassination. With regard to this chapter's overall scope, however, in the following discussion I will look primarily at Barelvi authors and preachers. Their voices have been some of the most audible during Taseer's villainisation. Part of the book *Muḥammad Malik Mumtāz Ḥasīn Qādrī Śahīd*, for example, composed after Taseer's death by Ahmad Zia Sayalvi, recapitulates some of the religious right's wide allegations against the governor.

> The reasons for his death were that [Taseer] called a woman who has insulted the Prophet and has been proven to be a blasphemer in a court investigation 'innocent' and 'downtrodden', he took the

law in his own hands and [thereby] broke his oath [as a governor], he committed blasphemy himself by advocating for a cursed blasphemer, he called the blasphemy law (295-C) – that has been installed in the light of the Quran and the Sunna – a black law, he ridiculed the *ulama,* and he called the unbelievers of the finality of the prophet [i.e. the Ahmadiyya] Muslims (Sayalvi 2016, 6f.).

According to Sayalvi, Taseer's murder was due to his support of a convicted blasphemer, which in the eyes of many within the Barelvi *ulama* itself amounted to blasphemy. On top of this he dared to call section 295-C a 'black law' (Qureshi 2012, 25–6). Both of these statements do not directly involve 'derogatory remarks' in the sense that 295-C states, yet they were sufficient to be interpreted as blasphemy by some Barelvi scholars.

The smear campaign against Taseer, importantly, also extended to his private life. Taseer's support of a convicted, non-Muslim blasphemer was explained by his allegedly indecent and un-Islamic nature. Ahmad Qadri, another Barelvi scholar writing on this issue, summed up how he interprets Taseer's behaviour:

> … invisible powers have chosen a man like Salman Taseer to conspire against the law for the protection of the honour of the prophet. A person who, according to his own illegitimate children, eats pig every day, drinks scotch, and has never even come close to praying or fasting. One time in jail he got a Quran in his hands. [Taseer] said that this was the first time in his life that he had the chance to read the Quran from cover to cover but that there was nothing for him in it (Qadri 2012, 26).

This personal information was taken from the biography of Aatish Salman, one of Taseer's sons who lives in Delhi.[9] The governor's un-Islamic private life was revealed alongside his rejection of the Quran and his habit of eating pork and drinking alcohol. The passage above further implies that only people who do not fast or pray could even think of siding with a convicted blasphemer. In this way, Taseer's exclusion also reiterates the Barelvi community's moral understanding of good and evil.

There is yet another crucial nodal point structuring this discourse, seen in the way the above passage is introduced. Qadri implies that Taseer's personal character flaws are utilised by 'invisible powers' who conspire against Islam. Such powers usually come from outside the country and thus link the local discussions on the amendment of Pakistan's Penal Code to a global discourse of 'Islam against the West'. Khaula

Matin, author of a book on Ilmuddin which will be introduced below, tellingly expresses this resentment against the West in this passage:

> What kind of tolerance and enlightenment is it when unfortunate Muslims' most dearly loved personality, the holy dignity of the Prophet (pbuh) is desecrated [lit. vulgar words are said]. [What kind of tolerance and enlightenment is it] when the West rubs salt into Muslim wounds and as a result of their hostility towards Islam when they elevate [blasphemers] into 'heroes'. In this regard, the examples of Salman Rushdie and Taslima Nasrin are clearly in front of us (Matin 2007, 13).

These examples show how Taseer's comments on 295-C were not merely seen as an internal Pakistani issue, but rather as an expression of a much wider struggle of 'the West' against Islam (Favret-Saada 2015). Many similar statements re-framed Taseer's criticism against the PPC as yet another attack on the Prophet that was in line with the Rushdie incident, the *Jyllands-Posten* cartoons and the film *The Innocence of Muslims*. This connection to other events and characteristics (what Sara Ahmed calls 'stickiness', see below) also resurfaced in Mumtaz Qadri's defence in court. Qadri's opening statement, which aimed to prove that he had not acted unlawfully, was a rant against Salman Taseer's personal flaws and incorporates this reductionist world view.

> I have not committed murder of an apostate like Suleman Taseer (the then Governor Punjab), contrary to dictums of the Holy Quran and Sunnah ... Salman Taseer himself was responsible for commission of an offence U/s 295-C of P.P.C. punishable to death or life imprisonment. In spite of that, he was not dealt with in accordance with law, obviously he was the lieutenant of President Asif Ali Zardari and a bully of Americans [*sic*] ... [The] personal life of Salman Taseer shows that right from early times he proved himself as an infidel. He married three times. His one wife was "Sikh" by religion ... His lifestyle, faith and living with a lady of non-Muslim faith, reflecting his act of living in constant state of Zinna [*zinā*, 'adultery'] under the pretext of marriage (not permissible in Islam) speak volumes of his character and associated matters (Khosa, Alam and Khan 2015, 4–6).

Qadri's defence in court echoed feelings of rancour against the governor, and ultimately aimed to reduce him to *vājib-al qatl* by linking theological arguments, moral judgement and global politics. This discourse was mainly orchestrated by parts of the *ulama* who felt disrespected and who feared losing influence to the liberal elites if the blasphemy laws were amended. Most importantly, these statements portray a clear 'us against them' structure. Salman Taseer is not merely seen as a blasphemer, but rather a Western agent and an alien element within the Islamic Republic. Unified and stereotypical notions of 'the West' clashed with similarly stereotypical concepts of Islam and pious Muslimness. Both sides, 'the West' and 'Islam', are described in reductionist and crude terms to emphasise their mutual incommensurability. This affective style of writing associates a variety of characteristics with the description of *gustākh-i rasūl*, a blasphemer.

To present the pinnacle of this demonisation discourse, I want to provide an excerpt of one of Hanif Qureshi's speeches delivered only a few days before Taseer's assassination. Hanif Qureshi is a famous *naᶜt* singer and Barelvi preacher who had viciously condemned Taseer for his public support of Asia Bibi. Mumtaz Qadri eventually revealed that Qureshi's engaging sermons incited him to murder the governor (Khan 2011, 53).[10] The following speech is an example of how Qureshi conjured hostility against Salman Taseer.[11]

> Listen, we are the heirs of Ghazi Murid Hussain Shaheed,[12] we are the heirs of Ghazi Ilmuddin Shaheed, we are the lovers of Ghazi Abdul Qayyum Shaheed's soul,[13] we are the lovers and followers of Ghazi Abdul Rasheed Shaheed.[14] Don't you know that we say openly that we are not afraid of anything! If the law in our country does not call for the death penalty for a blasphemer, for 295-C, then Allah gave us the power that we take the weapons in our own hands. We know how to shoot a gun, or how to cut a blasphemer's throat. … Are we Sunnis not able to do this? Remove the cowardice from yourself! Allah has given us so much power and courage. We can strangle the blasphemer, we can cut his tongue, we can dismember his body with bullets. No law can catch us! The punishment for blasphemy is death! The punishment for blasphemy is death! The punishment for blasphemy is death! Somebody who insults the prophet has no right to live. [Crowd chanting in the back: We are the servants of the Prophet. In the servitude of the Prophet we also accept death. Without the Prophet's love life is in vain.]

These words were underlined by a capturing and highly fomenting physical performance, throughout which Qureshi repeatedly incited his audience towards violence against the perceived blasphemer. By recalling the names of Ilmuddin and Abdul Rasheed, Qureshi linked the current events to similar incidents in the past, thus connecting Taseer's attempt to revise the blasphemy laws to a long list of Western conspiracies and alleged attacks on Islam. Hanif Qureshi reduced the governor to *vājib-al qatl* in order to re-establish the former (Barelvi) order and to counter the perceived attacks on Islam. Incited by this and similar speeches Mumtaz Qadri, a member of Salman Taseer's personal security team, shot the governor with 28 bullets from his automatic weapon on 4 January 2011 (Khosa, Alam and Khan 2015, 3). Taseer died on the spot and Qadri was arrested by his own colleagues in the security team. Mumtaz Qadri later admitted guilt for the murder and stated that the government's refusal to persecute Taseer for his blasphemy had triggered a natural course of events which led him to the murder (Khosa, Alam and Khan 2015, 5–6).

Religious affect

Such texts and speeches quiver with hatred and disgust for Taseer's deeds. Additionally, many of them present us with an allegedly singular experience when it comes to how Muslims react to blasphemy. Some authors claim that blasphemy triggers a natural reaction among *all* Muslims, thus legitimising a blasphemer's reduction to *vājib-al qatl*. Khalid Mahmud Qadri, for example, writes that 'Muslims cannot bear when the honour of the Prophet (pbuh) is disrespected. It's impossible for them to remain calm in the eyes of blasphemy' (Qadri 2006, 142). Hanif Qureshi resonates a similar sentiment when he writes that 'whenever a blasphemer made blasphemous remarks then one or the other lover [of the Prophet] would make him pay for his evil deeds. Just look for some time at the subcontinent's history' (Qureshi 2012, 12). The ubiquity of such generalisations also echoes in Mumtaz Qadri's court hearing. Qadri's defence statement, too, chose to frame the incident as a natural and spontaneous outburst of emotion.

> On the faithful day, I being member of Elite Force I was deployed as one of the member of the Escort Guard of Salman Taseer, the Governor Punjab [sic]. In Koh-i-Sar Market, the Governor with another after having lunch in a restaurant walked to his vehicle. In adjoining mosque I went for urinating in the washroom and for making ablution. When I came out with my gun, I came across Salman Taseer. Then I had the occasion to address him, "your honour being

the Governor had remarked about blasphemy law as black law, if so it was unbecoming of you." Upon this he suddenly shouted and said, "Not only that it is black law, but also it is my shit."[15] Being a Muslim I lost control and under grave and suddenly provocation, I pressed the trigger and he lay dead in front of me. I have no repentance and I did it for "Tahafuz-i-Namoos-i-Rasool". Salman offered me grave and sudden provocation. I was justified to kill him … (Khosa, Alam and Khan 2015, 6).

These statements link 'being a Muslim' to a natural loss of control when confronted with blasphemy. In other words, certain emotions in the eye of blasphemy are constitutive of the interpellation of the Muslim subject. Within this discourse, being Muslim means to be enraged about the act of blasphemy: to be 'touched' or 'moved' in some way. The naturalisation of this link, however, is deeply political; it hallmarks arguments in favour of the blasphemy laws and in some cases even legitimises extrajudicial murder. To elaborate on the link between emotions and Taseer's assassination, I will briefly introduce recent theories of affect and their connection to the performative structure of language.

Over the last decades, theories of emotion and affect have increasingly gained ground within cultural studies (Gregg et al. 2009; Clough and Halley 2007; Ahmed 2014). On a very basic level, affects can be described as visceral reactions or 'moments of intensity' in the body (O'Sullivan 2001, 26), which are not yet caught within any symbolic order. Emotions or feelings, on the other hand, are already located within a symbolic order – they are of a 'qualified intensity' (Massumi 1995, 88). Theories of affect, in short, want to reduce the influence of the mind *vis-à-vis* the body and turn their attention to physiological sensations which are part and parcel of everyday life. Spinoza's sleepwalker might be a good example of how bodies make decisions without consulting conscious knowledge (Spinoza 2006, 62).

This line of thought also poses the biggest problem for an affect-sensitive social theory. Affects are crucial to understanding emotions as physical intensities in the body that 'move' us (note the link between 'emotion' and the Latin *emovere*, which means 'to move out' or 'to stir up'). Precisely this pre-subjective character, however, might lead us into interpreting affect as some kind of 'original' sensation which is later distracted by the mind. The dangers of such a non-political affect theory are obvious in the aforementioned texts, where affective reactions are elevated onto natural and non-discursive planes (think of 'Being a Muslim, I lost control'). It is crucial to note, therefore, that visceral affects do not imply a chronological or even ethical primary of body over mind. Affects are not closer to 'real' emotions, as their 'intensities' are always retroactively pulled into the realm of meaning.

This makes affects 'presubjective' (unlike emotions) but not 'presocial' (Mazzarella 2012, 291). Thus affect and emotion need to be treated as two sides of the same coin with its own perpetuated and mediatised social history. In her work on the protest against the Danish cartoons in Lahore, Blom has shown how emotions need a certain framework to stage indignation and 'righteous anger' (Blom 2008, 2). I want to further her argument of an 'emotional-institutional landscape' (Blom 2008, 3) by looking at the ways in which certain texts – what I will call below 'hagiohistoric' literature – naturalise a certain emotion when it comes to reacting to blasphemy.

But how do words move people? To answer this question, I suggest that we must understand affective responses as performative and 'citational' – that they need a framework of previous affects within which they can function as being such spontaneous outbursts. That is to say, such mobilising or triggering words build on already sedimented affective structures, rhetoric strategies and textual genres. For Derrida, the power of a performative act comes from a coded structure or its 'citationality' (or 'iterability', see Blom 2008, 18). This citationality points to an articulation's trace, or a history.

The words 'I love you', for example, need to have been spoken and understood for them to be apprehended. They need to be both unique to the respective situation and endlessly repeatable. Yet such arguments about language do not only pertain to the plane of the written or spoken word; they also relate to the realm of visceral affects.[16] This citationality, however, does not yet explain how one term, in our case, 'blasphemer' (*gustākh-i rasūl*), becomes affectively charged – to the extent that many authors claim that the only legitimate reaction to it is to reduce the accused to *vājib-al qatl*.

Sara Ahmed tries to answer this question in her analysis of the emotionality of texts (Ahmed 2014). She uses the metaphor of 'stickiness' to explain how terms become affectively charged by 'sticking' to other terms while simultaneously concealing this association. The term 'Paki', for example, obtains its affective value as an insult from its hidden association with other terms such as 'immigrant, outsider, dirty', etc. (Ahmed 2014, 92). This affective value is produced through the absence of any fixed referent, making flows and circulations possible. Ahmed imagines this 'affective economy' similar to Marx's famous formula M–C–M': that is, money is invested into commodities which then are resold to gain surplus value (Ahmed 2014, 44–9). In other words, hateful terms gain their 'value' because they circulate and adapt to various situations in which they are associated with other signs.

The repetition of such terms and their concealed associations invites the implied audience to take part in their respective 'trace' (Derrida 1977) or sedimented history. The term *gustākh-i rasūl* or the blasphemer can also be understood as such a 'sticky' sign, which accumulated its affective value through association with other (more less concealed) signs. As we have seen in the case study of Salman Taseer, the governor was not only villainised on the basis of his support of an alleged blasphemer, but also for consuming pork and alcohol, and even for being a 'bully of Americans'. Seen through Ahmed's methodological lens, these associations with the term blasphemer are usually concealed. Only through an analysis of the term's tropological shifts does the sign 'blasphemer' reveal its various other links within this discourse.[17] The term's association with many other signs is solidified through a constant repetition, inviting the audience to take part in its emotionally charged terminology. The term is never fully associated with a fixed referent, however, thus making endless affective associations possible.[18]

It is now clear how this theory will help in understanding the transference of emotions and affects in the texts under scrutiny. Words may be affectively charged and produce intensities in the body due to their concealed and endless associations with other similarly charged signs. The described affects in the aforementioned texts are thus no natural intensities in the body, but rather build on traces of former affective reactions. It is precisely this kind of affective archive to which I now want to turn.

'Hagiohistoric' writing and affective archives

The trope of a sole assassin who violently reacts to insults of the Prophet's honour does not start with Mumtaz Qadri, but is built on a larger corpus of writing.[19] Such texts link 'historic' events and persons with hagiographic elements for the purpose of making moral claims about the present. I call such writings 'hagiohistoric' to emphasise how they intertwine meticulous research with accounts of divine intervention for solidifying their moral declarations. In addition, such texts frequently use the second person plural in their accounting of events in order to emphasise the respect given to the protagonist.

I will use these texts as the main source to analyse how the term blasphemer (*gustākh-i rasūl*) is affectively charged and repeated. Furthermore, this discussion will reveal how Mumtaz Qadri's actions, portrayed in his court hearings as uncontainable affective responses to Taseer's blasphemy, are in fact also 'citational': they present him as a Barelvi hero on the basis of already established notions of local and global threats to Islam. While a full overview is beyond the scope of this chapter, the following will introduce two incidents of murder (or attempted murder) of an alleged blasphemer, which in later Urdu hagiohistoric prose lead to the celebration and glorification of the assassin.

Ilmuddin

In April 1929 a young, illiterate Muslim man named Ilmuddin killed a Hindu book publisher, Mahashay Rajpal, in Lahore. His victim's offence was to have published a text widely considered blasphemous among South Asian Muslims. The controversial book was called *Rangīlā Rasūl* (*The Colourful Prophet*), a title that bore an obvious sexual connotation. *Rangīlā Rasūl* was in fact a satire about the alleged love life of the Prophet, and it immediately sparked a wave of protests among various Muslim communities. Rajpal, who was also a supporter of the proto-Hindu nationalists Arya Samaj, was later charged by the colonial government for a religious offence under section 153-A of the Indian Penal Code, and *Rangīlā Rasūl's* second edition was banned in British India (Raj 2015, 151). The Lahore High Court acquitted Rajpal due to scanty evidence of his intention to incite religious hatred (Stephens 2014, 45) and because the Penal Code at that time did not prosecute any '*verbal* defamations' of '*deceased*' religious authorities (Ahmed 2009, 182; italics in original).

The decision was – and still is – seen by many Muslims as a conspiracy planned and jointly organised by the British government and the Hindu majority (Matin 2007, 25). On 6 April 1929 Ilmuddin, the son of a poor carpenter and unable to read the book himself, took the law into his own hands, stabbing Rajpal for his allegedly blasphemous behaviour. Ilmuddin was taken into custody after the murder, where he confessed to his deed and revealed his motive. The young man was sentenced to death and, notwithstanding the intervention of Muhammad Ali Jinnah who defended Ilmuddin in court, he was hanged in October 1929.

Rajpal's assassination took place at a time of heightened communal friction and public displays of devotion for the Prophet in the subcontinent

(Gilmartin 1998, 1078). Within this political turmoil Ilmuddin became celebrated as a man who had stood up against two perceived oppressors of South Asian Muslims: the Hindu majority and the British government. He became an admired figure who served to unify the subcontinent's Islamic sects. Ilmuddin's story has since been reproduced in hagiohistoric accounts, popular films and even Pakistan's current schoolbooks.[20] The book *Ghāzī ʿIlmaluddīn Śahīd* (*The Martyr and Defender of Islam Ilmuddin*, 2007) by Khaula Matin is a striking example of hagiohistoric writing and the glorification of the assassin in religious lore. Matin's introductory text *Dil kī bāt* (*Concern of the Heart*) explains Ilmuddin's significance for the author.

> When it comes to the issues of sacrifice for the honour of the Prophet (pbuh), then the person who influenced me the most, after the companions of the Prophet, is the martyr and defender of Islam, Ilmuddin, who notwithstanding his begrudging circumstance has proven by killing Rajpal the blasphemer that, as long as only one Muslim roams this earth, no blasphemer will be allowed to stay alive … If the government had punished the blasphemer, then no Muslim would have taken the law into his hand (Matin 2007, 13–14).

Ilmuddin is thus elevated onto a plane almost level with the Prophet's companions, his deeds perceived as representative of a natural reaction allegedly shared by all Muslims. In Matin's eyes, only the death of the blasphemer can relieve the believer's affliction and re-establish the broken order. Revenge for any form of disrespect becomes every Muslim's duty. Matin makes this clear with a later point: 'Rajpal is not even close to being human; his murder was not the murder of a human being, but the murder of a devil' (Matin 2007, 36). In this interpretation Rajpal needed to be killed and, since the government failed to persecute and punish the blasphemer, Ilmuddin took the law into his own hands. We will find similar tropes when analysing the recent writings on Mumtaz Qadri.

Ilmuddin's life story, recounted in one of the book's later chapters (Matin 2007, 19–42), further exemplifies what I call hagiohistoric writing. On the one hand, Khaula Matin gives a detailed historic account of Ilmuddin's life, including verifiable dates, historical *personae* and news headings. On the other, however, his descriptions incorporate hagiographic tropes such as the visit of holy men (Matin 2007, 22f.) or divine interventions (Matin 2007, 31). The reader also obtains access to Ilmuddin's innermost feelings as the text blends 'historical narrative with lyrical poetry' (Stephens 2014, 45). All of these elements combine to cast Ilmuddin into a positive light and present his actions and moral judgements as the will of God. An example from Matin's story should further illustrate this.

At one point in the story, Ilmuddin has a dream in which an old man instructs him to act quickly and kill Rajpal. Ilmuddin wakes up and wants to share the dream with his friend, Shide – only to discover that, coincidentally, Shide has had the same dream. This leads to a rather grotesque situation in which the two young men fight over who will be the publisher's killer. To solve the dilemma, each writes his name on a piece of paper and casts it on the ground. A child is asked to pick them up at random and so choose a 'winner'. In this way, Ilmuddin's name is picked three times in a row, making him Rajpal's rightful murderer.

Another divine intervention aims to paint the course of events as a divinely approved natural order. This revelation appears at the time when Ilmuddin finally meets Rajpal and hears a voice saying, 'Don't hesitate, Ilmuddin! You need to do this. Don't hesitate and get up!' (Matin 2007, 29–30). Such and similar stories paint an image of greatness around Ilmuddin. Meanwhile the publisher Rajpal is reduced to a non-human status – and is thus free to be killed without any religious remorse.

Amir Cheema

The events that surround a young textile student from Rawalpindi, Amir Cheema, are an example of how hagiohistoric literature may mix misinformation and 'sticky' tropes to produce a Barelvi martyr. In 2006 Cheema attempted an attack on the conservative German daily *Die Welt*, which had reprinted the controversial Muhammad caricatures that originally appeared in the Danish newspaper *Jyllands-Posten*. Cheema was arrested and, according to the German police, committed suicide in his cell in April of the same year. Notwithstanding the thwarted attack and his own suicide, Amir Cheema is celebrated today as a <u>ghāzī</u> and a śahīd in Barelvi lore. Representations of his case utilise emotionally charged tropes similar to those seen in Ilmuddin's depictions.

According to German, Pakistani and international reporting on the case, Cheema entered the Axel Springer Haus in Berlin armed with a knife on 20 March 2006.[21] Based on his own statement, Cheema intended to murder Roger Köppel, the editor-in-chief of the newspaper, whom he deemed responsible for the reprinting of the Danish cartoons. Security stopped him, however, before he was able to execute the planned attack. Cheema, who seemed confused and disoriented, was arrested by the police and transferred to a jail in Berlin. Here he later hanged himself using a noose made from his own clothes.

This version of events, however, is contested by members of Amir's family and various members of the Barelvi *ulama*, who deem Amir a *śahīd* – a martyr who gave his life for the Prophet's honour. Such sources claim, for example, that Amir successfully assassinated the editor-in-chief, Roger Köppel, and was later killed in a German torture cell (Qādrī 2006). Nobody supplied any proof for this statement, but the production of Amir's suicide note by the German police could not eradicate the rumours of torture and murder in Pakistan.[22] These sources have also ignored the fact that Roger Köppel is, as of 2019, an active politician in his home country of Switzerland, appearing in public on a regular basis. In a personal email correspondence Roger Köppel refused to reveal details of the attack due to security concerns.

The Urdu Wikipedia entry on Amir Cheema provides yet another version of the story.[23] There Cheema is reported to have attempted to kill Henryk Broder, a blogger based in Germany and known mainly for conspiratorial and anti-Islamic prose. Broder, in fact, only worked for *Die Welt* years after Cheema's attack and had nothing to do with the incident. Nevertheless, the article describes how Cheema walked into the office of *Die Welt* and repeatedly stabbed Broder, leading to serious injuries. Broder was never attacked, however. In a personal email of September 2017, he also had no answer to the question of why his name appeared in this entry at all.

The fabricated story of the tortured Pakistani man who killed a German journalist for republishing the Danish cartoons touches an affectively charged issue. Not surprisingly, it also instigated protests in Pakistan from the religious right. Members of the MMA (Mutahida Majlis-e Amal), an association of religious parties in Pakistan, exploited the case politically and attacked the government for its silence on this alleged extrajudicial murder.[24] Protesters at one point even demanded expulsion of the official German representative from Pakistan.[25] The presence of Pakistani officials during Cheema's autopsy in Berlin, and their confirmation that no traces of torture were found, also failed to silence the outrage and the rumours.[26] Cheema's funeral in his hometown in Pakistan was attended by up to 300,000 mourners and various members of Islamic parties.[27] The young man is now championed as an Islamic hero (*ghāzī*) and his grave in Saroki, Wazirabad has turned into a *mazār* (shrine), frequented by admirers and often utilised for political rallies.[28]

The book *Ghāzī ʿĀmir ʿAbdul Raḥman Chīmah Śahīd* by Khalid Mahmd Qadri, published in 2006, displays the Barelvi version of the story. Here, too, Amir Cheema is portrayed as a God-loving young man who regularly prayed and was disgusted by alcohol. He is said to have been miserable due to the desolate condition in which Muslims live in Germany, and to have wished to come back to Pakistan as soon as his studies were complete (Qadri 2006, 187). Most importantly, Amir is represented as a successful assassin who killed the editor-in-chief of *Die Welt*. The following is my translation of how the incident is described:

> ... when he had found out the whereabouts of the editor of the Danish newspaper *Die Welt* [sic] in Berlin, he tried to enter into the office. The security guards stopped him, but Amir Cheema wanted to meet his goal. He said, 'I carry a bomb on my body. I will blow up the whole building. Let me in!' Full of fear, [the guards] stepped aside. He was very brave and strong. He entered into the room of the chief editor and said in a thundering voice: 'I will not allow the blasphemers to stay alive.' Amir Cheema reached the fleeing editor and attacked him with a dagger. He repeatedly attacked him and slit his belly open with a dagger. Meanwhile the staff [working in the building] captured him. They brought the editor quickly to the hospital and the blasphemer was safe from being sent to hell at that time, but even though the doctors tried their best, he could not be kept alive. With this attempt, however, Amir Cheema held Islam's flag up and with his deed made the Muslims happy [since] the duty was done, the debt lifted. This message spread all over Germany like a wildfire (p.145).

In the book Cheema's maternal grandmother recounts a dream that foretold the birth of Amir. At a time when she performed the ᶜ*umrah* in Mecca, she dreamt that the *hūrs* (the virgins in paradise) allowed her daughter into the heavens, where they took care of her. When Amir's grandmother woke up, she interpreted the dream as a sign that God had chosen her daughter for something great. The next time she called her family at home, she was told that her daughter was expecting a child – and this child was Amir (p.37). In a similar way to the aforementioned work, this book also mixes allegedly historic research with genre-typical hagiographic elements and the glorification of the protagonist.

Qadri's book also establishes a link between Amir Cheema and Ilmuddin. Under the heading of 'Why did Cheema take up arms?' (ᶜ*āmir chīmah ne hathyār kyon uṭhāyā?*'), we find a description of the aforementioned case from 1929. Part of the narrative recounts the events of Ilmuddin's life, together with the miracles surrounding his death, such as the corpse's fragrance which convinced a Sikh man to convert to Islam (Qadri 2006, 139). In a later part of the book, Amir's sister is interviewed; she mentions that her brother's favourite person was Ilmuddin (Qadri 2006, 187). Reportedly, Amir used to say to his sister, 'I wish I could also do something like that' (*kāś kah main̲ bhī kuch aisā hī karūn̲*).

The text on Amir Cheema gains its affective value through associating the alleged blasphemer, Roger Köppel, with a wide range of concealed signs. Similar to the case of Salman Taseer above, Köppel also became the figurehead of an international conspiracy against Islam. Qadri's introductory text, for example, describes how Islam is in a state of decay: 'The Muslim world has fallen into decadence, decline, confusion and secession' (p.25).[29] This deterioration, he writes, is perpetuated by Western politicians who conspire with the Jewish media to harm Islam by infiltrating certain films, books, TV dramas and cartoons. The internet, CDs and cable networks are used to spread a wave of indecency over the Islamic world (pp.137–8). According to Qadri, however, Amir Cheema stood up against this conspiracy. His actions gave the Muslim community back their respect – and therefore, Qadri concludes, Amir is a son and an idol of Islam (pp.25–6).

In the final section of this chapter, I will show how similar tropes were utilised to make Mumtaz Qadri into a larger than life Barelvi hero.

'Ghazi Mumtaz Qadri Shaheed'

Pictures of Mumtaz Qadri's immediate surrender show a young man smiling contently and sitting handcuffed in the back of a police car. Videos released later, taken on mobile phones by the policemen arresting Qadri, show the suspect singing *nᶜats* while in police custody and soberly confessing to the murder. These initial images helped to frame Mumtaz Qadri as a pious Muslim committing murder out of his love for the Prophet and then voluntarily surrendering to the police (Qureshi 2012, 29). News recordings of subsequent public appearances show an angry crowd chanting slogans against blasphemy while throwing flowers at Qadri. Some members of the Islamabad Bar Association also championed Qadri as a defender of Islam and offered to fight his case in court for free (Abbas 2013, 68; Rizvi 2013, 14–15).[30] These initial representations set the stage for the subsequent veneration of Qadri, even leading later to the construction of a mosque in his name and the celebration of his first ᶜ*urs* – actually, the celebration of the death of a Sufi saint – on 1 March 2017 in Bara Kahu, Islamabad.[31]

While other religious sects, such as the Jamaat-e-Islami, or the Jamaat ud-Dawa, also supported Salman Taseer's assassination, the Barelvis spearheaded a veneration campaign that transformed Mumtaz Qadri into a saintly figure. Qadri's life became filled with hagiographic tropes similar to those revolving around Ilmuddin and Amir Cheema. The following is but one example of how Qadri's birth is portrayed in the hagiohistoric book, *Muḥammad Malik Mumtāz Ḥasīn Qādrī Śahīd*, written by Ahmad Sia Sayalvi.

> About two years before your birth, your father, Grami Malik Muhammad Bashir Avan, woke up from a deep sleep and saw an old bearded man with a bright face praying in one corner of the house. Mr. Malik got worried and wondered how the old man could have entered [the house] even though the door was locked. In this moment, the old man stood up and said while leaving the room: 'Bashir Sahab! Here where I prayed, a saint in the eye of god and a friend of the Prophet (pbuh) will be born, who will make your name famous in the whole world. From his roar the halls of four hundred unbelievers will tremble and Pakistan's geographical and ideological [*naẓaryātī*] borders will become permanent' (Sayalvi 2016, 2).

With its reference to Pakistan's geographical and ideological borders, Sayalvi's hagiohistory creates a nexus between religious mythology and state ideology. Such a discourse has become a significant characteristic of Barelvi public engagement in recent decades (Philippon 2014). To further emphasise Qadri's outstanding persona, Sayalvi describes additional stories from Mumtaz's period in jail. At Qadri's arrival, for example, thousands of inmates supposedly chanted, 'In serving the Prophet, we also accept death', and welcomed him with a garland (Sayalvi 2016, 15f.). Qadri allegedly also cured various diseases, including cancer, and people who met him claimed that his body emanated an extraordinary scent (Sayalvi 2016, 16).

In Muhammad Rizvi's book *Tazkirah Ghāzī Mumtāz Ḥasīn Qādrī*, we find another typical story about Qadri's birth. Here it is again Mumtaz's father, Bashir Avan, who describes how a wandering Sufi saint predicted Mumtaz's pious deed. The incident happened as Avan was walking home from a religious event: he suddenly came upon a travelling *qalandar* (a Sufi saint), asleep on the ground. Avan approached him and invited him home for dinner. The man accepted the invitation and also correctly predicted the meal that Avan's wife had cooked for that night. After dinner Avan invited the Sufi to stay for the night, but the man declined, explaining that he had just come from Kashmir and now needed to travel to Delhi. When the *qalandar* left, he predicted good news for Avan's family in the near future. Later, when Mumtaz was born, Avan understood that this is what the *qalandar* had meant (Rizvi 2015, 17–18).

Qadri's veneration, even apotheosis, has a large affective archive at its disposal. His portrayal, which has today increasingly shifted to other media – such as video or Facebook pages – connects to similar cases and their representations from the past. This is evident in the depictions of Ilmuddin and Amir Cheema. Qadri's outburst, represented as a natural Muslim reaction in court, thus refers to a vast archive of emotional history. He and his biographers simultaneously draw from a sedimented history of emotion, as well as producing further sediments and 'traces' for future archives. Such sediments of affect are not only found in hagiohistoric writing, but have also – due to the digitalisation of the everyday – proliferated within many planes of society (see chapter 5).

Conclusion

When Salman Taseer spoke out against the blasphemy laws, many members of the Barelvi *ulama* interpreted the move as yet another attack on Islam, declaring that the governor 'ought to be killed' (*vājib-al qatl*). This public condemnation served as an open invitation to the masses to punish the blasphemer and re-establish the Barelvis' tainted symbolic order. Mumtaz Qadri executed this re-establishment, subsequently becoming an object of admiration and awe. In this chapter I analysed the hagiohistoric archives of this and similar veneration as one part of the emotional framework that made Taseer's assassination possible. These texts not only provide a history of young men willing to commit murder for the protection of the Prophet's honour; their blend of meticulous research with hagiographic tropes also helps to corroborate and naturalise certain kinds of affects and emotions as intrinsic parts of what it means to be Muslim. Qadri's court testimony stating that he was 'justified to kill [Taseer]' because 'being a Muslim [he] lost control' is but one example for such a naturalisation.

Recent studies of emotions show how affects arise as intensities in the body, but become retroactively qualified within certain symbolic orders. Hagiohistoric writing is significant (albeit not alone) in this qualification, as it repeatedly associates the term 'blasphemer' (*gustākh-i rasūl*) with a variety of other concealed signs. Taseer's alleged blasphemy, for example, became associated with his liberal lifestyle, his taste for alcohol, his relationship with a non-Muslim woman and his rejection of religious rituals, as well as his disregard for the Quran. Furthermore, Taseer is represented as a foreign agent, thus associating his transgressions with the discourse on the global threat to Islam and its vast emotional archive. All these qualities additionally charge the term *gustākh-i rasūl* and help in obtaining its affective value.

Notes

1. Transliteration follows the guidelines given by the Library of Congress. Names (of individuals and parties, for example) are given in their English form (for example, Jamaat-e-Islami).
2. This number, however, needs to be brought into context with regard to the comparatively small number of non-Muslims in the Islamic Republic. While it is extremely difficult to rely on demographic numbers, recent studies claim that only around 3 per cent of Pakistan's population fall under the category of 'non-Muslims' (Ispahani 2017, 6).
3. http://www.dawn.com/news/1221103.
4. http://tribune.com.pk/story/265857/sunni-tehreeks-protest-against-qadri-verdict-turns-violent/.
5. http://tribune.com.pk/story/85412/blasphemy-case-masjid-imam-offers-reward-to-kill-aasia/; http://edition.cnn.com/2010/WORLD/asiapcf/12/23/pakistan.blasphemy.protest/.
6. https://www.youtube.com/watch?v=HxvlLpSy4BI (0:18–3:53). This and all other quotes from Urdu in this article have been translated by me.
7. https://www.theguardian.com/world/2011/jan/08/salmaan-taseer-blasphemy-pakistan-bibi.
8. https://www.youtube.com/watch?v=zKrFWIDQZfw.
9. http://www.huffingtonpost.com/aatish-taseer/salman-taseer-stranger-to-history_b_2121502.html.
10. http://www.dawn.com/news/597628; http://www.nytimes.com/2011/01/11/world/asia/11qadri.html.
11. https://www.youtube.com/watch?v=8QEtLWYY6Tk.
12. Murid Hussain became famous after he killed a Hindu veterinarian in 1935 because the man had named a donkey after the Prophet Muhammad.
13. In 1935 Abdul Qayyum stabbed Nathuram, the editor of the Sindhi newspaper, *Sindh Samacar*, who had published a pamphlet that was considered blasphemous. The British government executed Qayyum on 19 March 1935.
14. Abdul Rasheed killed Swami Shraddhananda, a member of Arya Samaj, in 1926.
15. The assumption that Salman Taseer had provoked Qadri by stating that the blasphemy laws were his 'shit' was not proven in court, as the main witness, Sheikh Wapas, who was present at the time of the incident, and could have confirmed the sudden provocation, was not summoned as a witness by Qadri's defence.
16. Here my point comes close to Wittgenstein's 'private language' argument. For Wittgenstein no language could be private, as all emotions and inner feelings need to make use of a language which has been used before and was publicly available (Wittgenstein 1969, 243–315).
17. It is important to note that such associations are context sensitive. While the term '*gustākh-i rasūl*' might have a fairly established association with the sign 'making-derogatory-remarks-about-the-Prophet', other associations such as 'bully of Americans' or 'scotch drinker' may be particular to this discourse.
18. Žižek makes a similar argument in one of his early works, when he describes the 'surplus X' within ideology using the discourse of anti-Semitism as an example. The term 'jew', he argues, is not defined through fixed characteristics, but rather through an 'unattainable X', which opens the term to an endless variety of new descriptions. In other words there will always be something missing when aiming to describe the term 'jew', which adds to its affective charge (Žižek 1989, 105–10).

19. These texts have historic links to older Sufi hagiographies. At this point, however, I will not be able to explore this connection.
20. http://www.huffingtonpost.com/bashir-ahmad-gwakh/-the-deep-roots-of-pakist_b_807788.html.
21. http://www.spiegel.de/politik/deutschland/karikaturenstreit-selbstmord-nach-versuchtem-angriff-auf-chefredakteur-der-welt-a-414669.html; https://www.dawn.com/news/191024; http://www.nytimes.com/2006/05/10/world/europe/10iht-islam.html.
22. https://www.dawn.com/news/191456/berlin-gives-amir.
23. https://ur.wikipedia.org/wiki/عامر_چیمی. The article is also written in a hagiohistoric way, using, for example, the second person plural when talking about Cheema.
24. https://www.thenews.com.pk/archive/print/6677-mma-slates-govt-for-inaction-over-amir-cheemas-murder.
25. https://www.expatica.com/de/news/Angry-protests-after-death-of-Pakistani-in-Germany_137563.html.
26. https://www.thenews.com.pk/archive/amp/6174-amir-cheema-committed-suicide-claims-burney.
27. http://news.bbc.co.uk/1/hi/world/south_asia/4768615.stm.
28. https://www.pakistantoday.com.pk/2016/01/16/violent-sufis-growing-barelvi-extremism/; https://www.dawn.com/news/245026.
29. Qadri hereby picks up ideas of an Islamic Golden Age which were already found in reform movements of the nineteenth century (Reetz 2006).
30. For a visual representation of this appearance, see https://www.youtube.com/watch?v=2VhplckGeDQ&t=3s.
31. Due to the high number of daily visitors, the mosque needed to be extended recently to accommodate the crowds. https://www.theguardian.com/world/2014/apr/30/pakistan-mosque-killer-mumtaz-qadri-salaman-taseer.

References

Abbas, Shemeem Burney. 2013. *Pakistan's Blasphemy Laws*. Austin: University of Texas Press.
Ahmad, Asad Ali. 2009. 'Specters of Macaulay', in *Censorship in South Asia*, William Mazzarella and Raminder Kaur, eds, 172–205. Indianapolis: Indiana University Press.
Ahmed, Sara. 2014. *Cultural Politics of Emotion*. Edinburgh: Edinburgh University Press.
Bibi, Asia and Anne-Isabelle Tollet. 2012. *Blasphemy*. Chicago: Chicago Review Press.
Blom, Amélie. 2008. 'The 2006 anti-'Danish Cartoons' riot in Lahore: Outrage and the emotional landscape of Pakistani politics.' *Samaj* 2: 1–32.
Clough, Patricia Ticineto and Jean Halley. 2007. *The Affective Turn*. Durham: Duke University Press
Derrida, Jacques. 1977. *Limited Inc*. Evanston: Northwestern University Press.
Farah, Sumbul. 2013. 'Aqeeda, Adaband Aitraaz: Modalities of "being" Barelwi.' *Contributions to Indian Sociology* 46 (3): 259–81.
Favret-Saada, Jeanne. 2015. 'An anthropology of religious polemics.' *HAU: Journal of Ethnographic Theory* 6 (1): 29–45.
Gilmartin, David. 1998. 'Partition, Pakistan, and South Asian history: In search of a narrative.' *Journal of South Asian Studies* 57 (4): 1068–95.
Gregg, Melissa and Gregory J. Seigworth. 2009. *The Affect Theory Reader*. Durham: Duke University Press.
Gugler, Thomas. 2015. 'Barelwis: Developments and dynamics of conflict with Deobandis', in *Sufis and Salafis in the Contemporary Age*, Lloyd Ridgeon, ed, 171–90. London: Bloomsbury.
Human Rights Commission of Pakistan. 2016. 'State of Human Rights in 2016.' Self-published.
Ispahani, Farahnaz. 2017. *Purifying the Land of the Pure*. New York: Oxford University Press.
Khan, Ismail. 2011. 'The assertion of Barelvi extremism.' *Current Trends in Islamist Ideology* 12: 51–72.
Khosa, Asif, Mushir Alam and Dost Muhammad Khan, eds, 2015. *Malik Muhammad Mumtaz Qadri v. State*.

Massumi, Brian.1995. 'The autonomy of affect.' *Cultural Critique* 31: 83–109.
Matin, Khaula. 2007. *Ghāzī ᶜilmaluddīn Śahīd (The Martyr and Defender of Islam Ilmuddin)*. Self publication.
Mazzarella, William. 2012. ' "Affect: What is it good for?"', in *Enchantments of Modernity*, Saurabh Dube, ed, 291–309. London: Routledge.
Moj, Muhammad. 2015. *The Deoband Madrassah Movement*. London: Anthem Press.
O'Sullivan, S. 2001. 'The aesthetics of affect: Thinking art beyond representation.' *Angelaki* 6 (3): 25–35.
Philippon, Alix. 2014. 'The role of Sufism in the identity construction, mobilization and political activism of the Barelwi movement in Pakistan.' *Partecipazione E Conflitto* 7 (1): 152–69.
Qādrī, Muḥammad Khalīl al-Raḥman. 2012. *Ghāzī Malik Mumtāz Ḥasīn Qadrī ka Iqdām*. Lahore: Islāmik Meḍyā.
Qādrī, Khālid Maḥmmūd. 2006. *Ghāzī ᶜĀmir ᶜAbdul Raḥman Chīmah Śahīd*. Jamaᶜyat ᶜulamā-i Pākistān.
Quresī, Muḥammad Ḥanīf. 2012. *Ghāzī Mumtāz Ḥasīn Qadrī*. Islamabad: Śabāb-i Islāmī Pākistān.
Raj, Richa. 2015. 'A Pamphlet and its (dis)contents: A case study of Rangila Rasul and the controversy surrounding it in colonial Punjab, 1923–29.' *History and Sociology of South Asia* 9 (2): 146–62.
Reetz, Dietrich. 2006. *Islam in the Public Sphere*. New York: Oxford University Press.
Rizvi, Muḥammad Sadiq Qādrī. 2015. *Tazkirah Ghāzī Mumtāz Ḥasīn Qadrī*. Lahore: Idārah Riẓāe. n.d.
Saeed, Sadia. 'Secular power, law and the politics of religious sentiments.' *Critical Research on Religion* 3 (1): 57–71.
Sayalvi, Sakur Ahmad Ziya. 2016. *Muḥammad Malik Mumtāz Ḥasīn Qadrī Riẓvī Śahīd*. Lahore: Jāmᶜyah Niẓāmiyah Riẓviyah.
Schaflechner, Jürgen. 2018. *Hinglaj Devi: Identity, Change, and Solidification at a Hindu Temple in Pakistan*. New York: Oxford University Press.
Siddique, Osama and Zahra Hayat. 2008. 'Unholy speech and holy laws: Blasphemy laws in Pakistan – controversial origins, design defects and free speech implications.' *Minnesota Journal of International Law* 17 (2): 305–85.
Simpson, Edward. 2008. 'The changing perspectives of three Muslim men on the question of saint worship over a 10-year period in Gujarat, Western India.' *Modern Asian Studies* 42 (2/3): 377–403.
Singh, David Emmanuel. 2012. *Islamization in Modern South Asia*. Berlin: Walter de Gruyter.
Spinoza, Baruch. 2006. *The Essential Spinoza*, edited by Michael L. Morgan. Indianapolis: Hackett.
Stephens, J. 2014. 'The politics of Muslim rage: Secular law and religious sentiment in late colonial India.' *History Workshop Journal* 77 (1): 45–64.
Turābī, Muḥammad Śahzād Qādrī. n.d. *Malik Mumtāz Ḥasīn Qadrī. Śakhṣiyat Aur Safar Ākhirat*. Karachi: Self-published.
Wittgenstein, Ludwig. 1969. 'Philosophische Untersuchungen', in *Schriften 1*. Frankfurt a. M.: Suhrkamp.
Žižek, Slavoj. 1989. *The Sublime Object of Ideology*. London: Verso.

Websites

BBC. 2006. 'Huge crowds at Pakistani funeral.' http://news.bbc.co.uk/1/hi/world/south_asia/4768615.stm.
CNN. 2010. 'Pakistan parties protest possible blasphemy law charges.' http://edition.cnn.com/2010/WORLD/asiapcf/12/23/pakistan.blasphemy.protest/.
Dawn. 2006. 'Berlin gives Amir's suicide note to FO.' https://www.dawn.com/news/191456/berlin-gives-amir.
Dawn. 2006. 'Pakistani student found dead in Berlin prison.' https://www.dawn.com/news/191024.
Dawn. 2007. 'Row over Amir Cheema's death.' https://www.dawn.com/news/245026.
Dawn. 2011. 'Sermons motivated killer of Governor Taseer.' http://www.dawn.com/news/1221103.

Dawn. 2015. 'Sit-in staged for review of Mumtaz Qadri's conviction in Karachi.' http://www.dawn.com/news/597628.
Der Spiegel. 2006. 'Selbstmord nach versuchtem Angriff auf Chefredakteur der "Welt".' http://www.spiegel.de/politik/deutschland/karikaturenstreit-selbstmord-nach-versuchtem-angriff-auf-chefredakteur-der-welt-a-414669.html.
Expatica. 2006. 'Angry protests after death of Pakistani in Germany.' https://www.expatica.com/de/news/Angry-protests-after-death-of-Pakistani-in-Germany_137563.html.
The Express Tribune. 2010. 'Blasphemy case: Cleric offers Rs 500,000 for Aasia's execution.' http://tribune.com.pk/story/85412/blasphemy-case-masjid-imam-offers-reward-to-kill-aasia/.
The Express Tribune. 2011. 'Sunni Tehreek's protest against Qadri verdict turns violent.' http://tribune.com.pk/story/265857/sunni-tehreeks-protest-against-qadri-verdict-turns-violent/.
The Guardian. 2011. 'Salman Taseer, Aasia Bisi and Pakistan's struggle with extremism.' https://www.theguardian.com/world/2011/jan/08/salmaan-taseer-blasphemy-pakistan-bibi.
The Guardian. 2014. 'Pakistan mosque built to honour politician's killer to double in size.' https://www.theguardian.com/world/2014/apr/30/pakistan-mosque-killer-mumtaz-qadri-salaman-taseer.
The Huffington Post. 2011. 'The deep roots of Pakistan's extremism.' http://www.huffingtonpost.com/bashir-ahmad-gwakh/-the-deep-roots-of-pakist_b_807788.html.
The Huffington Post. 2012. 'My book "Stranger to History" was used to defend my father's killer.' https://www.huffingtonpost.com/aatish-taseer/salman-taseer-stranger-to-history_b_2121502.html?guccounter=1.
The News. 2006. 'Amir Cheema committed suicide, claims Burney.' https://www.thenews.com.pk/archive/amp/6174-amir-cheema-committed-suicide-claims-burney.
The News. 2006. 'MMA slates govt for inaction over Amir Cheema's murder.' https://www.thenews.com.pk/archive/print/6677-mma-slates-govt-for-inaction-over-amir-cheemas-murder.
The New York Times. 2006. 'A death in Berlin reignites Muslim anger.' http://www.nytimes.com/2006/05/10/world/europe/10iht-islam.html.
The New York Times. 2011. 'Pakistani assassin says he acted alone.' http://www.nytimes.com/2011/01/11/world/asia/11qadri.html.
Pakistan Today. 2016. 'Violent Sufis: Growing Barelvi extremism.' https://www.pakistantoday.com.pk/2016/01/16/violent-sufis-growing-barelvi-extremism/.
YouTube. 2010. 'Governor Punjab-Aasia Bibi press conference.' https://www.youtube.com/watch?v=HxvlLpSy4BI.
YouTube. 2011. 'Mumtaz Qadri reception at court.' https://www.youtube.com/watch?v=2VhplckGeDQ&t=3s.
YouTube. 2011. 'Hanif Qureshi's sermon which made Mumtaz Qadri to kill Salman Taseer Gustakh e Rasool khanqah dogran.' https://www.youtube.com/watch?v=8QEtLWYY6Tk.
YouTube. 2014. 'Salman Taseer interview. BBC Urdu.' https://www.youtube.com/watch?v=zKrF-WIDQZfw.

9
Afterword: On the efficacy of 'blasphemy'

Ute Hüsken

This volume, *Outrage: The Rise of Religious Offence in Contemporary South Asia*, is a very ambitious project. It explores the sharp rise of blasphemy accusations in the twenty-first century, specifically those occurring in countries which were formerly under British colonial rule and thus inherited the Indian Penal Code. Six 'blasphemy' cases from Pakistan, India, Bangladesh and Myanmar are discussed in depth, while the historically and theoretically well-informed Introduction casts a wide net and pulls the threads together.

Aiming to look beyond single case studies and country-specific developments, both the Introduction and individual contributors address the common question: why has there been such an intensification of allegations of hurt religious sentiments, desecration and sacrilege? This Afterword analyses the 'blasphemy' cases presented in this volume from the angle of Ritual Studies. In so doing, it does not claim that blasphemy cases *are* rituals. Rather, looking at these cases *as* rituals helps us to better understand *how* they work (efficacy), including who or what are the driving factors in these processes (agency) and how these processes are related to or disconnected from individual intentions, irrespective of the specific local, historical and social setting.

Performative efficacy, intentionality, agency

The phenomenon of 'blasphemy', as it is addressed in the contributions to this volume, is the legacy of colonial law, which then became the Indian Penal Code. The Introduction emphasises that 'blasphemy' is a judgement that produces what it describes. In Ritual Studies this mode of producing effects is called 'performative efficacy'; it relies on the local agreement 'that this is the way to do it', as Podeman Sørenson puts it (Podeman Sørenson 2006, 526). Judicial courts mainly work through such performative efficacy. The verdict that a specific action constitutes 'blasphemy' is a performative speech act in the Austinian sense (Austin 1955): it produces what it pronounces – at least within the jurisdiction of the respective court.[1]

At the same time, the act of 'blasphemy' itself is endowed with performative efficacy, as Rollier shows in chapter 2. He points out that 'the necessity to uphold blasphemy laws implies a presumption of linguistic efficacy, if not the recognition of blasphemy's power to bring about prodigious disruptions'. This seems to hold true for all the case studies from Pakistan (chapters 2, 7 and 8). In these we consistently see that the words themselves constitute (or re-enact) the offence, even if they are framed differently – for example, when repeated within the context of the legal process. Prosecution witnesses sometimes refuse to produce or to repeat the incriminating evidence, since doing so would amount to desecration. The impact of the reference to 'the act' is also minimised in court records by invoking Allah's forgiveness, as Rollier reveals (chapter 2). Only through such linguistic strategies is the performative efficacy removed from the words.

However, in his case study Ahmed shows how multiple translations, representations and interpretations in the process of handling the words in court fundamentally change what might have been said originally. This process helps to *create* the offence, thereby successfully *adding* performative efficacy to a speech act that may never have taken place but is retrospectively constructed. Ahmed's study of the court case involving Yousaf Ali (who was charged with claiming to be the Prophet in 1997) shows how translation and mediation processes *produced* the blasphemer.

'Performative efficacy' is closely linked to agency and intentionality. In Pakistan's blasphemy provisions intentionality is largely irrelevant (see chapter 8). In contrast, intentionality is central in the relevant paragraphs of the Myanmar Penal Code. In chapter 3 Frydenlund presents two cases from Myanmar, in both of which the accused were found guilty of offending Buddhism. One – a bar owner who wanted to promote drinks on Facebook with an image of the Buddha wearing headphones – was found guilty of having 'intentionally plotted to insult religious belief' and sentenced to two and a half years in prison. The second – a writer who publicly made the point that the Buddha was not Burmese – was found guilty on charges of 'deliberate and malicious acts intended to outrage religious feelings of any class by insulting its religion or religious beliefs'. He was sentenced to two years in prison.

Although the Myanmar Penal Code's formulation of the relevant paragraphs explicitly includes intentionality ('… with intent to insult the religion of any class …', 'Deliberate and malicious acts intended to outrage …' and 'with the deliberate intent …'), intentionality was in fact not considered when the men in the two cases were convicted (see chapter 3). This disregard of the intentions of the 'blasphemers' implies their lack of agency and the irreversibility of 'the act'. The words or acts work by themselves, and therefore they – again – are intrinsically performative in the Austinian sense.

(Im)Materiality

Importantly, however, performative efficacy is not a characteristic of speech acts alone. In chapter 2 Rollier points to the important effects of the transformation of words (in his case, quranic words) into artefacts with material properties. On the one hand this transformation facilitates their dissemination, but on the other it increases the risk of desacralisation – for example, the paper on which quranic verses are written could be burnt or trodden on.

The importance of the (im)material is brought out in particular in chapter 5, 'Affective digital images: Shiva in the Kaaba and the smartphone revolution'. Frøystad's contribution extends the investigation into the visual realm; in her case study it is images, rather than words, that are found to be offensive. As a result of intensifying internet penetration through mobile phones and smartphones, along with the growing use of social media in South Asia, virtual connections between new users and new groups are accelerating exponentially. These technologies are a major driving force and an essential element in processes leading to blasphemy accusations. Even more than words, these immaterial images can be interpreted in a variety of ways. With images, the message can be far more ambiguous. Here it is the receiving public that decides not only on the efficacy, but also on the *content* of the message itself. In that sense, Frøystad argues, 'the medium has become the message'.

The medium, in this case social media, impacts society through the content it delivers, but also by virtue of its own specific characteristics (Michandani 2018, 21) – notably the immateriality of images, which facilitates reproducibility at minimal cost and effort, even as authorship and accountability are obscured. While it is obvious *that* the medium is one central agent in these processes, Frøystad shows that in each and every case we still need to consider the local details of *how* an agreement (if any) on the content and efficacy of these specific messages is achieved.

As I argue below with reference to Whitehouse's 'frequency and arousal theory' (Whitehouse 2005), the easy repeatability of visuals and messages through smartphone technology reinforces the message; it is thus an important factor contributing to its efficacy. In order to explore the agency of social media and technology in more detail, it would be instructive to look into the details of cases where a potentially offensive message or image did *not* create any significant response, and to investigate the circumstances and details of a *lack* of efficacy – what I refer to as 'failed blasphemy' below.

Mediation plays an important role in both Frøystad's and in Ahmed's case studies, as does the individual mastery of the technology (Frøystad) or language (Ahmed) which influences both the number and the outcome of these controversies. Yet clearly agency does not reside only with the users of new technologies. For example, web engines encourage specialisation and polarisation (Eriksen 2016, 121) and thus have agency on their own. We are also confronted with new industries (Udupa and McDowell 2017), busy with manipulation and shaping opinion behind the scenes, which usually is invisible to the average user. Functioning like a 'giant megaphone', smartphone apps can decontextualise and enlarge the smallest issues. This confirms the more general insight that new media work in unpredictable ways, no matter whether we are talking about the printing press, television or smartphones.

A future task is therefore to look into the agency of media, and in particular of images in this process. Such analysis necessarily includes critically looking at the neoliberal notions of 'choice' and 'freedom' in consumer societies. While social media do not stop at national boundaries, and are thus an expression of 'large scale phenomena' (Eriksen 2016), this agency mingles intimately with local practices and actors. Agency never rests solely with a person or a medium: it is better understood as a network of distributed agency (Sax 2010). We therefore have to qualify what was previously noted about 'performative efficacy'. Although 'performative efficacy' implies that the performance itself renders the ritual effective, this is not an infallible mechanism. Instead it depends on certain preconditions. The most important aspect, namely the local agreement that 'this is the way it works' (Podeman Sørenson 2006, 526), in many cases encompasses several other requirements with regard to the appropriate conditions, performers and mode of performance.

Thus, for 'blasphemy' to work it is not only necessary that there exists a basic (though often vague) agreement on what it constitutes, but also that this agreement includes an agreement as to who can and who cannot blaspheme. Whose words or deeds matter? A person has to be attributed the relevant agency for this performative act. Ruud rightly points out that 'blasphemy' is never just about the act; it is also about the alleged blasphemer, and what and who s/he represents. More often than not, s/he represents all that is wrong in the accuser's eyes. At the same time, as the editors have shown in their Introduction, 'blasphemy' as a value judgement is usually employed by one of the majority or dominant groups in a society, often to curb dissent. In this context Appadurai's concept of 'predatory identities' is helpful (Appadurai 2006). Such identities require the extinction of other, proximate social categories, on the basis of a majority that feels allegedly threatened (whether in religious, linguistic or racial terms); they aim at silencing or even eradicating minorities.

A good example is the case of the radical Buddhist monks described by Frydenlund in chapter 3. While the two men were convicted by the state, it was the Buddhist monastic community (*sangha*) and, more precisely, MaBaTha and the 969 network (both Buddhist monastic organisations concerned with the perceived Islamisation of Myanmar) who demanded their conviction. Yet this does not always work, as Sen shows in chapter 6. Here she raises the question of who can speak for whom in her study of an emerging, ritual-based alternative to the predatory Hindutva identity. Sen shows that only through paying attention to detail on the local level can we actually see the processes that either encourage or prevent the assessment of an act as an offence.

In chapter 6 Sen demonstrates how different agents assess specific situations differently. In her speech in New Delhi, the then education minister Smriti Irani condemned the JNU students' celebration of Mahishasur martyrdom day as 'blasphemy', claiming that the Durga-worshipping populace of Kolkata was certainly outraged by it as well. She was thus trying to *produce* a case of 'blasphemy'. Yet in Kolkata the entire affair translated into a multifaceted discussion of the status and subjectivity of 'Asurs', in part through staging them, but also by involving some Asur people in one of the *pandals* of Durga Puja in 2016. Sen shows how this *pandal*, and the publicity it generated, was brought into use by the diverse actors (including the Asurs themselves, who used it to negotiate their position *vis-à-vis* the state). In so doing the actors rendered Irani's accusation of blasphemy a failure – at least there and then.

Irani's ignorance of local actors resulted in 'failed blasphemy'. Understood in terms of Ritual Studies, a 'failed blasphemy' would be an act that has the potential or might even be designed to incite religious outrage in others, but fails to do so. In these cases, it is the *lack* of efficacy that produces 'failed blasphemy' (see Hüsken 2007b). This might be the case when criticism is taken lightly, or even used constructively, or when words are dismissed, overheard or ignored. 'Blasphemy' is not inherent in words nor in the act itself, but in the response: it is a negative evaluation which can be, but does not have to be, attached to other people's acts or words. Importantly, even a negative evaluation gives weight, focuses attention and places importance. 'Failed blasphemy', in contrast, points towards who or what does *not* matter, who or what does *not* pose a threat and can be ignored. This is why a 'blasphemy' case might result in mob lynching or simply dissolve in thin air.

The seemingly diametrically opposed effects that a blasphemy accusation can have could be understood with reference to what Eriksen terms 'clashes of scale' (Eriksen 2016). He points out that, despite globalisation, most people's 'global outlook remains firmly anchored in their worlds of experience'. However, he also shows that, more often than not, the dialectics of globalisation are about 'large scale impinging on and dominating small scale' (Eriksen 2016, 150). Thus even transnational 'blasphemy' cases are often translated *locally* into action. One such action that becomes increasingly popular is street protests, designed to perform outrage and stage a sense of offence.

Emotional efficacy[2]

In several contributions to this volume, we see staged and 'dramatised' public responses to perceived blasphemy in street protests, or in the public heroisation and veneration of those who assassinate alleged blasphemers, often after the state has 'failed' to punish them 'appropriately' (see chapters 7 and 8). In chapter 4 these public displays are compared by Ruud to '(street) theatre' – not least because they are planned in advance (banners and effigies are prepared, as are press releases etc.), carefully rehearsed and performed for an audience. And in fact, on these occasions, the actors 'perform' in the strict sense of the word: they act, and they are consciously on display.

Ruud addresses the seeming contradiction between the strong emotions displayed during such street protests and the idea of theatre. The fact that protestors display apparently uncontrollable emotions in response to a perceived violation may at first seem incompatible with the idea of staged theatre. Although the label 'theatre' emphasises the performance's entertainment value, rather than its efficacy, following Schechner we see that performances may in fact possess qualities of both: entertainment and efficacy (Schechner 1977). When efficacy outweighs entertainment, the ritual aspects are predominant, while a performance that aims mainly at entertainment is a theatrical performance.[3]

Considered in that way, most cases of street protest mentioned in the contributions to this volume would rather fall in the category of ritual, since the intended outcome is clearly a *change* of the state of affairs beyond the performance of street protest. The government, or anyone who dares, is urged to take action against the 'blasphemers'. When analysing these events as ritual or ritualised performances, it is important not to conflate 'ritual' with meaningless and empty actions. On the contrary: ritual is here understood as efficacious and transforming activity.[4] Yet, also as ritual, street protests such as those described by Ruud in chapter 4 are carefully planned and rehearsed, something that still seems to be at odds with the strong uncontrollable emotions there displayed. Pernau shows that such emotional responses have some of their roots in perceptions of, and discourses on, virility and masculinity that became prominent around the turn of the nineteenth to the twentieth century (Pernau 2015, 2019). For this and other reasons discussed below, it is important to understand emotions as learned evaluations.

This can be illustrated with religious transgressions in the context of South Indian temple rituals. Here major ritual participants often act out strong negative emotions (envy, anger, dislike and related feelings) towards other participants through verbal abuse and physical violence: ritual participants shout at each other and may on occasion even get into fist fights (for details see Hüsken 2007a). Most of the time, however, such disputes between rival groups and individuals participating in temple rituals are strategically enacted during public temple festivals and processions. Participants thus make public statements about their own position. However, the fact that these fights are *strategically* enacted does not imply that the emotions displayed are not 'real'. Emotions need not be beyond one's own control or overwhelming to be actually and truly felt.

There are in fact many shades of grey between pure acting and being overwhelmed by emotions. Rather, the intense negative emotions of the ritual participants are based on the perceptions that the ritual rights and duties connected to the temple, and the ritual honours that reward participants for their individual contribution to the ritual performance ('ritual shares'), are both part of the participant's unique relationship to the deity.[5] This unique relationship is highly valued and ardently defended. The right to participate in a ritual in a specific way is considered to be one's property, and as such as an extension of the identity of a group or an individual (Harrison 1992).

The transgressions of ritual etiquette are therefore perceived as violations of the boundaries of individual and group identity. The public nature of the temple worship (especially during festivals) intensifies the unpleasant emotions when the expectations of the diverse participants are not met. These negative emotions, and the occasional violence that accompanies them, provide ways of attributing value to the proceedings (Moenius 2004, 166). Emotions are thus appraisals. Usually thought of as the opposite of rational thinking, they are in fact 'judgments of situations based on cultural beliefs and values' (Lynch 1990, 8; Josephinides 2005, 85). Not only are emotions spontaneous evaluations of a situation, but they are often also culturally prescribed, moral requirements (Lynch 1990, 9; Josephinides 2005, 72). Sax, for example, describes the situation of young women in Garhwal (India) who are expected to cry when leaving home (Sax 2012). Shedding tears is the display of 'morally correct emotions' (Svašek 2005, 8) – a premise that becomes especially clear when we look at instances of failure to display expected emotions. If a young Garhwali woman fails to cry, for example, she is considered a 'bad daughter'. Not surprisingly, members of communities usually conform to these emotional moral obligations.[6] As Pernau points out, the relevant sections in the Indian Penal Code had a similar effect (Pernau 2018; see also Pernau 2019). By transforming 'hurt sentiments into a resource recognized by the court', the legislation incites people to show 'how much one's sentiments have been hurt'. In this context showing one's strong emotions is not so much a moral, but rather a legal requirement.

Irrespective of whether morally or legally required emotions are concerned, the value system that underlies the emotional evaluation of a situation is not self-evident. It is culturally specific and acquired through learning processes. Emotional responses are learned, which does not exclude the fact that they are also embodied responses.[7] Repetition here is key, as in most learning processes.

In order to gain a deeper understanding of the connection between repetition and emotion, it is helpful to turn to Whitehouse's 'frequency and arousal theory' (e.g. Whitehouse 2005). In a nutshell, he argues that repetition reinforces input in mammalian brains. We learn particular skills through practice. These embodied skills become 'second nature' to us, enabling us to 'carry them out without consciously representing the knowledge we have acquired' (Whitehouse 2005, 94).

Repetition and imitation are gradual ways of embodying not only postures, movements etc., but also of embodying the corresponding emotions. (Ritual) mimesis has the power to create or transform emotions. Thus emotions and evaluations do not reside in the event 'as such', but are always personal and culturally specific. Being embodied, they go along with physical reactions, yet are acquired in learning processes. Here the accelerating speed and frequency of messages and images in social media play a decisive role in intensifying and 'heating up' emotions during street protests. The visual repetition of specific evaluations in online 'echo chambers' reinforces the message and amplifies emotions, as Frøystad's case study in particular reveals.[8]

The strong emotions displayed during street protests can therefore also be understood as historically rooted embodied politics – complemented by aspects of manipulation, strategy *and* genuine passion – responding to perceived acts of attack on the protesters' subjectivities.

A blind spot: gender

Some contributions to this volume touch upon gender. However, this is a field of inquiry that will need to be theorised in much more detail in future investigations, acknowledging the depth to which gender norms shape human lives. We need to look closely at the gendered nature of conflict, of disruptions of individual lives, of protests and of attempts at reconciliation. Some glimpses are present in the contributions to this volume. As Ruud points out in chapter 4, for example, street protest – and the public display of hurt emotions – is in most cases an urban, young and *male* activity. This observation resonates well with Pernau's historical investigation. She shows that in India around the turn of the nineteenth to the twentieth century the display of passions became constructed as a 'form of virility safeguarding the honor' of both the women and the religion of a community, and so became a 'form of enacting politics' (Pernau 2018).

In chapter 3 Frydenlund explores 'religious transgression' in the context of Myanmar's political liberalisation. Her contribution shows that even a century later, after the turn of the twentieth century, this is still dealt with as a transgression and violation of the bodies of female members of a religious community. The 2015 Burmese 'race and religion' laws seek to regulate marriages between Buddhist women and non-Buddhist men, and also to regulate birth control and family planning, which mainly target female bodies. Meanwhile women actors in 'blasphemy' cases remain relatively invisible. This is connected in part to the fact that in the relevant religious traditions women are generally excluded from access to, and exercise of, public ritual and religious authority.

However, future projects will need not only to take female agents in these processes into account, but also to pay attention to intersectionality of gender and ethnicity, caste and age – all further complicated by transculturality. How do women willingly or unwillingly participate in blasphemy accusations, taking advantage of or benefiting from these processes in return for disadvantaging other women or men? It is obvious that Buddhist and Hindu nationalist ideologies reinforce aggressive patriarchal structures. Yet they also offer free spaces for women to find a semblance of emancipation with the blessing of the religious community and a protected kind of identity (Dietrich 1996, 57). How does, at times, a higher degree of gender equality within a religious tradition come at the expense of other subjectivities?

Final reflections

The acceleration of 'blasphemy' cases is part (or symptom) of an all-pervasive phenomenon. Eriksen argues that through the accelerated change in our social, physical, cognitive and temporal worlds, we are confronted with what he calls 'clashes of scale', namely between an abstract (often transnational) level of scale and the concrete level of daily local practices (Eriksen 2016, 10–15). Increasing mobility of people and intensifying flows of information trigger more misunderstandings, as well as cultural conservatism in the face of rapid change (Eriksen 2016, 30, 59). This is one important factor contributing to an increase in accusations of blasphemy.

At the same time, it appears that in many of the case studies in this volume, 'blasphemy' or religious offence is not precisely defined by the accuser. Sen's case study in chapter 4 reveals that what Irani considered blasphemous remained implicit: was it the likening of the goddess to a prostitute or was it demon-worship? Interestingly, in spite of its vague definition in the Penal Code, the inadmissibility of blasphemy in Pakistan is one of the few areas of quasi-consensus among religious parties, even when there is intra-religious competition. Yet even here the definition of what constitutes 'blasphemy' often remains very vague.

Rollier therefore suspects that the accusations of religious offence aim at simplifying the discursive possibilities and excluding ambivalence (chapter 2). In this way 'blasphemy' accusations help to establish coherence through the creation of a hostile attacker on a religious tradition. Such blasphemy accusations, especially defined in imprecise terms, therefore serve to simplify a complex reality and to homogenise an actually disparate group. Establishing a dividing line between the inside and outside of a group is a common way of defining the 'true' tradition.

It may be exactly this ambivalence that offers an entry point for scholars' intervention in 'blasphemy' processes. Taking Eriksen's advice, we should make use of the accelerating connectivity provided by globalisation: it is an opportunity for 'rebuilding the ship at sea' (Eriksen 2016, 155). For we need to draw upon all the opportunities we can get hold of for communication and discussion – not necessarily to reach consensus, but to increase mutual understanding.

Notes

1. In the way that temple disputes in India were – and still are – settled (or accelerated), we see a similar effect of colonial legal concepts and terminology. In the blasphemy issue as well as in temple disputes, the British attempt to create a uniform legislation rather than arbitration of disputes was a very decisive factor. Here, too, the language that describes the offence directly reflects the wording of the law. The law thus defines and 'produces' the offence (see Hüsken 2009; Mukund 2005).
2. While 'affect' is referred to in a number of contributions to this book, understood in these chapters as 'prepersonal', non-conscious experience of intensity, prior to emotion, I refer in this contribution only to emotions as culturally determined evaluations.
3. However, Köpping rightly remarks that the distinctions between 'acting' and ritual performance are often closely connected to the performance skills of the audience or participants (2004, 101–2). And as Kendall shows, a strict separation of ritual ('real', 'authentic') and theatrical ('false', 'only acting') performances often is a misconception (Kendall 1996, 19ff).
4. Importantly, Sax points out that the use of the term 'ritual' implies a supposed lack of efficacy, at least in Western discourse, both popular and academic. Those who perform ritual in general do not label their action 'ritual'; they rather see it as a specific technique to achieve certain ends (2010, 3–4).
5. See Appadurai and Breckenridge 1976 and Harrison 1992.
6. Driver goes even further and insinuates that it does not matter whether the crying is 'just' a moral obligation or done for payment, as in his case study from Haiti (Driver 2006, 87).
7. This might be similar to the controlled possession described by Brückner (Brückner 2012), or to the controlled procedure that leads to uncontrolled possession (Anne de Sales 2012).
8. Similarly, in the context of Pakistan, Schaflechner (chapter 8) documents a specific literary genre that glorifies assassins of blasphemers and helps to 'naturalise' specific kinds of affects and emotions towards alleged blasphemers.

References

Appadurai, Arjun 2006. *The Fear of Small Numbers: An Essay on the Geography of Anger*. Durham and London: Duke University Press.

Appadurai, Arjun and Carol Breckenridge. 1976. 'The South Indian Temple: Authority, honor and redistribution.' *Contributions to Indian Sociology* (NS) 10 (2): 187–211.

Austin, J. L. 1955. *How to Do Things with Words: The William James Lectures Delivered at Harvard University*. Oxford: Oxford University Press.

Brückner, Heidrun. 2012. 'Gods going wild? Enacting loss of control in Tulu possession rituals: A photographic case study', in *Emotions in Rituals and Performances*, Axel Michaels and Christoph Wulf, eds, 214–36. New Delhi: Routledge.

De Sales, Anne 2012. 'Ritual virtuosity, emotions and feelings in Shamanic rituals in Nepal', in *Emotions in Rituals and Performances*, Axel Michaels and Christoph Wulf, eds, 171–83. New Delhi: Routledge.

Dietrich, Gabriele. 1996. 'South Asian feminist theory and its significance for feminist theology.' *Concilium* 1: 101–15.

Driver, Tom F. 2006. *Liberating Rites: Understanding the Transformative Power of Ritual*. New York: Booksurge.

Eriksen, Thomas Hylland. 2016. *Overheating: An Anthropology of Accelerated Change*. London: Pluto Press.

Harrison, Simon. 1992. 'Ritual as intellectual property.' *Man (NS)* 27(2): 225–44.

Hüsken, Ute. 2007a. 'Contested ritual property: Conflicts over correct ritual procedures in a South Indian Visnu temple', in *When Rituals Go Wrong: Mistakes, Failure, and the Dynamics of Ritual*, Ute Hüsken, ed, 273–90. Leiden: Brill.

Hüsken, Ute. 2007b. 'Ritual dynamics and ritual failure', in *When Rituals Go Wrong: Mistakes, Failure, and the Dynamics of Ritual*, Ute Hüsken, ed, 337–66. Leiden: Brill.

Hüsken, Ute. 2009. *Visnu's Children: Prenatal Life-cycle Rituals in South India*. Wiesbaden: Harrassowitz.

Hüsken, Ute. 2012. 'One nine-yard sari, two elephants, and ten sips of water: Ritual and emotions at a South Indian temple', in *Emotions in Rituals and Performances*, Axel Michaels and Christoph Wulf, eds, 117–39. New Delhi: Routledge.

Josephinides, Lisette. 2005. 'Resentment as a sense of the self', in *Mixed Emotions: Anthropological Studies of Feeling*, Kay Milton and Maruška Svašek, eds, 71–89. New York: Berg.

Kendall, Laurel. 1996. 'Initiating performance: The story of Chini, a Korean Shaman', in *The Performance of Healing*, Carol Laderman and Marina Roseman, eds, 153–76. London: Routledge.

Köpping, Klaus-Peter 2004. 'Failure of performance or passage to the acting self? Mishima's suicide between ritual and theatre', in *The Dynamics of Changing Rituals: The Transformation of Religious Rituals within their Social and Cultural Context*, Jens Kreinath, Constance Hartung and Annette Deschner, eds, 97–114. New York: Peter Lang.

Lynch, Owen M. 1990. 'The social construction of emotion in India', in *Divine Passions: The Social Construction of Emotion in India*, Owen M. Lynch, ed, 3–36. Berkeley, Los Angeles, Oxford: University of California Press.

Mirchandani, Maya. 2018. 'Digital hatred, real violence: Majoritarian radicalisation and social media in India', ORF Occasional Paper # 167, August 2018.

Moenius, Anne E. 2004. 'Love, violence, and the aesthetics of disgust: Saivas and Jainas in medieval South India.' *Journal of Indian Philosophy* 32(2): 113–72.

Mukund, Kanakalatha. 2005. *The View from Below: Indigenous Society, Temples and the Early Colonial State in Tamil Nadu, 1700–1835*. New Delhi: Orient Longman.

Pernau, Margrit. 2015. 'The virtuous individual and social reform: Debates among North Indian Urdu speakers', in *Civilizing Emotions: Concepts in Nineteenth-Century Asia and Europe*, Margrit Pernau, Helge Jordheim, Emmanuelle Saada, Christian Bailey, Einar Wigen, Orit Bashkin, Mana Kia, Mohinder Singh, Rochona Majumdar, Angelika Messner, Oleg Benesch, Myoungkyu Park, and Jan Ifversen, 169–86. Oxford: Oxford University Press.

Pernau, Margrit. 2018. 'Communal riots and the new masculinity.' Oral presentation at the conference 'Containing Religious Offence in South Asia', 7–8 June 2018, Oslo University.

Pernau, Margrit. 2019. *Emotions and Modernity in Colonial India: From Balance to Fervor*. Delhi: Oxford University Press.

Podeman Sørenson, Jørgen. 2006. 'Efficacy', in *Theorizing Rituals: Issues, Topics, Approaches, Concepts*, Jens Kreinath, Jan Snoek and Michael Stausberg, eds, 523–31. Leiden and Boston: Brill.

Sax, William S. 2010. 'Ritual and the problem of efficacy', in *The Problem of Ritual Efficacy*, William S. Sax, Johannes Quack and Jan Weinhold, eds, 3–16. New York: Oxford University Press.

Sax, William S. 2012. 'Emotional detachment and expression in Garhwali possession rituals', in *Emotions in Rituals and Performances*, Axel Michaels and Christoph Wulf, eds, 152–60. New Delhi: Routledge.

Schechner, Richard 1977. *Essays on Performance Theory, 1970–1976*. New York: Drama Book Specialists.

Schieffelin, Edward 1998. 'Problematizing performance', in *Ritual, Performance, Media*, Felicia Hughes-Freeland, ed, 194–207. London; New York: Routledge.

Svašek, Maruška, 2005. 'Introduction: Emotions in anthropology', in *Mixed Emotions: Anthropological Studies of Feeling*, Kay Milton and Maruška Svašek, eds, 1–24. New York: Berg.

Udupa, Sahana and Stephen D. McDowell, eds, 2017. *Media as Politics in South Asia*. London: Routledge.

Whitehouse, Harvey 2005. 'Emotion, memory, and religious rituals: An assessment of two theories', in *Mixed Emotions: Anthropological Studies of Feeling*, Kay Milton and Maruška Svašek, eds, 91–108. New York: Berg.

Index

adhamma 22, 78, 81, 90, 99–100
Adivasis 36, 149, 153, 165–69, 174
affect 29, 124
Ahl-e-Bayt 193
Ahl-e-Hadith 53–54, 71, 210–12
Ahmadis 16, 19, 50, 56, 63, 71–72, 202, 209
Ahmed, Asad 8, 31, 36, 38, 72, 178, 182
Ali, Muhammad Yousaf 181, 187, 192, 194, 198, 204–5
apostasy 20, 38, 57, 114
Assistance Association for Political Prisoners (AAPP) 88, 100
Asurs 153, 158–59, 161–70, 174, 240
Awami League 20, 103, 109, 115, 117–19
Azam, Muhammad 67, 69

Babunagari, Allama Hafez Junayed 112–13
Bangladesh 1–2, 9, 12–13, 18–20, 23, 31, 34–35, 38–40, 104–5, 108–11, 117–18, 144
Bangladesh Nationalist Party (BNP) 19, 111, 117
Barelvis 37, 52–53, 71, 209–14, 220, 230–31
Batra, Dinanath 26
Barthes, Roland 106
Baviskar, Amita 167–68, 170
Bengal 152–53, 157, 161, 171
Bharatiya Janata Party (BJP) 36, 123, 149–50, 156, 170–71, 173
Bhivamsa, Aria 82
Bhutto, Zufliqar Ali 16
Bibi, Asia 37, 49, 54, 60, 208, 212–16, 219
Blackwood, Phil 79
blasphemy: affect and 28–29, 124; allegations and accusations of, online 33, 37, 49–50, 52, 69, 71, 179, 181; in Buddhism 21; as criminal offence 16; definition and conception of term 4–6; human rights and 7; as hurt sensibility 8; laws prohibiting 1, 3, 10, 12, 52–54, 56, 68, 70, 72, 181–82, 202, 209, 213, 219–21, 231–32; legislation banning 20, 27; Pakistan 48–49; as political tool 26, 28; protests against 15, 25; social media and 34
Blom, Amélie 15, 27, 29, 53, 72, 107–8, 222
Brown, Wendy 7
Buddha images 21, 23, 35, 78–82, 94, 96, 99, 237
Buddhism 21–22, 77–78, 80–82, 84, 86, 88, 91, 94–96, 100
Burke, Kenneth 205

censorship 6, 9, 14, 18, 24, 26, 150–52, 156
Chandipurana 161–63, 165, 174
Charlie Hebdo cartoons 17, 27–28
Cheema, Amir 15, 208, 226–31, 233
Chevalier de la Barre affair 25
Clinton, Hillary 200
codification 185–86, 203
Collins, Steven 81
Communist Party of India 171, 174

Danish cartoon controversy 1, 17, 28, 108, 222, 226–27
death penalty 20, 110, 112, 114, 219
Deoband 210–11
Deobandi network 36, 53, 71, 110, 210–12
Doniger, Wendy 14
Dumont, Louis 146
Durga 145, 152–56, 159, 161–63, 165, 168, 172, 174
Durga puja 152, 154–59, 161, 163–65, 167

East India Company 9, 210

Facebook 39, 71, 94, 112, 114, 120, 128–31, 133, 142, 144
fatwas 19, 38, 51, 211, 215
First Information Reports (FIRs) 3, 54, 71, 133, 174, 184, 204
Ford, Bill 135
The Friday Times (TFT) 178–80, 201–2, 205
Fuller, Paul 21, 81

Gandhi, Indira 13, 153
Ghaffar, Mian Abdul 183

Hacker, Paul 146, 149, 172
hajj 112
Hamid, Zayd Zaman 183, 203
Hanif, Mohammed 57
Hefazat Barta 112
Hefazat Islam 20, 104, 110, 112, 119–20
Hinduism 129–30, 133, 135–37, 139–43, 146, 149–50, 152–53, 163–66, 168, 170–73, 175, 224–25; deity images 132; offence against 14; Pakistan 71; pilgrimage 135; religious denunciations by 35; United Kingdom 28
Hindu nationalism (Hindutva) 24, 27–28, 35–36, 132, 135, 149–50, 152–53, 163, 165, 171–73
Htin Lin Oo 80–82, 94–95, 97

249

Human Rights Watch 88–89
Husain, M. F. 28, 30, 155

Ibn Arabi 199, 205
Ilmuddin 11, 15, 208, 218–20, 224–26, 228–31
India 2–3, 8, 13–15, 164–68, 171–72, 174, 236, 243–44, 246; blasphemy regulation 27; broadcast media 31; constitution 152–54; growth of religious offence 2; Hindu nationalism 24, 27–28, 36, 132, 135, 149–50, 153, 171–73; Islamic texting 129; killings for blasphemy 149; Pakistan and 1; Parliament 72, 152–54, 173; penal code 9–12, 15, 21, 23, 83, 185–86, 236, 243; religious minorities 26, 35; Rushdie affair 9, 38; social media use 40, 125, 129, 134
instrumentalism 25
Irani, Smriti 36, 154–56, 161, 164, 166, 171–72, 174
Islam: apostasy in 57, 114; fatwas 19, 38, 51, 211, 215; hajj 112; legal protection of 19, 26; prohibition of visual representation of the divine 30; Sunni 39, 54, 210, 219. *See also* Islamism; Muhammad; Muslims
Islamism 19–20, 49, 53, 104–5, 109–10, 114, 116, 119
Ittan Wali 213–14

Jaffrelot, Christophe 26, 149
Jahanghir, Mian Mohammed 182
Jamaat-e-Islami 1, 18–19, 103, 111, 120, 214, 230, 232
Jawaharlal Nehru University (JNU) 36, 153–54, 156, 164, 174
Jyllands-Posten 226

Kaaba 35, 123, 127, 134–45, 238
Kali images 130–31, 133
Khabrian 181–82, 205
Khan, Raza 210–11
Khatm-e-Nabuwaat 202–3
Knapp, Stephen 138
Knowing Buddha Organisation (KBO) 96
Köppel, Roger 227, 229

Laine, James 14
Latour, Bruno 39, 126–27
law 15–17, 24–26, 67–68, 70, 82–83, 86, 90, 93, 98, 216–19; anti-blasphemy legislation 1, 3, 10, 12, 52–54, 56, 68, 70, 72, 181–82, 202, 209, 213, 219–21, 231–32; framing role 33; India 24, 246; legal process 93, 183, 186, 237; Myanmar 82, 82–87, 92; Myanmar, race and religion laws 92–93; Pakistan 48–49, 71–72, 209, 215; Pakistan, religious minorities and 50
Lawton, David 4, 106
lawyers 50, 53–54, 58–59, 62, 71, 94, 98, 119–20, 183, 185–86

MaBaTha 77–82, 91–98, 100, 240
MaHaNa 90, 98, 100–101
Mahishasur 36, 150, 153–54, 157, 159, 161–64, 167–68, 170, 172, 174; Martyrdom Day 154, 174, 240; Movement 150, 152, 169
Mahmood, Saba 5, 7, 38, 72
Mahmud, Khalid 220
Malaysia 116–17
Mandalay 88, 100
Matin, Khaula 225
Maung Shwe Hpi 85
Mazzarella, William 24, 27, 29, 32, 126, 149, 151, 156
McDowell, Stephen D. 2–3, 31, 239
Meyer, Birgit 132
Milton, Kay 30, 39
Modi, Narendra 34, 123, 149
Mopyar case 90–91
Muhammad (Prophet of Islam) 38, 49, 210–11, 214, 232; Barelivism and 210; derogatory remarks toward 56, 112; Hinduism and 141; impersonation of 181, 188, 191, 193, 195, 198; perfection of 192; prohibition on images of 71–72, 138
Muslims (*see also* Ahmadis; Islam; Sufism) 78, 85, 113, 139, 142–43, 146, 149–50, 193–94, 202, 204–5, 217–18, 220–21, 224–25, 228, 231; blasphemy accusations against 53; India 13; Shia 39, 50, 52–54, 68, 71–72, 108, 137; stereotypes toward 7; Sufi 52–54, 71, 180–82, 189, 191–96, 198–99, 201–2, 204–5, 208–9, 212, 229–30, 233; Sunni 39, 54, 210, 219
Myanmar 39–40, 81–83, 88–89, 91–94, 96–99, 236–37, 240, 244; legal system 21; media 31; penal code 39; religious minorities 26; revivalist Buddhism 21; under colonial rule (Burma) 21, 82–86, 88, 90, 99–100

National League for Democracy (NLD) 80, 92–93, 95
Ne Win 86–87, 89–90

Oak, Purushottam Nagesh 136–8, 140
Organisation of Islamic Cooperation (OIC) 7–8

Pakistan: anti-blasphemy legislation 3; blasphemy as human rights violation 7; blasphemy protests 227; broadcast media 31; court system 50, 182; criminal code 9, 12; Election Act amendments (2017) 63; High Court 11, 16, 56, 59, 182, 184, 224; law and criminal code 20, 39, 56–57, 181, 196–98, 200–201, 205; lionisation of assassins 27; penal code 16, 56, 71, 209, 216, 218; religious demographics 50, 71, 232; social media use 40
paper book 19, 184
Pinney, Christopher 24, 132–33, 151
Punjab 1, 11, 13, 16–17, 66–68, 208, 213, 215
Punjabi Christians 54–55, 64–65, 72

Qadri, Ahmad 217
Qadri, Mumtaz 15, 17, 67, 69, 71, 209–10, 212, 216–20, 223, 225, 229–31, 233
Qayyum, Abdul 232
Quran 16, 51, 57, 65–66, 68–69, 71–72, 209, 217
Qureshi, Hanif 210, 219–20

Rajpal 224–26
Rangila Rasul 10–12, 15, 25, 30, 224
Religious Insults Bill 11
Rushdie affair 8–9, 12–13, 25, 27–28, 32, 38, 218

Saffron Revolution 22, 88, 98–99
Savarkar, Babarao 135–36
Shahbag movement 20, 111
Shankar, Sri Sri Ravi 139–40, 143
Shia 39, 50, 52–54, 68, 71–72, 108, 137
Shiva 35, 123–25, 127–30, 133–34, 136–46, 238
shoe controversy 21–22, 34, 83–85, 97
Siddique, Latif 35, 103–5, 107–8, 111–14, 116, 118–20
Sikhs 72, 218, 229
smartphones 2–3, 35, 37, 125–27, 132, 238–39
social media 2–3, 31–32, 35, 37, 94, 96, 98, 100, 124, 126, 128–30, 143–44, 203, 238–39
State Law and Order Restoration Council (SLORC) 87–88, 100
street protests 106, 108, 113, 241–42, 244

Sufism 52–54, 71, 180–82, 189, 191–96, 198–99, 201–2, 204–5, 208–9, 212, 229–30, 233
Sunni Tehreek (ST) 26, 53, 154, 212, 214

Taseer, Salman 1, 11, 37, 208, 213–20, 223, 229, 231–32
Tehreek-e Labbaik Pakistan (TLP) 17, 26, 212–13
Tehreek-e-labbaik ya rasool Allah 64
Turner, Alicia 84–85

United Nations Human Rights Council (UNHRC) 7–8, 17, 38–39

V Gastro Bar case 94, 96–97
vigilante justice 209, 211, 213, 215–17, 219, 221, 223, 225, 227, 229, 231, 235
Vikramaditya 136
vinicchaya system 90, 94

Welt, Die 228
WhatsApp 71, 128–30, 142, 145, 170

YouTube 27, 35, 71, 94, 99, 140, 174, 232–33

www.ingramcontent.com/pod-product-compliance
Lightning Source LLC
LaVergne TN
LVHW050008140426
836100LV00010B/55